THE RESTAURANT

THE RESTAURANT

FROM CONCEPT TO OPERATION

THIRD EDITION

John R. Walker, D.B.A., FMP.
Marshall, Professor, & Director
Hotel, Restaurant, and Tourism Management
United States International University
San Diego, CA

and

Donald E. Lundberg, Ph.D.
Professor Emeritus
California State Polytechnic University Pomona

JOHN WILEY & SONS, INC.
New York   Chichester   Weinheim
Brisbane   Singapore   Toronto

Library of Congress Cataloging-in-Publication Data:
Walker, John R., 1944–
    The restaurant : from concept to operation / by John Walker and Donald Lundberg.—
3rd ed.
      p.   cm.
    Lundberg's name appears first on the earlier edition.
    Includes index.
    ISBN 0-471-35606-9 (cloth : alk. paper)
    1. Restaurant management.   I. Lundberg, Donald E.   II. Title.
TX911.3.M27 W352 2000
647.95′068—dc21   00-035182

Printed in the United States of America.

10 9 8 7 6 5

DEDICATION

To Donald E. Lundberg, Ph.D., my mentor, colleague and friend. Don was admired and respected along the halls of academia as a scholar and pioneer of hospitality and tourism education.

To all the wonderful people who made this book possible.
The National Restaurant Association
The Educational Foundation of the National Restaurant Association
The professors, students and prospective restaurant owners

We wish you happiness and success . . .

CONTENTS

Preface   *xvii*
Acknowledgments   *xix*

Chapter 1   INTRODUCTION   **2**

Liabilities of Restaurant Operation   *6*
French Culinary History   *7*
The Birth of Restaurants in America   *7*
The Restaurant Failure Rate   *8*
Buy, Build, Franchise, or Manage?   *9*
    Franchise, Anybody?   *13*
Starting from Scratch   *15*
Restaurants as Roads to Riches   *16*
Summary   *16*
Key Terms and Concepts   *17*
Review Questions   *17*
Endnotes   *18*

Chapter 2   KINDS AND CHARACTERISTICS OF
RESTAURANT AND THEIR OWNERS   **20**

Kinds and Characteristics of Restaurants   *22*
The Big Boys Compared with Independent Operators   *23*
Quick-Service Restaurants   *24*
    Colonel Sanders   *25*
    Wendy's International Restaurants   *26*
    Carl Karcher   *26*
    Cleo R. Ludwing, Founder of L-K Restaurants   *27*
    Regional Burger Chains   *29*
    The Subway Story   *29*
The Mexican Restaurant   *32*
Steakhouses   *33*
    The Lore of Steak   *34*
Fine-Dining Restaurants   *36*
Seafood Restaurants   *38*
Italian Restaurants   *39*
Chinese Restaurants   *41*
Theme Restaurants   *42*

The Chef-Owner Restaurant   *44*
Women Chefs as Restaurant Partners   *46*
Notable Female Restaurateurs   *48*
The Bakery-Café   *49*
Centralized Home Delivery Restaurants   *50*
Truck Stops and Travel Centers   *51*
Summary   *52*
Key Terms and Concepts   *52*
Review Questions   *52*
Endnotes   *52*

Chapter 3   CONCEPT, LOCATION, AND DESIGN   **54**

Restaurant Concepts   *56*
   Concept: Clear-Cut, or Ambiguous?   *57*
Protecting the Restaurant's Name   *58*
   The McDonald's Concept and Image   *59*
Defining the Concept and Market   *60*
The Fine Line Between Junk and Funk   *62*
Successful Restaurant Concepts   *63*
Concept Adaptation   *67*
Changing or Modifying a Concept   *67*
Copy and Improve   *68*
Restaurant Symbology   *69*
When a Concept Fails   *70*
The Multiple-Concept Chain   *70*
Sequence of Restaurant Development: From Concept
   to Opening   *72*
   Planning Services   *73*
   Common Denominators of Restaurants   *73*
Utility versus Pleasure   *73*
Degree of Service Offered   *74*
Time of Eating and Seat Turnover   *75*
Customer Space   *75*
   Menu Price and Cost per Seat   *76*
Advertising and Promoting Expenditures   *77*
Labor Costs as a Percentage of Sales   *77*
Planning Decisions That Relate to Concept Development   *78*
Profitability   *79*
The Mission Statement   *79*
Concept and Location   *80*
High-Growth Areas For Locating a Restaurant   *81*
   Location Criteria   *82*
   Some Restaurants Create Their Own Location   *82*
   Sources of Location Information   *83*
   Traffic Generators   *84*
   Knockout Criteria   *85*
   Other Location Criteria   *85*
   Suburban, Nook-and-Cranny, and Shopping Mall Locations   *86*

Minimum Population Needed to Support a Concept   87
Downtown versus Suburban   87
  Average Travel Time to Reach Restaurants   88
Is the Location Right for the Concept?   88
The Correct Number of Seats   88
Restaurant Chain Location Specifications   89
Location Information Checklist   91
The Takeover Location   92
Restaurant Topographical Surveys   93
Is the Location Too Costly?   94
Visibility and Accessibility   94
Design Criteria   94
Summary   97
Key Terms and Concepts   97
Review Questions   97
Endnotes   98

Chapter 4   RESTAURANT MARKETING AND
BUSINESS PLANS   **100**

The Marketing Plan   102
The Difference Between Marketing and Sales   106
Solving Customer Problems   107
Marketing Planning   107
Marketing Strategy   107
Market Assessment   108
Market Demand   109
  Market Potential   110
  Market Segmentation, Target Market, and Positioning   110
Marketing Mix—The Four Ps   111
  Place   111
  Product   112
  Price   116
  Promotion   118
Olive Garden Marketing   124
Summary   125
Key Terms and Concept   125
Review Questions   126
Endnotes   126

Chapter 5   FINANCING AND LEASING   **128**

Sufficient Capital   130
Compare Interest Rates   131
Real Interest Rates   131
Loan Sources   132
The Small Business Administration   133
  SBICs   135

     Soliciting an SBA Loan   135
     Sequence for Securing an SBA Loan   136
Stockpiling Credit   *137*
Selling the Proposal   *137*
Other Sources of Money   *139*
Collateral   *140*
Keeping the Loan Lines Open   *141*
Avoiding Personal Liability   *141*
Leasing   *141*
     Lease Costs   142
     Drawing Up a Lease   142
     Lease Terminology   144
     Length of Lease   144
     Specifics of Most Restaurant Leases   145
     Fire Insurance   146
What Is a Restaurant Worth?   *147*
Summary   *147*
Key Terms and Concepts   *148*
Review Questions   *148*
Endnotes   *148*

Chapter 6   LEGAL AND TAX MATTERS   **150**

What Business Entity Is Best?   *152*
     The Sole Proprietorship   152
     The Partnership   154
     The Restaurant as a Corporation   156
Buy-Sell Agreement with Partners   *158*
Two Corporations Recommended   *159*
Business and Life Insurance   *160*
Business Search Expense   *160*
Legal Aspects of Doing Business   *160*
Depreciation and Cash Flow   *163*
     Accelerated or Straight-Line Depreciation   163
Buying a Loser   *164*
Two Choices of Accounting Methods   *164*
A Tax Avoidance Plan   *164*
Retirement Tax Shelters   *164*
     Tax-Free Compounding   165
A Reasonable Return on Investment   *165*
Business Expenses and Taxes   *165*
     Tax Credit for Van or Bus   166
     Tax Breaks for Children in Family Restaurants   166
Reminders   *167*
Local, State, and Federal Taxes   *168*
Federal Laws Governing Employment   *169*
     The Federal Wage and Hour Law (The Fair Labor
       Standard Act)   169
     Employee Information   170

The Federal Equal Pay Act of 1963 and Federal Child
   Labor Laws   *171*
Wage Garnishment Act   *171*
The Age Discrimination in Employment Act   *171*
The Employment Retirement Income Security Act   *172*
Civil Rights Act of 1964   *172*
Legal Aspects of Contract Services   *173*
Complications in Discharging Employees   *173*
Reporting Tips to the Internal Revenue Service   *173*
Selling Liquor to Minors   *174*
Time Off to Vote   *174*
In Case of Wage and Hour Audit   *174*
Interpretation and Clarification of Government Regulations   *174*
Slip and Fall   *175*
Summary   *175*
Key Terms and Concepts   *176*
Review Questions   *176*
Endnotes   *177*

Chapter 7   THE MENU   **178**

Capability/Consistency   *181*
Equipment   *181*
Availability   *186*
Price   *186*
   Menu Pricing Strategies   *187*
Nutritional Value   *188*
Contribution Margin   *192*
Flavor   *192*
Accuracy in Menu   *193*
Kids' Menus   *193*
Menu Items   *194*
Appetizers and Soups   *196*
Lunch and Dinner Menus   *196*
   Degustation Menus   *197*
Menu Types   *197*
Salads   *200*
Entrées   *200*
Desserts   *200*
Matching/Pairing   *200*
Restaurants in Las Vegas Represent the Best Countrywide   *201*
Menu Analysis   *202*
Menu Design and Layout   *203*
   What Kind of Paper?   *204*
Standardized Recipes   *204*
Food-Cost Percentage   *204*
Summary   *207*
Key Terms and Concepts   *207*
Review Questions   *208*
Endnotes   *208*

Chapter 8   BAR AND BEVERAGES   210

Alcoholic Beverage Licenses   213
How to Apply for a License   213
Bar Layout and Design   214
Placement of a Bar Within a Restaurant   216
The Speed Gun   217
Glass Washing   218
Bartenders   218
A Basic Bar Inventory   218
A Wine List   219
Wines with Food   222
Responsible Alcoholic Beverage Service   223
Third-Party Liability   224
Controls   224
    Controlling Losses   225
    99 Ways to Steal in a Restaurant or Bar   225
Summary   231
Key Terms and Concepts   231
Review Questions   231
Endnotes   231

Chapter 9   FOOD PURCHASING   232

A Food Purchasing System   234
    The Purchasing Cycle   237
    Who Sets Up the System? Who Operates It?   237
    Food Quality Standards   238
    Buying by Specification   238
    How Much Inventory?   239
    The Mechanics of Ordering   240
    Storage   241
Types of Purchasing   242
    Buying from Full-Line Purveyors   242
    Co-op Buying   242
    Beware   242
Buying Meat   243
    The Chicken versus Turkey Choice   243
Purchasing Eggs   244
Buying Fresh Fruits and Vegetables   244
    USDA Wholesale Produce Grades   245
    Canned Fruits and Vegetables   247
Selecting the Right Coffee   247
    Coffee Brewing Machines   247
Summary   248
Key Terms and Concepts   248
Review Questions   249
Endnotes   249

Chapter 10   PLANNING AND EQUIPPING THE KITCHEN   **250**

The Open Kitchen   *256*
Kitchen Floor Coverings   *258*
Kitchen Equipment   *258*
   Categories of Kitchen Equipment   *259*
   Select the Right Equipment   *259*
   Match Equipment with Menu and Production Schedule   *260*
   Total Cost versus Original Cost   *261*
   Select the Most Efficient Equipment for the People and
      Skills Available   *261*
   De-skilling the Job with Equipment   *261*
Equipment Stars   *262*
   The Stove/Oven   *262*
   Deep-Frying Equipment   *264*
   Tilting Skillets   *265*
   Low-Temperature Ovens   *266*
   Forced-Air Convection Ovens   *266*
   Microwave Ovens   *266*
   Infrared Cooking Equipment   *269*
   Steam Cooking Equipment   *269*
   Hot-Food Holding Tables   *270*
   Refrigerators and Freezers   *271*
   Ice Machines   *271*
   Pasta-Making Machines   *272*
   Other Specialty Cooking Equipment   *272*
   Other Equipment   *273*
Maintaining Kitchen Equipment   *274*
   Dishwashing Equipment   *274*
Meeting with the Health Inspector   *275*
Summary   *276*
Key Terms and Concepts   *276*
Review Questions   *276*
Endnotes   *277*

Chapter 11   BUDGETING AND CONTROLLING COSTS   **278**

Budgeting   *280*
Forecasting Sales   *280*
   A Method for Forecasting Sales   *280*
Income Statement   *282*
Budgeting Costs   *283*
Gross Profit   *283*
Controllable Expenses   *283*
Labor Costs   *284*
Rent   *287*
Uniform System of Accounts for Restaurants   *287*
Pre-Opening Expenses   *287*

Cash Flow Budgeting   *288*
Productivity Analysis and Cost Control   *288*
Seat Turnover   *290*
Controlling Theft and Accidental Loss   *291*
Guest Check Control   *293*
Computer Systems   *294*
   How Much Computer Assistance?   295
   POS Systems   298
Financial Management   *300*
   Ratio Analysis   301
Summary   *302*
Key Terms and Concepts   *302*
Review Questions   *302*
Endnotes   *303*

Chapter 12   ORGANIZATION, RECRUITING,
AND STAFFING   **304**

Task and Job Analysis   *306*
   Technical Tasks Vary with the Establishment   307
Job Descriptions   *308*
   The Job Specification   311
   The Job Instruction Sheet   311
Organizing People and Jobs   *312*
Staffing the Restaurant   *314*
Civil Rights Laws   *314*
   Equal Employment Opportunity   315
   The Americans with Disabilities Act   316
   Hiring People Who Are Physically or Mentally Challenged   317
   AIDS   318
Recruitment   *319*
Selection   *319*
Interviewing   *320*
   Ideal Employee Profiles   322
Employment of Minors   *322*
   Restrictions on Employing Minors   325
Employment of Undocumented Aliens   *326*
Employee Sources   *326*
Questions to Avoid on the Application Form and During
   the Interview   *327*
   Questions You Can Ask   328
   The Multiple Interview Approach   330
   Telephone References   330
Careful Selection of Personnel   *330*
Employment Testing   *332*
Screening Out the Substance Abuser   *332*
Pre-Employment Physical and Drug Examinations   *333*
Summary   *333*
Key Terms and Concepts   *333*

Review Questions   *333*
Endnotes   *334*

Chapter 13   EMPLOYEE TRAINING AND
DEVELOPMENT   **336**

Orientation   *338*
Training   *339*
Part-Time Employees Increase the Need for Training   *341*
Training and Development   *341*
  Combine Training with Development   343
  Slogans Help   343
  Step-by-Step Training   344
  Training Theory   345
Behavior Modeling   *347*
Learner-Controlled Instruction   *348*
Responsible Alcohol Beverage Service   *349*
A Professional Training and Development Program   *350*
The Manager As Coach   *350*
Leadership   *352*
  Better Management Behavior   352
  Characteristics of Effective Managers   352
  Subtleties of Supervision   353
Motivation Through Part Ownership   *355*
A Tipping Policy   *355*
Summary   *356*
Key Terms and Concepts   *356*
Review Questions   *356*
Endnotes   *357*

Chapter 14   SERVICE AND CUSTOMER RELATIONS   **358**

The Service Encounter   *361*
Gamesmanship   *362*
Greeters   *362*
The Server as an Independent Businessperson   *363*
Foodservice Teams   *363*
Hard Sell versus Soft Sell   *365*
Formality or Informality   *366*
Setting the Table   *367*
Taking the Order   *367*
Magic Phrases   *368*
The Servers' Viewpoint   *369*
The Difficult Customer   *370*
  Teen Confrontations   373
Service Personnel as a Family   *373*
Greeter or Traffic Cop   *373*
Tact: Always   *374*
Summary   *374*

Key Terms and Concepts   *374*
Review Questions   *374*
Endnotes   *375*

Chapter 15   FOOD PROTECTION AND SANITATION   *376*

Food-Borne Illness   *378*
Biological Hazards—Bacteria   *378*
Causes of Food-Borne Illness   *379*
Controlling or Destroying Bacteria   *382*
Acidity and Bacterial Growth   *382*
Bacteria and Temperature   *383*
Every Staff Member a Sanitarian   *384*
Viruses   *384*
Chemical Contaminants   *384*
Personal Safety   *386*
Hazard Analysis of Critical Control Points   *386*
Common Food Safety Mistakes   *388*
   Time/Temperature   *388*
   Cross-Contamination   *389*
   Poor Personal Hygiene   *390*
Approaches to Food Safety   *390*
Food Protection as a System   *391*
Contract Sanitation Service   *395*
Warewashing and Food Protection   *395*
Pest Control   *396*
Summary   *397*
Key Terms and Concepts   *398*
Review Questions   *398*
Endnotes   *398*

Glossary   *401*
Index   *409*

PREFACE

Opening a restaurant is a distinct challenge. It is also a thrill that gives one the opportunity for tremendous creative expression. Developing the menu, creating a new dish, designing the decor, attending to your level of service or establishing an ambiance—these factors all contribute to exceeding the expectations of your guests. However, there are numerous hurdles to overcome before opening day. The good news is that with careful planning, including the writing of a solid business plan, coupled with preserving and a touch of "BAM", the chances of success are improved. The opportunity to be the boss and call the shots is appealing. To be responsible for the 'buzz' created and orchestrated is a rush. Maybe the concept will have 'legs.' If successful, a restaurant operator might become a small town, or even large town, dignitary.

The 21st century finds the restaurant business enjoying record sales but also rising labor and other costs. The conditions for restaurant success may change quickly, leaving financial scars on some operators. The unprecedented rise in much of the American public's income in the 1990s has provided opportunity for new styles of restaurants and the delivery of their products and services. Foods formerly considered exotic are now routinely accepted and expected. Taste titillation comes by offering interesting foods and flavor combinations that challenge chefs and owners.

To help meet the continuing restaurant challenges are the oncoming wave of students, who have studied the culinary arts and restaurant management, and view the restaurant business as a career of choice. A restaurant can be fun to operate, and the profit margins substantial. It is interesting to learn that at least one billionaire, Tom Monaghan, made his fortune in the pizza business and that dozens of millionaires have acquired fortunes in quick service restaurants. Some of their stories are told in the book.

The chapters of this third edition take the reader step-by-step through the complicated process of creating and opening a restaurant. In this edition, we have introduced three new chapters and, by deleting dated material, merged three existing chapters—thus keeping the number of chapters at 15. The new chapters are: Kinds and Characteristics of Restaurants; Restaurant Marketing and Business Plans and Bar and Beverage Management.

Each chapter has been revised, updated and enhanced with numerous industry examples, sidebars offering advice, charts, tables, photographs, and menus. All improve the look of the book.

An **Instructor's Manual** and set of **PowerPoint Slides** to accompany this textbook are available to qualified adopters from the publisher.

John R. Walker, DBA., FMP
San Diego, California

Donald E. Lundberg, Ph.D.
Carlsbad, California

ACKNOWLEDGMENTS

For their insightful suggestions on the revision of this text, we thank Letty Uy, V.B.I., Professor Evan Enowitz of Grossmont College, San Diego; Susan Schultze Classen of Paragon Steakhouse Restaurant; Ken Rubin, CPA; Dr. Cora Gatchalian, University of the Philippines; Volker Schmitz of California Café Restaurants; Dr. Jay Schrock of San Francisco State University; Dr. Ken Crocker of Bowling Green State University; Karl Engstrom of Mesa College, San Diego; Brad Peters of Mesa College, San Diego; Dr. Andy Feinstein of University of Nevada, Las Vegas; David F. Schweiger of Mira Costa College, Oceanside; Dr. Charlie Adams of Texas Tech University; Anthony Battaglia, Glendale Community College; Dr. Paul G. VanLandingham, Johnson and Wales University; Dan Beard, Orange Coast College; Marco Adornetto, Muskingum Area Technical College; Thomas Rosenberger, Community College of Southern Nevada; and C. Gus Katsigris, El Centro College.

We are also indebted to the National Restaurant Association, Gerald Breitbart of the California Restaurant Association, the restaurants who allowed us to include their menus or photos, and the following restaurant companies for their provision of resource information:

Charlie Trotter
Red Lobster Restaurants
TGI Friday
The Lettuce Entertain You Group
The Hard Rock Cafés
David Cohn and the Cohn Restaurant Group
Dick Rivera, President, Red Lobster
Jim Lynde, Senior Vice President People, Red Lobster
Chart House Restaurants
The Olive Garden Restaurants
John C. Cini, President and CEO of Cini Little
U.S. Bank

We acknowledge, with great thanks, the expert assistance of Candida Wallang, Tania Gonzalez, Carrie Sellereite, Ann Jenson, Simone Trafford and Michael Thorpe.

To all those numerous restaurant operators who have graciously given their time and ideas, photographs and menus, our sincere appreciation.

THE RESTAURANT

Chapter 1

After reading and studying this chapter,
you should be able to:

Discuss reasons why some people open restaurants.

List some liabilities of restaurants operation.

Outline the history of restaurants.

Compare the advantages and disadvantages of buying, building, and franchising restaurants.

INTRODUCTION

Restaurants play a significant role in our lifestyle, and dining out is a favorite social activity. Everyone needs to eat—so, to enjoy good food and, perhaps, wine in the company of friends and in pleasant surroundings is one of life's pleasures. Eating out has become a way of life for families. In recent years, a buoyant economy has given us higher disposable incomes, which allows more meals away from home.

All industry segments have improved product and service and now offer greater variety, consistency, and value than ever before. Phyllis Richman, *Washington Post* food critic, says, "Restaurants are one of the primary ways we fill our bodies, occupy our social lives, spend our money, learn about the world and conduct our business."[1]

Chef-owner Bob Kinkead, of Kinkead's Restaurant, Washington D.C. Courtesy Bob Kinkead

For the winners, the restaurant business is fun—lots of people coming and going, lots of new faces. You never get lonely. The business is always challenging because other restaurant owners are striving to attract your guests—but with the right location, menu, atmosphere, and management, the winners continue to attract the market. The successful restaurant offers a high return on investment. One restaurant, then two, perhaps a small chain. Retire wealthy. It happens. However . . .

. . . the odds in favor of being a big restaurant winner are not good. More than 815,000 commercial restaurants are doing business in the United States. Each year hundreds of new restaurants open and hundreds close. Other hundreds just fade away. Relatively easy to enter, the restaurant business looks deceptively simple. Like people? Love cooking? Take your nest egg of life savings, borrow on your home and from friends, or get a SBA loan, and you are in business. But for how long?

To be a winner requires considerable experience, planning, financial support, and energy. Luck also plays a part.

This book takes you from day one—that time when you dream of a restaurant— through the opening and into operation. What kind of restaurant? Quick-service, cafeteria, coffee shop, family, ethnic, casual, or luxury? Most restaurant dreamers—perhaps too many—think of being in the middle of a dinner house with lots of guests, skilled, motivated employees, social interaction, and profits. This may not be for you. Other choices may have a much better chance of success. Should you buy, build, or franchise?

The kind of restaurant concept you select determines, to a large extent, the kind of talents required. Talent and temperament correlate with restaurant style. Managing a quick-service restaurant is quite different from being the proprietor of a luxury restaurant. The person who may do well with franchising a Taco Bell franchise could be a failure in a personality-style restaurant. The range of restaurant styles is broad. Each choice makes its own demands and offers its own rewards to the operator.

This book shows the logical progression from dream to reality, from concept to finding a market gap to operating a restaurant. Along the way, it gives a comprehensive picture of the restaurant business.

Going into the restaurant business is not for the faint of heart. People contemplating opening a restaurant come from diverse backgrounds and bring with them a wealth of experience. However, there is no substitute for experience in the restaurant business—especially in the segment in which you are planning to operate.

So why go into the restaurant business? Here are some reasons others have done so, along with some of the liabilities involved.

- *Money.* The restaurant is a potential money factory. Successful restaurants are highly profitable. Few businesses can generate as much profit for a given investment. A restaurant with a million-dollar sales volume per year can generate $100,000–150,000 per year in profit before taxes. On the other hand, a failing restaurant, one with a large investment and a large payroll, can lose thousands of dollars a month. Most restaurants are neither big winners nor big losers.

- *The potential for a buyout.* The successful restaurant owner is likely to be courted by a buyer. A number of large corporations have bought restaurants, especially small restaurant chains. The operator is often bought out for several million dollars, sometimes with the option of staying on as president of his or her own chain. The older independent owner can choose to sell out and retire.

- *A place to socialize.* The restaurant is a social exchange, satisfying the needs of people with a high need for socialization. Interaction is constant and varied. Personal relationships are a perpetual challenge. For many people there is too much social interplay, which can prove exhausting.

- *Challenge.* Few businesses offer more challenge to the competitive person. There is always a new way to serve, new decor, a new dish, someone new to train, new ways of marketing, promoting, and merchandising.

- *Habit.* Once someone has learned a particular skill or way of life, habit takes over. Habit, the great conditioner of life, tends to lock the person into a lifestyle. The young person learns to cook, feels comfortable doing so, enjoys the restaurant experience, and remains in the restaurant business without seriously considering other options.

- *A firm lifestyle.* People who are especially fond of food and drink may feel that the restaurant is "where it is," free for the taking, or at least available at reduced cost. Some are thrilled with food, its preparation, its service, and it can also be fun to be a continous part of it.

- *Opportunity to express yourself.* Restaurant owners can be likened to theatrical producers. They write the script, cast the characters, devise the settings, and star in their own show. The show is acclaimed or fails according to the owner's talents and knowledge of the audience, the market at which the performance is aimed.

When asked by the authors and others what helped most "in getting where you are today," the emphasis on steady, hard work came out far ahead of any other factor. Next in line was "getting along with people." Then came the possession of a college degree. Close also was "being at the right place at the right time." Major concerns were low salaries, excessive stress, lack of room for advancement, and lack of long-term job security.

LIABILITIES OF RESTAURANT OPERATION

Long working hours are the norm in restaurants. Some people like this; others get burned out. Excessive fatigue can lead to general health problems and susceptibility to viral infections such as colds and mononucleosis. A number of foodservice chains expect management personnel to work 55 to 70 hours or longer per week, too long for many people to operative effectively. Long hours mean a lack of quality time with family, particularly when children are young and of school age. Restaurants owners have little time for thinking—an activity required to make the enterprise grow.

In working for others, managers have little job security. A shift of owners, for example, can mean discharge. While restaurant owners can work as long as the restaurant is successful, they often put in so many hours that they begin to feel incarcerated. Family life can suffer. The divorce rate is high among restaurant managers for several reasons. Stress comes from both the long hours of work and the many variables presented by the restaurant, some beyond the control of the manager.

One big liability for owners is the possibility of losing their investment and that of other investors, who may be friends or relatives. Too often, a restaurant failure endangers a family's financial security because collateral, such as a home, is also lost.

Potential restaurateurs must consider whether their personality, temperament, and abilities fit the restaurant business. A few years ago, a well-known and highly successful football coach at Florida A&M once described the perfect football player as "agile, mow-bile, and hostile." In the same vein, the perfect restaurant operator could be described as "affable, imperturbable, and indefatigable." In other words, he or she is someone who enjoys serving people, can handle frustration easily, and is tireless.

Lacking one or more of these traits, the would-be restaurant operator can consider a restaurant that opens on a limited schedule, say for lunch only, or five nights a week. Alternatively, an operator can be an investor only and find someone else to operate the restaurant. However, most restaurants with limited hours or days of operation have problems with financial success. Fixed costs force operators to maximize facility use.

Operating a restaurant demands lots of energy and stamina. Successful restaurant operators almost always are energetic, persevering, and able to withstand pressure. Recruiters for chain restaurants look for the ambitious, outgoing person with a record of hard work. The trainee normally works no fewer than ten hours a day, five days a week. Weekends, holidays, and evenings are usually the busiest periods. Weekends may account for 40% or more of sales. The restaurant business is no place for those who want weekends off.

Knowledge of food is highly desirable—a must in a dinner house, of less importance in fast food. Business skills, especially cost controls and marketing, are also necessities in all foodservice businesses. Plenty of skilled chefs have gone broke without them. A personality restaurant needs a personality; if the personality leaves, then the restaurant changes character.

FRENCH CULINARY HISTORY

M. Boulanger, the father of the modern restaurant, sold soups at his all-night tavern on the Rue Bailleul. He called these soups *restorantes* (restoratives), which is the origin of the word *restaurant*. However, Boulanger was hardly content to let his culinary repertoire rest there. In 1767, he challenged the *traiteurs* monopoly by creating a soup of sheep's feet in a white sauce. The *traiteurs* guild sued, and the case went to the French Parliament. Boulanger won, and soon his restaurant, Le Champ d' Oiseau, was restoring hundreds of hungry patrons with its succulent, well-prepared dishes.[2]

In 1782, the Grand Tavern de Londres, a true restaurant, opened on the Rue de Richilieu; three years later, Aux Trois Frères Provençaux opened near the Palais-Royal. The French Revolution in 1794 literally caused heads to roll—so much so that the chefs to the former nobility suddenly had no employment. Some stayed in France to open restaurants and some went to other parts of Europe; many crossed the Atlantic to America, especially to New Orleans, the only truly French corner of the New World. They almost all went into the restaurant business.[3]

THE BIRTH OF RESTAURANTS IN AMERICA

The term *restaurant* came to the United States in 1794 via a French refugee from the guillotine, Jean-Baptiste Gilbert Paypalt. Paypalt set up what must have been the first French restaurant in this country, Julien's Restaurator, in Boston. There, he served truffles, cheese fondues, and soups. The French influence on American cooking began early; both Washington and Jefferson were fond of French cuisine, and several French eating establishments were opened in Boston by Huguenots who fled France in the 18th century to escape religious persecution.

The restaurant often credited as the first in this country was Delmonico's in New York City, opened in 1827.[4] This claim is disputed by others. The story of Delmonico's and its proprietors epitomizes much about family-operated restaurants in this country. Few family restaurants last more than a generation, but four generations of the Delmonico family were involved in nine restaurants from 1827 to 1923. Delmonico's continued to prosper with new owners until the financial crash of 1987 forced it to close, and the magnificent old building sat boarded up for most of the 1990s. Delmonicos' renovation has restored the restaurant to its former opulence. It is just the kind of place to take someone you want to impress.[5] Restaurants bearing the Delmonico name once stood for what was best in the American French restaurant.

With most family restaurants, the name and the business fade into history. The last of the family-owned Delmonico restaurants, at 44th Street and Fifth Avenue in New York City, closed in humiliation and bankruptcy during the early years of Prohibition.

Prior to the American Revolution, places where food, beverage, and a place to sleep were called *ordinaries, taverns,* or *inns.* Rum and beer flowed freely. A favorite drink, called *flip,* was made from rum, beer, beaten eggs, and spices. The bartender plunged a hot iron with a ball on the end into the drink. It was said that flip was both food and drink—and, if you had enough of it, there was also lodging for the night.[6]

Restaurants are places where the public comes to be restored, nutritionally and psychologically.

THE RESTAURANT FAILURE RATE

The rapid expansion and competition at cutthroat levels seen in the restaurant industry during recent years have resulted in a significant number of restaurant firms going out of business. In Dun and Bradstreet Corporation's Business Failure Record, the segment of eating and drinking places—or the restaurant industry—had the most business failures of all segments in the retail trade sector during the six-year period from 1992 through 1997.[7]

Some studies show that the reported failure rates of restaurants are exaggerated, that restaurants in bankruptcy can recover their financial health, sell out, or acquire partners and remain in business. Whatever the true rate of business failure, it is clear that starting a restaurant involves high risk and that many startups are undercapitalized. Restaurants may require a year or two, or longer, to become profitable and need capital or credit to survive, usually for a longer period than anticipated.

One reason family-owned restaurants survive the start-up period is that children and members of the extended family can pitch in when needed and work at low cost.

Presumably, also, there is less danger of theft by family members than from employees who are not well known. Chain restaurant owners reduce the risk of startup by calling on experienced and trusted personnel from existing units in the chain. Even restaurants started by families or chains, however, cannot be certain of a sufficient and sustainable market for the new restaurant's success.

One study of restaurant failure found a failure rate of 27% during the first year, about 50% by the end of year three, and about 60% at the end of five years of operation. Over ten years, failures amounted to less than 70%. If a restaurant survives for three years, its chances of continued operation are high. This suggests that in buying a restaurant, you should choose one that is more than three years old.

When the economy is in a downturn or a recession, it is probably the wrong time to open a restaurant. Even existing restaurants are at greater risk of failure.

Are there too many restaurants? The answer is *yes* for many areas, as the failure rates indicate. When a new restaurant opens in a given area, it must share the market with existing restaurants unless the population or the per-capita income of the area is increasing fast enough to support it.

Whatever the failure rate, the perception of bankers is that restaurants are a high-risk business and they are notably reluctant to lend money for restaurant ventures. When it is loaned, a higher rate of interest may be charged.

Many restaurants fail because of family problems. Too many hours are spent in the restaurant, and so much energy is exerted that there is none left for a balanced family life. These factors often cause dissatisfaction for the spouse and, eventually, divorce. In states such as California, where being married means having communal property, the divorce settlement can divide the couple's assets. If a divorcing spouse has no interest in the restaurant but demands half of the assets, a judgment of the cost can force a sale of the operation.

When a husband and wife operate a restaurant as a team, both must enjoy the business and be highly motivated to make it successful. These traits should be determined before the final decision is made to finance and enter the business.

BUY, BUILD, FRANCHISE, OR MANAGE?

A person considering the restaurant business has several career and investment options:

- To manage a restaurant for someone else, either an individual or a chain
- To purchase a franchise and operate the franchise restaurant
- To buy an existing restaurant, operate it as is, or change its concept
- To build a new restaurant and operate it

In comparing the advantages and disadvantages of buying, building, franchising, and working as a professional manager, individuals should assess their own temperament, ambitions, and ability to cope with frustrations as well as the different risks and potential rewards. Buying a restaurant may satisfy an aesthetic personal desire. If the restaurant is a success, the rewards can be high. If it fails, the financial loss is also high, but usually not as high as if the investment were made in a new building. When buying an existing restaurant that has failed or is for sale for some other reason, the purchaser has information that a builder lacks. The buyer may know that the previous style of restaurant was not successful in that location or that a certain menu or style of management was unsuccessful. Such information cuts risks somewhat. On the other hand, the buyer may find it difficult to overcome a poor reputation acquired by the previous operator over a period of time. There are no quick fixes in overcoming a poor reputation or a poor location, but clearly, knowledge of these circumstances decreases risk.

Without experience, the would-be restauranteur who builds from scratch is taking a great risk. Million-dollar investments in restaurants are fairly common. Finding investors who are ready to join in does not reduce that risk.

A 100-seat restaurant, fully equipped, costs anywhere from $6,000 to $10,000 or more per seat, or $400,000 to $600,000. In addition, a site must be bought or leased. Examples can be given of inexperienced people who have gone into the business, built a restaurant, and been successful from day one. More examples can be given of those who have failed, unfortunately.

On the other hand, a sandwich shop can usually be opened for less than $30,000. As one entrepreneur put it, "All you really need is a refrigerator, a microwave oven, and a sharp knife."

Franchising involves the least financial risk in that the restaurant format, including building design, menu, and marketing plans, already have been tested in the marketplace. Even so, franchises can and have failed.

The last option—being a professional manager working for an owner—involves the least financial risk. The psychological cost of failure, however, can be high.

An Olive Garden restaurant, which offers Italian cuisine. Courtesy Olive Garden Restaurants

Luckily, no one has to make all of the decisions in the abstract. Successful existing restaurants can be analyzed. Be a discriminating copycat.

Borrow the good points and practices; modify and improve them if possible. It is doubtful that any restaurant cannot be improved. Some of the most successful restaurants are surprisingly weak in certain areas. One of the best-known fast-food chains has mediocre coffee; another offers pie with a tough crust; yet another typically overcooks the vegetables. Still another highly successful chain could improve a number of its items by preparing them on the premises.

The restaurant business is a mixed bag of variables. The successful mix is the one that is better than the competition's. Few restaurants handle all variables well. In all of France, only 18 to 20 restaurants are granted the Michelin three-star rating. In the United States, hundreds of restaurants do what they were conceived to do and do it well—serve a particular market, meeting that market's needs at a price acceptable to that market. The advantages and disadvantages of the buy, build, franchise, or manage decision are shown in Table 1–1.

The person planning a new dinner house should know that even huge companies like General Mills make big mistakes. Once owner of two profitable dinner house chains—Olive Garden and Red Lobster—General Mills bombed with Chinese, steak, and health-food restaurants.

The small operator lacks the purchasing power of the chain, which can save as much as 10% on food costs through mass purchasing. The new operator is usually unsophisticated in forecasting. Compare this with Red Lobster's system, which provides the manager with the numbers of each menu item to be prepared the next day. Each night, the manager uses a computer file on sales records to forecast the next day's sales. Based on what was served on the same day in the previous week, and on the same day in the previous year, sales dollars for each menu item are forecast for the next day. Frozen items can be defrosted and pre-prepped items produced to meet the forecast. Wholesale purchasing and mass processing gives the chain an additional advantage. The Red Lobster chain processes most of its shrimp in St. Petersburg, Florida. Shrimp are peeled, deveined, cooked, quick-frozen, and packaged for shipping daily to Red Lobster restaurants. Swordfish and other fish are sent to several warehouses, where they are inspected and flown fresh to wherever they are needed.

TABLE 1–1
Buy, Build, Franchise, or Manage—
Advantages and Disadvantages

	Original Investment Needed	Experience Needed	Potential Personal Stress	Psychological Cost Failure	Financial Risk	Potential Reward
Buy	medium	high	high	high	high	high
Build	highest	high	high	highest	highest	high
Franchise	low to medium	low	medium	medium	medium	medium to high
Manage	none	medium to high	medium	medium	none	medium

Red Lobster is the largest seafood restaurant chain. Courtesy Red Lobster

Quality control is critical; all managers should carry thermometers in their shirt pockets so they can check at any time that food is served at exactly the correct temperature. For example, clam chowder must be at least 150°F when served; coffee must be at least 180°F and salads at 40°F or lower. Swordfish is grilled no more than four or five minutes on a side with the grill set at 450°F. A one-pound lobster is steamed for ten minutes. In chains, illustrated diagrams tell cooks where to place a set number of parsley sprigs on the plate.

Individual operators can institute similar serving-temperature and cooking controls. They may be able to do a better job of plate presentation than chain unit managers can. Independent operators can develop a personal following and appeal to a niche market among customers who are bored with chain operators and menus. This is a distinct advantage that individual owners have over chain competitors. Their presence on the job and their personality make the difference. This is a game where you must be present to win!

The restaurant business has both the element of production (food preparation), and delivery (takeout). One product (food) is unique because in order to experience the exact taste again, the customer must return to the same restaurant. The atmosphere is important to the patrons. Some would argue that restaurants are in the business of providing memorable experiences. Successful restaurateurs are generally streetwise, savvy individuals, as evidenced in *The Life of the Restaurateur*, attributed to a consummate restaurateur, Dominique Chapeau, of the Chauntaclair Restaurant, Victoria, British Columbia, appears:

> It's a wonderful life, if you can take it. A restaurateur must be a diplomat, a democrat, an autocrat, an acrobat, and a doormat. He must have the facility to entertain presidents, princes of industry, pickpockets, gamblers, bookmakers, pirates, philanthropists, popsies, and a ponders. He must be on both sides of the "political fence" and be able to jump the fence. . . . He should be or should have been a footballer, golfer, bowler, and a linguist as well as have a good knowledge of any other sport involving dice, cards, horse racing, and pool. This is also useful, as he has sometimes to settle arguments and squabbles. He must be a qualified boxer, wrestler, weight lifter, sprinter, and peacemaker.
>
> He must always look immaculate—when drinking with ladies and gentlemen, as well as bankers, swank people, actors, commercial travelers, and company representatives, even though he has just made peace between any two, four, six, or more of the afore mentioned patrons. To be successful, he must keep the bar full, the house full, the stateroom full, the wine cellar full, the customers full, yet not get full himself. He must have staff who are clean, honest, quick workers, quick thinkers, nondrinkers, mathematicians, technicians, and who at all times must be on the boss's side, the customer's side, and must stay on the outside of the bar.
>
> In summary, he must be outside, inside, offside, glorified, sanctified, crucified, stupidified, cross-eyed, and if he's not the strong, silent type, there's always suicide![9]

Francise, Anybody?

The International Franchise Association reports that there are 552 separate restaurant franchise concepts.[10] Several corporations offer a number of concepts. Host Marriott uses more than 60 concepts and operates in more than 200 airports, shopping malls, and travel plazas. Several franchisers have stopped adding new franchisees because of area saturation and complaints from current franchise holders that additional units cannibalize existing stores. The successful franchiser wants people with restaurant experience and money, or ready access to it. Ten representative franchisers are listed in Table 1–2. Also given is the franchise fee charged to a franchisee, the royalty fee paid to the franchiser, and the fee percentage for marketing that all franchisees must pay. The last column shows the amount of capital, borrowed or otherwise, that the franchisee can expect to pay.

■ **Franchise Risks and Rewards.**   It may be believed that buying a franchise is without risk. Not so. The restaurant owned or leased by a franchisee may fail even though it is part of a well-known chain that is highly successful. Franchisers also fail. A case in point is the highly touted Boston Market, based in Golden, Colorado. In 1993, when the company's stock was first offered to the public at $20 per share, it was eagerly bought, increasing the price to a high of $50 a share. In 1999, after the company declared bankruptcy, the share price sank to 75 *cents*. The contents of many of its stores were auctioned off at a fraction of their cost.[11] Fortunes were made and lost. One group that did not lose was the investment bankers that put together and sold the stock offering and receiving a sizable fee for services. The offering group also did well; they were able to sell their shares while the stocks were high.

■ **TABLE 1–2**

Franchise System, Franchise Fee, Royalty Fee, Advertising
Royalty, Total Investment

Franchise System	Franchise Fee	Royalty Fee	Advertising Royalty	Total Investment
Carl's Jr.	$35,000	4%	4%	$500,000
KFC	$25,000	4%	2–4%	Approx. $1 million
Taco Bell	$45,000	5.5%	4.5%	$236–515,000
Arby's Restaurants	$37,500	4%	—	$212–400,000
Denny's	$35,000	4%	3%	$1.1–1.7 million
Golden Corral	$40,000	4%	2–6%	$1.2–3.3 million
Steak N' Shake	$30,000	4%	1%	$1.1–2.3 million
Subway Sandwiches	$10,000	8%	2.5%	$61–170,000
Village Pancake House	$25,000	3%	—	$500,000–2 million
Big Boy	$35,000	3%	3%	$450,000–1.8 million

Source: Ira Apfel, "The Art of Franchising," *Restaurants USA* (August 1997).

Quick-service food chains as well-known as Hardee's and Carl's Jr. have also gone through periods of red ink. Both companies, now under one owner, called CKE, experienced periods as long as four years when real earnings, as a company, were negative. (Individual stores, company owned or franchised, however, may have done well during the down periods.)

There is no assurance that a franchised chain will prosper. At one time in the mid-1970s, A&W Restaurants, Inc., of Farmington Hills, Michigan, had 2,400 units. In 1995, the chain numbered a few more than 600. After a buyout in 1995, the chain expanded by 400 stores. Some of the expansions took place in nontraditional locations such as kiosks, truck stops, colleges, and convenience stores, where the full-service restaurant experience is not important.

A restaurant concept may do well in one region but not in another. The style of operation may be highly compatible with the personality of one operator and not another. Most franchised operations call for a lot of hard work and long hours, perceived as drudgery by many people. If the franchisee lacks sufficient capital and leases a building or land, there is the risk of paying more for the lease than the business can support.

Relations between franchisers and the franchisees are often strained, even in the largest companies. The goals of each usually differ; the franchisers want maximum fees, while the franchisees want maximum support in marketing and franchised service such as employee training. At times, franchise chains get involved in litigation with their franchisees.

As franchise companies have set up hundreds of franchises across America, some regions are saturated—more franchised units were built than the area can support. Current franchise holders complain that adding more franchises serves only to reduce sales of existing stores. Pizza Hut, for example, stopped selling franchises except to well-heeled buyers who can take on a number of units.

Overseas markets constitute a large part of the income of several quick-service chains. As might be expected, McDonald's has been the leader in overseas expansions, with units in 85 countries. Of its roughly 18,000 restaurants, some 6,500 are overseas. About half of the company's profits come from outside the United States.

A number of other quick-service chains also have large numbers of franchised units abroad. While the beginning restaurateur quite rightly concentrates on being successful here and now, many bright, ambitious, and energetic restaurateurs think of future possibilities abroad. Once a concept is established, the entrepreneur may sell out to a franchiser or, with a lot of guidance, take the format overseas via the franchise. (It is folly to build or buy in a foreign country without a partner who is financially secure and intimate with the local laws and culture.)

The McDonald's success story in the States and abroad illustrates the importance of adaptability to local conditions. The company opens units in unlikely locations and closes those that do not do well. Abroad, menus are tailored to fit local customs. In the 1999 Indonesian crisis, for example, french fries that had to be imported were taken off the menu and rice substituted.

Reading the life stories of big franchise winners may suggest that once a franchise is well established, the way is clear sailing. Thomas Monaghan, founder of Domino Pizza, tells a different story. At one time, the chain had accumulated a debt of a half-billion dollars. Monaghan, a devout Catholic, said that he changed his life be renouncing his greatest sin, pride, and rededicating his life to "God, family, and pizza." A meeting with Pope John Paul II had changed his life and his feeling about good and evil as "personal and abiding."

Fortunately, in Mr. Monaghan's case, the rededication worked well. In 1999, there were 6,250 Domino Pizza outlets worldwide, with sales of about $3.3 billion a year. Monaghan sold most of his interest in the company for a reported $1 billion and announced that he would use his fortune to further Catholic church causes.

In the recent past, most food-service millionaires have been franchisers, yet a large number of would-be restaurateurs, especially those enrolled in university degree courses in hotel and restaurant management, are minimally excited about being a quick-service franchisee. They prefer owning or managing a full-service restaurant.

Prospective franchisees should review their food experience and their access to money and decide which franchise would be appropriate for them. If they have little or no food experience, they can consider starting their restaurant career with a less expensive franchise, one that provides start-up training. For those with some experience who want a proven concept, the Friendly's chain, which began franchising in 1999, may be a good choice. The chain has more than seven hundred units. The restaurants are considered family dining and feature ice cream specialties, sandwiches, soups, and quick-service meals.

Smith's Restaurant

Ethnic background did not stop Barbara Smith, an African-American woman who owns three Smith's restaurants in New York and Washington, D.C. She also finds time to host a weekly show, "B. Smith with Style," and publishes, with the American Express Publishing Corp., the magazine, *B. Smith Style.*

Lucques

Many highly successful restaurateurs work as husband-and-wife teams, the man usually serving as chef, the woman as front manager. Some single women are chef-partners.

Lucques in Los Angeles is an example. Suzanne Goin, chef-partner of Lucques, graduated from Brown University but took to cooking and moved up the culinary ladder at

Chez Panisse in Berkeley, subsequent restaurant work in Paris, and Olives in Boston prepared her to become executive chef at Companile in Los Angeles.

Let us emphasize this point again: If at all possible, work in a restaurant you enjoy and perhaps would like to emulate in your own restaurant. If you have enough experience and money, you can strike out on your own. Better yet, work in a successful restaurant where a partnership might be possible or where the owner is thinking about retiring and, for tax or other reasons, may be willing to take payments over time.

STARTING FROM SCRATCH

Would-be restaurant operators may have already worked in their family's restaurant, perhaps starting at an early age. Hundreds of thousands of aspiring restaurant operators have tasted the restaurant business as employees of quick-service restaurants. For others, their first food business experience was as a student in one of the 740 cooking school programs offered in vocational school or community college programs or at cooking institutes like the Culinary Institute of America in Hyde Park, New York, and the Johnson and Wales University in Providence, Rhode Island. "Too many cooks?" a *New York Times* article asks. The answer, says the article, is "not nearly enough."[12] The article notes, however, that "unfortunately the pay is often peanuts." The tens of thousands of young people who work in restaurants know that, but also welcome the experience and enjoy working with other young people who never consider the job as a career. One message comes through loud and clear: The restaurant business is highly competitive and requires inordinate energy, the ability to work long hours, and the willingness to accept a low salary. The jobs are there and, according to the Bureau of Labor Statistics and the National Restaurant Association, job growth for food preparation and service workers is projected to require 3.30 million new workers through the year 2006.[13]

The cost of attending culinary training programs varies from none, at the many public high school programs offered around the country, to the $22,760 charged at New York City's French Culinary Institute for a six-month course (this includes uniforms, tools, and books). The Culinary Institute of America offers a two-year associate degree program at $15,400 a year; uniforms, tools, and books are extra. A number of strong apprenticeship programs are offered by the American Culinary Federation and local community colleges, as well as area chefs in restaurants, hotels, and clubs.

Following the European tradition, students who wish to become known as master chefs often seeks jobs at the name restaurants in big cities like New York, San Francisco, and Los Angeles. Many go abroad for the same reason, building their skills and rounding out personal resumes.

RESTAURANTS AS ROADS TO RICHES

Probably the biggest reason thousands of people seek restaurant ownership is the possible financial rewards. With relatively few financial assets, it is possible to buy or lease a restaurant or to purchase a franchise. Names like Ray Kroc of McDonald's, Colonel Sanders of KFC chicken, and Dave Thomas of Wendy's exemplify the potential success one can experience in the restaurant business.

Dozens of McDonald's franchise holders are multimillionaires, yet some McDonald's restaurants fail. Some owners and franchisees of KFC stores are also wealthy. A surprise billionaire is Tom Monaghan, the Domino Pizza entrepreneur. Hundreds of lesser-known people are also making it big, some by building or buying restaurants, others by becoming franchisees. Three success stories exemplify fast-track restaurant success. The sidebar profiles of Suzanne Goin and Barbara Smith are based on information in the January 1999 issue of *Nation's Restaurant News*.[13]

SUMMARY

The purpose of this book is to take the would-be restaurateur through the steps necessary to open a successful restaurant. Actual operation of the restaurant is left largely untouched. Management, however, is such a critical part of a restaurant's success that the subjects of management and control are introduced.

Sitting in a busy coffee shop can be a fascinating experience. Food servers move deftly up and down aisles and around booths; lights flash, orders are placed and picked up, the hostess escorts waiting customers to tables, the cashier handles a steady stream of people paying their bills and leaving. The flow of customers, the warm colors, and the lighting creates a feeling of comfort and style.

Food servers are usually young, enthusiastic, and happy; the broiler cooks tend to their grilling and sandwich making with a fierce concentration. Food orders are slipped onto a revolving spindle to be taken in succession, the orders prepared, plated, and placed on the pickup counter. A bell or light informs the food server that an order is ready. The entire operation could be likened to a basketball team in action, a ballet of movement.

Among the players, the restaurant personnel, the emotional level is high. This ensures that players each perform their assigned role, their actions meshing with those of the other players. The observer may perceive an elaborate choreography paced to the desires of the customer; the restaurant is orchestrated and led by a conductor, the floor manager. How intricate, how simple, how exciting, how pleasurable—perhaps.

When the characters are in their places, know their assigned roles, and perform with enthusiasm, the restaurant operates smoothly and efficiently. To keep it that way means attention to detail and product, its preparation, its service; the personnel, their training and morale; cooking equipment, its maintenance and proper use; cleanliness of people, the place—and don't forget the toilets. A hundred things can go wrong, any one of which can break the spell of a satisfying restaurant experience for the guest. Most responsible positions require that the jobholder control a number of variables. Many jobs require precise timing and deadlines, but few are conducted in settings that, as in a 24-hour coffee shop operation, feature one deadline followed by another, on and on, around the clock, every day of the week. Few jobs have the degree of personnel turnover found in a restaurant. Few jobs require the attention to detail, the constant training of personnel, the action, the movement, the reaction to and the attempt to satisfy the multitude of personalities appearing as customers and personnel, day after day, week after week, year after year. The variables that must be controlled to ensure a smoothly operating restaurant can be overwhelming; the restaurant can, indeed, become a multivariate nightmare. Good luck on your way to becoming a small-town or, perhaps, a large-town dignitary!

KEY TERMS AND CONCEPTS

Liabilities

High-risk business

Restaurant failure rate

Uniqueness of restaurant industry

Types of restaurants

Restaurant concept

REVIEW QUESTIONS

1. Give three reasons why someone would want to own and operate a restaurant.
2. The restaurant business is a high-risk venture. Why is the risk higher than in many other businesses?
3. Success in any business requires effort, perseverance, self-discipline, and ability. What other personality traits are especially important in the restaurant business?
4. In entering the restaurant business as an owner/operator, the individual has a choice of buying, building, or franchising. Which would you choose for minimizing risks? For expressing your own personality? For maximizing return on investment?
5. How important do you think it is to have restaurant experience before entering the business as an owner/operator?
6. Give three reasons people patronize restaurants.

ENDNOTES

[1] Beth Panitz, "Year of the Restaurant: Unwrapping What the Industry Has to Offer," *Restaurants USA* 19, no. 2 (February 1999), 26.

[2] Linda Glick Conway, ed. *The Professional Chef,* 5th ed. (Hyde Park, N.Y.: The Culinary Institute Of America, 1991), 5.

[3] John R. Walker, *Introduction to Hospitality,* 2nd ed., (Upper Saddle River, N.J.: Prentice-Hall), 1999, 11–12.

[4] Thomas Lastely, *Delmonico's: A Century of Splendor* (Boston, Mass.: Houghton Mifflin, 1967).

[5] Ruth Reichl, "In a Steak Palace, a Timely Turn to Pasta," *New York Times,* October 14, 1998, 62.

[6] Donald E. Lundberg, *Inside Innkeeping,* Dubuque, Iowa: W.M. Brown, 1988, 23.

[7] Zheng Gu, "Predicting Potential Failure, Taking Corrective Action Are Key to Success," *Nation's Restaurant News,* 21 June 1999, 31.

[8] Steve Perez, "Auction Set for Stores' Wares," *North County Times* (Oceanside, Calif.), 17 February 1999, p. B2.

[9] Personal correspondence.

[10] The information comes from Ben Van Houten, "Franchisees Go a Courtin' " *Restaurant Business* 96, 21 (November 1997): 62–68.

[11] Perez, "Auction Set for Stores' Wares."

[12] Amanda Hesser, *"Too Many Cooks? Not Nearly Enough,"* New York Times, 25 October, 1998, sect. 3.

[13] *Restaurant Industry Pocket Book* (Washington, D.C.: National Restaurant Association, 1999).

[14] Ron Ruggles and Steve Ells, "National's Restaurant News," January 1999, 66–69.

Chapter **2**

After reading and studying this chapter,
you should be able to:

List and describe the various kinds and characteristics of restaurants.

Compare and contrast chain and independent restaurant operations.

Briefly describe the lives of prominent past and present restaurateurs.

Discuss the contributions made by various chain, independent, and prominent restaurateurs.

KINDS AND CHARACTERISTICS OF RESTAURANTS AND THEIR OWNERS

KINDS AND CHARACTERISTICS
OF RESTAURANTS

There is no complete agreement regarding restaurant categories. New ones appear in the literature from time to time. For example, the bakery-café and ethnic restaurants are sometimes considered separate restaurant categories and are so treated in this book. The coffee shop as a separate category of restaurant is not so considered in some restaurant magazines. Soft ice cream shops such as Dairy Queen, Starbucks Coffee, bagel shops, cookie shops, and convenience stores are not restaurants in the traditional sense. Broadly speaking, commercial restaurants can be divided between quick-service fast-food restaurants and other kinds. They are then segmented into sandwich, noodle, pizza, chicken, or casual seafood restaurants, steakhouses, dinner houses, and so on.

Leading restaurant concepts in terms of sales have been tracked for more than 35 years by the magazine *Restaurants and Institutions*. Their 1999 survey of the top 400 restaurants in sales is summarized in Figure 2–1. It shows burgers and pizza leading in sales, followed by family dining, lodging establishments, dinner houses, and chicken restaurants. As seen in the charts, steak/barbecue restaurants did 4.5% of sales tracked by *Restaurants and Institutions*. Mexican, seafood, and Italian restaurants followed. Cafeterias did just 1.8% of sales and Asian restaurants came last.[1]

Of course, McDonald's is at the top, with $36 billion in sales a year. Surprising to many is the $17.7 billion sales racked up by pizza restaurants. In the family dining seg-

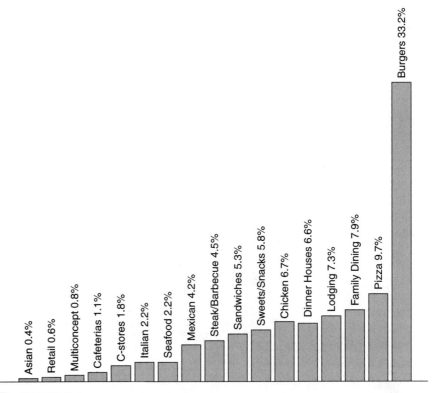

■ **FIGURE 2–1**

Percent of Top 400 Sales Total

ment, Denny's was the 1999 leader, with close to $2 billion in sales. Dapper Colonel Sanders, were he alive, would be pleased to see KFC leading in chicken sales. Applebee's Neighborhood Grill and Bar led the dinner house group.

Permutations of restaurant service styles and concepts continue to appear. Some prosper, others don't. Some restaurant periodicals classify restaurants broadly into quick service, family, casual, dinner house, and fine dining. Coffee shops like Denny's are labeled casual dining. Family restaurants, at one point, were called that because they were operated by a family and/or catered to families. The term now indicates restaurants that offer some table service and appeal to the family trade with price, location, and service. Few, if any, restaurants advertise themselves as family restaurants.

Restaurants called diners, usually found in the Northeast, offer both counter and table service. Originally, they resembled a railroad diner and could easily be physically relocated. Today, some are quite large but continue to feature traditional diner characteristics of bright light, lots of stainless steel, and both counter and booth seating. Cafeterias, popular in Texas and parts of the South and Southeast, are mostly self-service.

Coffeehouses, whose lineage goes back to 17th-century England, have grown in number—this time as espresso shops and coffee shops, some offering rolls, sandwiches, and light meals. The franchised chain Starbucks, a good example, has spread quickly across much of the country. Their guests are not pressured to leave and the various kinds of coffee are relatively expensive.

The large family restaurant chains today are corporate owned and may be franchised. In 1999, the largest in sales were Denny's, Shoney's, Big Boy, IHOP (International House of Pancakes), Cracker Barrel, Coco's, Perkins Family Restaurants, Friendly's Restaurants, and Bob Evans Farm.[2]

A major difference between what is usually called quick-service and family restaurants: Servers in family restaurants expect to be tipped, while quick-service employees do not. The beginning restaurateur can often buy into or directly purchase a family-style restaurant and forego the franchise route.

In the past, dinner house restaurants usually opened at 5:00 P.M. for dinner only, but remained open until 10:00 P.M. or later to serve the late theater market. Many dinner house restaurants could be classified otherwise. Among the large chains is Applebee's, with sales exceeding $1.5 billion a year. Other large chains calling themselves dinner houses are TGI Fridays, Chili's, Ruby Tuesday, Bennigan's, Hooters, Red Robin, Houlihan's, The Black Eyed Pea, Houston's, and the Chart House.

THE BIG BOYS COMPARED WITH INDEPENDENT OPERATORS

The impression that a few huge quick-service chains completely dominate the restaurant business is misleading. Unless our habits and taste change drastically, there is plenty of room for independent restaurants in certain locations.

Franchisees are, in effect, entrepreneurs, many of whom create chains within chains. The highest systemwide sales of a quick-service chain is McDonald's, followed by Burger King. Wendy's, Taco Bell, Pizza Hut, and KFC came next. Subway, as one among hundreds of franchisers, gained total sales of $3.1 billion. There is no doubt that ten years from now, a listing of the companies with the highest sales will be different.

Nobu is a good example of a high-style restaurant that is successful because it offers great cuisine, service, and ambiance and is located in a highly populated area, New York City. Photo credit: Steven Freeman

Some of the present leaders will experience sales declines, some will merge with or be bought out by other companies—some of which may be financial giants not previously engaged in restaurant business.

Restaurants come and go. Some independent restaurants will grow into small chains and larger companies will buy out small chains. Once small chains display growth and popularity, they are likely to be bought out by a larger company or will be able to acquire financing for expansion.

A temptation for the beginning restaurateur is to observe large restaurants in big cities and to believe that their success can be duplicated in secondary cities. Reading the restaurant reviews in New York City, Las Vegas, Los Angeles, Chicago, Washington, D.C., or San Francisco may give the impression that unusual restaurants can be replicated in Des Moines, Kansas City, or Main Town, USA. Because of demographics, these high-style or ethnic restaurants will not click in small cities and towns.

QUICK-SERVICE RESTAURANTS

Americans in a hurry have opted for quick-service food, especially that served in the cities, since the 1870s, when a New York City foodservice establishment called the Plate House served a quick lunch in about ten minutes. Patrons then gave up their seats to those waiting. Today, many quick-service restaurants precook or partially cook food so that it can be finished off quickly.

Seconds count in fast-food productions. The challenge for the quick-service operator is to have the staff and product ready to serve the maximum number of customers in the least amount of time.

To make the system work, a computer may be used to anticipate sales volume by placing advance orders on a screen when a sale is made. Time, temperature, and meat thickness are key in determining meat doneness. Appearance alone is not a good indicator of doneness.

Colonel Sanders

The restaurant business has many winners and many losers. One of the more inspirational stories is that of Harland Sanders, better known as the Colonel (an honorary title). Sanders and his wife, Claudia, built a thriving business in the little town of Corbin, Kentucky. They were known for their Special Graham Cracker Cream Pie and his self-taught knowledge of food. The restaurant, Sanders Café, was doing well when financial disaster struck: An interstate highway was built that bypassed Corbin. The Colonel was forced to sell his restaurant at auction to cover his debts. He was 66 years old and down to a monthly $105 in Social Security checks.

The Colonel took to the road with his "secret blend of herbs and spices," his home-style pressure cooker, an old car, and a lot of motivation and sales ability. Sleeping in the back of his car at night, he traveled from restaurant to restaurant, producing samples of his fried chicken, which could be fried in under eight minutes and tasted wonderful. The restaurants often agreed to pay him five cents for every order of the chicken served.

The Kentucky Fried Chicken concept was first franchised in 1952. In 1964, the Colonel sold most of his franchising idea to John Y. Brown Jr. and a group of investors

The Norman Brinker Story

Norman Brinker, CEO of Brinker International, climbed the corporate ladder with ambition and ability. President of the then fledgling Jack-in-the-Box burger chain, he started his own company, Steak & Ale, which was bought out by Pillsbury. Brinker became the largest stockholder of that company as well as executive vice president and board member. He went on to become CEO of Chili's and, finally, head of Brinker International, now numbering over 1,000 restaurants worldwide.

Brinker is credited with leading much of the growth of the casual dining sector of the restaurant business, including, Steak & Ale, Bennigan's, Macaroni's Grill, and Chili's. Similar casual dining restaurants opened in the 1980s, characterized by table service, often provided by college students, bright cheerful decor, and moderate prices—a step above the fast-food level. Often there is something new in style. Bennigan's became known for the plants arranged around its bar.

Norman Brinker, CEO of Brinker International, gives inspirational leadership talks. He says, "If you have fun at what you do, you'll never work a day in your life. Make work like play—and play like hell." Courtesy Brinker International

Brinker believes restaurants have a seven-year life cycle, after which they need a major change. The original concept, he says, gets tired. Upgrading, however, must be ongoing.

Brinker's type of casual dining restaurants lend themselves to rapid expansion via franchise, joint venture with financial partners, or issuing new public stock with which to buy other restaurants.

Brinker, very athletic and an avid horseman, suffered a devastating polo accident in 1993. He was in a coma for two and a half weeks and suffered partial paralysis. With physical therapy and prodigious determination, he recovered completely.

Brinker gives addresses on leadership and on making life an adventure. Take risks, he says. "If you have fun at what you do, you'll never work a day in your life. Make work like play—and play like hell."

From Norman Brinker and Donald Phillips, *On the Brink* (Arlington, Texas: Summit Publishing Group, 1996).

for $2 million, unwisely foregoing partial payment in $10,000 of company stock. (The group later sold out to Huebleins and hundreds of franchisees went on to become millionaires with the Colonel's "Finger-Lickin' Good" chicken.) Known for his devotion to quality, he insisted that franchisees adhere to rigid standards. The oil in which the chicken was fried had to be filtered and replaced when it began to foam or deteriorated in flavor. At one point, he sued his employer, the Hueblein Company, for a huge sum, charging it with producing an inferior mashed potato.

While representing Huebleins, the Colonel traveled some 250,000 miles a year. He would show up unannounced at franchises to demonstrate how to fry his chicken. He loved being in the limelight and at one time was one of the world's best-known figures, dressed in white suit, wearing a white goatee, and carrying a cane.

Later in life, he became a dedicated Christian, stopped using profanity, and gave much of his estate to the Salvation Army. Death came to him at age 90.

Successful restaurant operators, more often than not, share traits valuable in most businesses: high energy, ambition, and perseverance. The ability to overcome adversity, physical or otherwise, is part of most success stories.

Wendy's International Restaurants

For the person with experience in restaurants, who has at least $500,000 in capital, and who wants to be directly involved in opening a franchised restaurant, Wendy's International is a good choice—provided the restaurant being franchised is well located, meaning the area is not already saturated with competing quick-service restaurants.

Quick-service restaurants depend on national and local advertising to reach target markets.

Like most restaurant chains, Wendy's has had its ups and downs, in part because of turns in the economy. R. Davis Thomas, the founder, never really let go of the reins of the company and has had a large role in keeping Wendy's front and center by being himself, the smiling, old-shoe salesman for Wendy's. In 1999, he made 65 commercial appearances.

His family says he is actually a typical hard-driving quick-service chain president and, until recently, a workaholic: "Beneath the smile is a warrior." Though he started working a night shift in a restaurant at age 12, by age 35 he was a multimillionaire.

Thomas's sense of public relations is excellent. He dropped out of school at an early age; at age 61, he got his high school diploma—an event that made for great publicity (in spite of his earlier acquisition of 11 honorary degrees).

With a ghostwriter, Thomas wrote two books that detail his life, philosophy, and business principles. He stepped away from active management of Wendy's years ago but devotes much of his time to producing commercials and campaigning for his favorite charities, one of which is promoting the value of child adoption.[3]

Carl Karcher

Carl Karcher, founder of Carl's Jr., a fast-food chain that is a step up from the typical burger chain, is living testament to the good health, good living, and family values view of what it takes to succeed in the restaurant business. Raised as a farm boy, Mr. Karcher grew to be a 6 foot, 4 inch dynamo. His associates claim he is never tired. Rising at 3:30 A.M., he watches cable news, reads the newspapers, then attends Mass at 6:30. The first appointment of the day is at 7:15 A.M.

Carl's Jr. started in 1941 as a hot dog stand with money borrowed against Mrs. Karcher's automobile. The cash register was a muffin tin. By the 1990s, the name Carl's Jr. was on several hundred restaurants, with most food delivered from a huge commissary headed by a food scientist. Distribution to unit stores is by refrigerated truck. Carl Karcher Enterprises, the commissary operation, also supplies food and other supplies to a variety of other food establishments, such as hospitals, airports, parks, and zoos, in Southern California.

Carl's Jr. was one of the first quick-service chains to provide booths and self-serve salad bars. Customers place their orders at a counter, then seat themselves. Their orders are delivered to their table. Soft cushioned seats and quiet decor are elements that appeal to the middle-aged as well as younger customers.

Karcher, along with Al Levie, Pattrick Terrail, and James A. Collins, were early supporters of the fledgling hospitality school at California State Polytechnic University in Pomona.

International expansion took the company into markets in Asia, Australia, and New Zealand. When the company moves abroad, a licensing agreement that brings in fees without financial commitments by Carl's Jr. is set up.

His restaurant career, says Mr. Karcher, reminds him of a roller coaster ride, with its many highs and lows. The trips to the top, he says, have been exciting—while reaching the crest, thrilling; the plunges sent him reeling but, he says, "It's always been exhilarating."[4]

Karcher brought a sustaining faith from his Catholic upbringing. His wife, Margaret, and their 12 children are a source of strength and pride. Outspoken and political, he is in demand as a public speaker and TV guest. His message: faith in family, faith in people, faith in our country, and faith in the free enterprise system.

Carl's Jr. employs a number of people who are mentally and physically disabled, including many who are blind or deaf. The Braille Institute developed overlays for the keys on the cash register that enable employees who are blind to take orders. Some Carl's Jr. restaurants place Braille tags on the drink taps.

By 1998, CKE revenues were at an all-time high when a health problem necessitated a heart valve replacement for Karcher. In 1999, he was chairman of the CKE board of directors and still getting up at 4 A.M.

Emblematic of his philosophy of life, Karcher's business cards entitle the receiver to a free Carl's Jr. hamburger. The recipient also gets a tiny pamphlet about St. Francis of Assissi, a beloved Catholic saint.

Karcher is fond of asking, "Where else can 16-year-old counterpersons advance to manager positions in which they oversee $1.5 million businesses by the time they're 22?" He points out that Carl's Jr. managers are responsible for a million-dollar-plus investment and for overseeing the personnel development of 40 people. The average age of district managers is 33.[5] The average employee, however, does not see fast food as a career choice.

Cleo R. Ludwig, Founder of L-K Restaurants

Before McDonald's, hundreds of restaurants could have been called fast-food or quick-service regional restaurants. The stories of these entrepreneurs and the problems they faced are instructive and can help others anticipate similar problems. The L-K story illuminates the ups and downs of many restaurateurs—the need to cut and run when necessary, what to do when cornered by corrupt politics, and how, even at the best-run restaurant, difficulties will arise that are impossible to overcome.

Cleo R. Ludwig, a farmer's son, attended a one-room school that housed first through eighth graders, used the weekly newspaper instead of toilet paper in the out-house, and took a bath once a week. He grew to be big and strong, hard driving, God-fearing, and honest.

In 1940, having become successful as an insurance sales director, he began building homes on speculation and selling them at a fixed price—no changes allowed in the plan unless paid for by the buyer. That year, he became a partner with Bob Kibbey, a young schoolteacher, and together they continued building homes.

Their entry into the restaurant business was by happenstance. The partners knew nothing about the technical aspects of the restaurant business. They had been eating lunch at a little place called Wilson's Sandwich Shop and enjoyed chatting with the assistant manager, who interested them in buying a lot in a neighboring town and building a restaurant there. Only Ludwig had the cash to pay the building costs. Though involved in building homes, Ludwig and Kibbey found themselves working after hours washing dishes, frying hamburgers, and mopping the floor in their new restaurant. Mistakes were inevitable. One that was made was placing complete trust in their food vendors and the vendor drivers, expecting the suppliers to deliver what was paid for.

The partners soon discovered that the restaurant business provides a lot of room for dishonesty among vendors, delivery personnel, and employees. Vendors sent charges for which no deliveries had been made. Records were falsified. Employees took cash from the cash registers and stole food. The partners quickly installed accounting and control procedures and followed a policy of trying to remove temptations to steal.

The first L-K was opened in Marion, Ohio. By 1950, there were nine L-Ks and the plan was to have 40 restaurants. When Ludwig retired, there were over 200 stores, and more were being built at the rate of one a week.

After retirement, Ludwig looked back on his career and remembered some of the highlights. L-K had installed one of the first chicken fryers in the country in 1945, and he states that it was L-K who taught Colonel Sanders how to make Kentucky Fried Chicken in his little restaurant in Corbin, Kentucky. The Colonel parboiled his chicken in big ovens along with some vegetables to add flavor. The next day he rolled the chicken in flour and pan-fried it. Later, L-K had a hand in developing a pressure cooker called a broaster that took only six minutes to cook chicken.[6]

L-K used an 18-month training period for restaurant managers. All prospective managers were interviewed three times, at least once by a woman to obtain the feminine viewpoint, and a decision made only after a discussion among the interviewers. The final step was to visit prospective managers in their homes to size up the quality of their marriage and view how the house was kept.

The ratios of food and labor costs to income, key figures in restaurant operations, change over time and vary with the menu offered. When the chain started, food cost ran 50% of sales; labor cost 20% and overhead (other costs) 20%. This left a 10% profit. When Ludwig retired, the costs were 30% food, 35% labor, and 30% or more for overhead. Today, promotion and advertising costs as a percentage of sales have increased for restaurants and may be critical in attracting and retaining customers. An effective advertising slogan can make the difference in differentiating one quick-service chain from another.[7]

Ludwig believed strongly in the activities of the Salvation Army and that helping a person to self-sufficiency and self-respect is the best gift possible, but his true measure came in 1960 in Florida, during the civil rights movement. African-American students were staging sit-ins at white restaurants to call attention to the movement. An L-K manager called Ludwig to report a rumor that students from Florida A&M university, a traditionally African-American school, were going to march on the L-K restaurant in Tallahassee even though a city ordinance prohibited serving African Americans in a white restaurant.

Ludwig asked, "Do you have plenty of food and help on hand?" "Yes" was the answer. "Then let's stay open and serve them like anyone else." The upshot of the event was that from then on the L-K policy was "We will serve anyone who is respectable and pays the check."

Regional Burger Chains

With the multimillion-dollar advertising done by the big fast-food chains, it is easy to overlook regional burger chains and assume that it's no use competing with the big boys. Several regional chains and independents compete with the big names and do very well. In-n-Out Burger is one regional chain that knows full well the advantages of having customers supply their own dining room, thereby allowing In-n-Out the luxury of a relatively tiny preparation area and reduced rent. The customer remains in the car. The meat is delivered fresh, not frozen. Leaf lettuce, ripe tomatoes, and sweet onions are used. Fries are made from scratch using real potatoes. Shakes use real ice cream; buns are baked fresh.

Some regional chains go against conventional wisdom. Good Times Drive-Thru Burgers increased its prices in order to lose customers—those at the low end. Sonic Drive-Ins has made time stand still by providing carhop service, which was popular in the 1960s and early 1970s. Crew members walk or skate to customers' cars, which are parked in carstalls. On occasion, the Sonic quick-services chain serves cherry limeades and Chocolate-Covered Cherry Sweetheart Shakes or corn dogs on a stick, which appeal to kids.

The regional chains prove that they can compete with their huge fast-food brethren, the national and international chains, and offer franchise opportunities for those who qualify.

The Subway® Story

One major franchise that requires a low investment and offers a range of possible locations to franchisees is Subway, owned by Doctor's Associates, a Florida corporation with headquarters in Milford, Connecticut. Started in 1965, Subway has over 14,000 units in more than 72 countries and annual sales exceeding $3.5 billion. Franchisee responsibilities include:[8]

- Paying franchise fee
- Improving the leasehold
- Leasing or purchasing equipment
- Hiring employees and operating the store
- Paying 8% royalty to company (weekly)
- Paying 2.5 to 3.5% advertising fee (weekly)
- Paying additional advertising fees if the local market elects to participate in the program

In return, the company promises to provide:

- Access to product formulas and operational systems
- Site evaluation
- Training program at headquarters
- Operations manual
- Representative on site during opening
- Periodic evaluations and ongoing support
- Informative publications
- Marketing and advertising support

Subway publishes a franchise offering circular for prospective franchises that includes the names, addresses, and phone numbers of active franchise holders, listed by state. Subway encourages the prospective franchise buyer to visit and observe the restaurant in which they are training.

The initial fee is $10,000 for first-time franchise buyers. This fee is reduced to $4,000 for qualified owners purchasing additional franchises. Total initial investment by the franchisee ranges from $62,200 to $175,000, depending on location and equipment needs.

Subway units are located in a wide range of sites that include schools, colleges, offices, hospitals, airports, military bases, grocery stores, and truck stops—even casinos. Most remarkable is the company's statement that less than 1% of the units fail, partly accounted for by franchise holders' options to sell their unit or resell it to the company.[9] Depending on company approval, the location, hours of operation, and additional food items offered are flexible. The standard Subway menu cannot be omitted.

Capital requirements for traditional locations is shown in Table 2–1. Non-traditional locations may require considerably less capital.

No one should purchase a Subway franchise—or any other restaurant—without backup learning and experience. Subway franchise buyers attend the Franchise Training Program at headquarters at their own expense. Some 2,000 franchisees each year attend the two-week course covering management, accounting and bookkeeping, personnel management, and marketing. On-the-job training in nearby Subway restaurants is scheduled as well, totaling 34 in-store hours. Three to four trainees are assigned to a training restaurant.

The buyer pays a weekly franchise fee of 8% and a 3.5% advertising fee based on sales. The buyer has the option of life insurance; health insurance is another purchase option. Each franchise buyer gets a copy of a confidential operations manual containing about 580 pages.

■ **Menu Selection.**   Subway's flexibility in offering service in various types of locations is also seen in the kinds of food offered—submarine sandwiches, salads, cookies, and a low-fat menu featuring seven sandwiches with less than 6 grams of fat.

Subway features bread items that are prepared from frozen dough and served fresh from the oven. The frozen dough is thawed in a retarder unit in a refrigerator. The bread rises in a proofer and is then baked in a convection oven, in which a fan speeds the baking process. Bread formulas are specified at company headquarters and uniformly followed worldwide. Fresh-baked goods include white and wheat scored break, deli-style

TABLE 2–1

SUBWAY® Franchise Capital Requirements For Traditional Locations in the United States[a]

General Breakdowns	Lower-Cost Store	Moderate-Cost Store	Higher-Cost Store	When Due
Initial Franchise Fee	$10,000	$10,000	$10,000	upon signing Franchise Agreement
Real Property	2,000	5,000	10,000	upon signing Intent to Sublease
Leasehold Improvements	20,000	37,500	69,000	paid pro rata during construction period
Equipment Lease Security Deposit	2,500	2,500	2,500	before equipment is ordered
Security System (not including monitoring costs)	1,000	1,500	2,000	before order is placed
Freight Charges (varies by location)	2,000	2,900	3,400	on delivery
Outside Signage	2,000	4,000	8,000	before order is placed
Opening Inventory	2,000	3,000	4,000	within one week of opening
Insurance	500	1,250	2,000	before opening
Supplies	500	750	1,000	before opening
Training Expenses (including travel and lodging)	900	1,500	2,300	during training
Legal and Accounting	500	2,500	4,500	before opening
Opening Advertising	2,000	2,000	2,000	around opening
Miscellaneous Expenses (business licenses, utility deposits, small equipment and surplus capital)	6,000	8,000	10,000	as required
Additional Funds—3 Months	10,000	25,000	40,000	as required
Total Investment**	$61,900	$107,400	$170,700	

[a]U.S. dollars. Effective 1 April 1998.

rolls, wraps, breakfast selections (at some stores), cookies, and specialty items such as apple pie.

A company as large as Subway, working with thousands of franchisees of course, has complaints, among them being that a given market may be overcrowded with other franchisees who can be seen as competitors. However, the site selection process has been modified and is more sophisticated in evaluating market areas than in the past.

■ **Subway History.** The Subway story began when Fred DeLuca, its cofounder, was 17 years old. He and a family friend, Dr. Peter Buck, worked together on a business plan for a submarine sandwich shop. It took them four hours to produce and was implemented with a loan of $1,000 from Dr. Buck.

The first restaurant was opened in Bridgeport, Connecticut, in 1965. It did well in its first summer with the help of advertising slogans like "Put a foot in your mouth," emphasizing the foot-long sandwich, and "When you're hungry, make tracks for Subway." When summer ended, so, too did most of its sales. Dr. Buck suggested opening a second restaurant. "That way people will see us expanding and think that we're successful." It was not until they had five stores and better locations that the stores began making money.

DeLuca has changed the company's system of franchise development several times over the years and kept the concept simple and relatively inexpensive for franchise buyers. Operating the restaurant requires no special skills, except the desire to build a successful business in one's community.[10]

One of the many Subway Restaurants franchisees. Courtesy Subway

---

THE MEXICAN RESTAURANT

The food of Mexico covers a wide range of choices, much greater than that found in the usual Mexican restaurant in the United States. The menu is built around tortillas, ground beef, cilantro, chiles, rice, and beans. In the past, the food was commonly fried in lard, a practice almost guaranteed to add to the waistline and frowned on by the American Heart Association. Today, some Mexican restaurants use vegetable oil in their recipes. Generally, Mexican style food is relatively inexpensive because of the small percentage of meat used, which results in a food cost of less than 28% of sales. Labor costs are also low because many of the employees are first-generation Americans or recent immigrants willing to work at minimum wage.

The restaurant industry has a history of employing recent immigrants. Before 1900, and later, restaurants hired thousands of recent European immigrants. For example, fine New York City restaurants had kitchens headed by a French-born chef and backed by a brigade of his countrymen. Other national and ethnic groups filled restaurant jobs. In the South, it was African Americans; in the Southwest, Hispanics. Mexicans and Central Americans have experienced financial, political, and natural disasters that have sent hundreds of thousands seeking jobs in the United States. Among these thousands are many ambitious, intelligent people who become dedicated, loyal, and appreciative workers. Many go on to become restaurant managers and owners. As an example, Dick Rivera, of Hispanic origin, is president and CEO of the Red Lobster chain.

Other immigrant groups whose members have found jobs in the food service industry are the Vietnamese and Koreans. Numerous employers have built successful restaurants, including the large chains, using African Americans and now the new wave of Latino and Asian immigrants.

Ray and Gertrude Marshall and Acapulco Restaurants

The Ray and Gertrude Marshall story is inspirational. Ray was raised in an orphanage in Randolph, New York—where, he said, he was the worst-acting child so that he could get kitchen duty. Hitchhiking and working his way West during the 1930s Depression, he was first introduced to Mexican food in Denver. During World War II, he served as a chief commissary steward.

In 1960s, Marshall put down $1,000 for an existing four-table, six-counter restaurant that he reopened as the Acapulco and Los Arcos restaurant (he kept the name of the former restaurant to avoid spending money on a new sign). His restaurants became known for their famous double margaritas and 18-page menu.

Marshall took over failing restaurants, and by serving authentic Mexican food in exciting and comfortable surroundings became highly successful. Many of his recipes came from Mexican family recipes.

Chef Ray and Gertrude Marshall, founders of Acapulco Restaurants.

Calling himself "the gringo," Marshall's associates at the restaurants called him Pepe Ramon, while he defined himself as a

"Scotch, Irish, English, with a Mexican heart." A sense of humor and a big smile colored his relations with all he met. About his wife, Trudy, he joked, "I had to marry Trudy because she was making more money in our first restaurant as a waitress than I was as the chef-owner."[11]

Always proud of being a chef, he entered and won international awards at several chef contests. He researched food and kept a 10,000-item library. Marshall was fortunate in having as his lawyer and financial mentor the longtime mayor of Los Angeles, Richard Riordan, himself a restaurateur.

Among his several large-scale gifts, Marshall gave a half-million dollars to the hospitality program at the United States International University in San Diego. He has also endowed many scholarships for students interested in the study of food and food production.

Menus, decor, and music in Mexican restaurants are often colorful and exciting. Menus may include tasty seafood items and spicy sauces. Burritos—tasty ingredients wrapped in a flour tortilla—can be hand-held meals in themselves.

Before the day of the big chain Mexican restaurants there were Mom–and–Pop places, typically owned and operated by a Mexican family. These still abound in the Southwest and California. After World War II, Mexican chain restaurants began to appear.

STEAKHOUSES

Entry into the steakhouse category of restaurants is appealing to people who may wish to be part of a business that is simplified by offering a limited menu and caters to a well-identified market—steak eaters. A number of steakhouse franchisers are looking for franchisees. Steakhouse concepts feature steak, but the range in service offered is wide— from walk-up service to high-end service. The size of the steak served varies from a few ounces of a less expensive cut of beef to a 24-ounce porterhouse served on a white tablecloth. At the lower and mid-end of the steakhouse business are 6,454 casual steakhouses, a number that is growing.

The Chipotle Mexican Grill

Few restaurants move quickly into the success column. In 1993, Stephen Ells, a 32-year-old with a degree in art history at the University of Colorado, Boulder, and a degree from the Culinary Institute of America, opened a quick-service restaurant just off the campus of the University of Denver, calling it the Chipotle Mexican Grill. The restaurant has only 800 square feet of space but features burritos made with fresh lime juice and cilantro, wrapped in a big flour tortilla.

One of the salsa accompaniments is roasted chile and corn. The traditional guacamole and beans contain the best ingredients Ells can buy. A meal with a drink averages about $6 per person.

Blending and cooking the chicken, pork, or beef, grilled peppers, and onions draws on his food training skills and sense of flavor. His goal, Ells says, was to create a gourmet experience that could be enjoyed in 15 minutes—a big hand-held burrito. The concept is not

new; however, the way Mr. Ells does it and the setting for his restaurants make the difference. His first store does $1 million a year in sales—and by 1999, there were 17 more. The restaurant design fits the concept: stained floors, corrugated metal barn siding, steel pipe for table bases and foot rails. Plywood is used for the building's trim, part of a package that fits together.[12]

Steakhouses present the operator with food and labor cost combinations that are found in few restaurants. It is common for food costs to be as high as 50% of gross sales, whereas the labor cost may be as low as 12%; compare this to full-service restaurants, with about 34% food cost and 24 to 28% labor costs. Another difference: A high percentage of steakhouse customers are men. They enjoy aged beef, in which the enzymes have broken down much of the connective tissue, yielding a distinctive flavor and tenderness.

The prototypical steak eater likes his steak slapped on a very hot grill or griddle so that the surface is seared and the next layer yields a cross section of flavors.

Meat that has been wrapped in cryovac, sealed, and refrigerated for several days is called wet aged. The meat is not dried out. Dry aging takes place under controlled temperature, humidity, and air flow, a process that causes weight loss of 15% or more. The two processes result in different flavors.

■

The Lore of Steak

Steak lovers rhapsodize about their favorite form of steak and its preparation. Tenderloin steak is the most tender, cut from the strip of meat that runs along the animal's backbone and gets the least exercise. T-bone steaks are cut from the small end of the loin and contain a T-shaped bone. Porterhouse steaks, taken from the thick end of the short loin, have a T-bone and a sizable piece of tenderloin. (The Peter Luger Steakhouse in Brooklyn, New York, is known for serving a single steak dish—porterhouse, cut thick to serve two, three, or four people.) Most steakhouses promote their rib-eye steak and roasted prime rib. However, according to the Beef Association, tenderloin and top sirloin are the most popular cuts at upscale steakhouses.[13]

The New York strip steak, served in hundreds of steakhouses around the country, is a compact, dense, boneless cut of meat. A Delmonico steak (or club steak) is a small, often boned steak taken from the front section of the short loin. Sirloin steaks come from just in front of the round, between the rump and the shank. The age of the meat and its treatment affects flavor, but the amount of marbling created by fat between the meat fibers affects flavor even more.

High-end operations feel that about a million people are needed as a customer base. They require considerable investment in building, fixtures, and equipment. They may not be in competition with the Outback, Lone Star, Steak and Ale, or other steak-houses at the low end or middle of the market. Midpriced steakhouses like the Stuart Anderson's Black Angus chain compete in another price bracket. Forty percent or more of the high end is serving well-aged beef and may have sales of over $5 million a year. The low end may do well with sales of $500,000 a year. The high end expects to have a high percentage of wine and hard liquor sales. The low-end steakhouses may stick with beer and moderately priced wine. The high end may stock Kobe beef, imported from Japan, which may sell for $100 a pound.

In the year 2000, steakhouses were thriving and expanding, bucking the common knowledge that red meat, particularly highly marbled red meat, is good neither for the waistline nor the vascular system. Steak connoisseurs, however, say that the taste is exquisite.

Steakhouse sales can be quite high. Outback Steakhouse, in 1999, had gross sales of close to $1.5 billion and an average check of $17, an amount that places the chain in the mid- to lower price range.[14] Beverage sales constitute a large part of steakhouse prof-its. Fleming's, with restaurants in Newport Beach, California, and Scottsdale, Arizona, offer more than 100 by-the-glass wine selections, served in mini-carafes at prices rang-ing from $6 to $14.[15]

Outback Steakhouse Restaurants had gross sales of close to $1.5 billion in 1999, and an average check of $17, an amount that places the chain in the mid- to lower price range. Courtesy Outback Steakhouse

FINE-DINING RESTAURANTS

Fine dining refers to the cuisine and service provided in restaurants where food, drink, and service is expensive and usually leisurely. Turnover per table may be less than one an evening. Many of the customers are there for a special occasion such as a wedding or birthday. Many customers bring business guests and write off the meal cost as a business expense. The guests are often invited because they can influence business and other decisions favorable to the host. Fine dining is usually found in enclaves of wealth and where business is conducted—cities such as New York, San Francisco, and Palm Beach. Las Vegas has several fine-dining restaurants catering to tourists and high-stakes gamblers. The restaurants are small, less than 100 seats, and proprietor- or partner-owned.

The economics of fine dining differs from that of the average restaurant. Meal prices, especially for wine, are high. The average check runs $60 or more. Rents can be quite high. Large budgets for public relations are common. Because of the expertise and time required for many dishes and because highly trained chefs are well paid, labor costs can be high. Much of the profit comes from wine sales. Flair and panache in service are part of the dining experience. Tables, china, glassware, silverware, and napery are usually expensive and the appointments can be costly, often including paintings and interesting architectural features.

Daniel is an example of a fine-dining restaurant showcasing elegance in its cuisine, service, and ambience.
Courtesy Daniel

Charlie Trotter's, in Chicago, has established itself as one of the finest restaurants in the world. Charlie Trotter stresses the use of pristine seasonal and naturally raised foodstuffs. Courtesy Charlie Trotter

The menus usually include expensive, imported items such as foie gras, caviar, and truffles. Only the most tender vegetables are served. Colorful garnishment is part of the presentation. Delectable and interesting flavors are incorporated into the food and the entire dining event is calculated to titillate the guests' visual, auditory, and psychological experience. Expensive wines are always on hand, offered on an extensive and expensive wine list.

Food fashions change, and the high-style restaurant operators must keep abreast of the changes. Heavy sauces have given way to light ones, large portions to small. The restaurant must be kept in the public eye without seeming to be so.

If given a choice, the restaurant operator selects only those guests who will probably be welcomed by the other guests. It helps to create an air of exclusivity—one way of doing it being to park the most expensive autos near the entrance for all to see (Rolls Royces does well). It also helps to have celebrities at prominent table locations.

Very expensive restaurants turn off many well-to-do guests and make others uncomfortable when they feel they don't fit in or dislike the implied snobbery of the guests or staff.

Luxury hotels, such as the Four Seasons and the Ritz Carlton chains, can be counted upon to have restaurants boasting a highly paid chef who understands French, Asian, and American food and who likely attended an American culinary school or trained at a prestige restaurant and who has mastered French cuisine. Would-be restaurant operators should dine at a few of these restaurants, even though they are expensive, to learn the current meaning of elegance in decor, table setting, service, and food. (To avoid paying the highest prices, go for lunch and do not order wine.) Better yet, the person planning a restaurant career should take a job in a luxury restaurant, at least for a while, to get the flavor of upscale food service—even if they have no desire to emulate what they see.

SEAFOOD RESTAURANTS

In Colonial America, seafood, plentiful along the East Coast, was a staple food in the taverns. Oysters and other seafood were cheap and plentiful. In New England, cod was king, a basis for the trade between Boston, the Caribbean islands, and England. Dried cod was shipped to the Caribbean islands as a principal protein for the islanders. Sugar and rum made by the islanders were shipped to England, where manufactured goods were made and sold to the American colonies.

Seafood restaurants present another choice of operation for would-be restaurant operators, a choice that, in the year 2000, was continuing to gain in consumer favor

A Red Lobster restaurant. The largest seafood restaurant chain, it does approximately $2 billion worth of sales annually. Courtesy Red Lobster

and, according to NPD Foodservice Group's Recount Census, tallied more than 7,600 restaurants.[16]

Many seafood restaurants are owned and operated by independent restaurant owners. Red Lobster, with 661 restaurants, is the largest chain, with close to $2 billion in annual sales and an average sale per restaurant of almost $3 million. With the vigorous economy, customers do not hesitate to spend as much as $30 for a seafood meal.[17]

At the low end of the menu price range is a chain like Shoney's Captain D's, with an average check of $4.50. Seventy percent of sales is batter-dipped items, which reduces portion costs. (Batter is inexpensive compared to the fish itself.) Captain D's franchises its concept.

Farm-bred fish is changing the cost and kind of fish that are readily available. French-farmed salmon, grown in pens, outnumber wild salmon from the ocean by 50 to 1. Aquaculture has made marine biologists and many farmers into marine farmers, who are concerned with water temperature and fish breeding. Tilapia, grown in ponds in Mississippi and other southern states, is relatively inexpensive. Pollack, used widely in fish fingers, is also less expensive for the restaurant market. Other seafood, such as stingray and squid, are growing in popularity.

Seafood prices continue to rise but are in competition with shrimp grown in Mexico, India, and Bangladesh. Aquaculture is predicted to grow and may bring the price of seafood down dramatically.

ITALIAN RESTAURANTS

Of the hundreds of types of ethnic restaurants in the United States, Italian restaurants boast the largest number. They also offer an array of opportunities for would-be franchisees and entrepreneurs, and the possibility of coming up with a concept modification.

Italian restaurants owe their origins largely to poor immigrants from southern Italy, entrepreneurs who started small grocery stores, bars, and restaurants in Italian neighborhoods in the Northeast. The restaurants began serving their ethnic neighbors robustly flavored, familiar foods in large portions at low prices. The foods were based on home cooking, including pasta, a paste or dough item made of wheat flour and water (plus eggs in North Italy). Spaghetti, from the word *spago*, meaning string, is a typical pasta. Macaroni, another pasta, is tubular in form. In the north of Italy, ravioli pasta is stuffed with cheese or meat; in the south, it may be served in a tomato sauce without meat. Pastas take various shapes, each with its own name.

Pizza is native to Naples and it was here that many American soldiers, during the World War II, learned to enjoy it. Pizza eventually made Tom Monaghan a billionaire; his Domino's Pizza chain has made hundreds of small businesspeople wealthy.

While independent Italian restaurant owners typify the Italian restaurant business, chain operators are spreading the pasta concept nationwide and selling franchises to those qualified by experience and credit rating. The range of Italian-style restaurants available for franchise is wide, from stand-in-line food service to high-style restaurants where the guest is greeted by a maitre d'hotel, seated in a plush chair, and served with polished silver. A restaurant with a plebian name, Romano's Macaroni Grill, is said to cost $3 million to build, equip, and open.[18] As is true in upscale Roman restaurants, guests get to review fresh seafood, produce, and other menu items as they enter the restaurant. An extensive menu lists more than 30 items, including breads and pizza baked in a wood-burning oven.

Romano's Macaroni Grill is a restaurant with a plebian name, which is said to cost $3 million to build, equip and open. Courtesy of Romano's Macaroni Grill

The Olive Garden chain, with nearly 500 units, is by far the largest of the Italian restaurant chains. Its story is told in Chapter 4.

As might be guessed, many Italian-styled restaurants feature pizza and might be properly called stepped-up pizzerias. Pasta House Co. sells a trademarked pizza called Pizza Luna in the shape of a half moon. An appetizer, labeled Portobello Frito, features mushrooms, as does the portobello fettuccine. Spaghetti Warehouses are located in rehabilitated downtown warehouses and, more recently, in city suburbs.

Paul and Bill's (neither owner is Italian) sells antipasto, salads, and sandwiches for lunch, then changes the menu for dinner. The sandwiches are replaced by such items as veal scallopini with artichokes and mushrooms in a Madeira sauce. Osso bucco (veal shank) is another choice. Potato chips are homemade and a wood-fired oven adds glamour to the baked breads and pizza.

Fazoli's, a Lexington, Kentucky, chain, describes itself as a hybrid, positioned between fast food and casual dining. Customers place their orders at a counter, then seat themselves. A restaurant hostess strolls about offering unlimited complimentary bread sticks that have just been baked. The menu lists spaghetti and meatballs, lasagna, chicken Parmesan, shrimp and scallop fettuccini, and baked ziti (a medium-sized tubular pasta). The sandwiches, called Submarinos, come in seven varieties. Thirty percent of sales come via a drive-through window. The chain franchise has some 355 units and is growing. Kids are attracted by the offer of a surprise toy for under $2.00. The average sales per unit is about $1.1 million.[19]

Italian restaurants based on northern Italian food are likely to offer green spinach noodles served with butter and grated Parmesan cheese. Gnocchi are dumplings made of semolina flour (a coarser grain of wheat). Saltimbocca ("jumps in the mouth") is made of thin slices of veal rolled with ham and fotina cheese and cooked in butter and Marsala wine. Mozzarella cheese is made from buffalo milk. Risotto, which makes use of the rice grown around Milan, is cooked in butter and chicken stock and flavored with Parmesan cheese and saffron.

CHINESE RESTAURANTS

Though they represent a small percentage of all restaurants, Chinese restaurants find a home in most corners of North America, becoming part of the community and, in many towns and cities, staying for many years. Historically, they are owned by hard-working ethnic Chinese families who offer plentiful portions at reasonable prices. The cooking revolves around the wok, a large metal pan with a rounded bottom. The shape concentrates the heat at the bottom. Gas-fired woks are capable of reaching the high temperatures required for quick cooking. Small pieces of foods are cut into uniform, bite-sized pieces and quickly cooked. Bamboo containers, perforated on the bottom and fitted with a domed cover, are stacked in the wok to quickly steam some dishes.

China is divided into three culinary districts: Szechuan, Hunan, and Cantonese and Northern style centered on Beijing. Cantonese food is best known in the United States and Canada for its dim sum (small bites) steamed or fried dumplings stuffed with meat or seafood. Szechuan food is distinguished by the use of hot peppers.[20]

Chinese cooking styles reflect the places in China from which the chefs came. In the early 1850s, many Chinese joined the gold rush and opened restaurants in Western states. The cooking styles have been blended in many Chinese restaurants. The typical Chinese dinner was an extended affair, with guests each choosing an entrée and passing it around to share with the others. New Chinese chain restaurants are appearing, some financed by public stock offerings.

P. F. Chang's China Bistro came on the culinary scene as Chinese chic. In 1999, it had 35 restaurants and was opening more. The average check was about $17 per person, including entrée, appetizer, and beverage.

Panda Express is on a roll and looks to grow. Courtesy Panda Express

China Bistro departs from the often dimly lit restaurant operated by a Chinese family and offers, instead, an exhibition kitchen. Guests can see the woks as they flame and sputter. The chain has made a public offering of its stock.[21]

Panda Express has more than 300 units. Formerly located in malls and a few supermarkets, Panda Express is headed by an immigrant husband-wife team, the wife with a doctorate in electrical engineering, the husband with a master's degree in applied mathematics. Panda Express is on a roll and looks to grow.[22]

THEME RESTAURANTS

Theme restaurants are built around an idea, usually emphasizing fun and fantasy, glamorizing or romanticizing an activity such as sports, travel, an era in time (the good old days), the Hollywood of yesterday—almost anything. Celebrities are central to many theme restaurants. Some celebrities are part owners and show up from time to time. Michael Caine, the British movie star, for example, owns, with partners, six restaurants. George Hamilton operates several restaurants in hotels. Michael Jackson is associated with Chicago restaurants named for him. A number of football stars have participated in restaurants as partners. (Over time, many have stopped operations.)

As early as 1937, a Trader Vic's restaurant in California became popular with its South Sea Island theme, which was licensed for operation in a few hotel dining rooms over the next several years. Jack Dempsey, world heavyweight boxing champion in the 1920s, was associated with a New York City restaurant called Jack Dempsey's.

Joseph Baum created several theme restaurants in New York City beginning in the 1950s. He was well-known for La Fonda del Sol (Inn of the Sun), a theme restaurant that featured foods from Latin America. Another of his early restaurants, The Forum of the Twelve Caesars, was built on a Roman theme; the food servers dressed in modified togas. Roman helmets were used as wine coolers.

Theme restaurants like Planet Hollywood, which for a time experienced huge popularity, have a comparatively short life cycle. They do well located just outside major tourist attractions. Local residents, however, soon tire of the hype and, as is often the case, the poor food. Much or most of the profit in many theme restaurants comes from the sale of high-priced merchandise.[23]

Large theme restaurants involve large investments and employ consultants, such as architects, colorists, lighting, and sound experts. Color, fabrics, wall and floor treatments, furniture, and fixtures are blended to create excitement and drama. Theme restaurants of the kind found in Las Vegas and in large cities require large budgets and often fail because the food and food service are swept up and lost in the drama and high theater.[24] Novelty wears thin after a time and customers seek a more relaxing meal. In many theme restaurants, food is incidental to the razzmatazz.

The cost of most of the large theme restaurants is high both in capital costs and in operations. The rainforest Cafés, for example, spend large amounts on creating and operating the illusion that guests are in a rainforest. In addition to a regular full time staff, each restaurant has a full-time curator with a staff of four—an aquatic engineer with an assistant and four bird handlers. The decor includes electronic animals (a 9-foot crocodile, live sharks, and tropical butterflies). A scuba diver talks about the fish and their habitat.[25] The concepts, says its creator, Steven Schussler, won't work unless the restaurant has at least 200 seats.

Martin M. Pegler, a noted writer on retail and restaurant design describes sixty successful theme restaurants in Europe and America in his book *Theme Restaurant Design*. He divides theme restaurants into six categories:

- Hollywood and the movies
- Sports and sporting events
- Time—the good old days
- Records, radio, and TV
- Travel—trains, planes, and steamships
- Ecology and the world around us[26]

Some theme restaurants appeal to an older generation and present a time for reflection and nostalgia. Flat Pennies in Denver, supports a railroad theme. Steel railroad tracks holds up the bar canopies and are used as footrails. Lampposts suggest telegraph poles that once bordered railroad tracks. A huge Santa Fe train front, a mural, seems to be heading directly into the restaurant.

Motown Café, New York City, was designed to reflect elements of music and American musical history. Nostalgia for the 1950s and the 1960s is part of the theme. A two-story merchandise shop accounts for much of the revenue. As in most high-style theme restaurants, vibrant primary colors are widely used.

The restaurant Dive in Las Vegas creates the illusion of eating in a submarine. A team of architects, designers, and consultants using color, sound, and imagination assembled the place at considerable expense. It is a restaurant that is so costly and unusual that it could be successful in only a few places where large numbers of people congregate for pleasure. Dive, like most unlikely theme restaurants, does not depend on repeat customers for profit. The featured food is a submarine sandwich and prices are high enough to cover the large cost of planning and construction. Dive, like so many theme restaurants, is more about entertainment than food. Much of the income comes from merchandise, which yields higher profits than food does.

Tinseltown Studios, Anaheim, California asks if you want to be in the movies. Go to Tinseltown and enter the $15 million extravagant theme park and dinner complex. Tickets are $45 each. The place seats 700, covers 44,000 square feet, and an excited bunch of teenagers surround the visitors, seeking autographs and photos. Photos can be bought at the end of the evening. Some visitors are taken to a backstage studio and edited into a movie scene. Everyone is famous, with no effort on their part. Spotlights, cameras, applause from the Tinseltown employees give visitors a taste of celebrity. Appropriately, the place is near Disneyland—home of fantasy and good cheer. Steak and salmon are dinner choices. There is plenty of merchandise for purchase. Ogden Entertainment is the owner.

Would-be restaurant owners can visit one of the Irish pubs of Fado, the casual chain that offers a composite view of pubs in various stages of Irish history. Nearly all of the decor items are made in Ireland. They are clustered together into five sections within Fado, each forming a little piece of Irish history and artifacts. The word *fado* means "long ago" in Gaelic. Informality begins at the pub entrance with a sign reading "please seat yourself." As in Ireland, patrons are expected to become part of the atmosphere. Plenty of named draft brews—like Guinness Stout, Harp Lager, Bass Ale—stimulate the merriment. (Alcohol accounts for 70% of the revenue.)[27]

Food and beverage servers are trained in the Irish serving tradition, which prizes individuality. Each Fado pub has one or more Irish citizens on hand to impart the authentic accent and philosophy. Managers come from either Ireland or from the city where the pub is located.

Music is part of the entertainment mix and includes traditional jigs and live musicians for special occasions. Background music is placed during lunch and dinner; after midnight, it is moved to the foreground. The music changes with the age of the customer from—mellow for older customers in the early evening, to more-lively for a 23- to 40-year-old group as the evening goes on.

Both Irish mainstays and contemporary dishes are served. A potato pancake stuffed with fillings like corned beef and cabbage or salmon is popular. Cottage pie, which has chunks of chicken breast, mushrooms, carrots, and onions, is another favorite. Average sales of the six Fados in the United States in 1999 was $3.5 million a year.[28]

There is almost no end to what can be done with themes, some expensive, others much less so. As with any restaurant, there needs to be a market of people who will patronize the place, preferably as repeat customers.

Would-be restaurant operators who have the time—and they should take time— can visit these restaurants to get ideas to use or adapt for their own plans. The works of 31 restaurant designs are beautifully displayed in *Restaurant Interiors,* published by Rockport Publishers in 1998.[29] Charles Morris Mount has collected and comments on 57 restaurants in the book *The New Restaurant: Dining Design 2.*[30] Another related book is *Restaurants That Work* by Martin Dorf.[31]

The Benihana chain of Japanese-style restaurants can be considered theme restaurants. The razzle-dazzle of the highly skilled knifework of the chefs chopping and dicing at the separate table grills is memorable theater. Examples of other ethnic restaurants that border on being theme restaurants are:

- The Evvia Estiatorio in Palo Alto, California, which suggests a Greek taverna with a California aesthetic
- Tapas Barcelona in Chicago, which features regional Spanish tapas (hors d'oeuvres) and mariscos (seafood)
- Cucina Paradiso in Oak Park, Illinois, which features Northern Italian cuisine. Vivid murals, exposed brickwork, and a stainless-steel pasta sculpture add to the atmosphere.

It can be argued that every ethnic restaurant that is well designed is a theme restaurant emblematic of the cookery, food, and decor of a national culture. The restaurant can be Mexican, Moroccan, Chinese, Korean, and so on, or a combination of cuisines— Thai-French, Italian-Middle Eastern, Japanese-Chinese for example. If the restaurant is exciting because it presents an exotic cuisine and features serving personnel in national costumes and furnishings using traditional ethnic colors and artifacts, it is a theme restaurant.

THE CHEF-OWNER RESTAURANT

Chefs who own restaurants have the advantage of having an experienced, highly motivated person in charge, hopefully helped by a spouse or partner equally interested in the restaurant's success. However, hundreds of chefs are less knowledgeable about costs,

Spago Beverly Hills, one of Wolfgang Puck and Barbara Lazaroff's creations. Courtesy The Beckwith Company

marketing, and "the numbers" that is requisite for restaurants success. Many chef-owners learn the hard way that location and other factors are just as important for success as food preparation and presentation. Working in a name restaurant as an employee may bring a chef as much as $70,000 a year in income, while owning and operating a restaurant entails considerable risks. Gaining acclaim as a chef-owner has made a few chef-owners quite rich and made some chefs poor.

Chef-owners are part of the American tradition of family restaurants in which papa is the chef and mama is the hostess who watches over the operation from her post at the cash register. The family's children start work young and fill in where needed. Ethnic restaurants—Chinese, Greek, German, Mexican, and others—have flourished in this category since the days of the colonial taverns.

Chef-owners seeking fame and fortune can consider contracting with publicists to get the restaurant's name in the press a certain number of times over an agreed-upon period. The effective publicist knows a lot about restaurants as well as who to court and how to devise interesting stories about the restaurant and the chef. Promotion-minded chef-owners and other restaurant owners are adept at gaining public attention by appearing on TV programs, doing charity work, and making sure that the press knows that a film or sport star who is an investor in the restaurant appears in person occasionally.

The first thing a chef-owner should do is get a good backup person to share in management, food preparation, and, hopefully, marketing. This move anticipates periods of illness, family emergencies, and vacations, ensuring that an experienced hand remains at the wheel.

Consider the possibility of marital or partner dispute. Much of successful restaurant keeping is stressful—meeting meal hour deadlines and coping with delivery delays, plumbing breakdowns, and other unpredictable events. Co-owned restaurants can be beset by disagreements. Husband-and-wife teams are subject to divorce, resulting in often ugly litigation that is costly and stressful.

The best-known husband-and-wife culinary team in the year 2000 is Wolfgang Puck and Barbara Lazaroff. Puck, a native of Austria, gained some prominence as the chef-partner at Ma Maison restaurant in Los Angeles (later closed) and then he and his wife became well known for their restaurant Spago, also in Los Angeles. His personality, open and friendly, and his passion for restaurants are part of the reason for his success. Also responsible is his ability to work 16 hours a day in the kitchen when necessary. His work-day at Spago started at 8:00 A.M. and lasted until 1:00 the next morning. Puck's wife, Barbara Lazaroff, handles the marketing, much of the planning for new restaurants.

While at Spago, Puck went to the fish market in downtown Los Angeles five times a week because, he says, it is important to touch and feel the food you are about to cook.

Starting the first restaurant, Spago, in 1982 was a real trial with his new wife Barbara Lazaroff. The couple had only $3,500 and could not have opened without having a friend consigning a $60,000 loan. Later, they had to spend $800,000 to purchase land for more parking. Two other partners invested $30,000 each and $15,000 was raised, and, finally, the remainder was raised from more than 20 other investors.

By 1999, Puck and Lazaroff were said to be worth more than $10 million.

Puck's career speaks of the ups and downs of restaurant keeping and what can be achieved with determination, perseverance, a high energy level, good health, and good will. With the partnership of his wife, who designs the properties, Puck enjoys wide-spread recognition as a chef-entrepreneur.

His cooking style has been imitated from Tokyo to Paris and his Wolfgang Puck Food Company, which markets a line of frozen gourmet pizzas nationwide, is carried by a number of grocery chains. Puck and Lazaroff are known for their interest in and sup-port of several charities and social issues.

Puck's advice to the new restaurateur: Work hard and be patient. All of his restau-rants, he says, have been a struggle. Success does not come easily. His history bears him out. He started as an apprentice at age 14 and worked for several years in France. In 1974, he became a partner at Ma Maison restaurant with Patrick Terrail, who is French born and a graduate of the Cornell School of Hotel Administration. At Ma Maison, Puck also conducted the Ma Maison cooking school.

Since beginning Spago restaurant, they have gone on to open a number of restau-rants. The Puck-Lazaroff partnership has done what few others have—design and man-age a number of different styles of restaurant. Each restaurant is headed by an executive chef and a sous chef. Each chef, says Barbara Lazaroff, adds his or her own accents and personality, and each is a star in his or her own right.[32]

The skills, talents, and perseverance required to become a chef are told in detail in *Becoming a Chef* by Andrew Dornenberg and Karen Page. The book is valuable read-ing by anyone wishing to know about the skills, temperament, and the time required to undertake a chef training course.[33]

WOMEN CHEFS AS RESTAURANT PARTNERS

There are numerous examples of women chefs who are partners and do well as restau-rateurs. Susan Feninger and Mary Sue Milliken, co-owners of the award-winning Border Grill in Santa Monica, California, illustrate what can be done when trained chefs with food knowledge and a flair for showmanship become partners. It is often said that restaurants are at least 50% theater. In many restaurants, including the Border Grill, it's true.

Trained at American culinary schools, the partners met in 1978 while working at Le Perroquet in Chicago. Later, they both took the food pilgrimage to France so often pursued by Americans who want hands-on experience in French cuisine. Feninger worked at Oasis on the Riviera, Milliken at Restaurant d'Olympe. Back home, they became partners and opened the tiny City Café in Los Angeles.

Before opening the Border Grill in Santa Monica, they traveled extensively and added the City Restaurant in La Brea, California, to their responsibilities. Ebullient and fun loving, and with seemingly unlimited energy, the partners have become food and restaurant celebrities and written five cookbooks. They also have a TV series called *Too Hot Tamales*. Feninger and Milliken bring a casual yet highly informed knowledge of food to the television screen and to the radio. Both enjoy teaching classes and mingling with customers.

In 1999, they opened a sister Border Grill in Las Vegas, offering appetizers such as green corn tamales and ceviche (raw fish and seafood marinated in lime juice with tomatoes, onions, and cilantro), and luncheon items such as turkey tostada and a variety of tacos, including those made with fish, lamb, and carnitas (small pieces of cooked meat). A full bar offers more than 20 premium tequilas. At the entrance to the restaurant they

Alice Waters, a pioneer of California cuisine. Courtesy Alice Waters

Alice Waters, the Idealist in the Kitchen—Chez Panisse

Outspoken, yet speaking softly, Alice Waters has a mission—to awaken our thinking about food selection and its relationship to the planet. She might be called a kitchen philosopher whose writing reemphasizes the importance of using only the freshest locally grown organic and seasonal produce and animals that have been raised in a humane, wholesome manner.

Her degree from the University of California, Berkeley, was in French Cultural Studies. Waters says that the goal of education is not the mastery of a discipline but the mastery of a self and responsibility to the planet.

Waters's entry into the restaurant business had financial problems. Her father mortgaged his house to help get her started. In 1971, when Chez Panisse opened, it was overstaffed; she had 50 employees who received $5 an hour. It took little time before

the restaurant was $40,000 in debt. A woman who ran a cookware shop loved the restaurant so much that she picked up all the charges and paid the bills, but soon became disenchanted with Alice's lack of monetary motivation. Other business partners bought out the Good Samaritan, but it was eight years before the restaurant showed a profit. Waters never gave up her requirements for "the perfect little lettuces and the most exquisite goat cheese." The restaurant now operates on a budget and some of the staff share stock in the restaurant—and the place is a moneymaker. To assure that the "best and freshest" foods are selected, Waters employs a "forager" to search out and get the best from about 60 farmers and ranches in the area.

Both her restaurants and her publications have brought Waters national attention and won her numerous honors. Not only do

steady patrons come to her two restaurants, Chez Panisse Café and Chez Panisse Restaurant, but chefs, food writers, and others come great distances to eat there. Chez Panisse prints its menu seven days in advance; its diversity proclaims the place's virtuosity. The café menu changes twice daily, at lunch and at dinner.

The menus for the week of 3 August–4 September 1999, are shown in the menu chapter.

To spread the gospel of ecology and the need to eat only fresh, organic food, Waters has fostered the idea of having children's gardens as a part of school curriculum, the Edible Schoolyard project. She is also involved as an advisor to the horticultural project in the San Francisco County Jail and its related Garden Project. In 1997, she was named Humanitarian of the Year by the James Beard Foundation.

placed the Taqueria, where a variety of tacos are served (thin disks of unleavened bread made from cornmeal or wheat flour rolled around beans, ground meat, or cheese.)

More about this restaurant can be seen at the web site www.bordergrill.com. The color, vivacity, and menu of their latest restaurant, Cuidad, can be seen at www. ciudad.la.com.

Of course, few restaurant owners or franchisees have the zest or special talents of Feninger and Milliken. Be sure to get people like them on the staff—people who enjoy fun and are full of life lift the spirits of both employees and patrons. Professional public relations people can also put a fun spin on a restaurant's image.

NOTABLE FEMALE RESTAURATEURS

The restaurant business is democratic; its practitioners come from a variety of social, educational, and ethic backgrounds. A number of women have made it big in the restaurant business as heads of chains. For example, Ruth Fertel, founder of Ruth's Chris Steak House, led the nation's largest upscale restaurant chain. Its 70 restaurants sell more than 15,000 steaks daily and gross more than $260 million in sales a year.[34]

Auntie Anne's Anne Beiler introduced her rolled soft pretzels in 1988 at an Amish farmer's market in Gap, Pennsylvania. The pretzels were hand-rolled in front of the customers and served fresh from the oven. Sales from 580 stores in 1998 exceeded $167 million a year. Beiler has had the marketing smarts to come up with pretzel glazes like whole wheat, jalapeño, and raisin. The pretzel lover also has a choice of dips like chocolate, caramel, and marinara. Hard to believe, unit sales are about $1.13 million a year. Qualified franchisees may find pretzels produce a nice bottom-line.[35]

Julia Steward, president of Applebee's Neighborhood Grill and Bar, has scaled the corporate restaurant ladder. The company, based in Overland Park, Kansas, grew from 54 restaurants to more than 1100 stores and sales of more than $669 million in 1999. It is classified as a dinner house; labor costs run at 31.9% of sales—low compared to some full-service restaurants and one of the factors in the chain's success.[36]

Some African Americans have made it big as franchisees of large fast-food companies working in inner-city locations. Valerie Daniels-Carter is one example. As president and CEO of C&J Holdings, she is the largest minority owner of Burger King and Pizza Hut franchises in the United States. Daniels, who is in business with her brother, is a self-described workaholic—as, she says, was her father. In 1984, she bought her first franchise and in 1999 had 98 stores in Wisconsin, Michigan, and New York. Many of the company's units are in poor inner-city locations.

As for her view of employee relations: "When I hire people, I look for a moral stance, work experience, drive, and initiative." When buying an additional unit, she says, "It must make economic sense for everyone and, most importantly, offer opportunity for all of us, whether it's the manager or the dishwasher." Reflecting her concern for employees, she negotiated with Burger King to allow some stores to schedule shorter evening working hours so that workers and employees would feel safer.

It is possible that the typical restaurant manager of the future will be a woman. In 1997, according to the National Restaurant Association, 68% of all the supervisor positions in food service were held by women. Women managers, those in charge of a restaurant, accounted for 45% of those jobs.[37] Even though women with families sacrifice much of their personal life and time to managing a restaurant, those with stamina and ambition may be better suited for management than men with similar backgrounds. Women, it is agreed, are more concerned with details, sanitation, and appearance. Plus, they are likely to be more sensitive to and empathetic with customers than are men. Two national organizations—Les Dames d'Escoffier and The Round Table for Women in Foodservice—are both excellent networks for female professionals in the restaurant industry.

THE BAKERY-CAFÉ

When does a bakery become a café? The thin dividing line is blurred when coffee, sandwiches, salads, and soups are on the bill of fare. The smell of fresh-baked bread and cookies triggers memories of home cooking. Many independent bakery-cafés and chains are expanding. Some are mainly take-out; others are sizable restaurants. The small ones are quick-service establishments distinguished by skilled bakers who start their labors at 3:00 A.M. Many bakery-cafés mislead customers; they do not bake from scratch but bake off goods prepared elsewhere, a practice that drastically reduces the need for highly skilled personnel on premise. An in-between approach has the basic product being produced centrally, then delivered to the bakery-cafés where final proofing and bake-off is done.

Boston-based Panera Bread Company formerly Au Bon Pain, largest of the chain bakery-cafés, bakes some breads throughout the day and the company conducts training for bakers. Unit employees learn about breads and are able to suggest to customers which breads go best with which sandwiches.

Other large bakery-café chains also use the central commissary system. Corner Bakery, Chicago based, has a central commissary where bakers turn out 150 products from scratch.

Bakery-cafés offer a variety of settings and products. The La Madeleine chain, based in Dallas, Texas, presents a leisurely French country ambiance, with wood-beamed dining rooms and authentic French antiques. Some units have libraries; others, a wine cellar. The luncheon menu has, in addition to soups and sandwiches, such items as Chicken Friand, made with mushrooms and béchamel sauce and placed between layers of pastry crust. A patisserie carries such items as chocolate éclairs, crème brulée, and napoleons. The dinner menu features beef Bourgignon and salmon in dill sauce. Between 4,500 and 5,000 square feet in size, each La Madeleine unit seats from 120 to 140 guests.

Carberry's, an independent restaurant in Boston, has 72 seats and does sales of $2 million. Its owner, Matthew Carberry, says he offers an aromatic experience that customers can taste with their noses. His place produces 40 types of bread, including unusual sourdoughs such as sour cherry walnut and one with raisins, dates, figs, apricots, and sour cherries. Salads, sandwiches, and focaccias are offered. All baking is done from scratch.

Bakery-cafés can start small, but the owners should expect long hours of work and a slow buildup of customers. As with most restaurants, the best way to start is to learn the ropes as an employee working for a successful operator and then, with a knowledge base and capital, try for a high-volume location or become a franchisee of a chain with a proven track record.

CENTRALIZED HOME DELIVERY RESTAURANTS

Meals are being ordered and delivered via the Internet in the same way as fresh flowers. Existing food courts lend themselves to being changed into order and preparation centers where four or five popular food items such as pizza and Mexican, Italian, and Chinese foods can be prepared and delivered within a local area. Delivery can be by car, motorcycle, or bicycle. The center can be where a bank of phone operators and clerks take orders via the Internet or by telephone. The home delivery centers verify and process credit card information and use computers to perform the accounting.

Home delivery has been well established by individual pizza parlors and pizza chains. Much of the delivery cost is shifted from the pizza producer to the delivery person, whose income comes partly from customer tips.

Centralization reduces the costs of order taking, food preparation, and accounting; marketing costs, however, may not decrease. Competition will continue to force most players to advertise heavily. Economies of scale (efficiency resulting from high volume, automation, staffing efficiency, buying power, and specialized equipment) can reduce food, labor, and overhead costs.

In theory, the order taking and accounting can be done any place connected to the Internet, locally or internationally. The system does not even require that operators know what the customer has ordered; they simply transmit the order to a delivery person.

An order for pizza, theoretically, can be processed in China and prepared and delivered in California or New York. The Internet is inexpensive to use, faceless, formless, and global. The real question is whether the food can be delivered hot, tasty, and ready to eat.

Home delivery is being offered for upscale dining as well. Steak dinners are offered for home delivery by Steak-Out Franchising, an Atlanta company. Its home-delivered steak dinner comes with baked potato, tossed salad, dinner roll, beverage, and dessert for about $14.00.[38]

To promote home delivery in affluent communities, meals are delivered in special boxes or baskets. For example, a Japanese meal may be packed in a partitioned lacquered box called a bento box.

A variation on the home delivery theme is found in Chicago, where room service, in some hotels, distributes the menus from 12 selected restaurants to their patrons. The guest can call room service, which faxes or e-mails the order to the restaurant of choice. The hotel picks up the meal in 25 or 30 minutes and charges the restaurant $6 to $8 delivery.

Several chains are contemplating home delivery for more complicated, more expensive meals. The concept has worked for years via Meals on Wheels, a service provided for people who have difficulty moving out of their apartments or homes. The meals are nutritionally balanced and are delivered mostly by volunteers. An entrepreneur could learn home delivery by participating in the program.

Take-out meals have been available for many years. The old corn beef and cabbage meal available in several northeastern cities was essentially take out. In cities, take-out-meals are delivered to the address in minimal time. In cases where customers do their own pick-up, requests for meals can be phoned in or faxed to restaurants, thereby cutting wait time at the restaurant.

TRUCK STOPS AND TRAVEL CENTERS

Spread across the country are hundreds of truck stops and their big brothers, travel centers and travel plazas, where professional drivers as well as RV, auto, and tour bus travelers are offered fuel, restaurants, motels, and convenience store items. The large travel stops offer full-service restaurants and, clustered around the fuel stops, franchised quick-service outlets. In the West, these travel stops appear like oasis, often miles from towns, a respite from driving the interstate highway, beacons of hospitality. The food services offer business opportunities as franchisers and franchisees. Franchiser names prominent on these highway complexes are Carl's Jr., Pizza Hut, Subway, Sbarro, Popeyes, Blimpie, TCBY, and Dairy Queen.

Two pioneers of the road stop business are Stuckey's and Howard Johnson's. Travelers on the eastern seaboard in the 1930s were pleased to have a place to stop, gas up, and try one of 28 ice cream flavors offered at Howard Johnson's restaurants. The restaurants built a reputation for high-quality ice cream (12 percent butterfat), tender sweet clams, Simple Simon pies, and a limited restaurant menu. The restaurants spread across the country to number about 1000.

Mrs. Ethel Stuckey and her homemade pecan rolls and candies made her shops a must-stop along major highways in the South in the 1930s. Today, Stuckey's Express franchisees can stock some 400 items including caps, T-shirts, and hand-loomed Mexican blankets. Also on hand are jars of old-fashioned horehound candy and coconut bars. Mrs. Stuckey would probably also approve of books on tape, which truckers listen to while driving. These are available at Cracker Barrel Old Country Stores, 376 units in 36 states, located mostly on interstates and in tourist areas. An added attraction: Tapes can be returned for credit toward another tape.

More than 1,360 truck stops are in operation across the country; some, like the travel plazas, have 24-hour service and parking for 100 trucks. Truckers can get food and showers—often free, if they buy at least 50 gallons of fuel. Everything from truck parts to public fax machines and postal services are available at some stops. There may be ATM machines, a convenience or retail store, laundry service, truck and tire repair, truck washers, recreational vehicle facilities, even church services. Some stops offer e-mail and barbers. Travel Centers of America provides dumping stations for RV guests. In other words, everything to make life on the road easier is available.

Truck stops have developed their own character. Food service at travel stops can be minimal to fairly elaborate, from vending to full-service restaurants. Travel Centers of America offers breakfast around the clock. Its restaurant, Country Pride, has three separate menus for the East, Midwest, and West. The Flying J's restaurant, the Country Market and Buffet, typically seats 135 to 208 customers. Portion sizes are large partly because truckers may eat only two meals a day—a hearty breakfast and dinner. Flying J's has more than 100 Crossroad Delis and full-service restaurants. Travel Centers of America are located on all north-south and east-west interstate highways. The company tries to place a travel plaza every four hours of driving time, located at exits off the interstate. Their signs are large enough to be seen a mile away.

High-profit souvenir sales are a big part of many travel stops. The Flying J complexes have 24-hour convenience stores stocked with clothing, CB radios, mini-TVs—and, of course, radar detectors, insurance against being charged with speeding.[39]

SUMMARY

Chapter 2 describes the kinds and characteristics of restaurants and their owners. Restaurant categories have not been universally agreed upon and new segments are, from time to time, conceived in the literature. A comparison of corporate-owned and independent restaurants is made. Some leading restaurateurs of the past and present are discussed. Chef-owner restaurateurs and notable female restaurateurs are also discussed.

KEY TERMS AND CONCEPTS

Independent restaurant	Quick-service restaurant
Diner	Coffeehouses
Family restaurants	Chain
Corporate-owned restaurant	Dinner house restaurant
Regional chain	Ethnic restaurant
Steakhouse restaurant	Fine dining restaurant
Theme restaurant	Chef-owned restaurateur
Female restaurateur	Bakery-café
Centralized home delivery restaurant	Truck stop and travel center

REVIEW QUESTIONS

1. Briefly describe the kinds and characteristics of restaurants.
2. Briefly describe the life of Harland Sanders and the development of KFC.
3. What kind of restaurant would you be most interested to work in? Why?
4. What kind of restaurant would you most like to own? Why?
5. Briefly describe the life of R. Davis Thomas and the birth of Wendy's International.
6. Briefly describe the life of Carl Karcher and the birth of Carl's Jr.
7. What are the responsibilities of the franchisee under Subway's franchise agreement? What does the company promise?
8. What are the highlights of Mexican restaurant menus?
9. Name elements that make for "fine dining."
10. Name three women chefs who are restaurant partners and describe their activities.

ENDNOTES

1 Scott Hyme, Combine and Conquer. *Restaurants and Institutions* 109, no. 19 (15 July 1999). p 52.
2 Ibid.
3 Much of this information draws on Dave Thomas, with Ron Beyma, *Well Done! The Common Guy's Guide to Everyday Success* (Grand Rapids, Mich.: Zonderman Publishing house, 1994).
4 Personal conversation with Karl Karcher, November 23, 1992.
5 Carl Karcher, *Never Stop Dreaming: 50 Years of Making It Happen* (San Marco, Calif: Robert Eidman Publishing, 1991).
6 Leo R. Ludwig, *I Am What I Am . . . and Where's Why* (Caledonia, Ohio: Ludco, 1986), p. 43.

7 Op. Cit., p. 69.

8 Subway's Corporate Report, 1999.

9 Courtesy of Subway, Milford, CT.

10 Courtesy of Subway, Milford, CT. Vol. 19, no. 2. pp. 8–12.

11 Personal conversation with Ray Marshall, March 26, 1990.

12 Personal conversation with Stephen Ells, August 16, 1993.

13 National Cattlemen's Beef Association, Washington, D.C. Website: www.Beef.org.

14 Outback Steakhouse press kit, 1999.

15 Nancy Brumback, "The Catch," *Restaurant and Business* 96, no. 16 (15 August 1999): 55–72.

16 NPD Foodservice Group press release, November 1999.

17 Red Lobster press kit, December 1999.

18 Pamela Goyan Kittder and Katheryn Sucher, *Food and Culture in America* (New York: Van Nostrand Reinhold, 1989), 98, no. 4, 250–267.

19 Hoover's On Line company capsule, April 22, 2000.

20 Laura Kaufman, *Los Angeles Times*, 19 August 1999, C1. For a more complete comment on Chinese cooking styles, see Allen Davidson, *The Oxford Companion to Food* (New York: Oxford University Press, 1999), pp. 171–173.

21 Hover's On Line P. F. Chang's China Bistro, Inc., company capsule, April 22, 2000.

22 Restaurants USA, *National Restaurant Association*, February 1999, Washington D.C. 43.

23 Charles V. Bagli, "Novelty Gone, Theme Restaurants Are Tumbling," *New York Times*. 27 December 1998, Y1.

24 Ibid.

25 Cheryl Ursin, "Theme Restaurants Play to Diners' Appetite For Fun," *Restaurants USA* (19 February 1999).

26 Martin Pegler, *Theme Restaurant Design—Entertain and Fun in Dining* (New York: Reporting Corporation, 1997), 11.

27 Gina Lavecchia, "Irish Invasion," *Restaurant Hospitality*, 83, 1 (January 1999): 56–60.

28 Ibid.

29 *Restaurant Interiors* (Gloucester, Mass.: Rockport, 1998).

30 Charles Morris Mount, *The New Restaurant: Dining Design 2* (Glen Cove, N.Y.: PBC International, 1995).

31 Martin E. Dorf, *Restaurants That Work: Case Studies of the Best in the Industry* (Whitney Library of Design, 1992).

32 Ibid.

33 Andrew Dornenberger and Karen Page, *Becoming a Chef* (New York: John Wiley & Sons, Inc., 1995).

34 Hoover's On Line Ruth's Chris Steakhouse, company capsule, April 22, 2000.

35 Hoover's On Line Auntie Anne's, company capsule, April 22, 2000.

36 Hoover's On Line Applebee's International, Inc., company capsule, April 22, 2000.

37 Nancy Brumback, "Replacement Parts," *Restaurant Business*, 98, no. 11 (June 1999): 49–68.

38 Nancy Ann Tasoulas, "Are We There Yet?" *Restaurant Business* (15 February 1999).

39 "On Target," *Restaurant Business* 97, no. 19 (1 October 1998).

Chapter **3**

After reading and studying this chapter,
you should be able to:

Realize the advantage of a good restaurant name.

Explain the relationship between concept and market.

Be able to write a restaurant concept.

Understand restaurant knockout criteria.

CONCEPT, LOCATION, AND DESIGN

RESTAURANT CONCEPTS

The objective in planning a restaurant is to assemble, on paper, the ideas for a restaurant that, when operating, will be profitable and satisfying to the guest and owner/operator. The formulation of these ideas is called the *restaurant concept*, the matrix of ideas that constitutes what will be perceived as the restaurant's image. The concept is devised to interest a certain group of people (or groups of people), called a *target market* or *niche*. Marketing is the sum of activities intended to attract people to the restaurant. This includes determining what group or groups (target markets) are most likely to react favorably to the concept.

In this section, we discuss restaurant concepts. Later sections discuss the relationships between concept, business plan, site selection (restaurant location), and marketing. Concept, location, ambiance, and marketing are interdependent. Concept development applies to any foodservice operation, from a hot dog stand to a luxury restaurant, from quick-service to theme restaurants.

The challenge is to create a restaurant concept that fits a definite target market, a concept better suited to its market than that presented by competing restaurants, and to bring it into being. This is known as being *D&B*—different and better. The restaurant business is intensely competitive. There is always a better concept coming on stream—better in atmosphere, menu, location, marketing, image, and management. If a restaurant is not competitive, another restaurant down the street, across town, or next door will take away its customers.

This challenge does not mean that a new restaurant must be built. Plenty of existing restaurants and other buildings can be taken over. The challenge is to develop and install a new concept, acknowledging the possibility that it may be necessary to modify it as competition and other conditions change.

> The best concepts are often the result of learning from mistakes. Just when you think you have your concept figured out, guess what? You don't. Also, just when you think it's hopeless, a light's going to come on, a rainbow is going to appear, and the concept will be reborn. And it may not be the one you started out with. Restaurants are essentially about food and service. The success of your concept is going to depend on both.[1]

Every restaurant represents a concept and projects a total impression or image. The image appeals to a certain market—children, romantics, people celebrating special occasions, fun types, people seeking a formal or a casual venue. The concept should fit the location and reach out to appeal to its target market(s). In planning a restaurant concept, location, menu, and decor should intertwine. When a concept and image lose appeal, they must be modified or even changed completely.

Concept comprises everything that affects how the patron views the restaurant: public relations, advertising, promotion, and the operation itself. Concept frames the public's perception of the total restaurant. It includes the building, its curbside appeal, its exterior decor. Does the restaurant invite people to venture in, or is it neglected and dirty in appearance? Decor, menu, and style of operation are part of the concept. Concept includes the personality of the owner, the appearance of the dining room staff, the music, and the tone of the place. Particularly important are the menu, the food, and its presentation. Symbols, as seen in the sign, logo, colors, upholstery, and lighting, are aspects of concept. The right music reinforces the concept. The concept provides the framework on which to hang the image.

Concept: Clear-Cut or Ambiguous?

Many restaurants lack clear-cut concepts. The symbols, furnishings, service, and all of those things that make up the atmosphere of a restaurant are not integrated into an image that is projected for everyone to see. Logos (identifying symbols), signs, uniforms, menus, and decor should fit together into a whole that comes across to the public as a well-defined image.

Concepts can be purposefully ambiguous, but most restaurants are made more visible psychologically if they project a theme, a character, and a purpose.

A concept is strengthened if it immediately establishes an identity, one that is vivid, easily remembered, and has a favorable ring. "Wendy's" was chosen because of its identification potential and because it was easy to pronounce; it also tied in easily with the theme "old-fashioned hamburgers." It also happened to be the nickname of the daughter of R. David Thomas (the president). Taco Bell gained instant recognition because the word *taco* is synonymous with Mexican food.

The name of the restaurant is part of the image. The Spaghetti Factory suggests quick service, low cost, and a fun place for Italian food. El Torito suggests a Mexican theme restaurant and TGI Friday's portrays a fun image—however, people who do not know TGI Friday's, would not know what to expect. Coco's is even less descriptive—a patron would hardly know what to expect.

The restaurant name can tell the customer what to expect—Pizza Palace, New China House, Taco Bell, Hamburger Heaven. No one really expects to meet grandma

Park Avenue Café in Chicago suggests a homey, friendly ambiance. Photo by Peter Paige

Don't open a restaurant unless you:

1. Have experience in the restaurant business, especially in the segment in which you plan to operate.
2. Don't mind giving up your evenings and long weekends—not to mention mornings and afternoons.
3. Are able to accept personal risk. Have money to lose—oops! we mean capital to start a high-risk business.
4. Have a concept in mind and menus developed.
5. Have completed a detailed business plan.
6. Have personal and family goals established for the next several years.
7. Have the patience of a saint and two active thyroid glands!
8. Have identified a quantifiable need in the market for the type of restaurant you are considering opening.
9. Have an exit plan—the restaurant business is easy to enter but potentially costly to exit.
10. Can afford a lawyer and an accountant experienced in the restaurant business.

at Grandma's Kitchen, but the name suggests a homey, friendly place, one without escargots on the menu.

The Seven Grains suggests a health-food restaurant, as does The Thinnery. Well-known British names like Trafalgar Square suggest a British atmosphere and menu. Mama Mia's reflects an Italian menu. La Campagne projects a country French theme restaurant; Long John Silver's and Red Lobster suggest a seafood restaurant; Olive Garden implies an Italian restaurant.

> Here's the difference between a concept and a theme: A soup-and-sandwich place that sells sandwiches on whole-wheat bread is a concept; American food in an art decor restaurant is a theme. Be sure of your concept and stay with it.[2]

Naming a restaurant after the owner has proven successful for centuries, even though the restaurant may use a first name, as in Al's Place. The personal name implies that somebody by the name of Al is going to be around to see that things go well. Stuart Anderson is not likely to be found at any one of the many Stuart Anderson's Cattle Ranch restaurants, but the feeling is that Stuart may be somewhere in the wings watching out for his customers. Naming a restaurant after the proprietor suggests someone who has pride of ownership. The personally named restaurant evokes an image of someone who cares hovering in the background.

PROTECTING THE RESTAURANT'S NAME

Lawsuits over restaurant names do happen. Even if an owner of a new restaurant were named Howard Johnson, he would be wise not to call his restaurant Howard Johnson's because of trademark regulations. Once selected, a name may be difficult to change without serious financial loss. Ray Kroc, who built McDonald's restaurants, had to pay several million dollars to the original McDonald's owners to continue using that name and format. The proprietary right to a restaurant name not already in use begins with usage and signs, promotional campaigns, and advertising material.

If another party uses your restaurant name, you should take action against that person by proving that you, the challenging party, used the name first. Loss of the right to use a name means changing signs, menus, and promotional material. It can also mean court costs and, perhaps, the loss of power that has been built into the name by a superior operation.

The McDonald's Concept and Image

To illustrate concept, look at McDonald's—the greatest restaurant success story of all time. The concept is the all-American family restaurant—clean, wholesome, inexpensive, and fun. Ray Kroc would not allow a jukebox, cigarette machine, or telephone in McDonald's because it encouraged people to "overstay their welcome." In the company's advertising, McDonald's food servers are wholesome, bursting with health and good will. Ronald McDonald, the jolly clown, is better known in the minds of children than any other fictional character except Mickey Mouse and Santa Claus. Ronald is fun; therefore, McDonald's is fun. McDonald's TV advertising has reached into the American psyche and implanted the idea that eating at McDonald's is unalloyed joy. Image presentation is consistent and easy to understand; simplicity is portrayed in uncluttered, quick, efficient service.

The simple, straightforward menu is one key to the effectiveness of McDonald's advertising.

While the term *concept restaurant* is relatively new, concept restaurants have been around for some time. The person who took the retired railroad dining car in the 1920s and made it into a diner had the makings of a concept restaurant. In the 1930s, Victor Bergeron converted a garage into a schmaltzy Polynesian restaurant and called it Trader Vic's—a concept restaurant. The Rib Rooms, popular in the 1950s and 1960s, were an adaptation of Simpson's on the Strand in London, a famous rolling-beef-cart restaurant going back many years.

The so-called theme restaurants, which follow a particular ethnic menu and decor or are built around a particular idea, are concept restaurants. The concept can be ambiguous, as is the case with Bennigan's, Chili's, Houlihan's, and TGI Friday's, where it is difficult to ascertain any particular theme other than bric-a-brac or American bistro.

Decor and menu at these restaurants are fun and stimulating. In the men's room, straps from an old trolley car may be hanging over the urinals. The customer may find himself facing a mirror enclosed by a horse collar. Decorative surprises are the norm. The exterior may be painted an odd color, such as blue-green, or sport a brightly colored red-and-white awning. The concept features are humor, self-deprecation, full service, high-quality food, good value, and a place where people can relax.

Some concept restaurants make a virtue of the rustic and the antique by using exposed wood and unpainted, old barn siding. An array of antique artifacts can produce

Godzilla

One restaurant in San Francisco, named Godzilla after the original movie, was recently forced to change its name. This happened when the more recent version of the movie opened across the street. TV cameras noticed the restaurant name and crowds; a reporter interviewed the owner and when what amounted to a 30-second TV clip was seen by a movie executive, he contacted the copyright owners. A few days later, a letter arrived from the lawyers of the movie's copyright owners advising the restaurant owner that he was capitalizing on the movie's name and that he must change the name or face a lawsuit.

The decor of Spago inspires a casual elegance. Courtesy The Beckwith Company

a novel effect and, if selected and placed well, can be an inexpensive way to decorate. The owner can count on minimum maintenance.

DEFINING THE CONCEPT AND MARKET

In selecting a concept for a restaurant, define it precisely in the context of which markets will find it appealing. A typical coffee shop with counter and booth service, for example, may appeal to the working family or the traveler on an interstate highway. Ask yourself:

- Will a quick-service place with drive-through, walk-up, and table service appeal to the young family, teenagers, and children?

- Will an upscale restaurant with a view, opening at 5:00 P.M. to serve dinners, appeal to upper-middle-class patrons?

- Is a Mexican restaurant with hybrid Mexican decor and inexpensive food appealing to the middle class for an evening-out?

- Is a pizza house with beer and wine appealing to the young family as a fun place?

- Is a coffeehouse menu in a dinner-house setting, including a few European menu touches (for example, Coco's or the Grinder's) the right concept? Or should it be a stepped-up coffee shop with a few dinner items, like Jo Jo's?

- Does the restaurant offer authentic French, Chinese, or Japanese food? If so, does it have an authentic French, Chinese, or Japanese family operating it? La Campagne, for example, depends on a chef who is highly skilled in classical French cuisine. The authentic Mexican restaurant needs a few Mexicans or at least a few Mexican Americans to authenticate it. Japanese chefs are expected to be behind the grills at Benihana restaurants.

A quick-service ethnic restaurant does not need the authenticity required of a full-service ethnic restaurant. This fact is amply demonstrated in such chains as Taco Bell and Del Taco, which are staffed by teenagers without regard to ethnic background. A quick-service Mexican or Italian restaurant can be operated easily once the format is learned.

Whatever the concept, there must be a market to support it, a clientele who walks or drives to the restaurant and who want the kind of service, food, price, and atmosphere offered. A restaurant cannot exist without a market. One must fit the other. The market may constitute only a small percentage of the total population in an area—for instance, travelers on a nearby freeway, occupants of office buildings in the area, passersby in a shopping mall, or people willing to drive half an hour or more to experience the sort of excitement offered by the restaurant. There must also be a market gap, a need for the concept offered.

Figure 3–1 suggests the relationship between the market and the restaurant. The concept and market are central to the restaurant, supported by the menu, prices, service, quality, location, atmosphere, food, and management.

All aspects of the concept help determine whether a location is right for a particular market. Chuck E. Cheese's Pizza Parlors cater to children and specialize in children's parties. A shopping mall site offers the parking, security, and convenience that define a good location for this restaurant; the market consists of the families who patronize the mall. Coffee-shop patrons are often freeway travelers but also can be families within the community. All factors—the food, the seating, the type of service, the entire format—select out a particular market, perhaps an age group and an income level. Promotion and advertising can change the image to attract new markets, to a certain extent. Usually, however, promotion and advertising concentrate on an established market—teenagers, families, drivers, office personnel, mall shoppers, and so on.

Census tract surveys are helpful in assessing the number of people in the proposed restaurant catchment area and their demographics (age, occupation, income, sex, ethnic

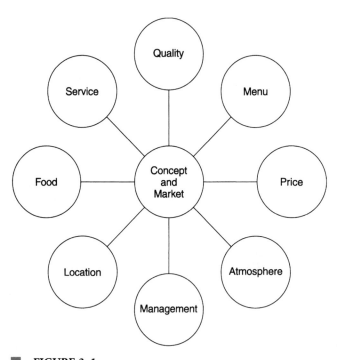

FIGURE 3–1

The Concept and Market comprise the hub around which the restaurant develops.

background, religion, family formation, and composition). This information assists in determining whether or not the concept has the market to support it.

THE FINE LINE BETWEEN JUNK AND FUNK

A number of concept restaurants in the 1960s, 1970s, and 1980s, could be labeled funky. These include takeoffs on warehouses, railway depots, meat markets, grocery stores, old mills, peanut factories, airplane hangars, and so on. They were not intended to be taken seriously but rather offered a fantasy, a return to childhood and to play. The symbols of real life are there, but only the symbols. A number of these restaurants faded quickly because they were not credible even as fantasies. The symbols were allowed to deteriorate. Funk turned to junk . As long as it evokes fantasy and not something merely worn out, the concept succeeds. Otherwise, it fails.

Victoria Station, a chain built around a London railroad depot theme, did well, allowing patrons to escape into nostalgia for the heyday of the old British railroad. The appointments were obviously expensive, and the patron could drift back in time as a member of the British middle or upper classes. The railroad theme appealed to children of all ages, and anglophiles were particularly pleased with the concept. But adults, like children, tire of playthings, and the fun of having dinner in a boxcar faded. The diner seeking an experience is constantly looking for a new one. After a few years, the fantasy faded and Victoria Station, once a big winner, failed.

SUCCESSFUL RESTAURANT CONCEPTS

TGI Friday's has remained successful over the years because they have stayed close to the customer and concentrated on quality and service combined with a theme of fun.

Most cities have an array of exciting restaurants. Some are owned and operated by celebrity chefs, such as Wolfgang Puck's Spago and Chinois in Los Angeles.

Some restaurants are owned or part-owned by celebrities. Arnold Schwartzenegger owns the Planet Earth restaurants. Naomi Campbell, Claudia Schiffer, and Elle MacPherson are part owners of Fashion Café. Michael Jordan used to own a restaurant in Chicago called Michael Jordan The Restaurant, but it closed in 1999 and reopened as Sammy Sosa's (move over number 23, here comes number 21!).

Other sports celebrities who own restaurants include Dan Marino, Walter Payton, Junior Seau, and Wayne Gretzky. Television and movie stars have also gotten into the act. Dustin Hoffman and Henry Winkler are investors in Campanile, a popular Los Angeles restaurant. Dive, in Century City, California, is owned by Stephen Spielberg; House of Blues, by Denzel Washington, George Wendt and Dan Ackroyd. Musicians Kenny Rogers and Gloria Estefan are also restaurant owners.

A concept created by Lettuce Entertain You Enterprises is Papagus, an authentic Taverna that offers hearty Greek delights in warm, friendly, rustic, surroundings. Mezedes, a variety of traditional bite-sized offerings, may be enjoyed with Greek wine and ouzo. The display kitchen adds an experiential atmosphere and offers specialties such as spit-roasted chicken, whole broiled red snapper, traditional braised lamb, spanakopita, and baklava.

The Lettuce Entertain You Group has several outstanding theme restaurants in the Chicago area. They include Scoozi, which recalls an artist's studio and serves Italian country cuisine; Café Ba-Ba-Reeba, a Spanish restaurant featuring tapas, the popular hot and cold "little dishes of Spain"; Un Grand Café, a Parisian cafe featuring pâtés, salads, fresh grilled fish, game, and steak, as well as daily specials; and Gino's East, which serves a world-famous deep-dish pizza rated number one by *People* magazine; R. J. Grunts, the original Lettuce Entertain You restaurant, has catered since 1971. Music and decor are reminiscent of the 1960s and 1970s, in a casual eclectic setting. The restaurant is known for its award-winning chili, oversized cheddar burgers, and daily vegetarian specials. Room Service will deliver some of your favorite Lettuce restaurant dishes right to your door.

The Hard Rock Café is one of the most successful restaurant chain concepts of all time. Peter Morton, then a young American college graduate in England, realized that London did not have a true American-style hamburger joint. He borrowed $60,000 from family and friends and opened the Great American Disaster in 1970. It was an immediate success, with a nightly line up around the block.[3]

Morton quickly realized that London really needed a restaurant that not only served American food but also embodied the energy and excitement of music past and present. With this objective in mind, he opened the first hard Rock Café in London in 1971. The restaurant offered a hearty American meal at a reasonable price in an atmosphere charged with energy, fun, and the excitement of rock and roll.

HRC was an immediate success. Each HRC restaurant is decorated with memorabilia of rock-and-roll stars, including David Bowie's two-tone black-and-white Vox guitar from the movie *Absolute Beginners*, Jimi Hendrix's beaded and fringed suede jacket, Elvis Presley's gold-studded white stage cape, one of John Lennon's guitars, Madonna's bustière, and one of Elton John's outfits.

Café Ba-Ba-Reeba has a successful concept featuring tapas, the popular hot and cold "little dishes" of Spain.
Courtesy Lettuce Entertain You

In 1982, with backing from film director Steven Spielberg, actor Tom Cruise, and others, the first Hard Rock Café in the United States opened in Los Angeles. There are now Hard Rock Cafés in San Francisco, Chicago, Houston, Honolulu, New Orleans, San Diego, Sydney, Maui, Las Vegas, and Aspen, to name a few.

Morton said he created Hard Rock Café because he wanted people to have a place to go where they could experience the fun of rock and roll, past and present, while enjoying a great meal.

All Hard Rock Cafés are dedicated to the same basic theme: rock-and-roll halls of fame. Tribute is paid to music industry legends and the hot artists of today by displaying their prized memorabilia.

On a chainwide basis, the Hard Rock Cafés are the highest-volume restaurants in the United States, hosting over 600,000 patrons per restaurant per year.[4]

Nearly all restaurants have an almost human life cycle—birth, growth, maturity, senescence, and death. There is nothing mystical about the life cycle of restaurants, nor is there an absolute inevitability about a restaurant's success. Restaurants can be revived on occasion, and a few seem to improve with age. The Delmonico restaurants in New York City had a lifespan of over 75 years but finally expired as successive generations of the Delmonico family lacked the interest and enthusiasm of earlier generations. Chain operations rise and fall in a similar manner. The largest restaurant chain in the United States during the 1930s was Child's Restaurants, also in New York City. The chain was finally purchased by a hotelier because of its tax-loss value to him.

Horn and Hardart had a successful concept that represented the Art Deco generation and the new industrial strength that emerged after the Great Depression. The concept was the Automat. Customers placed coins in a slot over a row of boxes and remove a food item from the box. There was a full selection of good-quality food ranging from hot entrées to petit fours. Behind the boxes were people working in the kitchen to

*Scoozi is an outstanding theme restaurant that gives the impression of an artist's studio. **Courtesy Lettuce Entertain You***

The Hard Rock Café's theme is a rock-and-roll hall of fame. Courtesy Hard Rock Café

prepare and put up the food. The concept worked well for a number of years, but over time, Automats became history.

A major reason for a restaurant's decline comes in the changing demographics of the area in which it is located. Areas rise and fall economically and socially. The restaurants within them are likely to follow suit. Fashions change. The all-white decor of some of the hamburger chains that flourished in the 1950s became less attractive when other chains moved to color. Top management ages, and the aging is reflected in the operations. The restaurant concept that excited the public when first introduced becomes tired after several years, and its power to excite fades as newer concepts are introduced in the same community. Menus that were entirely satisfactory at one time are no longer appealing.

Restaurant designs and buildings that were novel and attractive when new lose their luster when compared with newer, larger, more expensive designs. In the 1960s, a restaurant investment of a few hundred thousand dollars was enough to produce an imposing building—which by the mid-1970s looked uninteresting compared with restaurants with investments of $1 million to $3 million. As restaurant chains were pur-

The Hard Rock Cafe's motto, "Save the planet," represents a commitment to environmental and humane concerns. The restaurants have helped several charities and nonprofit organizations by donating food, services, and funds. Because of their distinct image, the Hard Rock Cafés have been highly successful in marketing and merchandising T-shirts, jackets, sweatshirts, and other memorabilia that feature the Hard Rock Café logo and location.

chased by conglomerates such as W.R. Grace and General Mills, huge sums of money became available for glamour restaurant investments that introduced a new dimension of scale and luxury into the restaurant business.

Current popular restaurant concepts are high-tech, casual contemporary, ethnic, designer, and celebrity restaurants. In the past few years, Mexican, Chinese, Japanese, and Thai restaurants have become popular. Northern Italian restaurants have become the hottest concept. Pizza and pasta offered at below $10 provide around two hours of affordable upscale dining. In saturated markets, a restaurant's being new no longer guarantees customers.

CONCEPT ADAPTATION

Most concepts that have not been tested need some adaptation to the particular market. In Ontario, Canada, a highly successful restaurant opened featuring seafood. The menu, however, was not popular, so it was altered. Several months passed before the place was profitable, but the owner wisely had adapted to the market demands. One of the superhotels in downtown Los Angeles featured dessert soufflés in its restaurant for several months. The soufflés were so popular that four extra personnel had to be employed to keep up with the demand. Restaurant volume of sales increased to the point that the sweet soufflés were no longer needed to entice patrons to the restaurant, and the soufflés were dropped from the menu. They had been used to build volume, but because they were high in labor cost and tended to show down seat turnover, they were deleted from the menu with no appreciable drop in patronage.

Concept development has always been important in the restaurant industry, but it is becoming more so now that dining districts are developing in almost every community. The restaurant cluster may include family restaurants, luxury restaurants, and a variety of quick-service restaurants. An area of just a few blocks may include chain representatives from Taco Bell, Burger King, Sizzler, Arby's, Red Lobster, and Pizza Hut, plus a Chinese restaurant. Each has its own identity. Are they all competing with each other? To an extent, yes; these restaurants may cannibalize each other's guests. Generally however, different menus and prices attract different markets.

As soon as a restaurant format goes stale for a market, a new concept must be developed. Nearly every major chain is undergoing renovation, adding color, changing its seating arrangements, perhaps trying garden windows, hanging plants, private booths, menu variety, different uniforms, or new menu items.

CHANGING OR MODIFYING A CONCEPT

Many highly successful concepts that have worked well for years gradually turn sour. The customer base and the demographics change. Morale and personal service falls off. Anthony's Fish Grotto, a well-established seafood restaurant, experienced sales decline over five consecutive years. Radical changes were called for and the owners hired consultants Rudy Mick and Victor Penedo of Los Angeles.[5]

Changes in management policy and operations turned Anthony's around. First, the owner wrote a mission statement that included a vision of what Anthony's would look like in 2005. The books were opened to employees—a major innovation. The top-down style of management was replaced by teams that worked on employee scheduling and ideas for a new image. A serving team came up with wait-staff schedules that satisfied all 40 services at one unit. A savings team reduced costs of linen and china.

The concept team worked with designers to create a dining area in the La Mesa, California, store that creates the impression of being in an underwater cave, brightly lit and colorful. The design includes waterfalls and sea animals jutting out from the walls. The new design has helped to attract baby boomers, along with their children.

Another restaurant, Alps Chalet in Niagara Falls, was in a declining market area. The town's population, once 100,000, had decreased by half. Consultant Edmund Michalski was called in and was surprised to find that servers forgot to charge $12 worth of menu items he had ordered. A competing pancake house nearby, he found, was selling steak for $10.95; at the Alps Chalet steak was priced at $8.50. The owner changed to a better grade of meat and raised his steak price by $2.00. Menu items like breaded pork chops, once an everyday item, became an occasional special. An outside patio was built for grilling and nightly entertainment was added. Adding live nightly entertainment is a major decision, one that can considerably affect a restaurant's image. A new point-of-sale system that made accounting more accurate was introduced. The outcome of these changes was an increase in Alps Chalet's sales by 30%.[6]

COPY AND IMPROVE

In coming up with a concept for a new restaurant, be a copycat. Look around for winners. Examine their strong points; look for their weak points; find a proven format. Learn the system to avoid mistakes—then improve on it. Initiate and adapt. Great composers build magnificent symphonies on borrowed melodic themes. Similarly, great restaurants take over elements of established restaurants.

There is no such thing as a completely new restaurant concept—only modifications and changes, new combinations, changes in design, layout, menu, and service. It is pure braggadocio to claim to have a completely new concept. If that were true, there would be no customers because the restaurant would be so strange people would avoid it. Accepting the fact that every restaurant builds on hundreds of predecessors makes good sense and can help avoid big mistakes. So be a copycat—but a critical, creative copycat.

Besides copying the format, learn the system by actually working with it before trying to establish your own restaurant. Merely observing an operation is not enough. Dozens of details must be learned, any one of which, if not known, may spell unnecessary trouble. Buying from the wrong vendor, using the wrong temperature for cooking an item, omitting a particular spice in a dressing, or using the wrong formula for a bun can result in high costs and stress for the operator.

A number of Mexican restaurants have been put together by non-Mexicans and are successful partly because several of the key kitchen personnel and waiting personnel are Mexican Americans, who lend authenticity to the restaurant.

It is probably not wise to try a full-service ethnic restaurant unless the owner/operator is from that ethnic background or has been immersed in it. Another alternative: Go with a business associate who is of the appropriate ethnic background.

You need not be a social analyst to define carefully the potential market if you copy an already successful restaurant. Creative copycats may borrow ideas from a number of operations, reconfiguring them as needed. The style of service may be drawn from a coffee shop, the method of food preparation from a dinner house; the menu can be drawn from a combination of several successful operations in the area, plus one or two modifications in preparation, presentation, or service. The pricing policy could be a combination of policies already well received by the public. Do not try to establish new taste patterns or vary far from the norm.

RESTAURANT SYMBOLOGY

Restaurant symbology—the logo, the line drawings, even the linen napkins and the service uniforms—helps to create atmosphere. In the 1890s, Cesar Ritz dressed his waiters in tails, which helped entice the elite from their mansions to his hotel restaurant, the Carlton in London. Chart House restaurants create a different image by dressing their servers in attractive Hawaiian shirts and dresses. Chart House restaurants have a contemporary nautical decor and are designed with a natural look that harmonizes with the setting. Extensive use of wood and glass give their restaurants a warm feeling. Their biggest draw is their locations, which are nearly all at water's edge.

Is it the Picasso hanging in the entrance foyer to the Four Seasons Restaurant in New York City that impresses the patrons? Is it the rheostat in the private room, which dims the lights during a particular party? Are the high prices part of the image? Undoubtedly.

Chart House restaurants have a nautical theme and most have spectacular ocean or water views. Courtesy Chart House Restaurants

Symbols include people, clowns, and kings. Ronald McDonald is part of McDonald's restaurants' decor and a personalizing element. So, too, are the miniature playgrounds offered by some of McDonald's restaurants. Burger King, which gives children cardboard crowns, competes for customers' attention with Ronald McDonald and Mickey Mouse.

Large companies spend tens of thousands on the graphics that represent them. Restaurant chain logos, often replications of their outdoor signs, are carefully crafted to fit the image the company wishes to project. The independent operator can take cues from the larger companies to come up with symbols and signs that reflect the restaurant's concept.

WHEN A CONCEPT FAILS

Provided the operator is competent, a failing restaurant need not be sold. The concept can be changed to fit the market. Conversion from one concept to another can take place while the old restaurant is doing business. The name, decor, and menu can be changed, and the customers who have left may return if the new concept appeals to them. The old concept may have gotten tired. Customers simply may be bored. The customers who enjoyed the old concept may have moved away and been replaced by a new market. Or a new concept, complete with decor, price, and service, may better appeal to the same market and siphon customers away from the competition.

In the worst case, a recession hits and customer count at all restaurants drops. Customers may trade down. Those who formerly patronized an upscale dinner house now go to a neighborhood coffee shop. The coffee-shop patron turns to quick service. Those who cannot afford to eat out at all drop out of the market completely. The smart restaurateurs downscale their menu prices to retain market share and even build volume. Luxury restaurants seldom lower à la carte prices; instead, they offer a fixed-price meal at a lower price than if the same food were taken à la carte.

THE MULTIPLE-CONCEPT CHAIN

Single-concept chains, such as McDonald's and KFC, have had the greatest success of any restaurants in history. Having a single concept permits concentrated effort on a single system. Nevertheless, the single-concept restaurant chain is changing to a multiple-concept chain, which offers several advantages. Conceivably, a multiple-concept restaurant chain could have five or more restaurants in the same block, each competing with the others, each acquiring a certain part of the restaurant market.

In fact, this has been done for a long time in order to minimize costs, and will probably be seen more often in the future because of its success in attracting different markets. As early as the 1950s, Lawry's had two separate-concept restaurants, one across the street from each other, in Los Angeles. The general public had no idea that they were owned by the same company. One aspect of the concepts was directly competitive: both restaurants featured beef. The company felt that if it did not add another competing restaurant, someone else would, and the particular area would support two, but only two, beef restaurants.

Generally, where restaurants are clustered, each concept is somewhat different from the others, and as many as 12 or 15 different concepts can be enclosed in the same mall

Chili's is a popular restaurant specializing in grilled Mexican cuisine. Courtesy Chili's Grill & Bar

shopping area—as at Marina Del Rey, a comparatively small area near the Los Angeles Airport, which has more than 36 restaurant concepts clustered together.

The concourse of the former Pan Am building in New York has three totally different restaurants utilizing the same kitchen—The Trattoria, Zoom Zoom, and Charlie Brown's. These are next to each other, yet utilize the same large kitchen.

Ruben's and Coco's also share some locations and reduce labor costs by having one general manager for both restaurants with an assistant manager for each.

Within a large market area, such as Los Angeles, Chicago, or New York, the same company may have several concepts, all close to one another but with slightly different decor and menus. Customers do not like to feel they are eating in the same restaurant all over the area, so the restaurants are varied somewhat and carry different names.

The largest of all restaurant companies, Tricon Global Restaurants, Inc., has three concepts—KFC, Taco Bell, and Pizza Hut—that do not compete directly with each other.

SEQUENCE OF RESTAURANT DEVELOPMENT: FROM CONCEPT TO OPENING

From the time a concept is put together until a location is obtained, architectural drawings made, finance arranged, the land leased or purchased, approvals for building secured, construction bids let, a contractor selected, and—finally—the building put in place can take two or more years. The sequence of events (Figure 3–2) may include the following:

1. Business marketing initiated.
2. Layout and equipment planned.
3. Menu determined.
4. First architectural sketches made.
5. Licensing and approvals sought.
6. Financing arranged.
7. Working blueprints developed.
8. Contracts let for bidding.
9. Contractor selected.
10. Construction or remodeling begun.
11. Furnishings and equipment ordered.
12. Key personnel hired.
13. Hourly employees selected and trained.
14. Restaurant opened.

In some cases, the time may be reduced, especially when taking over an existing restaurant or altering an existing building. Restaurant chains with pre-planned restaurant concepts generally reduce the time line by 6 to 12 months.

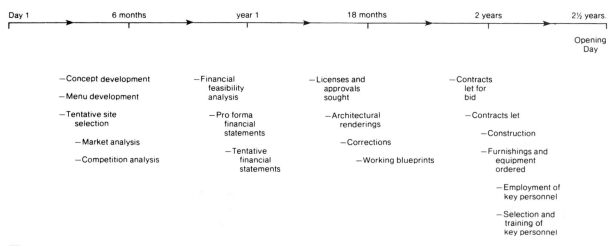

FIGURE 3–2

Time line showing the sequence of restaurant development

■ *Planning Services*

The person building a restaurant should employ an architect experienced in restaurant design. The architect, in turn, may hire a restaurant consultant to lay out the kitchen and recommend equipment purchases.

The builder may employ one of the relatively few restaurant consultants or can turn to restaurant dealers who double as planners or employ planners. The consultant works for a fee or a percentage of cost. The dealer may also charge a fee, but is likely to reduce or eliminate it if the equipment is purchased from him or her.

The best guide in selecting a planner/consultant is that person's experience and reputation. It should be remembered that any kitchen can be laid out in a variety of ways and still function well.

The consultant/planner will require a signed design agreement, including agreed-upon fees. The agreement spells out what services will be completed by the designer and usually includes:

- Basic floor plan
- Equipment schedules
- Foodservice equipment electrical requirements
- Foodservice plumbing requirements
- Foodservice equipment
- Foodservice equipment elevations
- Refrigeration requirements
- Exhaust air extraction and in-take requirements
- Seating layout

■ *Common Denominators of Restaurants*

In formulating a restaurant concept, the planner considers the factors common to all kinds of restaurants. An analysis of these common denominators may suggest a concept that is a hybrid of two or more classifications. Fast-food restaurants taken on the character of coffee shops, vending operations may offer limited service, cafeterias take on the appointments of luxury restaurants, and so on.

Common denominators of restaurants can be compared: the human needs met by the restaurant, menu prices, degree of service offered, space provided for each customer, rate of seat turnover, advertising and promotion expenditures, productivity per employee, labor cost, and food cost.

The planner picks and chooses from among the common denominators to come up with a concept believed to be most appealing to a particular market.

UTILITY VERSUS PLEASURE

What is the purpose of a particular restaurant? Is it there to provide food for nutritional purposes or for pleasure? Up to 75% of the meals eaten away from home are for utilitarian purposes, while the other 25% are for pleasure. The distinctions are not clear-cut. Depending on the individual, the quick-service experience may be thrilling or boring.

For the child, McDonald's may be full of excitement and fun. For a sophisticate, McDonald's can be a drag. The family that visits a Burger King or a Wendy's may find the experience as exhilarating as depicted in the TV commercials. For them, the utilitarian restaurant is a fun place, perhaps more pleasurable than an ultraexpensive French restaurant.

Pleasure dining increases as service, atmosphere, and quality of food increase. Presumably, pleasure also increases as menu price increases. Many factors intrude on such straight-line correlation.

DEGREE OF SERVICE OFFERED

As seen in Figure 3–3, restaurant service varies from none at all to a maximum in a high-style luxury restaurant.

As menu price increases, so, usually, does service—the higher the price, the more service provided. At one end of the spectrum, the vending machine is completely impersonal—no service at all. At the other end, the luxury restaurant, a captain and two buspersons may attend each table. Service is maximal. The customer pays for the food but also for the ambiance and the attention of service personnel. It is interesting to compare the productivity and profitability of a luxury restaurant with a coffee shop or popular-concept restaurant. The coffee shop can quickly train personnel replacements and pay relatively low wages. The French restaurant relies on years of experience and polished skills. It is also relatively inefficient. The chain restaurant relies on system and replication, the French on individuals. The chain markets its restaurants; the French restaurant attracts limited patronage by ambiance, personality, word of mouth, and public relations.

Restaurant service breaks down into seven categories: vending, quick service, cafeteria, coffee shop, family restaurant, dinner house, and luxury restaurant. Figure 3–4 shows that different kinds of restaurants have different seat turnover levels.

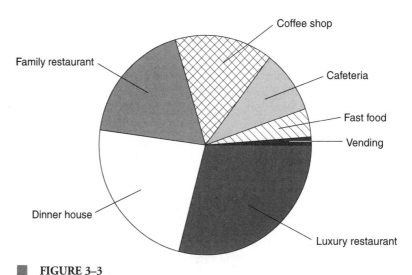

■   **FIGURE 3–3**

Different kinds of restaurants require different levels of service.

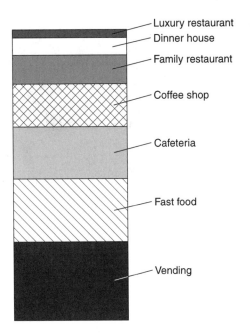

Luxury restaurant
Dinner house
Family restaurant
Coffee shop
Cafeteria
Fast food
Vending

■ **FIGURE 3–4**

Different kinds of restaurants have different seat turnover levels.

The degree of service offered probably correlates with menu price and pleasure—at least, that is the expectation of the diner. Here again, there are many exceptions, and as the expectations are purely psychological, a number of factors can intrude on the correlation.

TIME OF EATING AND SEAT TURNOVER

Utilitarian eating is often accomplished in double-quick time, while the customer of a luxury restaurant who spends $75 to $100 per person for an evening out may savor every minute of the total experience, plus the pleasure of anticipating the dining experience and the pleasure of remembering it. Telling one's friends about the truffled turkey can be worth the price of the meal, a conversation piece adding luster to the dinner. At the other end of the spectrum, the stand-up diner in New York City can hardly be expected to be enthralled by the experience.

The seat turnover and speed of eating correlate with the restaurant classification, but not perfectly (Figure 3–4). In some restaurants, the family style can offer speedy service, fast turnover, and still provide an enjoyable atmosphere for its customers. Turnover is also highly correlated with the efficiency of the operation; turnover in two restaurants of exactly the same type can vary widely because of layout and management.

CUSTOMER SPACE

Figure 3–5 suggests the amount of space per customer needed by type of restaurant. The restaurant customer, in effect, rents space for dining. The drive-through restaurant provides no dining space at all; the customer's automobile is the dining room. Coming up the scale a bit, the customer may walk to a counter and receive some service. The

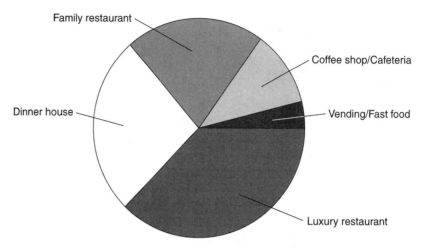

FIGURE 3–5

Different kinds of restaurants have different space-per-customer requirements.

coffee shop provides counter and booth seating and a nominal kitchen, while the luxury restaurant needs upholstered chairs and 15 to 20 feet of space per patron, plus the kitchen equipment to handle the more extensive menu.

The square-foot requirements and the turnover in patrons per seat per hour are listed in Table 3–1.

■

Menu Price and Cost per Seat

Menu pricing correlates highly with the degree of service offered, the time of eating, the labor cost, the amount of space offered the customer, and the cost of the restaurant itself.

It might be expected that the cost per seat of a restaurant varies directly with the other factors mentioned. This is true, to an extent, but there are wide variations. Some of the chain dinner houses cost at least $10,000 per seat, whereas each seat of the little French restaurant may cost $4,000. Some of the quick-service restaurants are very costly

■ **TABLE 3–1**

Square-foot Requirements and Turnover Rates

	Dining Room (square feet per seat)	Turnovers in Patrons (per seat per hours)
Commercial cafeterias	13–18	1.5–2.5
Coffee shop with counter and table service	15–17	2–3
Deluxe restaurants	13–18	0.5–1.25
Popular-priced restaurants	11–15	1–2.5

Source: Arthur C. Avery, *Commercial Kitchens* (New York: American Gas Association, 1989).

per seat, much more so than the family restaurant. Cost per seat thus does not correlate well with the restaurant classifications presented.

ADVERTISING AND PROMOTION EXPENDITURES

In advertising and promotion, expenditures may vary according to the type of restaurant. Figure 3–6 shows the percentage of sales spent on advertising and promotion among types of restaurants. The vending machine operator spends little or nothing in advertising. Quick-service restaurants are likely to spend 4 to 5% of their income on advertising, twice as much as the usual coffee shop, cafeteria, family restaurant, or dinner house. At the far end of the spectrum, the restaurant featuring fine food may spend heavily on public relations. Promotion may take the form of entertaining food columnists, the proprietor's being seen at the right places at the right time and with the right people, and the cost of paying a public relations firm for keeping the restaurant in the news.

LABOR COSTS AS A PERCENTAGE OF SALES

Productivity per employee correlates highly with the various elements, moving from a high point at the quick-service end of the classification scale to a low point in a luxury restaurant or at a country club. Here, too, there are exceptions, depending on management skill, the layout of the restaurant, and the menu.

As might be expected, labor costs vary inversely with productivity, as shown in Figure 3–7. Quick-service restaurants operate at comparatively low labor costs.

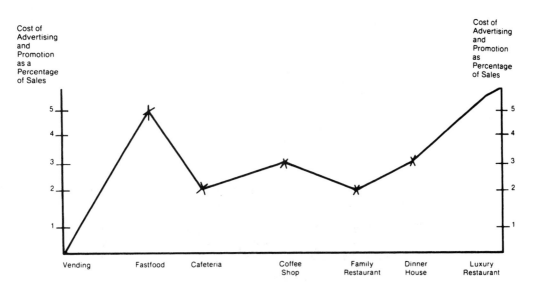

■ **FIGURE 3–6**

Advertising and promotion expenditures

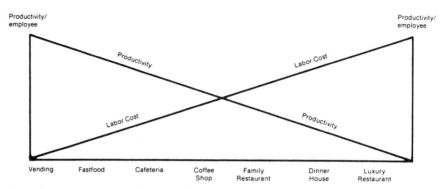

FIGURE 3–7

Productivity per employee

PLANNING DECISIONS THAT RELATE TO CONCEPT DEVELOPMENT

Who Are the Target Markets, the Customers?

Children, teenagers, young married couples, families, businesspeople, retirees, low-income people, high-income people, the adventurous, the sophisticated— anyone who is hungry could be your target market.

A particular restaurant may try to reach several markets, but the operator should know which.

Buy, Build, Lease, or Franchise?

Building is usually the most time-consuming of these options and can require two or more years from concept to completion. Arranging for financing, employing an architect, buying the land, getting the necessary approvals, and formulating contingency plans all eat up time and money. In franchising, the problem is to pick the right operation and to recognize that most major decisions have already been made and will continue to be made by others.

Food Preparation from Scratch or from Convenience Items?

How much of the food will be prepared on the premises? How much will be purchased ready for heating? How many of the menu items will be prepared from mixes, soup bases, and other convenience food items? Some restaurants prepare everything possible from fresh ingredients. Others prepare everything possible from convenience items and have a definite policy of cutting preparation time to the minimum. Most restaurants make some items and buy others. Chain operations often produce some foods in a commissary, then have them delivered for final preparation at the various unit restaurants. Even upscale restaurants usually purchase most of their desserts and pastries.

A Limited or an Extensive Menu?

Will the location and the concept support a limited menu, or does the concept call for an extensive menu requiring a large population base to support it?

How Much Service—Limited or Full?

The operator can pick from a wide range of service degrees, from vending to walk-up, carry-out, cafeteria, drive-through, and on up to luxury full service. Which best fits the concept and market?

Young Part-time Employees or Older Career Employees?

Much of today's foodservice industry is staffed by teenagers, people in their early twenties, and people who receive minimum or slightly above minimum wage. Some restaurants employ a range of age groups and depend on career employees rather than part-timers. Most restaurants offer at least some part-time positions.

Paid Advertising or Word-of-Mouth Advertising?

How will the target markets be reached—paid advertising, public relations, promotions, or largely by word of mouth? A number of successful restaurants have a definite policy of no paid advertising. Others rely heavily on paid advertising, still others on promotion or a combination of advertising and promotion, particularly the use of coupons.

Grand or Quiet Opening?

Will you open with a bang and fanfare or open quietly on Monday morning and allow the crew to ease into volume operation?

Electricity or Gas?

This decision is not an either/or proposition—some pieces of equipment can be gas fired, others wired for electricity—but the decision is an important one because installation costs are only part of the total costs. What is the cost of operating gas versus electric equipment, and what are the advantages of each type? Regional utility rates are a factor. In some locations, electricity is cheap; in others, expensive.

PROFITABILITY

Now for the famous last-but-not-least factor—profitability. Without a doubt, the most profitable restaurants are in quick-service category. McDonald's and KFC, the two largest quick-service purveyors, have produced dozens of millionaires and more than a few multimillionaires. A number of franchisees have acquired chains within the chain, multiple units clustered within an area. With predominantly minimum-wage personnel, high sales volume, the use of systems, and excellent marketing, the quick-service business is the all-out winner. Oddly enough, few restaurant-management students opt for quick-service management, believing it lacks the variety, glamour, and opportunity for self-expression found in restaurants offering more service and style. The professional restaurateur sees the restaurant as an ego extension. The investor usually cares most about profitability and what it takes to maximize profits.

THE MISSION STATEMENT

A mission statement drawn up by the restaurant owner can encapsulate the owner's objectives for the business. The statement may be brief, such as the one for Creative Gourmets, a catering company based in Charleston, Massachusetts: "Excellence Through Caring"[7] or much more encompassing, as in Chili's Grill and Bar, whose home office is in Dallas:

> We aim to be a premier growth company with a balanced approach toward people, quality, and profits; to cultivate customer loyalty by listening to, caring

about, and providing customers with a quality dinning experience; to enhance a high level of ethics, excellence, innovation, and integrity; to attract, develop, and retain a superior team; to be focused, sensitive, and responsive to our employees and their environment; and to enhance long-term shareholder wealth.[8]

A mission statement can be explicit about the market(s) served, the kinds of food offered, and the atmosphere in which the food will be served. The ethical standards to be followed can be stated as part of the mission statement or written as a separate code of conduct. The goals to be followed in relating to patrons, employees, vendors, and the community can be included. Restaurants Unlimited, a dinner-house chain based in Seattle, states something of the moral character of the company, the way it views the guest and the employees:

> To build a growing, financially successful business through increasing sales and excellent profits. This is achieved by living these values. We act Guest First. We deliver high-quality food every time at reasonable prices. We give great service and engage each guest. We hire the best and care about them. We are clean![9]

Several advantages accrue to the restaurant owner/management in taking the time to spell out a mission statement. The exercise forces owners to think through and put in writing an explicit statement about what the restaurant is all about, a statement that is sharp and to the point and can focus the energies of management and employees and set forth the responsibilities of the enterprise in its relations with patrons, employees, vendors, and the public.

Mission statements can include input from employees. Discussions with employees can mobilize their thinking about the restaurant's purpose and reason for existence. There should be no hesitation about stating the profit motivation and such goals as cleanliness, customer service, and customer delight.

A code of ethics may strike some people as naive. Codes of ethics place a burden on restaurant owners and managers to live up to the code, reminds them that ethical behavior begins at the top, and presumes a commitment to following the highest standards in personal cleanliness, food protection, service, and employee relations. One clause can address striving to price food to provide fair value and fair profit to investors. It does no harm to state that the restaurant expects employees and vendors to be scrupulously honest and pledges to do the same.

Some business writers say that a mission statement contains four elements:

1. The purpose of the enterprise
2. Its business strategy
3. The behavior standards it will follow
4. The values that the management and employees will hold foremost[10]

A mission statement is a useful part of the work plan needed to support a loan application from the Small Business Administration, bank, or other loan source.

CONCEPT AND LOCATION

What makes a good location for a restaurant? The answer depends on the kind of restaurant and the clientele to which it appeals. Is the location convenient and accessible for the potential clientele, the target market of the restaurant? The restaurant appealing to the professional for lunch usually must be relatively close to where professionals work. For some groups, the only food service in which they are interested is one within the building. For others, it is anywhere but within the immediate area, providing they can be back in their offices within an hour.

Roadside restaurants, especially those on superhighways, are favored by the automobile traveler. Location within a community (rather than on the edge of town) and on a major highway are plus factors. Brand-name restaurants such as McDonald's, Olive Garden, and Outback Steakhouse appeal to the stranger in the community looking for a known standard of quality and price. The traveler knows the menu prices and is fairly certain of the food quality and sanitation standards in a McDonald's, whether it is located in Massachusetts or New Jersey.

Will the size of the potential market support a particular type of restaurant? A hamburger quick-service restaurant may need only a population of 5,000 to support it, while a Polynesian restaurant might require 200,000. A coffee shop may do well with only a few thousand potential customers, while a gourmet restaurant may need 100,000 people in its potential market. The marketing manager for one upscale dinner-house chain feels that a population of 250,000 within a five-mile radius of one of their restaurants is needed for support. If the unit is located on a freeway, the radius might be extended to ten miles.

The price structure of a restaurant is a major determinant in establishing its market. The $45.00-average check seafood restaurant may appeal to 5 to 10% of the population, while a $12.00-average check Mexican restaurant may appeal to 60%. Neither restaurant needs a major highway location to be successful. The public is more apt to search them out because of the specialized menu and service and because, normally, there are fewer of them from which to choose.

HIGH-GROWTH AREAS FOR LOCATING A RESTAURANT

The semimonthly magazine *Restaurant Business* publishes an annual Restaurant Growth Index, the purpose of which is to list the best and worst places to open a restaurant in the United States. Quite correctly, the editors say that selecting a restaurant site or a restaurant city is both a science and an art. Certain areas have too many restaurants. A few are good places to buy or build a restaurant, depending on the area's share of employed persons, working women, income level, population age, and food consumed away from home. Certain towns are losing population, others gaining. Pittsfield, Massachusetts, in the 1998 survey, was ranked last as a growth market partly because it was losing population and its business future was not promising. Chicago was at the other extreme, ranking number one in restaurant sales in the country. It was followed by New York City, Los Angeles, Washington, D.C., Atlanta, Boston, Detroit, and Philadelphia. (Chicago had restaurant sales of $3.62 billion in 1997; New York, $3.55 billion.) The same ranking held for fast-food sales. Per capita restaurant sales was quite a different story. The five winners in this category were Myrtle Beach, South Carolina; Flagstaff, Arizona; Santa Fe, New Mexico; Naples, Florida; and Barnstable and Yarmouth, Massachusetts.[11]

The survey for 1998 says to look to the Midwest to plant your next restaurant and avoid New England. A one-page synopsis of economic data for each state is part of the survey.

While this information is valuable, more important is the amount and intensity of competition already existing, information that can only be learned by on-site study or experience. Help can be had from a local or regional expert on the local situation. It is well known that restaurant competition is intense in the major cities. Restaurants open and close by the hundreds.

Location Criteria

Restaurant personality, style of service, menu price, and management call for particular criteria in site selection. What is good for one restaurant may not be good for another. The focus is on the potential market. How convenient will it be to their place of residence or work? Will they feel that they are getting value for their money whether the menu price is low or high? Chain-restaurant executives ordinarily define site or location criteria carefully based on experience. Some of the more obvious location criteria are:

- Demographics of the area: age, occupation, religion, nationality, race, family size, educational level, average income of individuals and families
- Visibility from a major highway
- Accessibility from a major highway
- Number of potential customers passing by the restaurant (potential customers might be only travelers going through a community, drivers, local workers)
- Distance from the potential market
- Desirability of surroundings

These factors are then weighed against costs: leasehold cost, cost of remodeling an existing building, cost of buying an existing restaurant.

Some location factors are critical, and if a site does not meet them, it must be ruled out as the restaurant location. Establishing the critical factors in determining location is your first job.

The atmosphere of a restaurant must fit the location. Even though it may be a part of a chain, your restaurant can be different from the other units. The ethnic background of a community, its income level, and number of children per family are important. McDonald's, Burger King, and Wendy's are moving away from having a standard design for all locations. If the neighborhood is affluent and the demographics indicate an older population, the restaurant is likely to be broken up with more partitions, suggesting gracious dining rather than the fast-food look favored by younger populations.

Some Restaurants Create Their Own Location

Dinner or family-style restaurants need not place the same high priority on convenience of location necessary for coffee shops and quick-service establishments. In effect, the restaurant creates the location if the food service and atmosphere are desirable. The point is proved by the many undesirable locations that have failed as restaurants for as many as ten different owners but are taken over by an eleventh and within a few weeks are packed with customers.

Because this is true, developers and community officials are often eager to entice a successful restaurant operator into a new shopping center or an area that has fallen on bad times. Decaying communities offer particularly attractive terms to operators with a proven track record. A successful restaurant can attract hundreds of people and rejuvenate a shopping center, mall, or other area.

A colorful personality restaurant may be successful in a location relatively poor with respect to surroundings, distance from market, accessibility, and convenience. Such a restaurant would be that much more successful in a prime location. The owner of a highly successful chain of Mexican restaurants in California considers the usual location factors relatively unimportant. He feels, and experience has proved, that people will search out his restaurants. Consequently, he buys failing restaurants located in relatively undesirable locations, remodels them, and attracts a large clientele. Other restaurateurs say that "even with the best location, it is difficult to succeed in the restaurant business—therefore, go only for the best." Prime locations, however, require a good deal more money for lease costs.[12]

Sources of Location Information

A comprehensive book on site selection and its ramifications is John C. Melaniphy's *Restaurant and Fast Food Site Selection*, an in-depth analysis of the factors, amply explicated, that go into picking the site for a particular kind of restaurant.[13] Though the book was published in 1992, the principles and methodologies it propounds are enduring. Location decisions are based on asking the right questions and securing the right information. Real estate agents are prime sources. A few specialize in restaurant brokerage. The real estate agent(s) involved (there is usually at least one) are primarily interested in making a sale and gaining a commission. Real estate commissions are ordinarily based on 6% of the building selling price and 10% of the selling price of raw land. A $200,000 land deal brings the agent up to $20,000 in commission. (Keep in mind that commissions can often be negotiated.) With this kind of incentive, it is little wonder the agent may push a sale to the disadvantage of the buyer or the seller. To protect their interests, owners need multiple sources of location information. The agent can usually provide valuable information about the site and probably knows the community, its income level, growth patterns, traffic flows, restaurant competition, and the restaurant scene in the area.

Other sources of information are the chamber of commerce, the banks, the town or city planner, and, believe it or not, other restaurant operators. Town and city planning officials can provide traffic and zoning information. Current zoning information is critical, but no more so than what zoning officials are planning for the future. Is an area scheduled to be rezoned? Can a lot be split? Zoning reflects politics, and even if one group of officials plans one way, the next group may change the plan. The builder hopes for a lot to be rezoned up. Sometimes it is rezoned down. A change in zoning classification can mean a change in value of hundreds of thousands of dollars.

A number of communities have placed moratoriums on building for reasons such as protecting the environment or maintaining the status quo. Rapidly growing communities sometimes stop all building because utility or sewage systems are incapable of keeping up with the growth. In areas not served by a public sewage system, the construction of a restaurant may not be feasible because of the need for a sewage system with a large drainage field. An existing restaurant in such an area may be in a favorable competitive position for several years.

Building a restaurant is always nerve-racking, but it can be disastrous for an investor who encounters unexpected delays in getting permits, materials, and labor. A Howard Johnson's franchisee who was building a restaurant was unable to get the orange-colored roof for a number of months, which almost sent him into bankruptcy. Some communities refuse to allow a particular design of restaurant, and more and more building codes are specifying low-key architecture with minimal signage.

A look at the highways on the outskirts of some cities tells why the planning commissions are placing more restrictions on restaurant buildings and signs. Restaurants and motels crowd each other, each with a large neon sign, giving the strip an unsavory appearance.

Basic demographic information about the people in the area can be obtained from the *Census Tracts for Standard Metropolitan Statistical Areas*, available in local public and university libraries. The number of renters or homeowners, income levels, and so on can be abstracted from these tracts in a few minutes for the particular site in question. A plethora of information about people in a given area is available from government sources. Specialized demographic research companies will provide the information within a day or two for a moderate price. The larger chains use such companies routinely, but the individual should probably also use them to save time. Information such as population growth, decline, density, income levels, number of children, ethnicity, and other consumer facts are readily available for any given area in the United States. These companies do not research information themselves; they merely collect it from other sources and put it into usable form. All such information is valid only if it is relevant. Location experts working for chains have made big mistakes, selecting sites that were not right for a particular restaurant. The novice site analyst may have more problems.

A mom-and-pop operation may produce a living for its owners in a small town, while a restaurant with a heavy capital investment would be a loser economically. What might be an excellent location for a posh restaurant in one year could be a loser the next, as competition moves in and the fickle elite restaurant diners move on to the new in place.

Locations wax and wane in desirability depending on a number of conditions, including the general economy, the nature of the residents of the area, the presence or absence of new or declining buildings, changing traffic flows, and security. This means that the restaurant operator must be continually alert to general conditions in an area and be ready to change the menu, change the concept, if necessary, or even move out.

Census tracts used to be the standard measure. Now Zip plus Four (extended ZIP codes), which can contain as few as 15 households or only one business park, is more widely used to gather information.

With the proliferation of chains and changing lifestyles, people are less inclined to travel far to a restaurant. As a result, decision makers have to be even more precise in determining where new restaurants should go.

■

Traffic Generators

Look for built-in generators such as hotels, business parks, ball parks, indoor arenas, theatres, retail centers, and residential neighborhoods. Olive Garden, the 450 plus–unit chain of Italian dinner houses operated by Darden Restaurants, pursues a two-pronged growth strategy in which it moves into new markets as well as fills out markets it already operates in. To reduce development costs, the chain purchases restaurant sites and converts them to its own units.

Faced with market saturation and high real estate prices, restaurant chain executives who select sites for future building say their jobs have become riskier and more difficult.[8]

Knockout Criteria

If any one of the criteria listed below is not met, this should knock out a site as a restaurant location. There would be no point in exploring that site further.

- *Proper zoning.* If a site is not zoned for a restaurant and it is not likely that it can be rezoned, there is no point in pursuing that site.

- *Drainage, sewage, utilities.* If a site is impossible to use because of the unavailability of certain utilities, or if there is a possibility of being washed out by a flood, or if it has major drainage problems, it must be rejected.

- *Minimal size.* The plot must be of at least the minimal size for a particular restaurant. A freestanding coffee shop ordinarily calls for something like 40,000 square feet. The plot must be big enough, in most cases, to permit adequate parking spaces. A 200-seat restaurant, for example, in some cities calls for a least 75 parking spaces. Other building codes specify at least half as many parking spaces as seats in the restaurant.

- *Short lease.* If a lease is available for less than five years, the site may be undesirable for most restaurant styles.

- *Excessive traffic speed.* If the traffic travels at an excessive speed (more than 35 mph) past a location, this distracts from a site. Throughway and interstate highways are exceptions when off- and on-ramps are convenient to the site.

- *Access from a highway or street.* This is most important. An easy left turn onto the lot may be an important criterion. In one instance, a traffic light preventing a left turn reduced the volume of sales of a restaurant by half. The site may be all right for a style of restaurant different than one that depends on high traffic flow.

- *Visibility from both sides of the street.* The fact that a site is cut off from view may rule it out as the location for some styles of restaurants.

Other Location Criteria

- *Market population.* Each style of restaurant depends on a certain density of foot or car traffic past the location and/or a minimum residential population within a given radius of the location. Many restaurants call for a resident population of 15,000 to 20,000 within a two-mile radius. Some sites call for 50,000 cars to pass the location each day.

- *Family income.* A high-average-check restaurant normally calls for families of high income within a two- to five-mile radius. A lower-average-check restaurant could well succeed in a lower-income area.

- *Growth or decline of the area.* Is the area getting better or worse economically? Is the population rising or declining? If worse, the restaurant's lifespan may be brief.

Restaurant Row in San Diego's Gaslamp Quarter caters to both locals and tourists. Courtesy San Diego Gaslamp Quarter Association

- *Competition from comparable restaurants.* Is the area already saturated with hamburger restaurants, coffee shops, family restaurants, or dinner houses?
- *The restaurant row or cluster concept.* The idea older than the medieval fair. It can be found in the row of snack bars, preserved in Vesuvian ash, in Herculaneum in Italy dating back to the first century A.D. Putting a number of restaurants together may add to the total market because people will come a greater distance to a restaurant row than to separately located restaurants. However, in a restaurant row, only one or two hamburger restaurants may be viable. The usual cluster concept may site 35 or 40 restaurants in a small area, but ordinarily each offers a somewhat different theme, menu, and atmosphere. If the restaurant row is located in a particularly charming area, such as Marina del Rey in southern California or the Wharf area in San Francisco, each restaurant adds to the total ambiance. The whole is greater than the sum of its parts. A restaurant row must be part of or near a large population base.

Suburban, Nook-and-Cranny, and Shopping Mall Locations

Depending on menu and style of operation, restaurants do well in a variety of locations: suburbs, cities, near schools, in shopping centers, industrial parks, stadiums, and in high-rise buildings. McDonald's, for example, after a heavy emphasis on suburban expansion, turned to the nooks and crannies, those locations that are completely walk-up, without parking. Being a part of a shopping mall has many advantages, but the high cost of rent may preclude the success of some restaurants. Also, some styles of restaurants do much better in shopping malls than others, although almost every type of restaurant does well in one shopping area or another. Finding the correct area is the real trick.

Should the restaurant be placed within the covered mall itself or freestanding on mall grounds? The management of Fuddrucker's restaurants chooses the latter. Their clientele, mostly children accompanied by parents, gains the security of the mall and its parking facilities without being lost among the dozens of other mall stores.

The character of the operation should fit the character of the shopping mall. The Magic Pan, with its high-priced crêpes and omelets, high-style appointments, and rotary crêpe-pan cooking center, should be located where value is appreciated in terms of decor rather than quantity of food—that is, a mall serving an affluent community. A McDonald's restaurant was put in a posh Lexington Avenue area of New York City— and failed. A McDonald's as part of a military base shopping center is usually a winner.

MINIMUM POPULATION NEEDED TO SUPPORT A CONCEPT

How much population is needed to support a particular style of restaurant—5,000 people, 10,000, 25,000, or 50,000? When a nationally advertised chain such as McDonald's or Burger King comes into a smaller community, that restaurant is likely to have a higher frequency of repeat patronage than the place would in a large city. The fewer resources for entertainment a town or city has, means the existing businesses will receive a larger portion of business. Big cities have shops, restaurants, and thousands of options for the consumer. Put a McDonald's in a quiet little town like Kona on the big island of Hawaii and see what happens. People who do not know how to spend their free time, because there are few choices, are more apt to frequent a center of activity like a quick-service restaurant. It is new, it is fairly inexpensive, the food is in the American menu stream, and that is where the people assemble.

DOWNTOWN VERSUS SUBURBAN

Many restaurants have faded or failed because of the exodus of the middle class from the downtown area, leaving the restaurant perhaps a luncheon crowd, but no one for dinner. The situation has changed back in a number of cities. Townhouses are being built, and the two-person income has enabled many families to rent high-priced downtown apartments. Due to the high density of people living on one city block of New York City, which helps account for the large number of New York restaurants.

A restaurant's business may be tied to entertainment. When a popular movie shows, crowds come; when a poor movie shows, the restaurant has empty seats. Downtown restaurants appear in unusual places: in basements, in lobbies of old apartment buildings, in storefronts, on riverfronts, in department store complexes. Old churches become restaurants, as do converted firehouses, railroad stations, and libraries. Rents can be cheaper, depending on the neighborhood, or they can be considerably higher than in the suburbs, as much as double per square foot.

That an area, be it downtown or suburban, already has more than enough restaurants does not necessarily mean that a new one will not succeed. Is there a market gap to step into? Most towns and cities have more than enough restaurants. The proposer of a new one thinks that his or her place will better satisfy a particular market, provide more interest, be more exciting, have a more charming decor, provide more theater, serve higher-quality food, and so on. New restaurants continually displace old ones.

■

Average Travel Time to Reach Restaurants

Most diners-out select restaurants that are close by, near home, work, or shopping. Generally, restaurant patrons will travel about an average of 15 to 18 minutes to reach a hotel, steak, full menu, or fish restaurant. People often spend about 10 minutes when going to cafeteria and department store restaurants. In other words, consumers are willing to spend more time traveling to eat in a full-service specialty restaurant and for meals that are family occasions. People will travel an hour or more to reach a restaurant with a high reputation, especially if the meal celebrates an occasion. The same people want fast food or take-out food to be only a few minutes away.

IS THE LOCATION RIGHT
FOR THE CONCEPT?

A particular site may be right for a coffee shop but wrong for a dinner house or a fast-food place. It may be right for an in-and-out burger restaurant but wrong for a sit-down hamburger restaurant. The size of the lot, visibility, availability of parking, access from roads, and so on, all have an impact on the style of restaurant that will fit a location.

Restaurant sites have been known to fail six or more times running and then become highly successful with a new concept that fits the area and the competition. Sometimes, when a restaurant begins to fade, the owner feels that nothing much can be done except to do a better job, spend more on advertising, perhaps replace the present employees. This may be true, but often the only thing that will save the restaurant is a change of concept.

THE CORRECT NUMBER OF SEATS

Theoretically, a given location will support a given number of seats with a particular concept. A 120-seat restaurant may be right for location *x*, while a 240-seat restaurant would be wrong. Restaurant chains go through a period of evolution to arrive at the right size to suit their concept. Companies such as McDonald's, Denny's, and Pizza Hut have developed as many as three sizes of restaurants to fit different locations.

Surveys show that 40 to 50% of all table-service restaurant customers arrive in pairs; 30% come alone or in parties of three, 20% in groups of four or more. To accommodate these parties, consultants recommend tables for two that can be pushed together. Booths for four, while considered inefficient for some restaurants, are ideal for family places. Larger groups can be accommodated at several small tables placed together, in booths for six, or at large round tables. The floor space required per seat will vary according to the restaurant's service or atmosphere. Luxury and table-service restaurants require 15 to 20 square feet per seat; coffee shops and luncheonettes should allot about 12 to 17 square feet for each seat, while cafeterias need just 10 to 12 square feet per seat or per stool.

For the beginning restaurateur, it is probably better to build too small than too large. If the restaurant is excessively large for the location, it will be only partially filled. A crush of customers creates ambiance and excitement.

Some restaurants are too large for their markets. Better to shut down some rooms, if possible, so that customers can be seated with other customers. Few people like to sit in a large room with only a handful of other people present.

RESTAURANT CHAIN LOCATION SPECIFICATIONS

Restaurant chains usually have location specification details spelled out for use by realtors and potential franchisees. For example, this list shows critical criteria selected by a restaurant corporation headquartered in California:

- Metropolitan area with 50,000 population
- 20,000 cars per 24 hours on all streets of exposure; 24-hour traffic, at least four-lane highways
- Residential backup, plus motels, shopping centers, or office parks
- Minimum 200-foot frontage; approximately 45,000 square feet of land. If the restaurant is in a shopping center, a freestanding pad for a 5,000 square-foot building and adequate parking are necessary.
- Area demonstrating growth and stability
- Easy access and visibility
- Availability of all utilities to the property, including sewer

The same company illustrates how their restaurant would be placed on a parcel of land. Minimum width of the parcel would be about 170 feet, length about 200 feet. Motorists must be able to enter the property by making left turns from the street. Typical layouts for this company are shown in Figure 3–8.

Here are the site criteria for a Carl's Jr. restaurant, a quick-service hamburger-approaching-a-coffee-shop chain headquartered in California:

- Freestanding location in a shopping center
- Freestanding corner location (with a signal light at intersection)
- Inside lot with 125-foot minimum frontage
- Enclosed shopping mall location
- Population of 12,000 or more in one-mile radius (growth areas preferred)
- Easy access of traffic to location
- Heavy vehicular/pedestrian traffic
- An area where home values and family income levels are average or above
- Close to offices and other activity generators

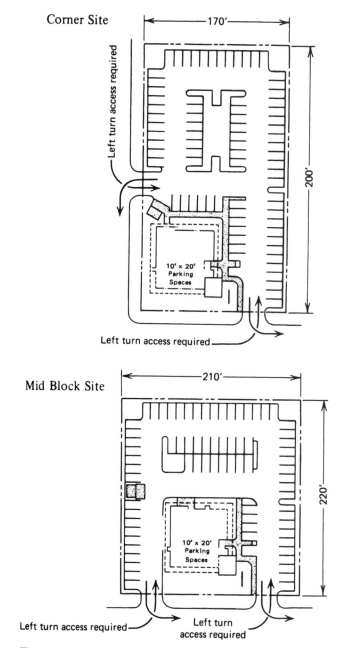

FIGURE 3–8

Typical coffee shop layouts

- A parcel size of 30,000 to 50,000 square feet
- No less than two or three miles from other existing company locations

Owners of nearly all new quick-service restaurants consider installing drive-through windows, which in some locations are used by more than half the patrons.

LOCATION INFORMATION CHECKLIST

To avoid overlooking location factors, the major chains develop checklists of information for evaluating a site, a recapitulation of the factors that experience has shown to be important for their style of operation. All of the information called for in the following checklist may not be needed to judge a particular site, but the list can call attention to factors that might otherwise be overlooked. The checklist is most relevant when evaluating a potential building site.

1. Dimensions and total square footage of site
2. Linear footage of site frontages
3. Distance and direction from nearest major streets
4. Average 24-hour traffic on each frontage street
5. Number of moving traffic lanes past location, widths, medians
6. Traffic controls affecting the location
7. Posted speed limits of adjacent streets (Some chains specify that traffic past a location not exceed 35 mph.)
8. On-street parking
9. Parking requirements: stall size, aisle width, number of stalls required
10. Landscaping and setback requirements for parking lot
11. Topography as regards necessary grading, slope characteristics, streams, brooks, ditches, flood conditions
12. Type of soil (natural and undisturbed, loose fill, compacted-fill soils); visible boulders, rock outcroppings, lakes, ponds, marshes
13. Drainage (public gravity-fed storm system; retention system on-site required)
14. Existing structures
15. Type of energy available (natural gas, LP gas, electric power).
16. Sanitary sewer availability
17. Underground utilities
18. Present zoning classification; any restrictions on hours of operation
19. Use and zoning of adjacent property
20. Building limitations
21. Character of surrounding area within one mile (office and industrial, tourist attractions, retail areas and shopping centers, motels and hotels, theaters, bowling alleys, schools, colleges, hospitals)

22. Population and income characteristics (number of people within one to several miles, typical occupations, median annual family income, ethnic makeup, housing value ranges, trade area population)

23. Agencies requiring plan approval:
    a. Federal Housing Authority (FHA)
    b. Water resources
    c. State conservation authority
    d. Local planning commission
    e. Local health department
    f. Environmental Protection Agency (EPA)
    g. Other

24. Status of annexation for sites not in municipal limits

25. Signage (pole-maximum area, height allowed, setback; building-area allowed; remote entrance signs, area allowed, height allowed)

26. Construction codes:
    a. Building
    b. Mechanical
    c. Plumbing
    d. Fire
    e. Building regulations covering design for people who are handicapped
    f. Other approvals required to obtain building permit

27. Restaurant competition within one mile of site (fast food, cafeteria style, family restaurants, coffee shops, dinner houses)

28. Offering price of property

In addition, real estate brokers submitting the information are asked to supply location maps, assessors' maps, plant maps, legal descriptions, zoning maps, chamber of commerce data, aerial photographs, and other available data.

THE TAKEOVER LOCATION

Being short of capital or wishing to minimize risk, the beginning restaurateur often starts by leasing or buying out an existing restaurant. The restaurant may be failing; the operator may wish to retire. If a restaurant is a failure, the new entrepreneur feels that he or she can do it better, or has a better concept for the location. Takeover situations can always be found.

Terms for the restaurateur can be favorable—little cash required and the building and equipment available for lease. The new restaurateur thinks: How can I lose? But he can and often does lose because the location is not right for the restaurant concept or format.

Often the entrepreneur changes the concept from a coffee shop to a dinner house or family restaurant with hammer and nails. The exterior may be covered or repainted, the interior decor changed by adding or removing booths, moving walls, lowering or raising ceilings, adding artifacts or color. If the restaurant is successful, a takeover in another location is undertaken. Once the concept has proved itself, the company begins

Blue Point Coastal Cuisine is a popular seafood restaurant in San Diego's Gaslamp District. Courtesy The Cohn Restaurant Group

to select its sites more carefully, according to strict criteria, and builds its own restaurants or finds interested investors to build according to specification.

RESTAURANT TOPOGRAPHICAL SURVEYS

Ray Kroc, founder of McDonald's, liked to pick locations for his restaurants from a helicopter. Flying over a community, he could see the churches, schools, and traffic patterns.

An alternative to this approach can be achieved using a town or city map and plotting the location of existing restaurants on the map. This birds-eye view provides a valuable perspective.

Nearly every restaurant in a community is listed in the yellow pages of a phone book, and it is not difficult to classify the restaurants in a way that will identify potential competition. If the planned restaurant is a coffee shop, all the coffee shops in the area should be marked on the map; they constitute direct competition. Seeing all of the restaurants in an area on a map gives some idea of the degree of restaurant saturation.

Of the hundreds of restaurants located in Pomona Valley, east of Los Angeles, quick-service restaurants predominate and compete vigorously with each other. The hundreds of restaurants might all do well in a more heavily populated urban area, which means that the number of restaurants is excessive, a not unusual situation. Only two or three high-style, high-check-average restaurants can be supported. Several Mexican restaurants can be sustained. A few other ethnic restaurants do fairly well, as long as the owner is the operator and is helped by family. The would-be restaurant operator in this Pomona Valley area would determine if the selected concept is needed. Is there a market gap, a group of people not being served the kind of food or offered the kind of service and atmosphere that the proposed concept would provide?

IS THE LOCATION TOO COSTLY?

Finally, and critically, can the concept and the potential market support the location selected? A restaurant has two potential values, its real estate value and its value as a profit generator. The two values should be considered separately. A restaurant building may actually detract from the real estate value, especially if the building has failed as a restaurant one or several times or is unattractive. On the other hand, the real estate value may be greater than the operational value.

A restaurant buyer is concerned with the real estate value, a potential lessee less so. A person wanting to lease a restaurant, however, must consider the real estate value (or its potential value) because, if the value increases, the owner will increase the rent—unless the lease agreement is written to prevent such an increase.

Affecting market value are potential changes in property zoning by local or state zoning boards. Will highway changes be made in the near future that will affect the value of the property? Is the area going downhill or being revitalized? Is the area getting better or worse for a particular kind of restaurant? As an area changes, the kind of restaurant that will be supported also changes. A declining income area may need a lower-check-average restaurant, a quick-service restaurant, or a coffee shop. As affluence grows, more dinner houses can be introduced.

The cost depends on location. The cost of construction may be $200 to $250 per square foot exclusive of land. A lease may run from $2.00 to $4.50 per square foot or more per month. This may translate into 6 to 9% of sales.

VISIBILITY AND ACCESSIBILITY

Visibility and accessibility are important criteria for any restaurant. Visibility is the extent to which the restaurant can be seen for a reasonable amount of time, whether the potential guest is walking or driving. Good visibility is vital to a quick-service restaurant and may be slightly less important to a full-service restaurant. There is a higher correlation between the quick-service restaurant and good visibility.

Accessibility relates to the ease with which potential guests may arrive at the restaurant. Parking, for example, may be a problem, as may access from the freeway or other traffic artery.

DESIGN CRITERIA

The restaurant has been likened to a theater. Restaurant design has two main components. The first is the stage setting and various props that the audience or guests experience; this is called the front of the house. The second is backstage, or the kitchen,

Le Cirque, in New York, is one of the most famous restaurants in the United States. Courtesy Adam Tihany International Ltd. Photo by Peter Paige

storage, and service areas. The space allocation for backstage is usually 30% of the total square footage, depending on the type of restaurant.

The design of both the back and front of the house needs to correlate with the theme of the restaurant. Design and the volume of business are reflected in each area: the exterior, the entrance and holding area, the bar or beverage area, the dining area (including the table arrangements), the kitchen, receiving (including access for deliveries), and storage and trash areas. Space is a major issue in restaurant design because it costs money, yet is vital to maintaining a balance between the overcrowded restaurant and the more spacious restaurant with too high an average check.

Lighting is the single most important element in restaurant design because incor-

Remi, in New York, is an Adam Tihany–designed restaurant that is both elegant and festive. Courtesy Adam Tihany International Ltd. Photo by Peter Paige

rect lighting can obliterate the effectiveness of all the other elements. Lighting is a critical psychological component as well.[15]

Color needs to be selected in tandem with lighting because the two need to be in harmony. Color and light interact with one another to create a mood. Darker colors tend to "come out" and make a room look smaller, although they may also give a feeling of greater intimacy. Lighter colors tend to recede and make a room appear larger. Pastel colors help guests relax more than primary colors. Quick-service restaurants use bold colors (and hard seats) combined with bright lights to ensure that guests move on after about 20 minutes.

Many restaurants use color as a mark of recognition, whether it is on the actual building or on awnings. These may have the psychological effect of attracting people to the restaurant.

The layout of the dining area, especially the tables and seats, the traffic lanes, and service areas, require careful consideration and usually several mock-up scale drawings. Designers can do this on computers. Will the tables have cloths? If so what color? Or will there be a wooden, tile, or other hard surface? Will there be cloth or paper napkins? Will the seats be wooden, upholstered in fabric, or vinylized? Will there be a hardwood floor, tile, or carpet? These and many other questions need answers that will conform to the overall theme of the restaurant.

SUMMARY

The concept should reflect the requirements of the market and location menu; service and decor should complement the concept.

Successful concepts exist for both independent and chain restaurants. Some concepts that were successful are now no longer in use. This suggests that fads come and go. Many so-called gimmick restaurants have stood the test of time. The restaurant life cycle varies from a few weeks to several years. The more focused the concept is on a target market, the greater the chance of success. Concepts often must change to keep in step with changing markets and economic conditions.

The sequence of restaurant development has many steps between concept and operation. A mission statement will help keep the restaurant operation on a straight course of action toward a common goal.

KEY TERMS AND CONCEPTS

Restaurant concepts
Clear versus ambiguous concept
Protecting the restaurant name
Defining the concept and market
The fine line between funk and junk
Some successful restaurant concepts
Concept adaptation
Copy and improve
Concept failure
Multiple-concept chain
Sequence of restaurant development
    from concept to opening

Utility versus pleasure
Degree of service
Profitability
Mission statement
Concept and location
Location criteria
Location information
Location checklist
Traffic generator
Topographical survey
Visibility and accessibility
Location specification

REVIEW QUESTIONS

1. In concept development, you select a given style of service: counter tray, cart, arm, or French. Which will fit your concept best, and why?

2. Which kind of restaurants is likely to have the greatest productivity per hour? Which will require the most advertising and promotion, the most dining room space per customer? Which has the greatest likelihood of the highest return on investment?

3. Roughly what percentage of meals eaten out are purely for pleasure?

4. Most college and university students majoring in hotel and restaurant management are not interested in fast-food restaurants. Why not? What distinct advantages do such restaurants have? What disadvantages?

5. What is the relationship between your logo and your restaurant concept?

6. Suppose your name is Joe Smith. Would you have any legal problem naming your restaurant Smith's?

7. Comment on the statement "Behind every restaurant there is a concept."

8. List five factors that together help formulate a restaurant concept.

9. How are restaurant image and concept related?

10. In what way do several existing restaurants close to a site affect the desirability of that site for another restaurant?

11. Can a particular site be wrong for one restaurant, right for another? Explain.

12. The desirability of a given restaurant location changes with time. Give three reasons why this is true.

13. In what way are management and decor related to the value of a given location?

14. Why may a community give favorable terms to a reputable restaurant operator to start a restaurant in a section of town that is deteriorating?

15. What location criteria would you suggest for a restaurant featuring diet foods?

16. What colors would you suggest for a high-style Italian restaurant?

17. A luxury, white-tablecloth restaurant has a rheostatic lighting control. How would you use it and for what purposes?

18. Why or why not would you use upholstered soft seating in a quick-service restaurant?

19. What kind of restaurant location can exist without parking?

20. In building a restaurant, what amount of money should you expect to invest per seat?

21. Suppose you have $80,000 with which to start a restaurant and no possibility of borrowing additional capital. What kind of restaurant should you consider and how would you go about getting started?

ENDNOTES

[1] Al DaCosta, FCSI, Cohn DaCosta International, "So You Want to Own a Restaurant?" *The Consultant* (Fall 1998): 57.

[2] Ibid.

[3] Nathan Cobb, *Boston Globe* magazine, June 4, 1989, p. 22.

[4] This section draws from information supplied by the Hard Rock American Restaurant Company (HRC). The authors acknowledge and appreciate the assistance given by HRC.

[5] Ira Apfel, "Is It Time to Change Your Concept?" *Restaurant USA*, Vol 18: No 10. November 1998, 22–26.

[6] Personal conversation with Edmund Michalski, December 1, 1999.

[7] "Best-Run Companies," *Restaurants and Institutions*, 29 May 1989.

[8] Courtesy Chili's Grill and Bar.

[9] Courtesy Restaurants Unlimited.

[10] Andrew Campbell and Sally Yering, "Creating a Sense of Mission," *Long-Range Planning*, Vol: 24 Iss 4 August 1991, 10–20.

[11] Cleo R. Ludwig, *I Am What I Am . . . And Here's Why* (Caledonia, Ohio, Vimach Associates, 1986).

[12] Personal communication with Ray Marshall, October 6, 1988.

[13] John C. Melaniphy, *Restaurant and Fast Food Site Selection* (New York: John Wiley and Sons, 1992).

[14] Keven Farrell, "Site and Saturation," *Restaurant Business* 90 no. 10 (1 July 1991): 72.

[15] Regina S. Barban and Joseph F. Durocher, *Successful Restaurant Design* (New York: Van Nostrand Reinhold, 1989), 47.

Chapter **4**

After reading and studying this chapter,
you should be able to:

Develop a marketing and business plan.

Conduct a market assessment.

Discuss the importance of the four Ps of the marketing mix.

Describe the best promotional ideas for your restaurant.

RESTAURANT MARKETING
AND BUSINESS PLANS

Before embarking on the complex task of setting up any business, especially a restaurant, it is essential to construct a marketing/business plan. This will help determine the probable degree of success of the restaurant. As with any plan, the more work that goes into it, the better informed the owner/operator is as to the feasibility and viability of the proposed restaurant. Some operators find that after preparing a detailed marketing/business plan, the numbers do not add up—or, in other words, it is unlikely that the restaurant would be successful. That's OK! All they have lost is the time and effort put into the plan—they have not lost their shirt!

THE MARKETING PLAN

A marketing plan sets objectives for identifying target customers and their restaurant needs and devises ways to satisfy those needs.

A marketing plan includes what marketing professionals call *positioning*. How does the public view your restaurant in relation to other restaurants in the market area?

How is your restaurant different from similar restaurants? What benefits will your restaurant offer that are not offered by competitors? Once these benefits are identified, they are built into the restaurant image you wish to project.

The image projected may be of efficiency, fun, and value (the quick-service restaurant). It can be laid-back, casual, or theme. It can be status, culture, and luxury (celebrity restaurant). It can be cheerful and friendly, formal and quiet, or conservative.

Markets can be defined according to the foods served. Certain foods appeal to particular groups of people. There is the hamburger market, the fried chicken market, the roast beef market, the health food market, and so on. Then there are those who like ethnic foods: Mexican, Italian, English, Chinese, French, and so on.

McDonald's restaurants appeal to children and teenagers; these groups, in turn, bring their parents. The market could be described as a young family market. McDonald's is extending its market to include older age brackets, and its advertising includes senior citizens. Wendy's saw a market gap in the hamburger market—age groups older than those attracted to McDonald's. Carl's Jr. also reaches an older hamburger market. The seating in some of these restaurants is more coffee shop in style, with banquettes and soft cushions. Advertising itself helps determine a market.

Each restaurant market has an economic dimension—low, middle, or high income. Some restaurants may cut across markets; others reach one particular market only. TGI Friday's attracts a younger, more affluent market than the average dinner house. The high-style French restaurant appeals to the movers, the doers, and the adventuresome. Prices generally exclude the less affluent, except for special occasions.

Ethnic restaurants may cut across age and economic brackets. Within the ethnic market, a particular Mexican restaurant may hit the upper end of the economic market, while another Mexican restaurant appeals to the lower end.

Coffee shop markets are differentiated; some appeal to the affluent, others to the less affluent. Depending on location, a coffee shop can cut across several markets.

An expensive restaurant selects a market: those people who may be gourmet minded and those who want to reinforce their own image by appearing or entertaining at an elegant restaurant.

Many Americans are keenly interested in unique food experiences. The over-50 affluent market is particularly interested in wineing and dining, with all of the accoutrements and special effects to make it as much an experience as a meal. Each restaurant appeals to a particular market or markets depending on the concept, its location, and the availability of other restaurant choices.

Hamburger, full-menu, and chicken restaurants are the least dependent on higher-income families and have the most even attendance among all family income groups. Low-income groups are more likely to pick a hamburger, chicken, or department or variety store restaurant.

Many people wonder why there are not more gourmet restaurants in a community. The answer is fairly simple—few customers are willing to pay the tab. It has been said that a gourmet is a person who, when invited out for an evening of wine, food, and song, wants to know what kind of food and wine. And the wine may cost more than the rest of the meal.

A good marketing and business plan will not only improve the chances of operational success, but also assist in obtaining financing, communicating to potential investors, and operational purposes. Marketing and business plans begin with an executive summary, which outlines the elements of the plan. These are listed as follows:

Cover Sheet

Executive summary
Statement of purpose

Description of the Organization

Management summary: mission, goals, objectives
Type of organization
Management qualifications, experience, and capabilities

Description of the Concept

The concept
The menu
Menu pricing

Market Analysis and Marketing Strategy

Description of target market
    Demographics, psychographics, lifestyles
    Market potential (size, rate of growth)
Competitive analysis
    Number of competitors
    Strengths, weaknesses, opportunities, and threats (SWOT) analysis
    Location
    Sales and market share
    Nature of competition
    Potential new restaurant competition

Pricing strategy
>   Menu and beverage list pricing
>   Location analysis
>   Description of the area
>   Commercial/residential profile
>   Traffic flows
>   Accessibility

Advertising and promotional campaign
>   Objectives
>   Techniques
>   Target audience, means of communication
>   Schedule

Other information
>   Schedule for growth
>   Financing schedule
>   Schedule for return on investment

Financial Data

Sources of funding
Proposed restaurant balance sheet
>   Pro forma income statement
>   First year—detail by month
>   Second year—detail by quarter
>   Third year—detail by quarter

Existing restaurant balance sheet
>   Previous three years' income statements
>   Previous three years'

Cash flow statement
>   Previous three years' tax returns

Appendices

Sales projections
Organization chart
Job descriptions
Resumes of management team
Legal documents
Leases
Licenses
Firm price quotations
Insurance contracts
Sample menu
Furniture, fixtures, and equipment (FF&E)
Floor plan, letters of intent
Anything else that is relevant[1]

The cover sheet also should have the name of the business, the logo or trademark (if any), the current or proposed address of the restaurant, the restaurant telephone number, the owner's name and associates' names, and their qualifications. In addition, it should list the name of the company, the addresses and telephone numbers of the executives, and an introductory statement. Each of the elements needs to be fully written up, and that takes research and critical thinking. Logically, the plan expects the operator to assess where the business is now and where it should be in five to ten years—and of course, how it is going to get there.

People do not purchase features, they purchase benefits, and each person purchases only those that specifically satisfy his or her personal or professional needs, wants, desires, hopes, aspirations, and dreams. We are really in the business of motivating people to purchase those benefits that satisfy their specific, and often changing, needs and wants.

Peter Drucker said we must frequently ask ourselves, "What business am I in?" Are we in the service business, the production business, or the entertainment business? The answer is yes to all of the above! The service aspect predominates, however, so we need to determine our guests' needs and wants.

Once we have established what business we are in, the next step is to come up with a mission statement (discussed in Chapter 3). The mission generally does not change. The goals and objectives, however, are reviewed as often as necessary. Goals should be established for each key operational area, e.g., sales, food, beverage, and labor costs, etc.

Objectives and strategies are the "how to reach the goal" and are more specific than goals and are generally short-term. Objectives are specific as to the date by which they are to be achieved and how much should be achieved. Based on objectives, a detailed action plan with individual responsibilities should be implemented.

A large factor in restaurant failure is the naive belief that if food, service, price, and atmosphere are good, patrons are certain to appear and will return in the future. An assumption is made that potential customers who want what is offered are waiting. Marketing makes no such assumption.

This chapter explores the meaning and ramifications of restaurant marketing and business plans. It also delineates marketing practices that, if followed, can help ensure success and avoid the financial costs and heartaches of failure.

Peter Drucker, the highly regarded management scholar and writer, states, "The only valid definition of business purpose is to create a customer." In the restaurant business, we should add, "and to keep a customer returning."

It is important to remember that the customer pays the bills and determines the level of profit—not the owner, manager, accountant, banker, or controller.

A vice president of marketing reviewing the corporation's marketing plan

The old joke sums it up well. "Do you know how to make a small fortune in the restaurant business? Start with a large fortune!" To be successful, a restaurant needs great food, service, and atmosphere. Some restaurants get by with mediocre service and atmosphere. Few survive with inferior food.

Restaurant marketing is based on a marketing philosophy that patterns the way management and ownership have decided to relate to customers, employees, purveyors, and the general public in terms of fairness, honesty, and moral conduct, needed in part because of greater importance being placed on the ethical and moral conduct of business. Building on the marketing philosophy, the techniques and practices of marketing include the efforts by managements to match what a particular group of people (the target market) wants in terms of restaurant food, service, price, and atmosphere.

Marketing is finding out what customers want and providing it at a reasonable price that leaves adequate profit. Marketing asks would-be operators to ask themselves, "Who will be my customers? Why will they choose my restaurant? Where will they come from and why will they come back?"

Marketing assumes that customers change, that they will want new menu items, new atmospheres, and, sometimes, new service. Marketing asks operators to expect change in the marketplace and to position or reposition the restaurant to meet those changes.

Many of us have been tempted to open a restaurant at one time or another. Perhaps Grandma passed down some good recipes and a desire to cook. Whatever the reason, the restaurant business is easy to get into because, apart from finances, there are no real barriers to entry.

The restaurant business, however, is complex. There are few businesses in which customers rely on all their senses to experience the product. In the restaurant business, our customers see, smell, touch, taste, and hear our offerings.

THE DIFFERENCE BETWEEN MARKETING AND SALES

It is important to distinguish between the terms *marketing, sales,* and *merchandising.* Marketing is the broad concept that includes the other two. Marketing implies determining who will patronize a restaurant (the market or markets) and what they want in it—its design, atmosphere, menu, and service. Marketing implies constant review of patrons and the identification of possible others. Marketing is an ongoing effort that matches patron with restaurant, matches patrons' desires with what the restaurant has to offer, and identifies people who would like the same thing. Marketing gets into the psyche of present and potential patrons. Once it is known what patrons want and what the restaurant has to offer, the two can be brought together.

Marketing focuses on the needs of the buyer; sales focuses on the needs of the seller. This distinction is important because restaurants often approach marketing with a sales mentality, which is a mistake.

Sales is part of marketing. Sales efforts are the activities that stimulate the patron to want what the restaurant offers. Selling is often thought of as the actions of restaurant employees that influence patrons after they have arrived at the restaurant.

The sales mentality exists when the seller thinks only of her or his needs—that is, pushing an item on the menu on to the customer. With this mentality, few customers would return to the restaurant.

Closely related to sales are advertising, promotion, and public relations. The three have similar objectives. Advertisements are purchased from newspapers, radio, TV, or similar businesses. Public relations is not. Public relations are those efforts to make the public favor the restaurant without resorting to paid advertising. Promotion is further elaborated on later in the chapter.

SOLVING CUSTOMER PROBLEMS

Marketing is about solving customer problems. Identifying and solving problems is not easy. Changing lifestyles lead to the different wants and needs of the customer, which vary from location to location. In California, people tend to grab a take-out meal on the way to the beach, whereas in New England, people may prefer to make a meal into a more social occasion.

The ideal restaurant experience is different for everyone; some diners look for elegance, some for convenience, some for value. Despite these differing expectations, surveys indicate that the quality of food is of primary importance to customers when selecting a restaurant.

All restaurant customers, however, have one basic need: hunger. In addition, they may also want entertainment, and they will seek a restaurant with a stimulating environment. Some may want recognition, so they will go to a restaurant that provides the feeling of importance that comes with recognition.

MARKETING PLANNING

Every marketing plan must have realistic objectives for sales and costs while leaving a reasonable profit margin. In addition, innovation—the development of new and better products—services, and processes, requires objectives for direction. Objectives for market share, sales volume, cleanliness, product quality, service, guest satisfaction, key ratios, and price also need to be set.

Before investing in a restaurant, it is critical to conduct a competition analysis, an assessment of the strengths and weaknesses of the competition, to determine if there is an open niche in the market for the type of restaurant being considered. See Figure 4–1 for a schematic of the planning process.

Competition analysis includes reviewing the competition within the market. Generally, this is done by analyzing the restaurants within the segment that the proposed restaurant will fit—for example, seafood restaurants or Mexican family restaurants. In recent years, this has become more difficult to do because the public has become less predictable and restaurants are offering a wider range of product. McDonald's is now offering a breakfast burrito! It is not a Mexican restaurant, but it is offering a Mexican dish and, if most Mexican restaurants were open for breakfast, they would have to be considered competition.

MARKETING STRATEGY

Marketing strategy will also position the restaurant in relation to competition regarding price, the food and service offered, atmosphere, and convenience.

The marketing strategy needs to conform to the circumstances of the restaurant. For example, a specific market entry strategy is appropriate for a new restaurant concept entering an existing market. We would need to find a competitive advantage based on the four *P*s: price, product, place, and promotion.

In taking over an existing restaurant, the goal could be market share. Any one or a combination of tactics could do this. For example, price reduction and heavy local advertising might achieve the strategy's goal.

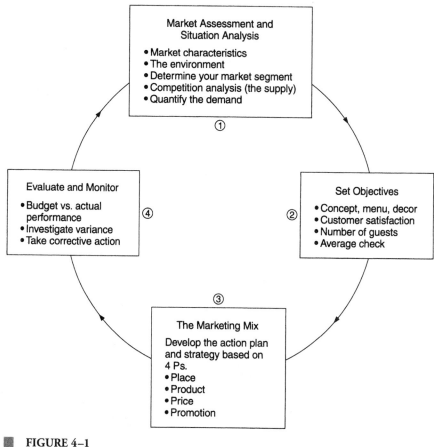

FIGURE 4–1

The planning sequence

Marketing strategy is the way the restaurateur accomplishes the goals set for the restaurant. One of the goals could be to increase the number of guests by 15%; this would be achieved by means of targeted flyers of the restaurant menu featuring certain dishes. The flyer could be distributed in selected postal zip codes.

Another goal might be to increase the average check by $1.00 at dinner. This goal could be reached by suggestive sales training. The strategy is the game plan for attaining determined goals.

The key ingredient in any marketing initiative is the marketing plan, which helps focus the marketing and direct it toward the target market. It analyzes the marketplace, the competition, and the existing or proposed restaurant's strengths and weaknesses.

MARKET ASSESSMENT

By examining the characteristics of the marketplace, we gain perspective on an operation being planned. The assessment provides initial information that is helpful in planning the success of the restaurant and hopefully avoids the loss of one's shirt! By scanning the horizon and anticipating changes, the odds against failure are raised.

A market assessment analyzes the community, the customers, and the competition:

- Is there a need for a restaurant?
- Potential customers:
  - How old are they?
  - What are their incomes?
  - What is their sex?
  - What is their ethnic origin or religion?
- What are customers' wants and needs?
- Why would people become customers?
- What will they like or dislike about the proposed restaurant?
- What do they like or dislike about existing restaurants?

MARKET DEMAND

The demand for a restaurant is not easy to quantify. At best, one arrives at a guesstimate—a calculated guess. The calculated part is derived from:

1. The population in the catchment area (the area around the restaurant from which people would normally be drawn to the restaurant)
2. This demographic split of this population by nationality, race, age, sex, religion, employment, education, and income

These data indicate the total number of people who might be customers. In recent years, demographic information has lost some of its relevance. One reason is the increas-

Mr. and Mrs. Damien Few reviewing their market assessment. Courtesy Damien Few

ingly multicultural nature of our society. Another is the changing characteristics of lifestyle. The blurring of demographic lines is evident when top executives eat at McDonald's. Using effective marketing techniques over the years, McDonald's has found the answer to that important question, "What do the people need and want and what price are they willing to pay?" Following the formula of founder Ray Kroc's—quality, service, cleanliness, and value—billions of hamburgers have been sold. McDonald's Corporation sales are greater than those of its three nearest competitors combined.

So, how does this relate to sound marketing prices? In the early 1960s, Ray Kroc realized that as families moved into the suburbs and adopted a more mobile lifestyle, they had less time in which to prepare meals. The fast-food hamburger was the answer, and it soon become an American favorite.

Market Potential

How many people in the market area are potential customers? What is the potential for breakfast, for lunch, for dinner? Will my restaurant attract customers from outside the immediate market area? Is my market the tourist, the businessperson, the highway traveler, the person in the neighborhood, or some combination of these? Breakfast and luncheon markets need convenient locations. Rapid service is prized, except in luxury restaurants. Dinner customers are something else. Customers will drive miles to a restaurant they like or one that has developed a reputation for food quality, atmosphere, service, or price.

Market Segmentation, Target Market, and Positioning

The market—that is, the total of all actual and potential guests—is generally segmented into groups of buyers with similar characteristics. Within these groups are target markets, which are groups identified as the best ones for the restaurant to serve. The reason for segmenting the market and establishing target markets is to focus limited marketing resources for maximum effectiveness.

Typical Segmentations

- *Geographic:* country, state/province, county, city, neighborhood
- *Demographic:* age, sex, family life cycle, income, and occupation, education, religion, race
- *Behavior:* occasions, benefits sought, user status, usage rates, loyalty status, buyer readiness stage

Once the target market is identified, it is important to position the restaurant to stand out from the competition and to focus on advertising and promotional messages to guests. The key to positioning is how guests perceive the restaurant.

Wendy's promotes never-frozen meat, hot off the grill; Burger King is known for its flame-broiled food, and Rally's double drive-through used low price to position itself in the marketplace.[2] Another example is Schlotzsky's, which recently announced new network TV ads to differentiate its product from sandwich-segment competitors as it seeks to lure first-time customers into its stores. The food photography is intended to enable people to distinguish the product from the other sandwich chains, such as Subway and Blimpie Subs and Salads.[3]

MARKETING MIX—THE FOUR *P*s

Every marketing plan must have realistic objectives for sales and costs while leaving a reasonable profit margin. Marketing plans are based on the four *P*s, known as the cornerstone of marketing—place, product, price, and promotion.

■

Place

The place or location of a restaurant is generally considered to be of major importance. In fact, many restaurateurs believe location to be the most critical factor in the restaurant's success formula.[4]

Good visibility, easy access, convenience, curbside appeal, and parking are the ingredients of a location's success. Visibility is necessary so that, as people approach the restaurant, they are able to easily identify it. Often, a prominently placed sign catches potential customers' attention; directions, if necessary, can be featured on it.

Restaurants are found in freestanding buildings on a lot with parking spaces, in city blocks with no parking, in shopping malls, in office buildings, in airports, train stations,

Maggiano's Little Italy, in Chicago. Celebrity visitors definitely boost marketing and promotional efforts. Courtesy Maggiano's Little Italy

A word of warning! If a restaurateur opts for the higher-rent district and spends heavily on lavish decor, the food and service should be excellent because customer expectations will be high. Would-be restaurateurs who find themselves in hot water due to spending a lot of money on the lease and alterations cut corners with the menu and service. This often leads to the restaurant's demise.

and bus depots. The University of California at San Diego has a Wendy's in the University Center and the Marine Corps Air Station at Miramar, California, has a McDonald's on the base. These restaurants are formulate in that, to a large extent, they have a built-in clientele.

A restaurant grouping, sometimes known as a *restaurant row*, is quite common. The approaches may attract people because of the wide choice of restaurants available. If two French restaurants are already on the block, it would be unwise to compete by opening another.

Most restaurants have little or no problem with Friday and Saturday nights. The big problem is how to fill up on Sunday through Thursday, and for both lunch and dinner to boot! This feat requires a magician who provides good location, conjures up an exciting atmosphere, and serves good food well.

Several established restaurant chains attempt to cluster their restaurants. Some franchise by territory. Proponents of this idea argue that economies of scale occur in purchasing, preparation, advertising, and management. Opponents of this view suggest that new stores simply take away business from existing stores. Clustering is, however, a tremendous advantage when there is positive customer awareness in the market for a particular restaurant chain.

The concept of adjacent complementary restaurants is catching on. For, example, one finds Kentucky Fried Chicken or Pizza Hut next to Taco Bell (all are companies within Tricon Global Restaurants, Inc.). Other quick-service companies are experimenting with sharing sites with other retailers. For example, Wendy's, Hardee's, and McDonald's have leased space in department and convenience stores.[5]

There is the occasional successful restaurant in an odd location, but the norm is to have high visibility, curbside appeal, easy access, and parking, all of which cost money. The better the location, the higher the rent, so there may have to be some compromise.

We have all seen restaurants whose prices are exorbitant. We may have gone there for dinner and cocktails once, but because our expectations were not met, we felt robbed and never returned. All too often, owners are talked into spending vast amounts on decor by interior design consultants. Design is important, and many smart restaurateurs have created expensive Italian, movie-theme, or nostalgia-theme restaurants, such as the Hard Rock Café. It is unnecessary, however, to spend a lot of money on the decor of a Greek restaurant close to a university campus because students—the target market—want a good price-value relationship. By contrast, patrons of an elegant New York restaurant—most of whom, no doubt, are on a company expense account—expect to pay for—and receive—excellent food, service, and decor.

■

Product

The product of restaurants is experiential; the complete package of food, beverages, service, atmosphere, and convenience goes into satisfying the customers' needs and wants and making for a memorable experience, one that customers will want to repeat.

The main ingredient is excellent food. People will always seek out a restaurant offering excellent food, especially when good service and ambiance accompany it.

Once the target market is selected, it is important to offer the total package in accordance with the wishes of the customers in this market. Menu items should reflect the selections of patrons within this group. In other words, if a restaurant is trying to attract a college crowd, it needs menu items popular with this group.

Food presentation as part of the product. Courtesy Chart House Restaurants

Food service and atmosphere are largely intangible. The purchase of a restaurant product is not like the purchase of an automobile, which can be inspected and driven prior to purchase. With restaurants, guests pay for the total dining experience rather than just the food. Restaurant product can be described as having three levels: the core product, the formal product, and the augmented product (Figure 4–2).

- The core product is the function part of the product server for the customer. Thus, a gourmet restaurant offers a relaxing and memorable evening.

- The formal product is the tangible part of the product. This includes the physical aspects of the restaurant and its decor. In addition, a certain level of service is also expected. When customers choose a family restaurant, they anticipate a level of service appropriate for the type of restaurant.

- The augmented product includes the other services, such as automatic acceptance of certain credit cards, valet parking, and table reservation service.

Product analysis covers the quality, pricing, and service of the product offered. How will the product—menu, atmosphere, location, convenience, price—differ from the competition? Will it include signature menu items—those that are unusual in some way or convey the stamp of uniqueness that customers will remember and associate with the restaurant? Will the decor and atmosphere be discernibly different from the competition? Is the service superior in some way, faster or more concerned, more professional or more elaborate? Is the value greater for the price than the competition's? Is the location more convenient, parking easier or more spacious?

■ **Atmospherics.** Restaurateurs are placing greater emphasis on atmospherics, the design used to create a special atmosphere. Based about 1970, the majority of restaurants were quite plain. Today, atmospherics are built into the restaurant concept to have an immediate sensory impact on customers.[6]

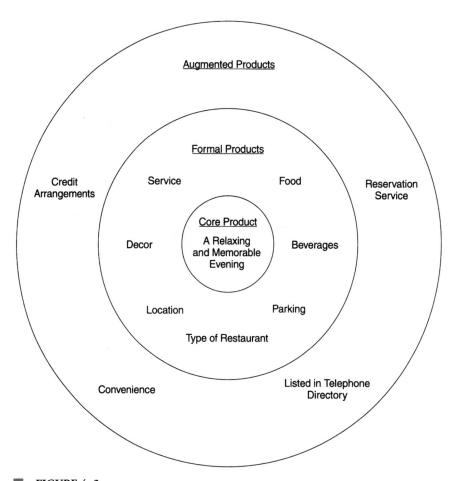

FIGURE 4–2

Three levels of product concept for restaurants

Perhaps the most noticeable atmospherics are found in theme restaurants. The theme employs color, sound, lighting, decor, texture, and visual preparation to create special effects for patrons. Sporting themes are definitely in with many people, as is the Hard Rock Café's rock-and-roll nostalgia. Some McDonald's restaurants rely on atmospherics. They have small play areas for kids. The restaurants are decorated with bright colors, bright lights, and hard seats, all of which are designed to persuade patrons to vacate in less than 20 minutes. Care should be taken when creating theme restaurants, because the life of the theme may be only a few years. The atmosphere must be appropriate for the target market.

■ **Product Development.**   Innovative menu items are added to maintain or boost sales. By keeping consumer interest stimulated, restaurants may increase market share and profit. The new items replace those with which the public has become bored. Dining menus have come alive in recent years. Gone are the heavy meat items with their calorific sauces. In their place is fresh pasta, fish, chicken, or other lighter dishes with a more wholesome sauce.

Most of the large chain restaurants test their new product in selected markets. If the new product is accepted, it is launched systemwide. This was the case with the breakfast menu that a number of restaurant chains introduced in recent years. It is interesting to note that as soon as one company rolled out a new breakfast menu, the competition felt compelled to follow suit. In some cases, this was done with too much haste, leading to an inferior product and consequent customer dissatisfaction.

■ **Product Positioning.**   Restaurant customers generally have a perception or image of the restaurant, its food, service, atmosphere, convenience, prices, and how it differs from other restaurants in the area. Positioning conveys to the customer the best face or image of the restaurant, what people like most about it, or how it stands out from the competition. If value is the best feature of the restaurant, it should be emphasized in the positioning statement and reinforced in advertising. Wendy's approach in underscoring the freshness of their product is an excellent way of positioning it.

■ **Restaurant Differentiation.**   Restaurant owners usually want their restaurant to be different in one or more ways, to call attention to the food or ambiance.

How does a burger restaurant differentiate itself from the competition? An early example happened by chance in 1937, before quick-service restaurants became widespread. In that year, Bob Wian, who four years earlier, as a high school student, had been voted most unlikely to succeed, sold his old DeSoto car for $350 and used the

Hard rock Cafés offer exciting interiors featuring rock-and-roll memorabilia.
Courtesy Hard Rock Café

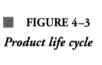

FIGURE 4–3
Product life cycle

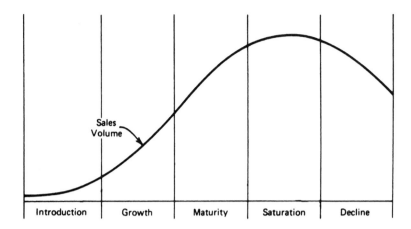

money as a down payment on a ten-stool lunch stand in Glendale, California. One day, a Los Angeles musician asked Wian for something different from a regular hamburger. Wian though for a moment, then took a standard hamburger bun and sliced it into three horizontal pieces instead of two. He then placed two cooked hamburger patties on the bun and wrapped the whole thing in paper to keep it warm.

Later, the double-pattied hamburger acquired a name when Wian wanted to call a boy who did odd jobs around the restaurant in exchange for hamburgers. Not remembering the boy's name, he called out, "Hey, big boy." On reflection, Wian thought, "What a name for my two-patty hamburger!"

A local artist was asked to draw a caricature[7] of a smiling, big-eyed, pudgy boy. It became the logo for the Big Boy chain, which grew to include hundreds of franchised restaurants. Wian had a flair for promotion and described his milkshake as "so thick you can eat it with a spoon." In 1967, Wian sold the chain to the Marriott Corporation and retired wealthy.[8]

■ **Product Life Cycle.** Restaurants, like all businesses, go through a product life cycle from introduction to decline. The trick is to extend the maturity and saturation stages.

■
Price

Price is the only revenue-generating variable in the marketing mix. Price is affected by the other mix variables—for instance, if a restaurant has a costly location, then the prices charged are likely to be higher—unless the volume is very high. Price is also an important consideration in the selection of a restaurant. Today, restaurant guests want value and will patronize those restaurants which they perceive give good value.

In restaurant marketing, several factors affect price:

■ The relationship of demand and supply

■ Shrinking guest loyalty

■ Sales mix

■ The competition's prices

- Overhead costs
- The psychological aspects of price setting
- The need for profit

The objective of a pricing policy is to find a balance between the customer's perception of value and a reasonable contribution to profit. Different strategies may be employed according to the objectives of the restaurant. For example, if an increase in market share is the objective, an extremely aggressive pricing policy would likely bring improved results, all other aspects being equal.

■ **Cost-Based Pricing.**   Many industry practitioners advocate a cost-based pricing strategy. This conventional-wisdom method calculates the cost of the ingredients and multiplies by a factor of say 3 to obtain a food cost percentage of 33. The price is rounded up or down a few cents based on the operator's pricing strategy. For example, if the cost of ingredients for a dish on the menu was $3.24, then the selling price would be $9.75 ($3.24 × 3 = $9.72, rounded up to $9.75).

■ **Competitive Pricing.**   A restaurant operator may use cost-based pricing to determine the menu price of an item and then check with the competition to see what they are charging for the same item. If there is a significant difference in favor of the competition then the operator must either choose another item or alter the ingredients of the existing item to bring its price in line.

■ **Contribution Pricing.**   Most operators do not price more expensive items using the cost-based method because it would make them appear too expensive. An expensive meat or fish item, for example, may cost $7.00 per plate, but there would not be many takers at $21.00; therefore, the price is adjusted down to an acceptable level. Remember that the contribution of the dish will be greater than one of the lower-priced menu items.

Contribution pricing is illustrated in Table 4–1.

Another important aspect of pricing is the amount of labor cost involved with the preparation and service of the menu items. Food and labor costs, when added together, are known as *prime costs*. Combined, they should, generally speaking, not go above 55 to 60% of sales.

- The relationship of demand and supply is crucial to the pricing equation. This basic factor controls all pricing policies. If demand is high and supply is limited, prices may be increased. Regrettably, as most restaurateurs know, the opposite is generally the case. In many markets, a saturation point has been achieved, with more and more restaurants opening. They mostly split up the available market just as a hostess divides up an apple pie when an unexpected

▨ **TABLE 4–1**
Contribution Pricing

	Food Cost	Selling Price	Food Cost Percentage	Contribution
Pasta (Fettucini)	$2.15	$ 6.25	32.80	$4.20
Fresh fish	$4.50	$12.75	35.29	$8.25

guest arrives for dinner. Each restaurant receives a smaller market share, assuming equal distribution.

It is important, therefore, to survey the market to determine demand and supply, and the prices in the marketplace being entered.

■ Shrinking guest loyalty has an effect on pricing. At one time, it was possible to increase guest loyalty, repeat business, and brand loyalty by dropping prices. Now, however, customers are more inclined to shop around for the best deal in order to make their dollar go further. One strategy that major chains in the airline and hotel business have adopted is to identify the heavy users and reward them for their loyalty with frequent-flyer programs and reduced accommodation rates. This concept, while good in theory, has, in a number of instances, run into serious difficulties and contributed to shrinking profits.

■ The price-value relationship is extremely important, especially in difficult economic times, when customers pay more attention to the value they receive for their dollar. If a customer is charged $6.95 for a soup, pasta, and salad bar with no service, he or she may think twice about returning if the restaurant across the street is offering a cooked entrée with a soup or salad starter with full table service for the same price.

■ This is why many pizza, Mexican, Chinese, and Italian restaurants are successful. Due largely to low food costs, they appear to offer greater value to customers.

■ Sales mix is an important aspect in setting pricing levels. Restaurants have a variety of items on the menu, some of which sell more than others. The trick is to have sufficient volume of popular items. While they may have a smaller contribution margin, they are able to offset the less frequent sellers, which may have a higher per-item contribution. Because they sell less frequently, they do not produce as great a contribution toward overhead and profit.

■ **Price and Quality.**   There is a direct correlation between price and quality. If high-quality ingredients are used, an appropriate price is charged. Ruth's Chris Steakhouse uses only USDA prime aged beef and charges more than Outback Steakhouse. Both restaurants are successful and balance price and quality.

Price is also discussed in the chapter on menus.

■

Promotion

Promotion is the activity by which restaurateurs seek to persuade customers not only to become first-time buyers but also repeat customers. Promotion, which includes communication, seeks to inform and persuade customers. A promotional campaign may have the following goals:

1. To increase consumer awareness of the restaurant
2. To improve consumer perceptions of the restaurant
3. To entice first-time buyers to try the restaurant
4. To gain a higher percentage of repeat customers
5. To create brand loyalty (regular customers)

6. To increase the average check

7. To increase sales at a particular meal or time of day

8. To introduce new menu items

Notice how this paradigm becomes a funnel. The large number of people at the top are the target market, customers that we need to first make aware of the restaurant. Other activities are undertaken until the customers become brand-loyal, regular customers.

Promotions are conducted to increase sales in several ways:

- To increase customer awareness of the restaurant or a particular menu item. Advertising often does this.

- To introduce new menu items, such as Jack in the Box's pita, or McDonald's Parfait or the McFlurry.

- To increase customer traffic, perhaps by advertising a menu special to act as a bring-them-in or a better deal than the competition.

- To increase existing customers' spending by building check average. This is often accomplished by personal selling and promotions.

- To increase demand during slow periods that are unproductive in that little or no contribution is made to overhead. Examples of efforts to boost sales during nonpeak periods are McDonald's McBreakfast and early-bird dinners for seniors that fill restaurant seats in the early evening, seats that would otherwise be empty.

Promotional programs take a variety of forms. In the early 1990s, some New York restaurateurs initiated a rollback of prices to the 1960s. Others downscaled their prices from an average check of $75 to $45 per person. When the economy turned sour, restaurateurs sought innovative ways to promote their restaurants. One restaurant substituted a three-course, $38 prix fixe menu for a $52 dinner.[8] The art of downscaling is to create exciting food from lower-costing ingredients.

Of the many promotional ideas for restaurants, some work and some do not. The degree of success varies and is often dependent on the relevance and value of the promotion as perceived by the target market. McDonald's does a great job not only of getting the attention of kids but also of enticing the kids to persuade their parents to take them to McDonald's. It's McMonday and here's the reason to go to Micky D's. . . . Joyce and Evan Goldstein of Square One, San Francisco, say that the relationship between a restaurateur and his or her customers is "like marriage or a relationship—the trick is keeping things fresh and interesting even after the passion period is over."[9]

A plan would be to ask the movers and shakers of the town to come up with a list of foods that they would like to see on the menu. The owners can then select their menu from the list.

Another idea would be to have a soft opening, meaning to open without a big announcement and spend a month working out the finer details. Then have a grand opening, with media in attendance, and enjoy rave reviews. Some restaurants have a camera handy to take photos of guests and then send them along with a thank-you-for-your-patronage note. The following examples are from the American Express booklets entitled *50 More Promotions That Work for Restaurants.*[10]

- In order to speed up lunch service, allow guests to fax and deliver orders. In some restaurants, this has boosted delivery and takeout by 20 to 25%.

- If your restaurant is in an area where you are likely to receive guests from other countries, have menus available in the relevant languages.

- Have reading glasses or menus with large print available for those who left their glasses at home.

- Create promotions around the many occasion days of the year. Example: Secretaries' Day.

- Create a dinner club to fill the slow nights. Focus around a theme and inform potential guests of the club night by mailings.

- Encourage guests to leave their business cards for a prize drawing. This creates a mailing list.

- One quiet night, say a Monday or Tuesday, announce to the restaurant and the media that one table's bill will be on the house, and that every Monday or Tuesday you plan to "comp" one table. The restaurant will likely fill up on those otherwise quiet nights.

- Give people something to tell their friends about or something to take home as a remembrance of their visit to your restaurant.

- Offer special birthday promotions.

- Send your menu and any relevant information to your catchment area. For example, if you have an Italian restaurant and decide to feature food from various regions of Italy, perhaps with a featured chef, mail an announcement to all the target market in the catchment area.

- Arrange a cook-off with a prize for the best pie (or whatever). Inform the local media and ask them to be the judges. That should ensure plenty of free coverage.

- Use coupons to build traffic and, once the goal is reached, phase them out. One of the difficulties is reaching the target market. The Penny Saver crowd may not be your market.

- Send postcard photos of your menu items to your guests.

- Invite guests to complete an application for dinner for two in another city. Purchase an open ticket and give a $500 spending allowance.

Many restaurants use coupons to promote their restaurants. Coupons may be a mixed blessing. They come in a variety of offerings and are generally distributed in the vicinity of the restaurant. The purpose of coupons is to build awareness and traffic in off-peak periods such as weeknights and early evenings, and to entice new customers into trying the restaurant. Some offer a price reduction, while others promote a two-for-one deal or other form of discounting.

Corporations like Taco Bell would not promote a discount value strategy with popular menu items already reduced to $0.49 or $0.59 if they did not feel this was sound common sense under the prevailing economic climate. Taco Bell's success in recent years is the envy of the restaurant industry.

Some promotions involve a tie-in to cartoon characters popular with children.

Off-hour dinner discounts are a means of capturing higher frequency from regular diners and more patronage from first-time customers. Entrée prices are chopped during nonpeak hours. This trades food costs for occupancy, which is good old-fashioned advertising, according to Mike Hurst, former president of the National Restaurant Association and a pioneer in early-bird discounting at the 15th Street Fisheries, his high-volume waterfront dinner house in Fort Lauderdale, Florida. The early-bird strategy has worked for Hurst, who discounts the entire menu. In fact, his restaurant does one and a half turns before 7:00 P.M., because, he says, early-bird patrons are so impressed with value that they insist on either sending or bringing their friends to dine. This appeals to retired individuals on fixed income!

Paul Dobson, a prominent San Diego restaurateur, has not only realized the benefit of early-bird pricing but also appeals to night owls. His restaurants build on the Latin custom of later dining, offered after mid-evening patrons have finished.

■ **Advertising.** The extent to which a restaurant needs to advertise depends on several variables. If the restaurant is part of a national chain, a percentage of sales is automatically taken for national advertising. A strictly enforced budget for local advertising is normally a percent of sales.

Most independent restaurants rely heavily on local customers, so advertisements are placed in city, town, and neighborhood newspapers. It is difficult to determine precisely the degree of success that advertisements have. Operators generally try an advertisement and check the response. The advertisements are coded to a particular telephone number or a person's name for tracking. Coupons are easy to track because people cut them out and bring them in themselves.

Many restaurateurs engage the professional help of an advertising agency. The agency can offer expertise in media services such as artwork, copy (wording), and media relations. The cost of these services can add up, so it is advisable to be well organized by having the key points of the message to be conveyed in order to achieve the maximum benefit from the advertising budget.

The advertising budget should be carefully planned and not limited to a percentage of sales, because if sales were to drop—as they do periodically—so would the amount spent on advertising—and this may be the time you need more advertising to help increase sales.

There are restaurants that refuse to spend money on advertising. Some would rather give every customer a $5.00 bill under every entrée plate, while others give coupons to encourage repeat visits.

Whatever method is chosen, care is required to ensure that the advertisement is appropriate to the target market and will induce the customer to come into the restaurant again and again.

Some restaurants deliberately take a low-key approach to marketing. Instead of expensive television, radio, and media advertising, they concentrate on producing the finest food, service, ambiance, and value. Reliance on word-of-mouth advertising has worked for Chart House, which attributes its success to a combination of location, food, and service. This is interesting because their locations often buck conventional wisdom. Many of the 64 Charthouse restaurants are in outstanding ocean locations in California, Hawaii, Florida, Puerto Rico, the U.S. Virgin Islands, and New England. Many restaurateurs would not touch a location where half the catchment area is in the ocean! Chart House locations are in "destination locations," most of which are close to major markets.

The first Chart House was opened in 1961 in Aspen, Colorado, with two cocktail tables and four dining tables. On the first night, four customers were served. In 1991, the opening in Scottsdale, Arizona, had sales of over $250,000 in the first month and a healthy operating profit. Patience has been a virtue for Chart House. This was underlined by the five-year wait to secure its prime Philadelphia location and seven years for the one in Indianapolis. The sites are not always successful, however. The restaurant in San Francisco struggled for several years because it was two blocks from the hub of the Embarcadero.

Another contributing factor to the success of the Chart House chain is that the restaurants are not faddish or "themeish." Tastefully and timelessly decorated, they feature a lot of wood and glass to harmonize with natural surroundings.

■ **In-House Advertising.** Some innovative restaurant operators embrace in-house advertising by other businesses by letting vacant space be used for advertising media. This either generates additional revenue or decreases costs such as menu printing, which may be as much as $20,000 per year. In-house advertising goes as far as bathroom stall doors and paper cups! Other restaurants have gone to a magazine-type menu advertising a variety of products and services, which patrons can read while they wait for their meal. The 14,000-unit Subway sandwich chain has bartered space on its large drink cups for promotional services. Subway cups were imprinted with Lilliputian-sized ads for the movie *Terminator 2*. More recently, Burger King was promoting Pokemon toys.

■ **Filling in the Periods of Low Demand.** Sales curves for restaurants vary by day of the week and time of the year. Sales for the typical restaurant start off the year at the lowest point in January and gradually increase until June or July, when sales reach their maximum. After that, sales decline through December. Weekly sales also follow a typical curve that is lowest on Monday and Tuesday and reaches a peak on Friday and Saturday. Sales usually drop off a little on Sunday, then the weekly cycle repeats. Each restaurant, moreover, has individual sales curves.

Marketing efforts are most needed during the low periods early in the week and the year. Fixed costs remain the same during the slow periods and efforts are needed to reach and exceed the break-even point during these times.

Tie-Ins and Two-for-Ones   Downtown restaurants often provide tie-ins with department stores, movies, and the theater. Dinner at the restaurant and tickets to the play or movie provide the buyer with a substantial discount.

Two-for-one promotions are an effective way of getting people into a restaurant for the first time, people who otherwise might not have been aware of the restaurant. Some restaurants give a 50% discount on the total food check for two persons. The usual two-for-one is made available by a newspaper advertisement or by sales of dining discount books. On certain days of the week during certain hours, two persons can dine for the price of one. The problem is that regular customers, who would come anyway, also take advantage of the promotion.

Loss-Leader Meals   While a restaurant is not likely to price a food item at cost, as is done sometimes at supermarkets, it may offer one or several items at a price that produces much less profit than normal. Some quick-service restaurants offer a free hamburger when one is bought. Discount coupons offer reduced prices for dinner houses, perhaps on selected days, usually on the slow first days of the week. The purposes are to gain market penetration, to attract new customers to the restaurant, and to get people into the restaurant so that they will buy more profitable items as well.

Some restaurants find such loss-leader advertising highly profitable because of the liquor sales generated. The operators reason that any such sales are likely to be above the break-even point and, even though the food cost may be high, fixed costs are already covered. Serving personnel are happy because they are busy and making more tips.

There are literally hundreds of innovative promotional ideas for bringing in new customers, building repeat business, building during slow periods, increasing average checks, and enhancing community relations.

■ **Advertising Appeals.**   The reasons for going to a restaurant vary all the way from plain necessity (the only restaurant around) to great adventure (a trip to a three-star restaurant in Provence). Several motivational forces may operate simultaneously: a respected friend has praised a restaurant, an anniversary is being celebrated, and time is limited.

Generally, there are six benefit appeals used in restaurant advertising: food quality, service, menu variety, price, atmosphere, and convenience.

Quality of food is the most important factor in choosing a restaurant. Each of the other factors is important and is featured with greater prominence according to the type of restaurant and target market for the advertisement.

■ **Travel Guides for Free Advertising.**   Listing in one or more of the three major travel guides can be worth thousands of dollars in extra sales at no cost to the restaurant operator. The National Restaurant Association states that travelers and visitors account for 50% of all table service restaurant sales with average checks of $25 or more (http://www.restaurant.org/research/pocket/index.htm). The Mobil Travel Guide lists 21,000 hotel/motels and restaurants located in more than 4,000 cities. Some 750,000 copies are sold each year. Solicitations from restaurant operators who wish to be rated are accepted.

Exxon's Travel Guide reaches 11 million Travel Club members and lists approximately 5,000 restaurants, again with no charge to the operator. The majority of restaurants that are reviewed are those that operate in vacation areas.

By far, the largest distribution of travel guides is that of the AAA Tour Book, which reaches more than 23 million AAA members. Those near major tourist attractions are preferred. Solicitations from restaurant operators are welcome.

■ **Yellow Pages Advertising.**   Probably the most widely used advertising medium in North America is found in the local telephone directory—the yellow pages, a medium that the restaurant operator is almost forced to use because it is available to everyone who has a telephone.

The operator opening a new restaurant must apply for a listing in the yellow pages several weeks in advance of publication—which could mean several months, because most directories are published yearly. The restaurant that opens without a published phone number and without a listing in the yellow pages is at a disadvantage. A small ad in the yellow pages can tell something of the character and menu of the restaurant— that the place serves vegetarian dishes, is "the most romantic dining spot," serves Cajun cuisine, has mesquite-broiled steaks, cooks fish using live oakwood, has fresh seafood, and so on.

■ **Developing a Mailing List.**   Restaurants that appeal to a fairly stable market—some coffee shops, some dinner houses and luxury restaurants—develop customer

Potential Benefits	Own Restaurant	Competition A	Competition B	Competition C	Competition D
Location					
Convenience					
Parking					
Food Quality					
Food Service					
Price					
Beverage Quality					
Beverage Service					
Rest Rooms					
Decor/ Ambiance					
Curbside Appeal/ Exterior					

FIGURE 4–4

Comparison benefit matrix

loyalty and increase sales by regular mailings. The mailings can be newsy and informational. Photos of customers, receptions held at the restaurant, descriptions of a new wine, or the announcement of specials can be sent to patrons on a mailing list. Restaurant party announcements, such as Halloween and New Year's parties, are examples of events that can be covered in a mailing.

Mailing lists can be purchased, but it is usually better to develop a list of people who are known or potential customers.

Charity affairs attended by the affluent are an occasion to collect addresses. Attendants can be asked to sign a register and give addresses. Persons calling for reservations can be asked their addresses. If the called asks the reason for the address request, the reservation taker can explain that regular customers are mailed information about special events and seasonal affairs offered by the restaurant.

Figure 4–4 shows a comparison benefit matrix that can be used to assess one restaurant's benefits or drawbacks in comparison to other restaurants.

OLIVE GARDEN MARKETING

How the big restaurant chains conduct their marketing is instructive for the independent restaurant restaurateur. The Olive Garden restaurants (owned by Darden) coordinate marketing through nine regional marketing managers who help the individual restaurants determine how best to promote their restaurants. Twenty-two public relations firms around the country also assist the restaurants. For some Olive Garden restaurants, print advertising is most effective. Others depend on TV.

The decisions are based on the market population size, the sum of the media costs, the number of Olive Garden restaurants in the market, and how well the individual restaurants are meeting their sales targets.

In bringing onstream a new Olive Garden, the company uses Darden specialists. These staff people identify business, shopping centers, and residential neighbors that can provide a sizable number of luncheon and dinner guests, including specific traits. Information is gathered that includes an area's major retail centers and office and commercial districts. Traffic patterns are studied; so, too, are the residential areas close to the proposed restaurant. Local planning officers are questioned about major highway projects under consideration. Competing restaurants are visited and information gathered about their decor, menus, pricing, and level of business activity.

The real estate department looks at vacant land, local building standards, and at the level of commercial development. There is always the option to purchase a defunct or operating restaurant, which cuts down the time required to open a new restaurant. Depending on the location, funding and acquiring a suitable site can take as few as six months or as long as five years. Some markets can support one or two Olive Gardens; others, such as Los Angeles, can support as many as 50. The Olive Garden is the most popular dinner house chain whose success hinges on the strong marriage of operations and marketing.

SUMMARY

Marketing is a major factor in the success of any restaurant. No restaurant can reach its potential without an understanding of the principles of marketing and a good business plan. Some streetwise owner managers do not possess formal marketing skills; however, their informal skills are often as savvy as those of any marketing expert. Marketing focuses on the needs and wants of guests, whereas sales focuses on the needs and wants of the restaurant operator. Once the potential market is identified, planning can take place.

The marketing and business plan is completed after an assessment of the marketplace, the competition, and the restaurant's strengths, weakness, threats, and opportunities. The marketing plan, if properly completed and executed, will greatly assist in ensuring that the restaurant's goals are met. The main components of the marketing plan are known as the four *P*s: product, place, promotion, and price.

KEY TERMS AND CONCEPTS

Marketing philosophy	Pricing
Marketing plan	Planning
Goals	Product
Levels of product	Marketing segment
Objectives	Atmospherics
Product development	Competition analysis
Product positioning	Product life cycle

Social analysis   Marketing mix
Place/Location   Product differentiation
Solving customers' problems   Marketing positioning

REVIEW QUESTIONS

1. Describe restaurant marketing.
2. What is the difference between marketing and sales?
3. Discuss marketing philosophy in the restaurant business.
4. Give examples of how marketing solves customer problems.
5. In your restaurant project, which will be your principal target market?
6. What is meant by *market positioning*?
7. In what way does market assessment aid the marketing process?
11. Some restaurant owners question the necessity of developing marketing plans. What is your response?
12. Develop an outline for your restaurant's marketing and business plan.
13. What are the differentiating characteristics of your restaurant?
    a. Product
    b. Atmospherics/Decor
    c. Service
    d. Place/Location
    e. Price
14. How will you advertise your restaurant? What percentage of total sales will be allocated to advertising?
15. Discuss which restaurant promotions are the most effective.
16. How will you determine your restaurant's pricing policy?
17. How will contribution pricing affect your restaurant's pricing policy?
18. Discuss how the four Ps of marketing are utilized in your restaurant.

ENDNOTES

1. *A Guide to Preparing a Restaurant Business Plan* (Washington, D.C.: The National Restaurant Association, 1992), 9.
2. Philip Kotter, John Bowey, and James Makens, *Marketing for Hospitality* (Upper Saddle River, N.J.: Prentice Hall, 1998), 257.
3. "New Schotzsky's TV Spots to Switch Focus to Food" *Nations Restaurants News* 34, no. 2 (10 January 2000): 14.
4. Tom Powers, *Marketing Hospitality* (New York: John Wiley and Sons, 1990), 157.
5. Monica Kass, "Downscaling in New York," *Restaurants and Institutions* 65, no. 28 (17 October 1990): 113.
6. Robert C. Lewis and Richard E. Chambers, *Marketing Leadership in Hospitality: Foundations and Practices* (New York: Van Nostrand Reinhold, 1990), 339–340.
7. Bob Semelgian, "The Rise and Fall of Bob's Big Boy," *Las Vegas Sun*, 6 January 1999. p 6.
8. Ibid.
9. Joseph J. West and Michael D. Olsen, "Grand Strategy: Making Your Restaurant a Winner," *Cornell Hotel Restaurant Administration Quarterly* (August 1990). Vol 31 No. 2.

[10] *American Express Establishment Services*, "50 More Promotions That Work for Restaurants," Leslie Ann Hogg, ed. (New York: Walter Mathews Associates, 1989), 18.

[11] Ibid., and American Express Establishment Services, *50 Promotions That Work*

[12] "50 More Promotions That Work for Restaurants." American Express Establishment Services, Leslie Ann Hogg, ed. (New York: Walter Matthews Associates, Inc., 1989).

[13] Ibid.

Chapter **5**

After reading and studying this chapter,
you should be able to:

Know what it takes to acquire a loan in order to start a restaurant.

Discuss the strengths and weaknesses of the various types of loans available to restaurant operators.

Explain the nuances of restaurant leases.

FINANCING AND LEASING

Ruth Fertel, founder of the Ruth's Chris Steakhouse chain, mortgaged her house in 1965 to raise the money to start her first restaurant. This was against the will and wisdom of her brother, lawyer, and banker. She was warned that she would not be able to handle the hard work and that she would lose her home because she didn't have any experience in the business.

Once the concept, location, and menu are chosen, the next step is financing the restaurant. Where does the money come from? Many restaurants have been started by borrowing money on property, including the family home. Others have been started by a loan from a relative, a friend, or a group of friends. An experienced restaurant operator may have a lawyer put together a partnership with the operator as managing partner and investors as limited partners. Still other restaurants are financed by groups of investors who form a corporation to buy or build and operate a place. Forming a corporation is simple and can be done quickly and at relatively low cost. The corporation becomes a legal entity that can take on debts and guarantee loans. To do so, however, a corporation must be creditworthy, just as an individual must. It must pay taxes, just as any individual with income must do, which can mean double taxation for the owner. The corporation pays a corporation tax and the individual owners receiving income from the corporation pay individual income tax as well.

SUFFICIENT CAPITAL

Many would-be restaurateurs try to start restaurants with only a few thousand dollars in capital. Such ventures usually fail. Although the number-one factor in restaurant failure is said to be lack of management, lack of finance and working capital may be a close second. No one knows the real rate of failure in the restaurant business because so many restaurants merely fade away, the owners taking severe losses and selling for what they can get. Dun and Bradstreet, the major firm that reports business failures, has no way of assessing the number of fade aways. Often, a restaurant opens, but the owners lack the working capital needed to keep it alive more than a few months.

In financing any business, astute businesspersons are concerned with risking somebody else's money rather than their own. Many individuals struggle and scheme for years to come up with a way of doing this. Some people have a knack for interesting other people in putting up their money for a venture that the promoter controls.

Few persons entering the restaurant business have the total capital necessary to enter as a complete owner, debt free. Such a course of action would mean owning the land, the restaurant building, and its equipment and furnishings, plus having working capital—that is, a standby amount of cash to open the restaurant and to get through possibly several unprofitable months of operation.

Experienced businesspersons seek to rent or lease the building and land and to search for a loan for the furnishings, equipment, and necessary start-up expenses. Ownership of the land on which the restaurant sits is usually left to a long-term investor. The same may be true for the restaurant building. Rather than using capital for the ownership of the real property, restaurant operators believe their expertise is their investment. They usually want to conserve capital or use it in the most productive way possible. Also, they want to face limited personal risk, should the business fail.

To accumulate enough assets to start a restaurant without borrowing is difficult. To borrow money wisely and to know how to get loans is a major part of a businessperson's acumen.

Where does one get the money for a restaurant? Commercial banks are common sources of funds, but the borrower must remember that the lending officers in the banks are only paid employees, not owners, and are also limiting their risks. They take minimal risks because their performance is largely judged by good loans. Lending officers tend to be ultraconservative.

Ordinarily, unless the individual has established a line of credit, the bank wants at least 20% (and usually more) of the total needs to be invested by the individual or corporation. This can be a considerable amount. The bank also wants collateral (assets that the bank can take should the loan not be repaid) to be pledged.

Loans are made for varying periods of time:

- A *term loan* is one repaid in installments, usually over a period longer than a year.

- *Intermediate loans* are made for up to five years.

- *Single-use real estate loans* typically run less than 20 years.

A construction loan is made in segments during the course of construction and is usually a term loan. The borrower should be clear as to when segments of a construction loan will be available—that is, before or after each phase of construction is completed. Borrowers often ask for a construction loan larger than the actual amount required, and, if granted, use the balance as working capital. (Never pay a contractor all of the money required up front.)

In buying or selling a restaurant, there is a simple rule to follow, say the experts: When you sell, get as much cash as possible. When buying, put as little cash down as possible.

COMPARE INTEREST RATES

When operators or would-be restaurateurs have a choice of lenders, they should, by all means, compare interest rates. A difference of 1% over a period of years is big money. Lenders often ask for "points," dollars added to the interest rate. If possible, these should be avoided.

Over the past years, interest rates have gone up and down like a yo-yo. Not so long ago, interest rates were in the 28% range. They then went down to 11%, then as low as 5.5%. If at all possible, delay borrowing during the very high range, even though it may mean delay in starting a restaurant or expanding it. For the past few years, the SBA loan interest rate has hovered around 8 to 10%, depending on the amount being borrowed and the collateral pledged.

Beware of bankers who demand interest discounted in advance or a compensating balance. Borrowers are often pleased to receive a loan no matter what the cost. They may overlook conditions placed on the loan. One such condition is when interest on a loan is discounted in advance. The borrower pays interest on a lower amount than was actually received.

Another condition that may be placed on a loan is the requirement of a compensating balance. The banker requires a certain amount to remain in the bank at all times. In effect, the borrower is not borrowing the full amount—rather, the amount minus the compensating balance.

REAL INTEREST RATES

The interest deductions allowable by the Internal Revenue Service (IRS) cut the real cost of a loan considerably. The net cost of the interest paid is lower, the higher the tax bracket.

Suppose a restaurant owner is in the 28% tax bracket and takes out a loan on his restaurant at 11% effective interest. The real cost of interest is less than 7.5% after tax deductions (on federal income tax return and considering the state income tax deductions). As federal income tax laws change, of course, the real cost of interest also changes.

Deduction of interest cost when paying federal income tax explains why the higher interest rates charged by banks do not seem quite so high to business borrowers. This also helps explain why companies are not dismayed at interest rates that seem overwhelming. Tax laws change frequently and the example above could become irrelevant at any time.

LOAN SOURCES

In seeking funds for financing a restaurant, an approach can be made to a number of possible sources:

- *The local bank.* Usually the banker wants at least one-third to one-half more collateral against the loan as a lien against the loan. In other words, if the individual wants to borrow $50,000, he must have collateral of perhaps $80,000 to $100,000. Banks are very reluctant lenders for restaurant ventures.

Bruce Barteldt, of Little and Associates Architects, suggests the following tips before signing a lease:

- *Don't guess about the size and shape of the building.* Do a feasibility study; all 2,500-foot retail spaces are not created equal. Depending on the shape of the space, you may be able to fit in 80 seats or only 50 seats. The difference could have a major impact on the restaurant's bottom line.

- *Don't let sunlight wash out your profit.* Harsh sunlight streaming in will annoy diners and wash out the effect of accent lighting and artwork. Window blinds or tinting will control the glare but, unless designed properly, create a less than welcoming atmosphere.

- *Negotiate for extra HVAC.* In most leases, the landlord will provide heating, ventilating, and air conditioning, or HVAC, or give a tenant an improvement allowance to cover HVAC costs. But as a result of new energy codes adopted around the country, restaurants are required to increase

the outside air coming in rate, which in turn increases the required HVAC capacity.

- *Know how the kitchen hood will exhaust.* Codes governing kitchens are strict and complicated. Before you sign a lease, inspect where the hood exhaust ducting will be located. That exhaust must run through the roof and be at least 10 feet from any door, window, or fresh air intake. In a multistory building, that may mean constructing a shaft through each tenant space above; that can be costly and should be negotiated into the lease.

- *Get the power supply plugged in.* Typical retail spaces are provided with 200 amps of electrical service, but even a small restaurant requires approximately 400 amps for running the appliances, coolers, and lights. Who pays if the retail space isn't equipped to handle such a heavy power load?

- *Preserve the roof warranty.* Restaurants require a large number of roof penetrations for hood, gas, and bathroom

exhausts, fresh air intakes, and HVAC ducting. The more times the roof is punctured, the more it is likely to leak. Always employ the roofer who installed the building's original roof to make the penetrations and holes. Often, the best option is to ask the landlord to coordinate the roofing work. Yielding it to the landlord and his or her roofing contractor will keep the roof's warranty intact and avoid you and your contractors' being blamed if a leak occurs.

- *Strive for perfect timing.* A retail store can be designed, given a permit, and become operational within 90 days, so most developers give retailers 60 to 90 days after the lease is signed before rent is due. But restaurants take longer to design, permit, and construct. Negotiate for a longer grace period before rent must be paid, or work into the budget the cash needed to pay the rent before the restaurant is opened.

Source: Bruce A. Barteldt, "Strategies for Negotiating the Best Restaurant Lease," *Nations Restaurant News* 31, no. 28 (21 July 1997).

Never sign a restaurant lease until you have had a thorough due diligence conducted. Due diligence is a legal term, borrowed from the securities industry, that means, essentially, to make sure that all the facts and figures are available and have been independently verified. In some respects, it is similar to an audit. All the documents of the firm are assembled and reviewed, the management is interviewed, by a team of financial experts, lawyers, and accountants. The health department, fire department, and Liquor Control Board are contacted to ensure that the restaurant is in compliance with all regulations,* the reason being that the one time licensing authorities can step in and require extensive alterations to bring a restaurant up to code is when there is a change of ownership. So make any lease contingent on gaining all necessary licenses.

*http://www.geocities.com/athens/forum/6297/hm048.html, 9 December 1999.

- *The local savings and loan association.* The local savings and loan association usually insists on similar security against any loans.

- *Friends, relatives, silent partners, syndicates.* Funds secured from these sources often have no security other than a lien against the property to be purchased or built. Individual arrangements vary considerably from non-interest loans to active participation and ownership in the project.

- *Limited partnerships.* A limited partnership, where the managing partner calls the shots, is a good way for some restaurants to start debt-free. The partners invest; the managing partner—often the one with the expertise but little or no money—makes the decisions and the other partners receive a percentage of any profits. The advantage of this method of financing is that the restaurateur may start up a restaurant using very little of his or her own money. The downside risk is that a piece of the business is given away in the form of profits. However, creative limited partnership agreements include clauses for buyouts, payback, and, possibly, a percentage of profit as rent for the first few months.

THE SMALL BUSINESS ADMINISTRATION

The Small Business Administration (SBA) is user friendly and has an excellent record of success in lending money to restaurants. In fact, there is a 65% success rate of the SBA loans to restaurants, compared to the often quoted failure rate of restaurants: 50% fail in two years and of that 50%, 50% are not profitable, meaning that only 25% of the restaurants that open are profitable after two years.

Over the years, the SBA guaranteed loan program has helped launch some of the nation's biggest entrepreneurial success stories—companies such as Apple computer, Federal Express, and Intel—that had no place to go for financing when they got started.[1]

In the past few years, thousands of restaurant owners have utilized the SBA loan guaranty program to start, acquire, or expand their business.

The SBA now guarantees loans up to 90%. The maximum guarantee on loans exceeding $155,000 is 85%. The SBA can generally guarantee up to $750,000 of a private-sector loan. It works like this: If you can borrow money from the banks, Uncle Sam consigns the loan.

There are three principal parties to an SBA-guaranteed loan: the SBA, the small business borrower, and the private lender. The lender plays the central role. The small business submits a loan application to the lender for initial review. If the lender finds

The SBA's Low Doc Program allows the participating bank not to have to submit all of the usually required financial data to the SBA for analysis and review. Rather, the borrower completes a one-page application form and the bank completes a one-page analysis. The SBA processes these loan applications quickly—usually in 48 to 72 hours. Most traditional SBA loans can be processed under this program as long as the amount is under $100,000. The approval process focuses on the lender, as well as certain income tax returns.

Source: Jenny Hedden, "The Bucks Start Here," *Restaurant USA* 16, no. 10 (November 1996): 13.

the application acceptable, it forwards the application and its credit analysis to the nearest SBA office. After SBA approval, the lender closes the loan and dispenses the funds. The borrower then makes loan payments to the lender.

Loans cannot be made at more than 2.75% over the prime lending rate, so if the prime rate is 6%, the total loan would be 8.75%. However, if banks are eager to lend money, they may drop that rate by up to 1%. There are no points involved and the borrower has only to pay out-of-pocket expenses. The bad news is that there is a 2% fee for the guarantee.

The best part about a SBA loan is that the government cosigns the loan by guaranteeing it. When applying for a SBA loan, the borrower must have 33 to 50% of the project cost and this must be debt-free; you cannot borrow $10,000 on your credit cards.

There are only three forms to complete in order to fulfill the SBA requirements: an application, a disclosure, and a personal disclosure.

The SBA cites poorly presented financial information as the number-one reason why loans are rejected. Loan applications to the bank and the SBA must contain accounts that are prepared in accordance with generally accepted accounting principals.

SBA loans require four basic steps:

1. The right type of business
2. A clear idea of which loan program is best for you
3. Knowing how to fill out the application properly
4. The willingness to provide the detailed financial and market data required[2]

Talking with an SBA loan officer. Being prepared for a meeting with a loan officer makes it easier to obtain a loan

Where to Find the SBA Pot of Gold

If you're eligible for an SBA-backed loan, the money may be in your own backyard, according to Mike Stampler, public relations officer in the SBA's office of Public Communications. All SBA loan paperwork is initiated at the local level, so Stampler recommends talking with your banker first to determine if an SBA guarantee would help you obtain the financing you need. If your banker doesn't handle SBA loans, call the SBA district office in your area to locate banks in your state that are approved SBA lending sources. To find the district office's telephone number, consult the Small Business Administration listings under United States Government in the Telephone book, or call (800) 8ASK-SBA or 827-5772. Internet users can access the SBA home page at http://www.sbaonline.sba.gov.

Source: Jenny Hedden, "The Bucks Start Here," *Restaurant USA* 16, no. 10 (November 1996): 13.

SBICs

Licensed by the SBA are the Small Business Investment Companies (SBICs). These are independently owned and managed companies set up to provide debt and equity capital to small businesses. They are permitted to leverage their private capital by using federal funds. A variation of the SBIC, Minorities Enterprise SBICs (MESBICs) specialize in loans to minority-owned firms. Amounts loaned range from $20,000 to $1 million or more. A free directory of SBICs can be obtained from the National Association of SBICs, 618 Washington Building, in Washington, DC 20005.

Soliciting an SBA Loan

The SBA was established for the purpose of getting small businesses like restaurants going. The federal government encourages small business, especially those owned by minority groups. Funded by the federal government, the SBA, headquartered in Washington, DC, has dozens of field officers spread over the country. The term *small business* is so defined that it includes almost every independently owned and operated or even contemplated restaurant. The SBA can help in a number of ways, but primarily through guaranteeing loans to start a business or to expand it and through providing expert consulting and counseling service via an auxiliary organization called the Service Corps of Retired Executives (SCORE). This organization is made up of successful retired businesspeople who work on a volunteer basis to help businesses with specific problems. In some areas, SCORE executives are among the most knowledgeable in the business and are available to consult with any restaurant operator, fledgling or veteran. As no one can know everything about the restaurant business, SCORE executives who are expert in disciplines such as accounting, layout, food purchasing, menu planning, and so on can be requested, and their services are provided at no charge.

The SBA is in business to make business loans, not outright grants, and the loan applicant must meet certain qualifications:

- Be of good character.
- Show ability to operate a business successfully.
- Have enough capital in an existing firm so that, with an SBA loan, the person can operate on a sound financial basis.

- Show that the proposed loan is of such sound value or so secured as reasonably to assure repayment.

- If the request is to cover an existing business, show that the past earnings record and future prospects of the firm indicate ability to repay the loan and other fixed debts, if any, out of profits.

- If a new business, be able to provide from the person's own resources sufficient funds to withstand possible losses, particularly during the early stages.

Like any other lender, the SBA, when guaranteeing a loan or making money available otherwise, wants collateral, which may take the form of mortgages on land, liens on equipment, guarantees, or personal endorsements.

The SBA also wants, in writing, a great deal of information concerning the proposed or present business. For a restaurant, the information desired by the SBA encompasses:

- A detailed description of the proposed restaurant

- A description of the experience and management capabilities of the applicant

- An estimate of the applicant's worth and how much he or she and others will invest in the business and how much will be borrowed

- A financial statement (balance sheet) listing the personal assets and liabilities of the owner(s)

- A detailed projection of earnings for the first year of the restaurant's operation

- Collateral offered as security for the loan, with an estimate of the present market value of each item listed

■

Sequence for Securing an SBA Loan

The SBA guaranteed loan-application process consists of four stages. First, the applicant requests a list of participating banks in the area from the SBA. Second, the SBA's six-to-eight page loan application (available at most commercial banks) is completed and submitted to a lender for review. The form may only take about an hour to complete *but* the supporting documents can take time to track down, and no one can ever predict what the SBA will request. A restaurant owner, for example, must provide a copy of the lease and liquor license. Third, on completion of the loan request, the lending bank sends the application to the local SBA for approval. Fourth, if the SBA approves the loan, the borrower is requested to visit the bank to sign the loan documents.

Keep in mind that the SBA also wants to see the following six items for all loans it guarantees.

- A current business balance sheet listing the company's assets, liabilities, and net worth

- Income statements for the current period and the three most recent fiscal years, if available

- A current personal financial statement of the proprietor or each partner or stockholder owning 20% or more of the corporate stock

- A list of collateral to be offered as security for the loan, along with an estimate of the present market value of each item, as well as the outstanding balance of any existing liens

- A statement noting the total amount of the financing you are trying to raise and the specific purpose of the loan
- Tax returns for the most recent three years, which may be your personal returns or your company's returns, depending on how long you've been in business[3]

The application first approaches the SBA for a list of participating banks, then selects five banks to ask for a loan under SBA's Loan Guarantee Plan. If a banker finds the application acceptable, he or she will contact the SBA. The SBA approves 50% of loans in three days and a further 35% in ten days.

The details for making a loan application can be extensive. The loan application can be a number of pages or it can be rather brief, depending on the relationship between the lender and the loan applicant and the amount of the loan requested. A detailed business plan, including a statement of resources, abilities, and experience of the applicant and a forecast for the business, tends to support the application.

STOCKPILING CREDIT

The borrower should not wait to request a loan until just before it is needed. Processing a loan may take time. Much of the required information can be put together in draft form, ready to be updated when a loan is needed. The kind of information that can be assembled and held ready for use includes:

1. A personal financial statement:
   a. Education and work history
   b. Credit references
   c. Copies of federal income tax statements for the previous three years
   d. Financial statement listing assets and liabilities and life insurance
2. If in business:
   a. Business history
   b. Current balance sheet
   c. Current profit and loss statement
   d. Cash flow statement for last year
   e. Copies of federal income tax returns for past three to five years
   f. Life and casualty insurance in force
   g. Lease
   h. Liquor license
   i. Health department permit

SELLING THE PROPOSAL

Borrowing money involves selling the lending officer on the belief that the borrower will be successful. To do this, the borrower must be able to convince the officer that a carefully thought-out business plan is ready and can be put into effect once the funds are available. The business plan not only presents what is proposed but also includes a financial and work history of the applicant—information necessary to support the view that the applicant will be successful in the restaurant. The business plan is evidence, to some extent, of the applicant's ability to think logically and project plans into the future.

The manner of presentation can be impressive and has an effect similar to a well-conceived resume. (Applicants sometimes turn to specialists who develop business plans for a fee.)

The Bank of America provides an outline (Figure 5–1) for a business plan that can be followed in drawing up a loan proposal package.

I. Summary
    A. Nature of business
    B. Amount and purpose of loan
    C. Repayment terms
    D. Equity share of borrower (equity/debt ratio after loan)
    E. Security or collateral (listed with market value estimates and quotes on cost of equipment to be purchased with the loan proceeds)
II. Personal information (on persons owning more than 20 percent of the business)
    A. Educational and work history
    B. Credit references
    C. Income tax statements (last three years)
    D. Financial statement (no older than 60 days)
III. Firm information (whichever is applicable—A, B, or C)
    A. New business
        1. Business plan
        2. Life and casualty insurance coverage
        3. Lease agreement
    B. Business acquisition (buyout)
        1. Information on acquisition
            a. Business history (include seller's name, reasons for sale)
            b. Current balance sheet (not older than 60 days)
            c. Current profit and loss statements (less than 60 days old)
            d. Business's federal income tax statements (past 3 to 5 years)
            e. Cash flow statements for last year
            f. Copy of sales agreement with breakdown of investors, fixtures, equipment, licenses, goodwill, and other costs
            g. Description and dates of permits already acquired
        2. Business plan
        3. Life and casualty insurance
    C. Existing business expansion
        1. Information on existing business
            a. Business history
            b. Current balance sheet (not more than 60 days old)
            c. Current profit and loss statements (not more than 60 days old)
            d. Cash flow statements for last year
            e. Federal income tax returns for past 3 to 5 years
            f. Lease agreement and permit data
        2. Business plan
        3. Life and casualty insurance
IV. Projections
    A. Profit and loss projections (monthly, for one year) and explanation
    B. Cash flow projection (monthly, for one year) and explanation
    C. Projected balance sheet (one year after loan) and explanation

---

■ FIGURE 5–1

Sample loan package outline. From "Financing Small Business," **Bank of America, Small Business Reporter,** *1976.*

The SBA places emphasis on the business plan required of the borrower as part of the loan application. The SBA suggests the plan be written in seven sections:

1. Cover letter, including the amount of the loan being requested, the terms, and the repayment period

2. Business summary with the restaurant's name, location, menu, target market, competition analysis, and business goals, and profiles of the management

3. Market analysis explaining the kind of restaurant and where it fits into the overall industry

4. Menu analysis, including a copy of the proposed menu, the signature (special) items that will be offered, and a comparison of the menu with those of the competition

5. Marketing strategy, including promotion and advertising plans for reaching the target markets

6. Management plan, including the organization chart, job descriptions, and resumes for the officers

7. Financial data, including a financial history of the borrower(s) and financial projections month by month for the first year, financial projections by quarter for the second year, and for the third year as a whole; projections of the key ratios such as food, labor, and beverage costs as a percentage of sales and how the projections compare with industry averages and those of competitors

Quite correctly, the SBA would like loan applicants to have had at least three years of experience working in a restaurant similar to the one being proposed.

The SBA also wants the loan applicant to personally invest at least 20% of the total cost of opening the restaurant.

OTHER SOURCES OF MONEY

Several other loan sources are often overlooked. These sources include:

- *Borrowing from the landlord.* Often, the landlord is as interested in the restaurant as the operator. He or she may help in financing the restaurant with start-up costs and allow the loan to be paid back in higher rent.

- *Borrowing from the landlord's bank.* The landlord may have more credit than the operator and may even be prevailed on to endorse a loan.

- *Borrowing from the local government.* Many municipalities have raised large sums of money by selling industrial revenue bonds. That money is usually available at rates lower than the going rate. A number of quick-service chains have tapped this source of money and saved large sums ordinarily paid in interest charges.

- *If the restaurant owns the land or restaurant building, selling it and leasing it back.* Several restaurant chains have been built on the sales-and-leaseback plan. Investors who buy the restaurant are promised a good yield on their money plus the depreciation on building and, sometimes, on the equipment as well.

- *Borrowing from the public.* Sell stock in the restaurant company to the public. Stock offerings of less than $1.5 million can be done simply with the help of good legal advisors.

- *Selling bonds or convertible bonds.* Bonds are debts, taken on by a company, that pay the bondholder a certain rate of interest and must be repaid in full by a fixed date. Convertible bonds are the same but can be converted into common stock of the issuer according to fixed terms.

- *Getting a bank loan guaranteed by the Farmer's Home Administration.* These loans are made to businesses in rural areas and cities with fewer than 50,000 people. The loan must be used to create jobs or add to the tax base of the community.

- *Borrowing from the Economic Development Administration (EDA).* The loans are made for businesses that can create jobs or add to the tax base of a community.

- *Borrowing from a city with the help of the Urban Development Action Grant (UDAG) program.* The UDAG was created to help 320 large cities and more than 2,000 small cities defined as "distressed." The borrower goes to such a city or town government with a proposal for an investment that will benefit the town or city. The government then applies for the grant.

COLLATERAL

What security does the borrower offer in return for the loan? Collateral, security for the lender, is the personal property or other possessions the borrower assigns to the lender as a pledge of debt repayment. If the debt is not repaid, the lender becomes the owner of the collateral.

The most important collateral is the character of the applicant. How does the lender determine character?

- By personal observation—knowing the borrower over a period of time

- By references provided by the borrower and records of previous borrowings and payments

- By credit reputation, established in previous credit transactions. Lenders, especially banks, refer to credit rating firms for credit reputation.

Unless the borrower has already established a line of credit with the lender (for example, a bank), the lender wants collateral (any asset acceptable to the lender). Customary forms of collateral accepted by banks are:

- *Real estate (homes, other buildings of value, land).* The lender determines the value of the property and the amount of insurance carried on it.

- *Stocks and bonds.* Banks use loan securities, discount stocks and bonds offered by as much as 50% to allow for decline in value.

- *Chattel mortgages.* Liens (legal claims) on specified physical assets, such as automobiles or machinery, are used.

- *Life insurance.* Insurance companies commonly loan money against paid-up insurance policies, usually at interest rates below bank rates. Banks will lend up to cash value of a life insurance policy provided the policy is assigned to the bank.

- *Assignment of lease.* Commonly, a bank lends money on a restaurant building and takes a mortgage. A lease is worked out between the operator and the franchiser such that the bank automatically receives rent payment. In this manner, the bank is guaranteed repayment.
- *Savings accounts.* Sometimes a loan can be made on a personal savings account. In this case, the account is signed over to the bank, which keeps the savings account passbook.
- *Endorsers, co-makers, and guarantors.* Closely related to other forms of collateral are loans guaranteed by others who must prove themselves capable of repaying the loan and who are liable for the debt if the borrower does not pay.

An endorser is contingently liable for the loan. If the borrower does not pay, the lender expects the endorser to do so. An endorser may be asked to pledge collateral in the same way as the borrower.

A co-maker joins the borrower on equal terms of obligation to the lender. The lender can collect directly from either the maker or the co-maker of the loan.

A guarantor signs the note and guarantees payment. Private and government lenders often require officers of corporations to sign as guarantors, which makes them personally liable for repayment.

KEEPING THE LOAN LINES OPEN

In seeking a plan, it is important to keep in mind that one loan may lead to another. The development of a line of credit is a valuable asset, one that is nurtured by businesspeople. Friendship with a lending officer can help, but more important is a series of loans that have been repaid as scheduled. In other words, try to borrow money under circumstances where you may go back for more when necessary.

AVOIDING PERSONAL LIABILITY

Large corporate chains usually have sufficient credit standing to command loans without the necessity of personal guarantees. The shrewd individual who guarantees a sizable loan sees to it that very few personal assets can be claimed in case of default. Ownership of automobiles, homes, land, and other personal assets is transferred to a spouse or other relative with the thought that, should the business fail, the creditor has little to claim. Giving one's assets to another, however, may be hazardous. For example, the spouse may end up with the assets after an estrangement or divorce.

LEASING

Restaurant buildings and equipment are more likely to be leased than purchased by the beginner because less capital is required for leasing than for building or buying. The beginner reduces the investment and, should the venture fail, reduces loss.

Caution When Taking Over an Existing Restaurant Location

Just as you think you've found the perfect location for your restaurant— think again! The transfer of restaurant ownership is the one time when licensing authorities may demand costly modifications to bring the restaurant up to code. Be sure to hire a lawyer skilled in restaurant leases and build in conditional clauses that say the lease is contingent on all necessary licenses and permits being obtained.

Keep in mind, however, that signing a lease obligates the signer to come up with the lease payments for the entire period of the lease. This means that if a building is leased for five years and the restaurant fails in the first year, the lessee has to find someone suitable to sublet or make the lease payments for the entire five-year period, or try to get the landlord to terminate the lease. If the lessee is truly in desperate financial straits, he or she can declare bankruptcy.

A restaurant lease should be good for both parties—the landlord (lessor) and the tenant (lessee). Established restaurant companies often sign 20-year leases. Beginners probably should try for a five-year lease with an option to renew for several additional five-year periods. If the beginning restaurateur is apprehensive about failing, a shorter lease period with options to renew, or even a month-to-month lease, might be desirable.

The option to renew can be a large financial factor if it permits a renewable at the same dollar amount as the original lease. If this is possible and inflation is high during the period of the original lease, the restaurateur can be a big gainer. Most leases, however, are in terms of a fixed dollar amount per month plus a percentage of gross sales. The percentage reflects the effects of inflation.

Beginning restaurateurs who are short of cash often lease restaurant equipment as well as the building. The building and equipment are sometimes available as a package lease. The beginner may also lease individual pieces of equipment. A coffeemaker may be leased from a coffee supplier. A dishwashing machine can be leased. Ice cream cabinets are frequently loaned, provided the ice cream is purchased from the lender.

■
Lease Costs

The cost of leasing a building or parts of one is counted in terms of cents or dollars per square foot per month. The restaurant operator forecasts the amount of sales to determine if the lease cost is fair. A choice location could be suitable for one restaurant concept, much too expensive for another.

Sales per square foot or per seat depend on the average customer check amount and the speed of seat turnover. California Pizza Kitchen, which has very high sales per square foot, has an average table turnover of 10 or 11 times on weekends. High seat turnover, an average check of about $10, and relatively small kitchens help account for the high per square foot sales. With high sales and relatively low labor cost, the California Pizza Kitchen can afford to lease in affluent malls and neighborhoods where rents are high.

The concept must fit the locations to be profitable. A full-service restaurant, for example, could not be successful in an airport location, where lease costs range as high as 20% of sales.

■
Drawing Up a Lease

Ask the following questions before agreeing on a lease:

1. Why is the building up for rent? Will an airport locate nearby? Is the highway being expanded? Is it a high crime area? Is there sufficient parking? Is the building in bad repair? Is it a bad location—for example, near a fertilizer plant? Are there rodents? fire hazards? Check with the fire department, police, and health department for information.

2. Who was the last tenant? Why did the tenant leave?

The following clauses are among those a lessee of a restaurant would want to consider for inclusion in the lease:

■ Names and addresses of the parties—landlord and tenant; period of time the lease is in effect

■ Amount of lease payment

■ How paid. Rent is payable on the last day of the month, unless there is a clause in the lease saying "Pay in advance."

■ Occupancy (how many people are allowed to occupy the space?); facilities available and time of availability

■ Parking (exact amount of space to be available)

■ Appliances and equipment included as a part of the lease

■ Specification of party responsible for repair or replacement of appliances

■ Security deposit to be returned at the end of the lease, provided tenant has not damaged property

■ An assignment or sublet clause—for example, "the tenant has the right to obtain a new tenant with the landlord's permission" (and this permission must not be unreasonably withheld) and the new tenant pays the rent directly to the landlord. The original tenant is released from further liability for the balance of the lease. In the sublet arrangement, "the new tenant pays the rent to the old tenant, who continues to pay the landlord. The old tenant remains liable to the landlord for the balance of the lease."

■ A clause stating "the landlord agrees not to withhold unreasonably his consent for the tenant to assign or sublet"

■ Common area maintenance costs (CAMs), yes or no. Landlords often try to pass on to tenants the tax, insurance, and maintenance expenses of operating the property, usually in proportion to the amount of occupied space. If you are paying CAMs, then the landlord has no incentive to control costs. If there are CAMs at the location you want, one suggestion is to insist on a cap—for example, 10% of minimum rents. Thus, if rent is $3.00 per square foot, CAMs would be 30 cents or less.[5]

■ A condemnation clause. A successful business housed in leased property may find that the leased property is condemned. A clause in the lease protects the tenant.

In the lease, include statements that you have:

■ The right to operate a restaurant

■ Permission to alter the building

■ Permission to erect a sign (a sign can be a risk that forces the landlord to pay higher insurance)

■ Permission to landscape and put up outside lighting

■ An exact amount of parking (describe it)

■ The right to paint the building the color you wish (interior and exterior)

- A wine and liquor license, health permit, business permit, fire department permit. Include a conditional clause stating "This lease will have no effect if any of the above permits are denied. The lease is conditional on obtaining the necessary licenses and permits."

- An option to renew the lease and the method of computing the rent at that time

- Include a clause that you can remove equipment that you have installed provided you put the building back in its original shape.

- Include an exclusive provision—a clause saying that the landlord will not rent to another restaurant within a certain radius

- Include a clause protecting the tenant in case of death or insanity, such as "wife or partner may terminate the lease"

- Include a clause stating that unpleasant odors that cannot be eradicated easily will terminate the lease.

- Insert the broadest use clause possible. You don't want to be restricted to selling subs if, after a while, you want to sell pizza or tacos as well. Also, a broadly defined use will be more attractive to prospective buyers.[6]

- Include a cotenancy clause. If you move to a shopping center and three months later the anchor tenant moves out—along with most of the foot traffic—you could lose a lot of money. Include a clause that says if there are major losses of occupancy in the center—to, say, 65% you have the option, after a certain period of time, to move out with 30 days notice. An alternative is to specify that rent will be reduced during times of low occupancy. Normally, landlords are permitted a reasonable period of time (say six months) to fill the vacancy before you can exercise your option.

■

Lease Terminology

In making a lease, both parties should consult a lawyer versed in real estate terminology to avoid misunderstandings. An example of lease language that has a specialized meaning is *triple net lease*. In short, the term refers to a lease in which the landlord, the lessor, passes on to the lessee the responsibility for building leasehold improvements, and paying for increases in taxes and insurance. This guarantees that the landlord incurs no expense beyond the investment made at the time the lease is signed. In other words, the restaurant operator who has a triple net lease assumes the burden of upkeep, taxes, and insurance on the building. Clearly agreeing on who is responsible for what avoids confusion and ill will.

■

Length of Lease

Operators have different opinions about the length and details of an ideal lease. Some specialists recommend obtaining a renewable lease for as long a period as possible—normally, a long lease is about 20 years (30, if you can get it). The option to renew for periods up to 20 years appeals to some. There is a security of knowing that the restaurant may be around for some time.

Others prefer a five-year term plus three five-year renewal options. The shorter the lease time lock-in, the better, they say. Be sure to lock in the renewal and a fair method of computing the rent at renewal time. The rationale for this option is that circumstances can and do change quickly in the restaurant business and you might not want to tie yourself into a business that you can't get out of.

Another possible option is a short-term lease with a clause that says that, at the end of five years of a ten-year lease, the operator can leave without penalty, providing one year's notice is given.[7]

A big point to remember in leasing anything: If the business does not survive, you, the lessee, are still liable for the payment if you have signed a personal guarantee and can be burdened with the debt for the rest of your life if it is not paid off.

■

Specifics of Most Restaurant Leases

The annual rent for lease space is calculated per square foot per month of space and is known as the base rate. Chez Ralph, a hypothetical restaurant, is a space of 5,000 square feet leased at $2.00 per square foot. The annual rent would be:

5,000 (square feet) $\times$ $2.00 per square foot = $10,000 per month

The annual rent would be:

$10,000 (monthly rent) $\times$ 12 = $120,000

On average, total rent cost should be about 7.3% of yearly gross sales. If the rent costs go as high as say 10% then other costs must be proportionately lower, in order to maintain suitable profit margins.

■ **Term of Lease.**   Most foodservice business leases are for five years, with two more five-year options for a total of 15 years. In addition to rent and percentage factors, it is not unusual to have an escalation clause in the lease detailing a "reasonable" rent hike after the first five-year term. The increase may be based on the Consumer Price Index (CPI) or the prevailing market rate (what similar spaces are being rented for at the time the lease is negotiated.) Make sure the basis for any rent hike is clearly spelled out in the lease agreement.

■ **Financial Responsibility.**   Early in the lease negotiations, you should cover the touchy topic of who will be responsible for paying off the lease in case, for any reason, the restaurant must close its doors. If an individual signs the lease, that person is responsible for covering these costs with his or her personal assets. If the lease is signed as a corporation, then the corporation is legally liable. As you can see, it makes sense to pay the state fees to incorporate before signing a lease.

Within your corporation, multiple partners must have specific agreements about their individual roles in running the business. You should probably also outline how a split would be handled if any partner decides to leave the company. Your attorney and accountant fees will be well worth the peace of mind to have these important contractual agreements written and reviewed.

■ **Maintenance Agreement.**   Another important part of a lease is the complete rundown of who is responsible for repairs to the building. Some leases give the tenant full responsibility for upkeep. Others give the landlord responsibility for structural and exterior repairs, such as roofing and foundation work, while tenants handle interior maintenance, such as pest control service or plumbing and electrical repairs. These items are easy to gloss over if you have your heart set on a particular site. Remember, however, all buildings need maintenance, and the cost can really add up. How much are you willing to do—and pay for?

■ **Insurance.**   Generally, the tenant is responsible for obtaining insurance against fire, flooding, and other natural disasters, as well as general liability insurance for accidents or injuries on the premises. The lease must specify how the policy should be paid—monthly or yearly are the most common stipulations—and also the amount of coverage required. Both tenant and landlord are listed as the insurance parties, so the landlord should be given copies of all insurance policies for his or her records.

■ **Real Estate Taxes.**   Each city and county decides on the value of land and buildings, and taxes an address based on its assessed value. These taxes are typically due once a year, in a lump sum, but most landlords ask that the taxes be prorated and paid monthly, along with rent and insurance. A triple net lease is the term for a lease that includes rent, taxes, and insurance in one monthly payment.

■ **Municipal Approval.**   Just because you sign a lease does not mean you will ever serve a meal at this site. Cover your bases by insisting, in writing, that this lease is void if city or county authorities do not approve the location to operate as a restaurant (or bar, or cafeteria, or whatever you're planning). Potential roadblocks: Do you intend to serve alcohol? Is your concept somewhat controversial—scantily clad wait staff, for instance? You will save yourself a lot of time and money if your lease allows these items in writing and if you also obtain permission from the county or city first. Politely inquire about all the necessary licenses and permits before you begin finish work on the site.

■

Fire Insurance

There is no need to point out the necessity of carrying fire insurance on a restaurant. However, we offer a few suggestions:

■ If leasing or renting the building, it must be very clear who carries the fire insurance—the operator or the landlord.

■ Is the restaurant insured by business interruption insurance—insurance that is paid over a definite period of time in case the restaurant is closed because of fire or other reasons? (Because of its expense, many—probably most—operators do not carry this insurance.)

■ Is insurance carried on inventory as well as on the building?

■ Is current insurance coverage sufficient to replace losses? Inflation and new equipment make it necessary to update insurance coverage periodically to reflect replacement costs.

- Is a sprinkler system in place and operative? Sprinkler systems reduce insurance costs. Insurance rates also reflect construction material, alarm systems, cooking hood protection, fire extinguisher protection, exit signs, and housekeeping practices.

WHAT IS A RESTAURANT WORTH?

What is a fair price to pay for a restaurant building? A restaurant has two potential values: its real estate value and its value as a profit generator. The two values should be considered separately. A restaurant building may actually detract from the real estate value, especially if the building has failed as a restaurant one or several times or is unattractive. The real estate value may be greater than the operational value.

A restaurant buyer is much concerned with the real estate value, a potential lessee less so. However, a person wanting to lease a restaurant nevertheless must consider the real estate value (or its potential value) because, if the value increases, the owner will increase the rent (unless the lease agreement is written to prevent such an increase).

What is the real estate value? The value is usually determined by competitive values in the community. The market value of real estate tends to follow the value set by similar properties in the area. Is the asking price above or below the market value for the area? Potential changes in property zoning by local or state zoning boards affect market value. Will highway or other changes be made in the near future that will affect the value of the property? Is the area going downhill or being revitalized? Is the area getting better or worse for a particular kind of restaurant? As an area changes, the kind of restaurant that will be supported also changes. A declining area may need a lower-check-average restaurant, fast-food place, or a coffee shop. As affluence grows, more dinner houses can be introduced.

A final note: just because a sweet financial deal has been put together, the success of the restaurant is not assured. Too often, a group of businesspersons are afflicted with the restaurant-ownership bug. They figure all of the angles, find a cheap source of money, contemplate the benefits of investment tax credits and depreciation, and can hardly wait to become restaurant owners. They fantasize about all of those wonderful meals they will provide their clients in their restaurant, all tax deductible. What they overlook is the need for concept development, menu development, location, and other planning. They may also lack a qualified general manager and chef. Financial planning is only one aspect of the success or failure of a restaurant.

SUMMARY

Each step in the process of the restaurant evolution, from concept to operation, is important. Finance and leasing are of equal importance to the overall success of the restaurant. The amount of capital required, how much to keep in reserve for the first few months of operation, where the capital is obtained, and how much it will cost to borrow the money are all critical issues. Soliciting a Small Business Administration loan is a lengthy and complex process. Other sources of loans are discussed.

Leases are also a complex commitment. Generally, leases are for a fixed-dollar amount per square foot per month plus a percentage of gross sales, depending on the negotiated terms of the lease. With triple net leases, the restaurant operator assumes the burden of upkeep, taxes, and insurance on the building.

KEY TERMS AND CONCEPTS

Capital

Interest rates

Loans

SBICs

SCORE

Collateral

Leasing

Money

Compensating balance

MESBICs

Stockpiling credit

Liability

Fire insurance

REVIEW QUESTIONS

1. List, in order of priority, four sources of financing you would approach in seeking funds for your restaurant.

2. In seeking a construction loan, would you expect to have the entire amount of the loan given to you in a lump sum? Explain.

3. Suppose you are in the 30% income tax bracket and you borrow money at 10%; what is the real interest that you pay?

4. The procedure in seeking a loan from the Small Business Administration is fairly elaborate. What is the usual sequence for this process?

5. The recommendation is made to "stockpile your credit." What does this mean?

6. Is it possible (not probable) to start a restaurant without any cash of your own? Explain.

7. What is the advantage to a company of selling bonds rather than stock?

8. Suppose you sign a ten-year lease on a building and open a restaurant in it. After a few months, you see that it is not going to be successful. What are your liabilities concerning the lease?

9. How do you know whether a building is worth what is being asked for it?

10. Define these terms:

    a. Prime rate

    b. Net worth

    c. Balloon payment

    d. Leverage buyout

    e. Collateral

ENDNOTES

[1] Joseph R. Mancuso, "The ABCs of Getting Money from the SBA," *Your Company* 6, no. 4 (June/July 1996).

[2] Ibid.

[3] Ibid.

[4] Some of the ideas on this section are based on "Capital Crisis: Where to Get the Money in Tough Times," *Institutions*, 15 April 1980, 23.

5 Michael J. Strausser, "The Language of Leases Part II: Why Give Landlords the Upper Hand? Do Your Homework Before Negotiating a Lease," *Restaurants USA* 13, 11 (December 1993): 45.

6 Ibid.

7 Ibid.

Chapter **6**

After reading and studying this chapter,
you should be able to:

Evaluate the various forms of business ownership and decide which is best for your restaurant.

Discuss the advantages and disadvantages of each form of business.

Realize the legal aspects of doing business.

LEGAL AND TAX MATTERS

Deciding on the concept, location, menu, and decor of a restaurant is a lot more fun than doing the paperwork.

A new restaurant operation has a choice of legal entities under which to operate. These are individual ownerships (sole proprietorship) or partnerships (with one or several co-owners, but with only a general partner or partners making decisions and legally responsible if things go wrong). There is also the corporation, a legal entity unto itself. An S corporation is a type of corporation that has advantages of both a corporation and of a sole proprietorship.

A lawyer and an accountant can aid in setting up a business to prevent future problems. Laws—state, federal, and local—must be considered. If you need a liquor license, get it before opening your restaurant. Health and fire department approval and permits must be obtained. Your lawyer or accountant can advise you concerning tax matters. What follows is general information; details and possible changes in laws should be checked with an experienced accountant and lawyer.

WHAT BUSINESS ENTITY IS BEST?

How should a restaurant be operated—directly by the owner, as a partnership with other owners, or as a corporation, a legal entity unto itself?

Under the law, all businesses are operated as proprietorships, partnerships, or corporations. Business ventures have a choice of these entities, each with different tax consequences, advantages, and disadvantages. At one point, one business entity provides more advantages; at another time, a different form may be better.

Always consider that one of four things will happen to the restaurant: It will be sold, it will be merged with another company, it will fail, or it will pass to heirs. Also consider that members of a family-operated restaurant will almost certainly disagree at times and that spouses may divorce. Almost inevitably, some one person must make final decisions, and some of these will be wrong. Divided responsibility and authority can be dangerous.

The choice of entity affects:

- Federal income taxes
- Liability to creditors and other persons
- The legal and/or personal relationships among the owners (if more than one exists)
- The legal life and/or transferral of the business entity

In addition to the choice of a form of business entity, certain other tax choices and elections are made prior to filing the new entity's first federal income tax return.

The Sole Proprietorship

The simplest business entity, for tax purposes, is the sole proprietorship. In the case of the sole proprietor, an attorney or accountant is not needed, though both should usually be consulted. In most states, the new proprietor is required to register the business name (if different from his or her own). From an income tax standpoint, only a Schedule C as part of Form 1040 need be filed as part of the federal income tax returns.

As sole proprietor, the restaurant operator does not draw a salary for federal income tax purposes. He or she reports as income the profit for the year or deducts as an expense any loss for the year. For tax purposes, the proprietor is not an employee; however, his or her income is subject to self-employment tax. The rate is slightly higher than the rate for social security taxes, with the same limitation on earnings subject to tax as is the case for an employee. This is paid along with the federal income tax. If both husband and wife work in a sole proprietorship, each pays the self-employment tax, up to the total income or the tax limitations, whichever is less.

An individual taxpayer normally reports on a calendar-year basis for federal income tax purposes. Consequently, each year, all of the earnings of the restaurant are taxed in addition to investment income and income earned by a spouse.

Ingrid Croce, who began as a sole proprietor, outside one of her restaurants. Croce was a pioneer in the development of the now popular Gaslamp Quarter

For example, assume Mr. X earns $65,000 in the year 2001 as a building contractor. Mrs. X opens a restaurant and operates it at a loss of $20,000 for the first calendar year. Mr. and Mrs. X would report only $45,000 of income for that year if Mrs. X is a sole proprietor. If Mrs. X lost $17,500 through September 30, 2001, and then began to earn a profit, she could incorporate as of October 1, 2001 (usually tax free), and allow the profits to be earned by the new corporation. If we assume Mrs. X draws no salary from her corporation until 2002, Mr. and Mrs. X would report $47,500 as income for the year 2002 (the profits from October through December would not be taxed to them).

■ **Advantages of the Sole Proprietorship.**   Advantages to being a sole proprietor, as opposed to doing business in corporate form, include the following:

- It is simple. You are required, for tax purposes, to keep a formal set of books. (This is highly recommended for financial purposes even when it is not required for tax purposes.) The tax laws and regulations require you to keep those records that will enable you to accurately report your income.

- Because all the earnings are yours, there is no problem about setting a reasonable salary that could be questioned when doing business in the corporate form.

- Funds can be withdrawn from the business, subject to their availability, without tax consequences.

- The business can be discontinued or sold with minimal tax consequences, compared with those arising in connection with the corporate form.

■ **Disadvantages of the Sole Proprietorship.**   Tax disadvantages in doing business as a sole proprietor include the following:

- Because you are not an employee, your company's group insurance cannot cover your insurance plan on a tax-deductible basis.

- You cannot be a participant in your company's qualified pension or profit-sharing plans. A sole proprietor can set up a Keogh retirement plan for self and employees; however, law limits the amount.

- The owner's liability for all of the restaurant's debts and any tort liability to third parties is unlimited. Theoretically, owners limit their liability by incorporating; however, in many cases—in fact, most—the owners are called upon to endorse or guarantee the corporation's liabilities.

- The sole proprietorship has no legal existence apart from the owner. The death or incapacity of the owner has severe legal implications and results in the termination of the business, unless it has been willed to another person or persons. Often, the willed property must pass through probate, which can be time consuming and costly in terms of legal fees.

■

The Partnership

A partnership is legally defined under the Uniform Partnership Act as any venture where two or more persons endeavor to make a profit. There are two kinds of partnerships: general and limited. General has complete liability but full management rights. Limited partnerships, on the other hand, share limited liability with no services performed.

David and Leslie Cohn at Tupelo American, one of their restaurants in San Diego's Gaslamp District. Courtesy of David Cohn

When two or more individuals plan to enter the restaurant business together, they may wish to employ the partnership form of doing business. The tax consequences of doing business as a partnership are basically the same as those for a sole proprietorship. The partnership, however, does file an annual tax return on Form 1065. This is an information return only, as the partnership pays no federal income tax. The partnership return requires a beginning and ending balance sheet, together with a reconciliation of each partner's capital account for the year. Consequently, formal bookkeeping must be done. Also, each partner receives a Schedule K-1 of the partnership tax return form and reports his or her respective income or loss from the Schedule K-1 on the individual tax return.

Partners do not draw deductible salaries from partnerships for tax purposes. Therefore, if a partner receives a salary from the partnership, no payroll taxes are deducted. At the end of the year, each partner reports his or her salary and share of the profits (or losses) on personal tax return Form 1040.

The partnership entity is quite flexible for tax purposes and lends itself to situations whereby one partner supplies the capital and another supplies only services or services plus a lesser amount of capital. It is possible to structure almost any type of business arrangement within a partnership as long as the tax consequences are consistent with the business realities.

The partnership, as an entity, has the same problems of legal liability as the sole proprietorship. In addition, each partner can create debts for the partnership. All partners must understand the dangers of this arrangement. Each partnership interest is an asset that can, under certain circumstances, be subject to the legal claims of an individual partner's creditors or other claimants.

Partnerships can be expected to dissolve someday. Death, disagreement, ill health, and other contingencies can make the perfect partnership into a perfect nightmare. Spouses setting up in the restaurant business as partners can see the business fall apart as they quarrel or divorce. In states with community property laws, each divorced spouse is entitled to half the assets, which may mean a forced sale of the restaurant. Partnerships usually work well when things go well. With losses, partners quickly see each other at fault.

Partnerships can be set up in a number of ways. Partners may have their liability for debts limited by the terms of the partnership. Limited partners have no voice in the restaurant operation; managing partners are given this responsibility. There may be dozens of limited partners, with only one or two managing partners.

The Restaurant as a Corporation

A corporation is a legal entity similar to a person in that it can borrow, buy, conduct business, and must pay state and federal taxes on profits. Working through a corporation offers advantages and disadvantages.

Deciding whether to incorporate can often depend on the amount of insurance coverage available. If insurance coverage is available, a restaurant may decide not to incorporate because the insurance will cover and limit the sole proprietor's liability, which might otherwise cause financial ruin in the event of a mishap or lawsuit. In situations where insurance protection is not available or affordable, incorporation and the limited liability it provides might be advisable.[1]

When incorporating, the first step should always be to consult an attorney. It may cost a bit more than doing it yourself, but in the long run should ensure that all necessary requirements have been met.

The second step should be to select a state in which to incorporate. This is an extremely important decision because regulations, incorporation costs, and other fees, taxes, and ownership rights vary widely among the 50 states.[2]

The big disadvantage of corporate ownership of a restaurant is that it opens the way for double taxation. Profits of the corporation are taxed and then passed on to the owners, where the profits are again subject to taxation as individual income. To avoid taxation, an S corporation (explained below) can be used.

In setting up a corporation, the entrepreneur must keep in mind that to maintain control, he or she must own 51% of the stock. Anything less could mean absolute lack of control and even expulsion from management.

Stock in a corporation can be sold to the general public or to individuals.

The entrepreneur can often find a landowner who is willing to subordinate ownership against a loan, the money from which can be used to erect a building.

The corporate form should not be used without legal and accounting advice. A corporation is a separate entity and is incorporated under the laws of the state in which it has its principal place of business. The rules for incorporation vary from state to state. The owners of a corporation are called shareholders or stockholders. They elect a board of directors, which has the final responsibility of operating the restaurant. Theoretically, the directors elect corporate officers. The directors can, under certain circumstances, have legal liability to third parties for their actions. The corporation has a legal existence apart from its owners, the shareholders. The latter are not responsible for the corporation's debts, provided they have fully paid for their investment in the company's capital stock and have not guaranteed its debts.

Before deciding to incorporate, the investors must make certain business and tax decisions that will have a vital effect on the future of the business. How much of the investment will be paid into the corporation? A portion may be paid in as capital stock and the balance may be loaned, to be repaid when the company has sufficient funds. From a tax standpoint, placing funds in the corporation as a loan is more advantageous than is stock. The repayment of a loan is tax free, whereas the repayment of stock is taxed as a dividend to the extent of the company's after-tax profits. Interest paid on a loan is tax deductible to the corporation, whereas dividends paid are treated as distribution of profits and are not deductible.

Enough must be paid in as stock to satisfy creditors. If the stock amount is too small in relationship to the amount of shareholder loans, the Internal Revenue Service (IRS) may claim that all of the money paid in is capital and that all repayments are taxable dividends to the extent of corporate after-tax profits. A "thin corporation" has the minimum allowable as capital, the maximum as debt. Because the corporation is a separate legal entity, the restaurant operator is an employee of the corporation. His or her salary is subject to all payroll taxes, just as that of any other employee is. The operator may also be covered for group insurance; the corporation may provide the person with up to $50,000 of group term coverage in addition to health insurance without its value being taxed. Other corporate fringe benefits can be arranged, such as medical expense reimbursement, sick pay, and pension and profit-sharing plans. What is a reasonable salary for shareholder employees? Shareholder employees naturally want to avoid double taxation, and the profits paid as salary to the management/stockholder must be "reasonable." If not, the "unreasonable" portion is treated as a dividend and is not deductible by the corporation.

■ **An S Corporation.**   An S corporation provides for a remarkable use of the corporation: It permits the business entity to operate as a corporation but allows it to avoid paying corporation taxes. It also avoids a double tax upon liquidation due to built-in gains from appreciation of assets.

If the corporation owners do not want to accumulate after-tax income in the corporation or if its shareholders are in low tax brackets or have personal tax losses, an S corporation is ideal. In addition to passing income to their shareholders, such corporations can pass through operating losses that can be reported pro rata by the owners and deducted up to the cost or adjusted basis of their stock and loans. This is an excellent arrangement for the first years of the company's existence, if it experiences losses. Once the company begins to operate at a profit, the S corporation election can be ended and the corporation taxed at regular corporate rates. The S corporation election is extremely useful in a family restaurant. If there are dependent children or parents, an S corporation offers a tax advantage. Gifts of the restaurant's stock can be made to these dependents who, when they receive the dividends, are taxed according to their income bracket. Corporation taxes are avoided and profits from the restaurant are taxed at the low rates experienced by the dependents.

The IRS requires that corporate officers draw a fair salary so that the company's earnings are not overstated; thereafter, the net income is allocated in proportion to the stock ownership.

One disadvantage of an S corporation is that shareholders of the corporation may not deduct benefits, such as medical disability and life insurance premiums of more than 2% of their annual salary.

■ **The Corporate Joint Venture.**   Still another variation of the corporation is possible. Suppose a qualified restaurateur and one or several investors wish to join forces in the restaurant business. The investors wish to avoid legal liability in case something goes wrong. The experienced restaurant person does not want to incorporate. A joint venture may satisfy both parties.

Together, a joint venture (partnership) agreement is reached, the joint venture to operate the restaurant. For tax purposes, salaries for management are paid as partnership withdrawals. Income from the restaurant is taxed as a partnership, not a corporation. Each party can elect to be taxed in the manner most advantageous to him or her. The management person can set up a corporation under an S corporation and spread his or her income to members of the family by gifts of stock. The investors can do the same.

Distributions of earnings of the joint venture partnership are tax free. In other words, there is no corporation tax on the joint venture. If the business is sold, corporate taxes are again avoided.

BUY-SELL AGREEMENT WITH PARTNERS

In closely held corporations and with partnerships, it is wise to arrange a buy-sell agreement with the co-stockholders or partners. Such agreements specify a price or a way of arriving at a price if a sale becomes necessary. This situation arises when owners die or, for some reason, want out. The buy-sell deal sets the tax value that the IRS will accept, even though the fair market value of the stock at the valuation date is actually higher. A buy-sell agreement can be funded by life insurance on the partners or stockholders. This means that the business carries the cost of the life insurance and collects the proceeds if the owner dies.

Setting an agreed-upon price or an agreed-upon way of pricing removes much of the potential for conflict among the owners when the time comes that one or more of the owners wants to sell or when an estate owning part of the restaurant must be settled.

▓ **TABLE 6–1**

Comparison of Corporate Forms

Corporate Structure	Ownership Rules	Tax Treatment	Liability	Pros and Cons
Sole proprietorship	One owner	Pass-through federal tax entity[a]	Unlimited personal liability for business debts	Is easy to set up but leaves your personal finances at risk. Plus, you miss out on all kinds of business deductions
S Corporation	Up to 75 shareholders; only one basic class stock; slight flexibility on voting rights	Pass-through federal tax entity[a]	Limited	Is easy to set up but limits your financing options later on
Corporation	Unlimited number of shareholders; no limits on stock classes or voting arrangements	Dividend income gets taxed at the corporate and shareholder levels; losses and deductions stay at the corporate level	Limited	Can be costly from a tax perspective but is investor friendly
Limited-Liability Company	Unlimited number of members; flexible membership arrangements, with voting rights and income divided as desired	Pass-through federal tax entity[a]	Limited	Has lots of advantages but makes investors leery, which could make financing the deal dicey; cost of switching forms from S or C corporation status is generally prohibitive
Partnership	Two or more owners	Pass-through federal tax entity[a]; flexibility about profit-and-loss allocations among partners	Personal assets of any operating partner at at risk from business creditors[b]	Allows lots of room to play with tax benefits, but in a general partnership, that personal liability can be scary
Limited-Liability partnership	Two or more owners	Pass-through federal tax entity[a]; some flexibility about ownership arrangements	Limited	As an alternative to traditional partnerships has many advantages; is easy enough to switch to but is a new form and hasn't gained acceptance in all states

[a]In a pass-through tax entity, income and losses "pass through" to owners and are taxed by the IRS at the personal level.
[b]In limited-partnership variation, limited partners' liability can be restricted to amount of original investment.

TWO CORPORATIONS RECOMMENDED

To maximize depreciation deductions, some tax experts recommend putting all real estate and equipment into an asset corporation. This is a company that owns the building, the land, and the operating equipment.

A separate corporation is set up as an operating company, which has as few assets in it as possible. Machinery and equipment can be depreciated and so can the building. In buying a business, buy the building and allocate as much as possible to any item that can be legally depreciated: carpets, trees, fences, roses, garbage cans, dust pans, brooms, vacuum cleaners, dish machines, stoves. The idea is to build as big a tax base—a depreciable tax base—as possible. Then, say the experts, depreciate it all as fast as possible. Those depreciation dollars are essentially tax-free dollars.

The operating company is quite distinct from the asset company and can carry a great load of expenses that, again, are tax free—a company automobile, a medical/dental plan for the officers, travel expenses, life insurance, entertainment expenses. Costs often borne by individuals become tax free.

BUSINESS AND LIFE INSURANCE

Restaurant owner/operators are obligated to take out comprehensive general liability insurance, workers compensation insurance, property insurance, and, if necessary, automobile insurance. Principals in closely held businesses need to insure against the death of other principals. In the case of a death, the remaining owners may end up owning the restaurant with the surviving spouse. Chances of this happening are higher than might be expected.

One way to prepare for such a calamity is to arrange a buy-sell agreement with the surviving spouse, an agreement that can be funded by life insurance carried by the business itself.

BUSINESS SEARCH EXPENSE

Anyone starting a restaurant should ordinarily spend adequate time thinking about the details of operation and evaluating potential buyouts and locations. Suppose the deal or deals fall through; are the search costs deductible as a business expense?

Yes, say the tax experts, if the searcher incorporates the business before beginning the search and buys stock equal to the amount of the expected search expense. This way, the costs can be charged to the corporation. If a restaurant never materializes, the corporation can be liquidated and a personal deduction taken for the amount of the loss. If the corporation is set up as an S corporation, the loss involved in the search is passed directly to the corporation owner, the searcher. If all of this sounds complicated, it only serves to emphasize the need to have the advice of a good accountant.

LEGAL ASPECTS OF DOING BUSINESS

Many legal requirements must be addressed when setting up a restaurant business. In California, for example, these are the required steps:

    I. Form a business entity.
      A. Sole proprietorship
      B. General partnership
      C. Limited partnership
      D. Subchapter S Corporation
      E. Corporation

II. Identify necessary permits and licenses.
    A. Local requirements
        1. Business licenses: county clerk's office
        2. Tax registration (county or city)
        3. Police, health, and fire department permits
    B. State requirements: check with your state. (For example, in California, the Department of Economic and Business Development has a book entitled "California License Handbook," 1120 N Street, Sacramento, CA 95814.)
        1. Liquor license
    C. Federal requirements
III. Identify local restrictions on proposed business licenses.
    A. Zoning requirements (City Planning Commission)
    B. Building inspections
IV. Obtain environmental or similar permit (new for coastal areas, shorelines, floodways, and wildlife habitats) as needed.
 V. Obtain state sales tax permit. Obtain from Board of Equalization Publication BT-741-1 (*Your Privileges and Obligations as a Seller*) and related Regulations, including 1698–1700.
VI. Determine applicability of employer registrations.
    A. Obtain federal employer identification number (Complete Form SS-4 at Social Security or IRS office.)
    B. Register with the State Employment Development Department (relates to unemployment insurance).
VII. Insurance
    A. Obtain mandatory workers compensation insurance.
    B. Join employers reciprocal exchange plans. Buy policy of insurance from broker or state comprehensive insurance fund.
    C. If self-insured, you need consent. Write to Director of Industrial Relations, Self-Insurance Plans, Room 5043 107 S. Broadway, Los Angeles, CA 90012.
    D. Dram shop insurance
    E. Real property insurance
    F. Auto insurance
VIII. Comply with relevant statutes and regulations with respect to employees' wages.
    A. Comply with State Industrial Welfare Commission orders with respect to employee wages, hours, and working conditions (post required posters).
 IX. Fulfill occupational and health requirements.
    A. Federal OSHA replaced some state regulations with comprehensive bottom line regulations.
  X. Assess applicability of other antidiscrimination laws.
    A. Title VII if 15 or more employees, comply (no discrimination in employment)
    B. Executive Order 11246: If you will have government contracts, then they must comply; affirmative action program required.
    C. Federal Equal Pay Act
    D. Federal Age Discrimination Act
    E. State Fair Employment Practices Act

XI. Check for eligibility for government assistance.
  A. Small Business Administration—special loans
  B. Minority Business Development Agency—assistance with obtaining loans
  C. Others: Purchase *A Survey of Small Business Programs* from U.S. Government Printing Office.
  D. State programs: Purchase *A Guide to Starting a Business* in a local bookstore.
XII. File fictitious business name.
  A. File with county clerk in your county within 40 days of purchase of business.
  B. Publish in paper on county.
  C. Sign Affidavit of Publishing.
XIII. Assure meeting posting requirements.
  A. Sales tax permit—conspicuous place
  B. Employment Development Department—reunemployment (from EDD office)
  C. Payday and right to vote.
  D. State OSHA notice—from Department of Industrial Affairs
  E. Wage and Hour poster—from Department of Industrial Relations, Division of Labor Standard Enforcement
  F. State Fair Employment Law poster—from Department of Fair Employment and Housing
  G. U.S. Equal Opportunity Commission and Age Disclosure Law posters from Public Information Assistance, Equal Employment Opportunity Commission (EEOC) [your state]
XIV. Obtain and arrange tax return filings.
  A. Sales and use taxes
    1. Collect or obtain exemption or resale certificate with each sale.
    2. File quarterly returns.
    3. Keep required records—see Regulation 1698.
  B. Federal and state employment taxes (Read Circular E.)
    1. Federal income tax, FICA, and FUTA (Federal Unemployment Tax Act) withhold, file records.
    2. Federal self-employment tax, if appropriate
    3. State employment tax and contribution includes income tax, SDI, and unemployment insurance tax.
  C. Corporate income tax
  D. Local property taxes
  E. Excuse, license, or privilege taxes probably not applicable
XV. Learn reporting and notice procedure in event of employee injury or exposure to toxic substances. (Read "Record-keeping and Reporting Requirements under [your state] OSHA from Department of Industrial Relations, Division of Labor Statistics and Research.)

It is essential to obtain these licenses and permits before opening a restaurant. Without them, costly delays in opening will occur. Protect yourself by making your lease contingent on these licenses and permits being granted. This is particularly important when taking over an existing restaurant because although the previous owner may have had the necessary licenses and permits, the authorities seize the opportunity of change of ownership to enforce codes. This can be costly. We suggest you consult with the requisite authorities in your area.

DEPRECIATION AND CASH FLOW

As a business generates income and pays its immediate expenses, including taxes, the money left over is not all profit. In a restaurant, the building, kitchen, and dining room equipment and furnishings depreciate year after year until finally they have no value or only a salvage value. Theoretically, at least, money is set aside for replacing these items— a depreciation allowance. Actually, this money is seldom set aside and very often the building, instead of depreciating in value, appreciates. Even so, for tax purposes, the depreciation allowance is a deductible item and can be used by the owner/operator. The money taken in before considering the depreciation allowance is called cash flow. The restaurateur is much concerned with keeping cash flow adequate to meet current obligations.

The owner of a restaurant gets a depreciation allowance. The owner of the equipment gets a depreciation allowance. The owner of the land on which the restaurant sits gets none; land is a nondepreciable item, whereas other tangible assets that have a life-span are depreciable. The matter of depreciation can be quite important in the success of a restaurant and is especially important to whoever owns the building. Restaurants are often owned by a corporation, which in turns owns a corporation that owns the land, and still another that owns the building and equipment. The idea is to maximize depreciation so as to pay the least amount of taxes possible, especially during the first several years of operation. For more authoritative reference for restaurants, refer to the latest edition of *The Uniform System of Accounts for Restaurants*, published by the National Restaurant Association.[3] In addition, the IRS has several bulletins on the subject.

Accelerated or Straight-Line Depreciation

Depreciation for tax purposes may bear little relationship to the actual decrease in the value of items being depreciated. A restaurant building, for example, may, for tax reasons, be completely depreciated over 31 years, yet the building may have appreciated during the period and may be sold at much more than construction cost. Market value and book value after depreciation usually are quite different.

Restaurant equipment, furnishings, and the building itself can be depreciated for tax purposes over their expected life. Everything that can be depreciated should be depreciated.

Most new restaurant operators want and need the cash that can be retained by choosing the accelerated method of depreciation. Accelerated depreciation methods allow greater depreciation during the early life of a building or equipment, less depreciation later. A start-up business usually needs all the depreciation dollars it can get. Rapid depreciation results in lower taxes during the early years of the restaurant, with greater after-tax income. Federal income tax guides provide instruction in depreciation methods, but tax advice by an expert is usually needed to make the best use of the depreciation provisions. In simple terms, the straight-line depreciation method assumes a fixed life for an item—seven years for an oven, three years for carpet, and so on. The cost of the item is then divided by the expected life to arrive at the depreciation allowance. If an oven cost $2,100 and is expected to last seven years, $300 depreciation can be deducted each year for seven years.

BUYING A LOSER

There may be advantages in buying a losing restaurant other than that it can be had at a fraction of its value. If the restaurant is in the form of a corporation, the corporation may have tax losses that can be bought and used against profits made in other restaurants or profits in the future. Tax losses are a valuable commodity and can be bought and sold like tangible property.

TWO CHOICES OF ACCOUNTING METHODS

Business can be operated under either the cash accounting method or the accrual method. The cash method is the easier to understand: Income is reported when collected and expenses reported when paid. Using the accrual method, computation of net income embraces amounts earned but not yet received. Liabilities are counted even though not yet paid. Unless accounts of accrued income or liabilities are carefully kept, the IRS insists on the cash accounting method. For most people, this method is easier to comprehend and follow.

A TAX AVOIDANCE PLAN

A corporation owned by you and maybe one or two others leases a piece of land to you, the principal owner. You, in turn, erect a restaurant on the leased land, then lease the building back to the corporation (of which you are the principal owner). This makes you, in effect, both a lessee and a lessor. You, the individual, have leased the land from the corporation. You, the individual, have erected the building and leased it back to the corporation. And you, the individual, own the restaurant and are able to take advantage of the depreciation on the building and to draw money from the corporation in the form of lease payments.

Sounds good, doesn't it? Just be sure you have an experienced accountant to advise you.

Until October 1999, the IRS held restaurant operators responsible for trying to get their employees to accurately report their tip income, a practice the industry urgently opposed, saying they did not want to act as police for the IRS. The IRS used its power to audit restaurant operators. The shift in IRS policy was welcomed by the industry.

Source: Associated Press, 29 October 1999.

RETIREMENT TAX SHELTERS[4]

Two popular federal government retirement plans are available. The individual retirement annuity (IRA) and the Keogh plans became legal in 1962. The Keogh plan makes it possible for a self-employed person or someone who has income from self-employment (in addition to whatever else is earned) to put up to $30,000 per year or 25% of the annual income from the self-employment into a tax-sheltered retirement plan. The earnings from money generated in a retirement plan are deferred from taxes.

Keogh and IRA plans can save a considerable amount of money for the individual. The total amount generated can be surprisingly large because the interest generated is also tax deferred and accumulates tax free while the plans are in effect. The participant eventually pays taxes, but at a lower rate because of usually being in a lower tax bracket upon retirement and because gains accumulated are taxed at capital gains rates rather than at straight-income rates. Many investment counselors believe these plans to be the safest and probably the best savings plans available.

For either plan, the money can be managed through a custodian as directed by the person having the account. The custodian of the account, usually a bank, charges fees.

Spouses can establish separate IRA plans if each works and has earned income. A restaurant owner can have either a Keogh plan, in which case employees must also be covered, or an IRA plan (no employees need be covered).

■

Tax-Free Compounding

A big advantage in government-approved pension plans is that the yearly contributions to the plan are deductible—that is, not taxable to the participants. Moreover, interest, dividends, and gains from investments made from the contributions (while the plan is being funded) are compounded tax free. The difference to the participant can be astounding.

■ **The Rule of 72.**   It is surprising how fast an investment like a Keogh plan doubles itself if no taxes are paid. A simple method of calculating this doubling is to follow the "rule of 72." Divided the rate of return into 72 and you get the number of years required to double your money at that rate of interest.

Suppose you invest $10,000 in a deferred annuity and receive 10% interest on it. In how many years will you have $20,000? The answer is 7.2 years (72/10). Here are other examples:

$$8\%(72/8) = 9 \text{ years}$$
$$9\%(72/9) = 8 \text{ years}$$
$$10\%(72/10 = 7.2 \text{ years}$$
$$11\%(72/11) = 6.5 \text{ years}$$
$$12\%(72/12) = 6 \text{ years}$$

A REASONABLE RETURN ON INVESTMENT

Businesspeople are concerned with their return on investment (ROI). If $100,000 is invested in a restaurant, what profit can reasonably be expected?

The answer depends partly on the yield that can be expected from similar investments with a similar amount of risk. If money market funds yield 6 to 10% with little or no risk, a restaurant investment should yield at least 15 to 20%. If municipal bonds yield 6 to 10% with almost no risk and are tax free, a restaurant investment should yield considerably more. Whatever the yield, it should be more than enough to cover the rate of inflation.

BUSINESS EXPENSES AND TAXES

Anything that is a cost of doing business is tax deductible (if the IRS agrees). Many things taken as deductions are in the gray area and some are highly debatable. For example, a restaurant operator attends the National Restaurant Show held in Chicago. All expenses are tax deductible. How about the expenses of the spouse? It depends. Is he or she active in the business? If the spouse were treasurer of the restaurant, there would be little question that his or her attendance at the show could be a benefit to the business.

What if the operator wishes to attend a similar show held in London? The cost would be deductible. (But no more than two such trips per year outside the United States or its possessions are deductible. Puerto Rico, the Virgin Islands, and the Pacific Trust Territories are not considered foreign for this purpose.) The deductions for such trips are limited in amount and require attendance at meetings and substantiation of expenses. (The requirements for a tax deduction change frequently and should be investigated.)

A company-owned car is deductible. Life insurance on key executives is also deductible, as is medical and dental insurance for the executive and his or her family.

The list of fringe benefits that are legitimate for tax purposes is extensive and imaginative. Here are a few being given to corporate officers:

- Club membership in country club, athletic club, tennis club, and so on
- Comprehensive medical plan, including annual medical checkup
- Vacation allowance in excess of company policy
- Supplemental retirement benefits over and above regular pension, profit sharing, and so on
- Low-cost loans
- Additional life insurance
- Financial planning by professionals on tax planning, investments, preparation of personal income taxes.

Remember, depending on the tax bracket, every dollar of benefits can be worth $1.50 or more of straight income.

Tax Credit for Van or Bus

Many restaurants find that providing free transportation, pickup, and delivery of employees from their homes to a central point works to the advantage of the employer as well as the employee. In some locations, such an arrangement becomes a necessity because of a lack of public transportation and of employees with automobiles. The big advantage to the employer is the investment credit allowed to a business owner for providing van pooling for employees. If the vehicle has a useful life of at least three years, the investment credit may be 100% of the investment in the vehicle if the arrangement meets certain specifications of the IRS. The vehicle must have a seating capacity of at least eight adults, not including the driver. At least 80% of the vehicle's mileage must be for van pooling, and the number of employees transported must be at least half of the adult seating capacity of the vehicle, not including the driver. Employees need not be picked up and delivered to their homes, but may be picked up from a central point or points.

From the employee viewpoint, the value of the transportation is not considered income and is not subject to FICA, FUTA (Federal Unemployment Tax Act), and income tax withholding.

Tax Breaks for Children in Family Restaurants

Children of restaurant owners get special consideration with regard to the necessity of withholding social security and federal employment taxes. Family restaurants operated as sole proprietorships or partnerships of spouses may employ members of the family up to age 18 and not report social security and federal unemployment taxes.

At age 18, the social security and federal unemployment exemptions vanish. Children can be claimed as dependents as long as the persons claiming them as dependents provide 50% of the total support.

REMINDERS

Taxes, we can be sure, will be with us always. Because laws and their interpretations change each year, the restaurant owner necessarily relies on the accountant or legal advisor to suggest the most advantageous way of conducting business and of avoiding taxes. As everyone should know, out-and-out falsification of tax returns or failure to report income is tax evasion. Avoiding taxes by legal means is something else. The difference between tax evasion and tax avoidance is often good tax advice.

Believe it or not, the IRS has a number of helpful publications. One, publication 583, entitled "Starting a Business and Keeping Records," offers helpful information, as does the IRS Web site at www.irs.ustreas.gov.

After deciding which form of business entity your restaurant will be, you need to obtain a taxpayer identification number so that the IRS can process your returns.

All business are controlled, some say, beset, by a multiplicity of laws and regulations. The best way to keep up to date is to become a member of the National Restaurant Association (NRA) and your state restaurant association. One of the association's responsibilities is to keep members informed of local, state, and federal requirements.

New restaurant operators must obtain a permit to operate and a building permit, if they are building or remodeling an existing structure. Applications for a building permit should be accompanied by blueprints and cost estimates from a designer or contractor.

A city or county health department issues health department permits, required for all owners. Usually these permits must be posted where they can be readily seen.

Many locales require a fire clearance. The local fire department officials issue a permit after an inspection. All restaurants must have fire exits, and owners should develop emergency evacuation plans. Officials are concerned about the hazards in range flues and grease hoods, the origins of many restaurant fires.

Some states require a seller's permit. States imposing a sales tax are concerned about having the restaurant operator collect and forward that tax. Operators should *never* dip into or borrow from the sales tax or other taxes for other uses. Infractions, when caught, are prosecuted vigorously.

Even assuming that the restaurant owner did not know he was violating the law, ignorance of the law is no excuse. Avoiding serious violations adds one more facet to being in business—keeping abreast of law and regulations.

Relations with the government begin some time before a restaurant is opened. Local zoning laws must be observed and any construction undertaken must be approved before construction begins. Most communities require that all businesses have a business permit obtained at a town, county, or city hall (depending upon jurisdiction). States, too, may require registration.

LOCAL, STATE, AND FEDERAL TAXES

One of the most onerous of the operator's tasks is keeping records and submitting tax reports. The operator not only pays taxes as required on restaurant sales but also is responsible for collecting and paying taxes to the city, state, and federal governments. California, for example, levies an unemployment tax (SUTA), an employment training tax, a disability tax, and an income tax.

Workers Compensation Insurance is federally mandated but administered by the states. It protects both the employer and employee in case of injury. The employer is protected against being sued by the employee. If injured, the employee receives medical care and may receive rehabilitation and retraining, if needed.

Separately, the federal government requires the operator to withhold from employees' pay federal income tax, as administered by the Internal Revenue Service (IRS), and Social Security taxes.

Every business with at least one employee in addition to the owner must register with the IRS, acquire an employer identification number, and withhold federal payroll taxes from employees' pay. The taxes withheld are submitted to the IRS at least quarterly. Amounts withheld depend on deductions claimed by the employee. The employer provides each employee with a W-2 form stating the amount of income taxes withheld and also the amount of the employee's contribution to FICA (Federal Insurance Contribution Act, commonly called Social Security), also withheld by the employer.

Law prescribes the business deductions. The percentage paid by the employee is 7.65% of up to $53,400. Any wages over this limit are not taxed for FICA purposes.

Then there is the Federal Unemployment Tax Act (FUTA), which requires the employer to contribute another percentage of the employee's gross wages or salary (up to a specified amount.)

If the restaurant business entity is in the form of a corporation, a federal corporate income tax return is filed. These filings are in addition to personal income taxes. Don't forget that most states have other tax filings and so do some municipalities.

Once in business, the operator must also instantaneously become a bookkeeper, or hire one. Small operators generally employ an independent accountant to do the bookwork and advise on tax matters. Large restaurants usually employ their own accountant for bookkeeping and pay for expert advice on tax matters.

Local health departments are active in promulgating and enforcing food protection regulations. State employment offices are charged with enforcing employment regulations, and other state agencies may be involved. In some states, more than one agency is involved in defining compliance with a particular regulation or law.

As discussed in Chapter 12, the Americans with Disabilities Act (ADA) prohibits discrimination against persons who are disabled and stipulates that "readily achievable" modifications be made in work practices and working conditions, including physical access.

Local and state agencies vary in their enforcement policy. A regulation that was on the books for many years but ignored may all of a sudden become of major importance to a new administration, with the result that heavy fines are laid against operators for things that have been common practice. This happened with the truth-in-menu enforcement policies. To keep abreast of changes, operators usually rely on associations serving the industry.

Because the regulations change so frequently, there is little point in spelling out the details of legislation here. By the time this book is published, the regulations may have been reinterpreted or changed. It is helpful to be familiar with the major legislative acts that affect the restaurant operator.

FEDERAL LAWS GOVERNING EMPLOYMENT

■

The Federal Wage and Hour Law
(The Fair Labor Standards Act)

Passed in 1983, this law was designed to increase wages and increase employment by reducing the hours of the average workweek.[5] The Act covers employees of a restaurant having an annual dollar volume of sales of at least $325,000 (exclusive of excise taxes at the retail level that are separately stated.) Operators with sales less than this amount are not subject to the federal wage and hour laws. They are, however, still subject to pertinent state laws. Operators in many states can and are paying less than the federal minimum wage. Operators who are covered by the Act must display a poster, obtained free from an officer of the Wage and Hour Division and outlining the Act's basic requirements, where employees can see it readily.

■ **Supervisors and the Minimum Wage.**   Persons who are in bona fide supervisory positions are not subject to the federal minimum wage law. The question is whether or not the trainee or bona fide supervisor must be paid time and a half for hours worked beyond 40 a week. Restaurant corporations often hire management trainees and require them to work 50, 60, or more hours per week at a straight salary, which may work out to a low hourly wage. The NRA explains that employees who are considered supervisors or managers must meet the following conditions:

- The employee's first and primary duty is managing a company or customarily recognized department or subdivision of a company.
- The employee regularly directs the work of at least two other employees.
- The employee has authority to hire or fire or to recommend on hiring and firing, transfer, and promotion.
- The employee regularly exercises discretionary powers.
- The employee's nonmanagerial duties take up no more than 40% of the work time.[6]

The employee who is in sole charge of a restaurant is considered exempt even though more than 40% of the work is nonmanagerial. In other words, the person in charge of a snack bar may do most of the physical work but is still exempt. The interpretations of these provisions change and must be checked periodically.

The Department of Labor (DOL) has set forth six conditions that must be met before an employee qualifies for exemption to the minimum wage law. The first five conditions are the same as those the NRA uses to define supervisors; the sixth is that the supervisor is compensated for services on a salary basis of not less than a certain dollar amount per week—check with your state restaurant association for the accurate amount—exclusive of board, lodging, or other facilities.

The condition most difficult to meet is the one relating to nonmanagerial duties. Historically, managers in restaurants are called on to do many kinds of nonmanagerial jobs, such as operating the cash register, cooking food, setting up tables—anything to keep the operation running smoothly and efficiently.

The DOL has disqualified chefs and shift managers in a sandwich shop. If disqualified, the employee must be paid time and a half for hours worked beyond 40 per week. In some cases, the disqualified employee's overtime wage greatly exceeds what was intended.[7]

■ **Hours Worked.**   Bona fide meal periods, ordinarily 30 minutes, are not counted as hours worked—time that must be paid for by the employer. Coffee breaks and time for snacks are considered part of the employee's work time and the employee must be paid for those times.

If, during a meal period, the employee is frequently interrupted by calls to duty, the meal period must be counted as hours worked and compensation paid.

■ **Overtime Pay.**   Covered employees are paid at least one and a half times their regular rate of pay for hours worked over 40 in a week. The legislature and government of California recently passed into law a bill stating that persons must be paid overtime if they work more than eight hours in one day.

■ **Child Care Leave.**   If other employees are allowed to take leave without pay or accrued annual leave for travel or education not related to their job, the same type of leave must be granted those wishing to remain on leave for purposes of taking care of an infant. Also, any health, disability, or sick leave plan made available to employees must treat pregnancy the same as other medical conditions, regardless of who pays the premium.

■ **And Yet More Regulations.**   Overtime pay at time and a half for all hours worked beyond statutory standards was set. From this act have come a number of minimum wage laws and reduced hours regulations. The law spells out tip credit that may be taken by the employees, overtime rates beyond the 40-hour week, deductions for meals provided to employees, and equal pay provisions for the sexes. State laws must conform minimally to federal legislation but may be more exacting; where they are more stringent than the federal regulations, the state laws apply. For example, there is no tip credit allowed in California, and the minimum wage, in the past, was higher than federal law requires.

■

Employee Information

As required by the federal government, operators must keep records covering employees, including the following information:

1. Name of employee in full

2. Home address, including zip code

3. Date of birth, if under age 19

4. Sex and occupation

5. Emergency contact

6. Time of day and day of week on which the employee's workweek begins

7. Regular hourly rate of pay in any workweek in which overtime premium is due; basis of wage payment (such as $6/hour, $48 days, $240 week plus commission

8. Daily and weekly straight-time earnings

9. Total daily or weekly straight-time earnings

10. Total overtime excess compensation for the workweek, where applicable

11. Total additions to or deductions from wages paid each day

12. Total wages paid each period

13. Date of payment and the pay period covered by payment

The Federal Equal Pay Act of 1963 and Federal Child Labor Laws

The Federal Equal Pay Act of 1963 is an amendment to the Fair Labor Standards Act, which prohibits employees from discriminating on the basis of sex by paying employees of one sex a lower rate than the opposite sex.

Under federal law, the minimum permissible work age is 14. Laws prohibit people of a young age from operating dangerous equipment, such as food slicers and grinders, food choppers and cutters, and bakery-type mixers. Minors under 18 cannot operate elevators, power-driven hoists, or bakery machinery.

A number of regulations apply to persons under 18 working in restaurants, and the restaurant operator must be careful to abide by these regulations. State agency representatives have placed heavy fines on restaurants for failing to have workers under 16 get required work permission from their school authorities. In general, child labor laws allow 14- and 15-year-olds to work only between 7:00 A.M. and 7:00 P.M. and 3 hours or less on a school day, 8 hours or less on a nonschool day, 18 hours or less in a school week, and 40 hours or less in a nonschool week. The DOL has the authority to check time sheets without a warrant if it suspects wage and child labor law violations. Each violation of the child labor law can result in fines up to $1,000.

Wage Garnishment Act

To protect employees from having excessive amounts of wages collected by a lender (wage garnishment), the Federal Wage Garnishment Act (Title III of the Consumer Credit Protection Act) was enacted. State garnishment laws may provide greater restrictions on garnishment.

The Age Discrimination in Employment Act

Most individuals over 40 years of age are protected from age discrimination in matters of hiring, discharge compensation, or other terms, conditions, or privileges of employment. Under the purview of the Equal Employment Opportunity Commission (EEOC), the Act prohibits arbitrary discrimination based on the ages mentioned by private employers of 20 or more persons. Regional offices of EEOC attempt to settle complaints by conciliation before going to court.

The Employment Retirement Income Security Act

The Employment Retirement Income Security Act (ERISA), passed by Congress in 1974, established a broad range of standards with respect to vesting, funding, and planned participation in pension plans. The regulations are so strict that many employers have opted to avoid the plans altogether. According to some observers, ERISA tries so hard to nail the bad guys (those who fail in their fiduciary responsibilities) that they also nail a number of good guys by overwhelming them with paperwork.

Civil Rights Act of 1964

Title VII of the Civil Rights Act of 1964 bans discrimination based on race, religion, color, sex, and national origin. Court cases have established precedents regarding sexual relationships between and employee and an employer. An employer cannot:

- Make sexual advances or demands as a condition of employment or advancement.
- Abolish an employee's job because the employee refuses sexual advances by the employer or supervisory personnel.
- Refuse to investigate complains from an employee that supervisory personnel have engaged in sexual harassment.[8]

Violations of Title VII of the Civil Rights Act of 1964 can take a number of forms. A federal district court judge ruled that an employee required to wear what would be considered a revealing and provocative uniform has the right to pursue a case.[9] According to the judge, employers do not have the unfettered discretion to choose employees' uniforms.

The direction of the law has alerted the EEOC to complaints from employees about sexual harassment. The cost of sexual harassment can be high. Three waitresses who were sexually harassed were awarded a total of $275,000 by the court.[10]

Harassment can take a number of forms, including fondling of a nonsupervisory female by a supervisory male, put-down joke with sexual overtones, pinching, and slapping. Touching another in a sexual way without his or her permission is an act of assault and battery.

Sexual harassment can be perpetrated by either sex. For example, a woman restaurant manager might extort sexual favors from a nonsupervisory male worker in order that he might retain his job as captain.

Since the Clarence Thomas hearing in 1992, sexual harassment claims have climbed considerably in restaurants. The informality of restaurants may actually encourage or at least tolerate sexual banter. The line between work and social interaction in a restaurant setting can easily be blurred and that makes monitoring harassment more difficult. Food servers being harassed by managers, owners, or even patrons might be the most obvious example of sexual impropriety, but it is by no means the only one. The most effective technique in preventing sexual harassment is the adoption and dissemination of a sexual harassment policy.[11]

Employers are liable for harassment conducted by their employees, supervisory and nonsupervisory. If complaints are made, the complainants must be told their rights and management must investigate the incident. If the investigation warrants, prompt and effective steps must be taken to remedy the situation. Lukewarm responses are not sufficient. The victims must be told of the action taken and of the steps taken to prevent retaliation by the harassers.

The responsibilities of managers to stop sexual harassment may extend to controlling the behavior of guests, persons who are not employees, depending on the degree of control that the employer has over the nonemployee. In one instance, a restaurant customer fondled a waitress and made grabbing gestures toward her breast. The waitress informed the restaurant owner and, although the owner said that he would talk to the customer, a friend of his, the customer never apologized. Even though the owner told the waitress he did not condone such sexual harassment, the waitress sued the owner for sexual harassment. The EEOC held in favor of the waitress.[12]

LEGAL ASPECTS OF CONTRACT SERVICES

Restaurant operators often contract out services such as air-conditioning repairs and maintenance, janitorial services, and pest control. Independent contractors have proved popular because, presumably, they are skilled in their field and because the restaurant operator avoids the liabilities for unemployment insurance, workers compensation, wrongful discharge, injuries to third parties by a worker's conduct, and other claims.

To ensure that the tax authorities also view that independent contractors are indeed independent and not employees, the operator should have a written agreement with the contractor that specifies the nature and duration of the work to be done. The operator should be sure that the contractor has an employer account with the state and carries workers compensation insurance. Employment of musicians as independent contractors may well be questioned by the state. Laws regarding musicians leave few cases in which they can be considered independent contractors.

COMPLICATIONS IN DISCHARGING EMPLOYEES

In the absence of a contract, managers used to have the power to fire at will employees—for good cause, bad cause, or no cause. Today, firing decisions are restricted by a maze of often overlapping statutes and executive orders. The National Labor Relations Act (NLRA) prevents companies from arbitrarily dismissing employees engaged in union activity. The Equal Employment Opportunity Act, state statutes, and executive orders protect employees against decisions based on race, age, sex, religion, or complaints to the Occupational Safety and Health Agency (OSHA) that working conditions are unsafe or unhealthy. An employer who wins in one forum can lose in the next because each forum establishes its own enforcement machinery.

REPORTING TIPS TO THE INTERNAL REVENUE SERVICE

A running controversy has existed for a number of years between restaurant operators and the IRS over tip reporting. The IRS requires tipped employees to maintain accurate records of tip income and report such income at least once a month to their employers. The problem is that it is suspected that most employees underreport their tips.

SELLING LIQUOR TO MINORS

The Alcoholic Beverage Commission (ABC) regulates the sale of alcohol. Selling alcohol is regarded as a privilege, not a right; as a result, a license may be withdrawn if a restaurant owner fails to comply with regulations. The ABC regulates the hours of the sale of alcoholic beverages, entertainment, and the food-bar ratio of sales.

State laws vary regarding the age at which liquor can be legally bought, but they all agree on the seller's responsibility to sell only to those persons legally entitled to buy. In California, for example, the California Business and Professions Code provides that:

1. Any person who sells or gives any alcoholic beverage to a person under 21 years of age is guilty of a misdemeanor.
2. Any person who gives or sells any alcohol beverage to an obviously intoxicated person is guilty of a misdemeanor.
3. Any employee of a retail license who permits any alcoholic beverage to be consumed by any person with a license after 2:00 A.M. is guilty of a misdemeanor.

Bartenders, waiters, and waitresses are subject to the code and can be prosecuted. In court cases involving the sale of alcoholic beverages to minors, eight of ten bartenders, waiters, and waitresses who were arrested failed to request proof of age from minors.

TIME OFF TO VOTE

Some 30 states have laws governing time off for elections; such laws vary from state to state. The amount of time off required is typically two to four hours. In some states, the employee must make specific application for time off to vote to be eligible for the right. The local state restaurant association is probably the best source of current information on such laws.

IN CASE OF WAGE AND HOUR AUDIT

The DOL or state labor department officials may demand that a restaurant operator produce wage and hour records within 72 hours. Investigators, after inspecting the records, may want to interview employees, and the operator should make current employees available for such interviews.

Interviews are conducted to verify the accuracy of employment records and what is stated as the employee's duties. If the investigator finds a violation, the operator may wish to employ an attorney to represent the restaurant. The attorney may accompany the operator to the interview with the investigator.

INTERPRETATION AND CLARIFICATION OF GOVERNMENT REGULATIONS

There is no way that the operator can keep posted on constant changes in regulations and their interpretation without help. It would be far too expensive to employ legally trained persons to keep the independent owner current on such matters as minimum wage and working conditions, unemployment disability insurance, and safety on the job regulations. The California Restaurant Association, for example, keeps its members informed on a host of rules and regulations affecting the food and alcoholic beverage service industries in the state. These are some of the areas of coverage:

- Minimum wage and working conditions regulations (complete state and federal labor law information)
- Alcoholic Beverage Control Act and related regulations
- Health and sanitation
- Unemployment insurance, including methods to prevent illegal and unwarranted claims
- State unemployment disability insurance
- Workers Compensation Insurance
- IRS taxes and regulations (Social Security, FUTA, etc.)
- Sales tax (cities and states)
- Business regulations affecting new construction or alterations
- Fair Employment Practice and Equal Employment Opportunity laws and regulations

The matter of insurance is also complicated, and some state restaurant associations provide insurance keyed to the industry's needs. Insurance coverage includes group workers compensation insurance, group life insurance program for owners and key personnel, and comprehensive group medical insurance.

SLIP AND FALL

The most common litigation for restaurants involves slips and falls. This happens when a guest or employee slips on a wet floor or something on the floor, falls, and is injured.

Restaurant owners and operators are required to provide a safe environment for guest and employees. When guests slip and fall, a lawsuit is likely; such suits are usually settled out of court for a substantial amount. Needless to say, insurance premiums are a good investment.

SUMMARY

Careful evaluation of the advantages and disadvantages of the various forms of legal entities under which a restaurant may operate will help the operator select the best one. The time and effort invested will be rewarded by fewer problems as the business matures. Depreciation, tax issues, and benefits are also important considerations for the restaurateur. Setting up a business entails considerable time and effort and involves meeting a number of legal requirements with which the average person will require help. This reinforces the value of experience in the restaurant business before operating as an owner.

There is no way the individual restaurant operator can keep abreast of all legal requirements alone. Most operators depend heavily on their state restaurant associations to keep them informed of changes in legal requirements and to answer questions about current requirements. Taxes—local, state, and federal—are assessed against businesses. Understanding and paying them on time is an unhappy chore and responsibility.

KEY TERMS AND CONCEPTS

Sole proprietorship
Partnership
Limited partnership
Depreciation
Individual retirement annuity (IRA)
Fringe benefits
Buy-sell agreement
Keogh plan
S corporation
Health, Fire, and Alcoholic Beverage
    commission results
Local, state, and federal taxes
Americans with Disabilities Act (ADA)
Federal Wage and Hour Law (The Fair
    Labor Standards Act)

Minimum wages
Child care leave
Equal Pay Act
Federal child labor laws
Age Discrimination in Employment Act
The Employment Retirement income
    Security Act (ERISA)
The Civil Rights Act of 1964
Sexual discrimination and sexual
    harassment
Interpretation and clarification of
    government regulations

REVIEW QUESTIONS

1. In setting up a restaurant business, you have a choice of operating as a corporation, partnership, or sole proprietorship. Which will you choose and why?

2. What are some dangers of operating a restaurant as a partnership?

3. If you wanted to operate your restaurant as a corporation but be taxed as an individual, how could you arrange this?

4. What is the advantage of setting up a buy-sell agreement with partners?

5. As a restaurant corporation owner, how would you decide how much salary to pay yourself?

6. In buying a going restaurant, what is the advantage of allocating as much value as possible to the building and its contents rather than to the operating company?

7. If buying an existing restaurant, would you want to buy the corporation that owned it if it had heavy losses in recent years? Explain.

8. As a restaurant owner/operator, what is the big advantage to you of taking part in a Keogh plan?

9. Name at least five benefits that restaurant owners can give themselves without income tax consequences.

10. Why would you want to take accelerated depreciation during the first years of a new restaurant?

11. What are some dangers in operating a restaurant as a partnership?

12. As a limited partner in a restaurant, what part do you have in making management and financial decisions?

ENDNOTES

[1] Mark E. Battersby, "Corporate Decisions," *Restaurants USA* (January 1997).

[2] Ibid.

[3] National Restaurant Association, *The Uniform System of Accounts for Restaurants.*

[4] Details of these plans change over time. The tax advantages remain substantial. Set up any plan with the advice of a good accountant.

[5] For a comprehensive explanation of the Act, see U.S. Department of Labor, *Restaurants Under the Fair Labor Standards Act*, (Washington, D.C.: GPO, rev. 1978).

[6] National Restaurant Association, *Washington Report*, 19 November 1979.

[7] National Restaurant Association, *Washington Report*, 23 July 1980.

[8] Ibid.

[9] National Restaurant Association, *Washington Report*, 6 August 1980.

[10] "Sexual Harassment: A Cheap Feel Gets a New Price Tag," *Restaurant Hospitality*, 84, no. 14 (June 1983), 28.

[11] K.T. Anders, "Bad Sex: Who's Harassing Whom in Restaurants?" *Restaurant Business* 92, no. 2 (20 January 1993), 46–52.

[12] Ralph H. Baxtor, *Sexual Harassment in the Work Place: A Guide to the Law*, 4th edition (New York: Executive Enterprises Publications, 1994), 71–72.

Chapter 7

After reading and studying this chapter,
you should be able to:

Plan a restaurant menu.

Price a restaurant menu.

Decide how to lay out and design a restaurant menu.

THE MENU

New restaurateurs who have found a great location often focus more on that than on the food. Many restaurateurs begin to plan the design and decor and even the marketing and promotional activities before they have completely decided upon the menu.

Kitchen space is often a limiting factor for many restaurants. Preparation, the cold kitchen, pastry and desserts, production, and service frequently require more space than most restaurants have available. Short of knocking out walls, something has to give. If the restaurant is open for lunch and dinner, the schedule may not leave sufficient time for desserts to be prepared (if it was open only for dinner, pastries and desserts might be prepared in the morning). Perhaps they can be purchased. It is not uncommon for restaurants to purchase special desserts rather than make them.

The menu and menu planning are front and center in the restaurant business. Guests come to restaurants for a pleasurable dining experience and the menu is the most important ingredient in this experience. Food quality, according to a *Restaurant and Institutions* magazine survey, is what restaurant patrons consider the most important factor when choosing a restaurant. Food quality is ranked above service, value, and even cleanliness (though that's a close second).[1]

This orientation presents today's operators with four major challenges:

1. Providing tastier presentations
2. Offering healthier food options
3. Pleasing savvy customers
4. Creating flavors that are nothing short of extraordinary[2]

These and other factors are critical to the menu's and the restaurant's success. The many considerations in menu planning attest to the complexities of the restaurant business.

Considerations in menu planning include:

- Needs and desires of patrons (guests)
- Capability of cooks
- Equipment capacity and layout
- Consistency and availability of menu ingredients
- Price and pricing strategy
- Nutritional value
- Contribution theory
- Accuracy in menu
- Type of menu
- The actual menu items
- Menu analysis
- Menu design and layout
- Standard recipes
- Food cost percentage

The menu is the most important part of the restaurant concept. Selection of the menu items requires careful analysis. An analysis of competing restaurants will help in terms of positioning the restaurant with respect to the competition and of product differentiation. In some restaurants, the guests and servers are also asked for input, which makes for consensus building and a feeling of ownership of certain dishes. The menu must reflect the concept and vice versa. The restaurant concept is based on what the guests in the target market expects, and the menu must satisfy or exceed their expectations. Responsibility for developing the menu may begin with the chef, individually or in collaboration with the owner/manager and, perhaps, cooks and servers. Even New York superstar chef Bobby Flay, who has three high-profile restaurants, television cooking shows, and cookbooks, admits that sometimes "your feelings will betray you." He remembers several years ago that when he opened Bolo, his Spanish-inspired restaurant, "I had this great idea for a lobster and duck paella using Arborio rice. I was so adamant about how good it would be and how well it would do. It bombed."[3]

A café menu for an 85-seat restaurant featuring pastas may consist of about five appetizers, two salads, soup of the day, and 12 to 14 entrees (chicken, meat, seafood, vegetarian—perhaps a steak, grilled chicken, and a couple of fresh fish dishes). The meat can be grilled, sautéed, or poached and the vegetables steamed. (If this café were trying to please an upscale clientele but were to open in a strip mall, the likelihood of success would be low.)

CAPABILITY/CONSISTENCY

The capability of the chefs or cooks to produce the quality and quantity of food necessary is a basic consideration. The use of standardized recipes and cooking procedures will help ensure consistency. The standardized recipe is one that, over time, has been well tested. It lists the quantities of ingredients and features a simple step-by-step method to produce a quality product. The menu complexity, the number of meals served, and the number of people to supervise are also elements that have an effect on the capability and consistency of the restaurant kitchen. Today, chefs and cooks are more innovative and creative in their approach to the culinary arts. The Culinary Olympics, the local chef association, and the many fine foodservice and culinary programs at colleges and universities have done much to improve the creativity of chefs and cooks.

EQUIPMENT

In order to produce the desired menu items, the proper equipment must be installed in an efficient layout. A systematic flow of items from the receiving clerk to the guests is critical to operational efficiency. The chain restaurants and experienced independent operators carefully plan the equipment for the menu so as to achieve maximum production efficiency. Menu items are selected to avoid overuse of one piece of equipment. For example, too many menu items that are broiled may slow service because the broiler cannot handle them. Most menus begin with a selection of appetizers that avoid using the stovetops and grills to avoid conflict with the entrée preparation. Some appetizers are prepared and placed in the refrigerator, ready to be served cold. Others may be prepared and then fried. More on this subject is covered in the chapter on planning and equipping the restaurant.

FIGURE 7–1

The menu of the Mesa Grill in New York City, where Chef Bobby Flay serves bold American flavors in a unique high-energy environment. Courtesy Chef Bobby Flay

APPETIZERS

**ROASTED PUMPKIN +
SMOKED CHILE SOUP**
with Mexican Cinnamon Creme Fraiche
+ Crispy Blue Corn Tortillas
$8.00

**PARMESAN CRUSTED
WILD MUSHROOM QUESADILLA**
with Caramelized Shallots,
Goat Cheese and a Smoked Pepper +
Roasted Garlic Relish
$12.50

ROMAINE SALAD
with Parmesan Crisps, Hominy Croutons
+ Spicy Caesar Dressing
$7.50

FRISEE SALAD
with Chorizo, Asiago Cheese,
Tomatoes + Roasted Garlic Vinaigrette
$9.00

BLUE CORN CRUSTED SQUID
with Cilantro Pesto
+ Smoked Chile Vinaigrette
$11.00

GRILLED QUAIL SALAD
with Pomegranate Molasses-
Horseradish Glaze, Spicy Pecans
+ Tangerine Vinaigrette
$12.50

CORNMEAL CRUSTED OYSTERS
with Green Chile-Coconut Milk
Sauce + Salmon Caviar
$13.00

**SHRIMP + ROASTED
GARLIC CORN TAMALE**
$13.50

SOPHIE'S CHOPPED SALAD
with Her Own Special Dressing
+ Crispy Tortillas
$8.50

BLUE CORN PANCAKE
filled with Barbequed Duck
+ Habanero Chile Sauce
$13.00

**BLUE CRAB + SALMON
GRIDDLE CAKE**
with Tequila Smoked Salmon +
Roasted Serrano Chile Buttermilk Sauce
$13.50

MOLASSES-BARBEQUED RIBS
with Molasses-Chipotle Sauce +
Peanut-Green Onion Relish
$13.00

LUNCH HOURS : NOON-2:30 MONDAY–FRIDAY
DINNER HOURS : 5:30-10:30 MONDAY–SUNDAY
BRUNCH HOURS : 11:30-3:00 SATURDAY AND SUNDAY
PLEASE REFRAIN FROM PIPE AND CIGAR SMOKING
WE ACCEPT AMERICAN EXPRESS, MASTERCARD, VISA,
DINERS + DISCOVER AS WELL AS CASH
18% GRATUITY ADDED TO PARTIES OF 8 OR MORE

MESA GRILL (212) 807-7400

FIGURE 7–1

Continued

ENTREES

YUCATAN STYLE GROUPER
with Cilantro Mashed Potatoes
+ Patty Pan Squash
$27.50

SHELLFISH + ANDOUILLE GUMBO
with Shrimp, Scallops, Clams +
Oysters with Toasted Blue Corn Bread
$26.50

NEW MEXICAN SPICE RUBBED PORK TENDERLOIN
with Ancho Chile-Mustard Sauce
Served with a Roasted Garlic
Goat Cheese Tamale
$26.50

RED CHILE CRUSTED SALMON
in a Roasted Vegetable Broth
with White Beans + Fresh Sage
$26.50

YELLOW CORN CRUSTED CHILE RELLENO
filled with Roasted Eggplant
and Goat Cheese +
a Salad of Grilled Vegetables
$18.00

PAN ROASTED RABBIT LOIN
with Cranberry-Habanero Chile Sauce
and Sweet Potato +
Toasted Pinenut Polenta
$28.50

GRILLED BLACK ANGUS STEAK
with House Made MESA Steak Sauce
+ a Double-Baked Horseradish Potato
with Green Onions + Creme Fraiche
$29.00

GRILLED TUNA
with a Spicy Mango-Black Pepper Glaze,
a Black Bean Risotto Cake + Spinach
$28.00

SIXTEEN SPICE CHICKEN
with a Caramelized Mango-Garlic Sauce
+ a Plantain Tamale
$24.00

PAN ROASTED VENISON
with Crushed Blackberry-Ancho
Sauce + a Pumpkin Tamale
with Spice Butter
$28.00

BLUE CORN TORTILLA CRUSTED RED SNAPPER
with Roasted Poblano Pepper Sauce
served with a Sweet Potato Tamale
$27.50

SIDE DISHES

**SWEET POTATO AND TOASTED
PINENUT POLENTA WITH SMOKED
YELLOW PEPPER SAUCE**

SOUTHWESTERN FRIES

PLANTAIN TAMALE

SPINACH
$6.50

**DOUBLE-BAKED POTATO WITH
HORSERADISH, GREEN ONIONS
+ CREME FRAICHE**
$7.00

CHEF: BOBBY FLAY

FIGURE 7–1

Continued

MARGARITAS

MESA GRILL MARGARITA
Made *with* Fresh Lime Juice + Triple Sec
Served On The Rocks, Frozen or Up
$6.50

PREMIUM MARGARITA
The Mesa Grill Margarita Made *with* a
Selected Tequilla

SAUZA HORNITOS	**EL TESORO PLATA OR REPOSADO**
CENTINELA BLANCO OR REPOSADO	**CHINACO BLANCO OR REPOSADO**
EL JIMADOR REPOSADO	**HERRADURA SILVER OR REPOSADO**
SAUZA COMMEMORATIVO	
GRAN CENTENARIO PLATA OR REPOSADO	**PATRON SILVER**
CUERVO GOLD	**SAUZA GALARDON**
CUERVO TRADICIONAL	**SAUZA TRES GENERACIONES**
	CUERVO 1800
$7.00	**$8.25**

ESPECIAL MARGARITA
A Premium Margarita made *with* a selected Tequilla
+ a selected Orange Liqueur

GRAND MARNIER

COINTREAU

GRAN TORRES

$7.75/$9.00

CACTUS PEAR MARGARITA
Made *with* Herradura Silver Tequila,
Cactus Pear Juice + Fresh Lime Juice
$8.00

■ **FIGURE 7–1**

Continued

AVAILABILITY

Are the menu ingredients easily available? A constant, reliable source of supply at a reasonable price must be established and maintained. High-quality ingredients make a high-quality product, and fresh must be just that—fresh! Almost all food items are available everywhere—at a price. The operator takes advantage of the seasons when items are at their lowest price and best quality. The ups and downs in food prices can be partially overcome by seasonal menus, or even daily menus, as is the case with the California Café where general manager Volker Schmitz has the menu on his computer. This enables him to quickly remove an item from the menu in the event a hurricane in the Gulf of Mexico or frost in California or Florida dramatically increases the price of fresh fish, fruit, or vegetables. A decision is made to either adjust the price or take the item off the menu.

PRICE

Price is a major factor in menu selection. The customer perception of the price-value relationship and its comparison with competing restaurants is important. Another important factor is a value-creation strategy. John Correll, writing in *Pizza Today*, stresses, "A value-creating strategy needs to create a higher perceived value than that of your competitors. Decide on (or perhaps clarify) your value-creation strategy."[4]

There are two basic components of value creation: what you provide and what you charge for it. To build perceived value, you need to (a) increase the perception of value of what you provide, (b) lower the price you charge for it, or (c) both.

Factors that go into building perceived price-value include:

- Amount of product (portion size)
- Quality of the product (dining pleasure)
- Reliability or consistency of the product
- Uniqueness of the product
- Product options or choices (including new products)
- Service convenience (such as speed of service)
- Comfort level (such as courtesy, friendliness, and familiarity with the business)
- Reliability or consistency of service
- Tie-in offers or freebies included with the purchase

Are you selling a Cadillac or Chevrolet? If you sell a costly Cadillac, you need to charge a Cadillac price; if it's a Chevy, a Chevy price. It is almost always a fatal strategy to attempt to sell a Cadillac at a Chevy price, and vice versa. The most common pricing mistake of independent operators is the former—trying to sell a Cadillac at a Chevy price.

The concept and target market will determine the parameters of menu prices. For example, an Italian neighborhood restaurant may select appetizers and salads in the $2.95 to $5.95 range and entrées in the $6.95 to $11.95 range. A quick-service Mexican restaurant may have a limited menu offering food in the $.99 to $3.89 range. The selling price of each item must be acceptable to the market and profitable to the restaurateur. Questions to ask when making this decision include:

- What is the competition charging for a similar item?
- What is the item's food cost?
- What is the cost of labor that goes into the item?
- What other costs must be covered?
- What profit is expected by the operator?
- What is the contribution margin of the item?

If the costs plus a profit cannot be covered, the restaurant should not be in operation and, over time, will fail. Consider each factor. In the dynamic marketplace of the foodservice industry, competition continually changes. Individual and chain restaurants rise and fall. New restaurants are opened, old ones closed. New marketing and promotional concepts are always in the making or being introduced. New management plans, new building designs, new advertising, and, more slowly, newer modified foods are forever appearing. Competition, however, usually determines menu price more than any other factor.

Menu items are selected to complement the restaurant image and appeal to its target market. For example, hamburgers come in a variety of prices, depending on whether they are self-served or table served, their size, their garnish, the atmosphere, and convenience in reaching the restaurant. No one expects to get a hamburger served on a white tablecloth at the same price as one served from a counter. At "21" in New York, a hamburger is over $21 and is served with french fries and snow peas. By contrast, McDonald's has reduced the price of their smallest burger to 59 cents. A walk-up select-your-own steak may cost a third less than if served at a table in a quiet, attractive dining room, such as Bern's Steak House in Tampa, Florida. Bern's reputation has been built over the past 40 years by creating an aura around its beef. The restaurant buys only U.S. prime beef, which is then aged for an additional four to ten weeks in specially built lockers controlled for humidity and temperature. The menu lists six basic cuts, from Delmonico to porterhouse, which are available in any thickness and broiled to eight levels of doneness. The large multiroom establishment is decorated with expensive antiques, gilded plaster columns, red wallpaper, Tiffany lamps, and murals of French vineyards.[5]

Menu Pricing Strategies

There are two main ways to price menus. A comparative approach analyzes the competition's prices and determines the selection of appetizers, entrées, and desserts. Individual items in each category may then be selected and priced. The cost of ingredients must equal the predetermined food cost percentage.

The second method is to price the individual menu item and multiply it by the ratio amount necessary to achieve the required food cost percentage. For example, to achieve a 40% food cost, multiply the cost of ingredients by 2.5; for a 33% food cost, multiply by 3. This method results in the same expected food cost percentage for each menu item. It is not the best strategy. An expensive fresh fish item may be priced too high when compared to the customer's perception of value or to the prices charged by the competition. A glass of iced tea might have a beverage cost of 15 cents and sell for 25 cents when it could be priced at $1.

This may lead to a weighted average approach, whereby the factors of food cost percentage, contribution margin, and sales volume are weighted. This strategy allows for the stars to save the dogs. The stars are the high-selling items with the greatest contribution margin (gross profit). These items are strategically placed on the menu at the focal point that will attract the greatest attention. A problem with this approach is that averages are relied upon to separate the high-selling items from the low-selling items. The customer's choice can tilt the food cost percentage.

NUTRITIONAL VALUE

Restaurant guests, some more than others, are becoming increasingly concerned about the nutritional value of food. Demand for the healthier chicken and fish items is increasing. In fact, two-thirds of all seafood is eaten in restaurants. Compared to other protein foods, fish and shellfish have far less fat; in addition, seafood has been found lower in cholesterol and sodium. Fish and shellfish are also rich in the highly polyunsaturated omega-3 fatty acids, which may prevent heart attacks.[6] Greater public awareness of healthy food and individual wellness has prompted operators to change some cooking methods—for example, they are broiling, poaching, steaming, casseroling, or preparing rotisserie chicken instead of frying. Kentucky Fried Chicken, to divert attention from the word *fried* in the title, changed its name to KFC. The company also changed its cooking oil, which included some animal fats, to 100% vegetable oil. Some restaurants place a heart sign next to menu items that are recommended for guests with special low-fat dietary needs. A few restaurants put the number of calories beside each item on the menu. Most chain restaurants have taken steps to provide lighter and healthier food. As an example, McDonald's publishes the complete nutritional breakdown of their menu items and has changed their cooking oil for potatoes from animal fat, high in cholesterol, to 100% vegetable oil, which is cholesterol free.

Consumers are more concerned about a food's fat content than about cholesterol and sodium. A number of restaurants offer menus with leaner meats and more seafood and poultry. Bob Wattel, executive vice president of Lettuce Entertain You Enterprises in Chicago, notes that, on the whole, heart-healthy menu items have sold well. Some of the best sellers in Lettuce's program include tuna asada with papaya relish, charred tuna pizza, and angel hair pasta with shrimp and artichokes. The trend toward foods that are lower in calories, cholesterol, sodium, and fat appears to be here to stay. Seafood is expected to play a major role in heart-healthy menu planning for years to come because of its taste and superior nutritional qualities.[7]

The National Restaurant Association recommends that restaurateurs offer meatless main dishes or vegetarian selections. About 15% of restaurant customers look for operations that serve vegetarian fare, and at least 20% of restaurant goers order meatless items. Blue Mesa, in Chicago, serves foods with a Southwestern accent. Its fresh vegetable burrito consists of flour tortillas filled with corn, broccoli, leeks, peppers, tomatoes, onions, and mushrooms, all topped with black bean sauce, Chihauhua cheese, sour cream, and guacamole. In Portland, Oregon, Wholesome and Hearty Foods sells its Gardenburgers, which are made with mushrooms, onions, oats, brown rice, cheese, walnuts, and spices, to businesses such as Disney operations, the Hard Rock Café, and the TGI Friday's chain. Avanti's, in Manhattan, Kansas, serves meatless sputini (little bites), including crostini with walnut-artichoke pesto, fried ravioli with spicy tomato sauce, and grilled polenta with mushroom ragout.[8] There is no doubt that much of the public believes that healthy eating contributes to prolonging our active lives.

FRESH FISH

*Our selection of fresh fish changes daily so that we can offer you the finest catch
available, prepared just the way you want it: baked, grilled or broiled. Served with
our irresistible Cheddar Bay Biscuits, salad, fresh vegetables & your choice of
white Cheddar mashed potatoes, rice, baked potato or French fries*

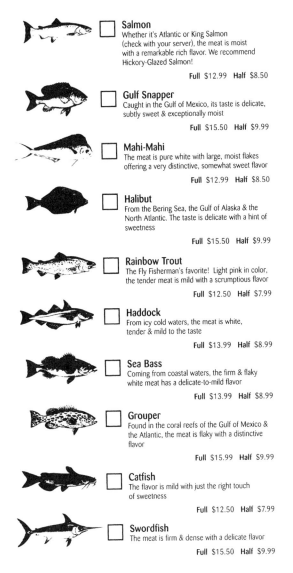

Salmon
Whether it's Atlantic or King Salmon
(check with your server), the meat is moist
with a remarkable rich flavor. We recommend
Hickory-Glazed Salmon!

        Full $12.99 **Half** $8.50

Gulf Snapper
Caught in the Gulf of Mexico, its taste is delicate,
subtly sweet & exceptionally moist

        Full $15.50 **Half** $9.99

Mahi-Mahi
The meat is pure white with large, moist flakes
offering a very distinctive, somewhat sweet flavor

        Full $12.99 **Half** $8.50

Halibut
From the Bering Sea, the Gulf of Alaska & the
North Atlantic. The taste is delicate with a hint of
sweetness

        Full $15.50 **Half** $9.99

Rainbow Trout
The Fly Fisherman's favorite! Light pink in color,
the tender meat is mild with a scrumptious flavor

        Full $12.50 **Half** $7.99

Haddock
From icy cold waters, the meat is white,
tender & mild to the taste

        Full $13.99 **Half** $8.99

Sea Bass
Coming from coastal waters, the firm & flaky
white meat has a delicate-to-mild flavor

        Full $13.99 **Half** $8.99

Grouper
Found in the coral reefs of the Gulf of Mexico &
the Atlantic, the meat is flaky with a distinctive
flavor

        Full $15.99 **Half** $9.99

Catfish
The flavor is mild with just the right touch
of sweetness

        Full $12.50 **Half** $7.99

Swordfish
The meat is firm & dense with a delicate flavor

        Full $15.50 **Half** $9.99

■ FIGURE 7–2

*A Red Lobster menu showing
a wide selection of seafood
items. Courtesy Red Lobster*

TODAY'S SPECIAL

Ask your server about our special fresh fish preparation

DIN-A-2   © Red Lobster 0607

GREAT STARTS!

Beer
Draft Beers "Too Cold to Hold!" Ask about our Domestic, Import or Microbrew selections
Bottled Beers (If you don't see it here, ask)
• Budweiser • Bud Light • Miller Lite • Coors Light • Heineken • Corona • Sam Adams • O'Doul's (non-alcoholic)

Painkillers
Lobsterita Treat yourself to a mega-sized frozen traditional or strawberry margarita made with premium tequila
Alotta Colada™ Quench your thirst with our humongous frozen piña colada
Bahama Mama A tantalizing tropical blend of spiced rum, orange & pineapple juices splashed with grenadine

Soups
New England Clam Chowder .... **Cup** 2.50 • **Bowl** 3.85
Bayou Seafood Gumbo With andouille sausage .... **Cup** 2.99 • **Bowl** 4.25
Soup of the Day .... **Cup** 2.50 • **Bowl** 3.85

Lobster, Crab & Shrimp
✦ Parrot Bay Coconut Shrimp Jumbo shrimp dipped in coconut batter flavored with
Captain Morgan's Parrot Bay rum, lightly fried & served with a piña colada sauce 6.99
Lobster & Crab Stuffed Mushrooms Lobster & deviled crab smothered with Cheddar cheese 6.50
Fiesta Lobster Rolls Olé! Crispy shells packed with lobster, spicy cheeses & vegetables 6.25
Ultimate Fondue Dip into a bread bowl filled with crab meat, crawfish, shrimp & Cheddar cheese 6.50
Shrimp Cocktail .... **Regular** 4.99 • **Jumbo** 6.99

Seaside Samplers
✦ New England Appetizer Sampler Lobster & Crab Stuffed Mushrooms,
fried clam strips & scallops broiled with bacon 7.25
Batterfried Calamari 4.99
Mozzarella Cheesesticks 5.25
Batterfried Chicken Fingers 4.99
Spicy Hot Buffalo Chicken Wings 5.99
Fried Fresh Mushrooms 4.50
Create Your Own Appetizer Sampler .... **Any two** 5.25 • **Any three** 6.99
• Batterfried Calamari • Mozzarella Cheesesticks • Batterfried Chicken Fingers • Fried Fresh Mushrooms
• Fried Clam Strips • Substitute Lobster & Crab Stuffed Mushrooms as a selection for $1 more

> Add delicious lobster or sweet crab legs to any meal...
> • Maine Lobster Tail 6.75 • Snow Crab Legs 5.99

FIGURE 7–2
Continued

SHRIMP & FISH

Walt's Favorite Fried Shrimp Walt (our first crew member) likes 'em, so will you!
Our best shrimp – butterflied & fried to order. Add another half-dozen for $3 .... 11.99
Boardwalk Popcorn Shrimp We invented 'em! Golden, bite-sized fried shrimp 8.99
Mix & Match Shrimp Combo .... **Any two** 9.50 • **Any three** 11.50
• Traditional Fried • Scampi • Lemon-Pepper Fried • Beer-Batterfried
• Shrimp Rockefeller with fresh spinach & bacon, over rice
Nantucket Baked Flounder Lightly seasoned or topped with roma tomatoes & Parmesan cheese (also available fried) 9.99
Farm-Raised Catfish Take your pick – blackened or fried 9.99
✦ **"Shrimp Lovers" Monday** It's shrimply irresistible! On Mondays only, enjoy all the peel & eat shrimp you'd care to eat.
Seasoned with OLD BAY® SEASONING & served chilled or hot. *(Please no sharing - Not available for take-out)* 11.99

SEAFOOD COMBINATIONS

Chesapeake Bake Baked flounder topped with roma tomatoes & Parmesan cheese, plus a terrific trio of
shrimp, scallops & deviled crab topped with Cheddar cheese 9.99
Dockside Shrimp & Chicken Tender baked shrimp scampi & grilled chicken breasts 9.99
Fried Seafood Platter Lightly breaded & fried shrimp, fish fillets, clam strips & deviled crab cakes 10.50
Cape Coral Caesar Salad Garlic-seasoned lobster & shrimp, topped with
Caesar dressing & freshly grated Romano cheese, plus Cheddar Bay Biscuits .... **Half** 7.50 • **Full** 8.99

S-20 © Red Lobster 1/17/00

SEAFOOD FEASTS

🦐 **Shrimp Feast** A regular shrimp cocktail plus shrimp scampi, fried butterflied shrimp & Shrimp Rockefeller with fresh spinach & bacon, over rice 16.25

Admiral's Feast An all fried platter of butterflied shrimp, scallops, clam strips & fish fillets 15.25

🦐 **Ultimate Feast** Our guests' favorite – broiled Maine lobster tail, snow crab legs, shrimp scampi & fried butterflied shrimp. 18.25

CREATE YOUR OWN COMBINATION PLATTER

Choose your two favorites from the selections below 12.99

Grilled Fresh Salmon Try it with our Hickory Glaze	**Fried Butterflied Shrimp**	**Farm-Raised Catfish** Blackened or fried
Shrimp Scampi	**Outer Banks Sampler** Baked shrimp, scallops & deviled crab topped with cheese	**Santa Fe Chicken**
Shrimp Pasta		**Grilled Sirloin Steak** Substitute as a selection for S2 more

LOBSTER & CRAB

🦐 **Live Maine Lobster** Pick one out of our tank! Served steamed or baked with a deviled crab stuffing . . . . Mkt. Price

Rock Lobster Tail Lightly seasoned & baked, served fluffed on the shell 19.25

RockZilla A HUGE Rock lobster tail, lightly seasoned & baked (when available) . . . . Mkt. Price

Snow Crab Legs One pound to crack, dip & enjoy! 15.99

SEAFOOD in every bite PASTA

Served with our irresistible Cheddar Bay Biscuits & your choice of Caesar or garden salad. Our pasta is topped with freshly grated Romano cheese

🦐 **Lobster & Shrimp Pasta** Linguini topped with a flavorful lobster & shrimp tomato-herb sauce, garnished with fresh broccoli . . . . Half 8.99 • Full 10.99

Shrimp Pasta Tender shrimp, garlic Alfredo sauce & sliced green onions over linguini . . . . Half 8.25 • Full 9.99

Crab Alfredo Linguini, creamy Alfredo sauce & sweet crab meat . . . . Half 8.99 • Full 10.99

Cajun Shrimp Pasta Lotsa' linguini topped with shrimp & green onions in a spicy cream sauce . . . . Half 8.25 • Full 9.99

STEAK & CHICKEN

We serve only USDA Choice center-cut steaks

Steak & Fried Shrimp Grilled top sirloin plus our fried butterflied shrimp 14.99

Steak & Lobster Grilled top sirloin & a baked Rock lobster tail 18.75

12 oz. New York Strip Steak 13.65

Santa Fe Chicken Chili-rubbed chicken breasts topped with melted white Cheddar & cool vegetable salsa 9.99

Mainlander's Chicken Salad Grilled chicken on top of crisp greens with tomatoes, cucumbers & Cheddar cheese, plus our Cheddar Bay Biscuits . . . . Half 6.99 • Full 7.99

Cajun Chicken Pasta Spicy chicken in a garlic Alfredo sauce over linguini, plus your choice of Caesar or garden salad & our Cheddar Bay Biscuits . . . . Half 8.25 • Full 9.99

> *Add delicious lobster or sweet crab legs to any meal…*
> • Maine Lobster Tail 6.75 • Snow Crab Legs 5.99

Dinners - except Salads & Pasta - include:
Our irresistible Cheddar Bay Biscuits, cole slaw or salad (Caesar or garden), & your choice of fresh vegetables, white Cheddar mashed potatoes, rice, baked potato or French fries. Add petite shrimp to your salad for just 75¢ more

🦐 We recommend our house specialties!

■ **FIGURE 7–2**

Continued

Restaurants are offering more choices for health-conscious customers. Among the trends restaurant operators reported in a recent National Restaurant Association study are an increase in customer interest in lower-fat menu items and that 40% of table-service restaurants feature or promote certain menu items because of specific or unique nutritional benefits.[9]

CONTRIBUTION MARGIN

The contribution margin is the difference between the sales and the cost of the item. The amount over (the gross profit) when the cost of the item is deducted from the selling price is the contribution that is made towards covering the fixed and variable costs. It works like this: If restaurant A offers a steak on the menu that costs $5.00 and sells for $10.95, the contribution margin is $5.95 for every steak sold. The margin of $5.95 goes to pay the fixed and variable costs, including 15% for surrounding plate costs such as vegetables and sauces, and leaves some over for profit.

FLAVOR

With the new millennium, its clear the American foodservice industry is on the expressway to a broader range of ethnic and international foods with expanded flavor profiles. Americans are embracing ethnic cuisines like never before, manufacturers are providing more flavor-added ingredients, and chain operations are bringing new flavors to the mainstream. Restaurateurs are beginning to realize that flavor is the heavyweight tool to differentiate themselves from others.[10]

There is no doubt that the American palate is craving an increase in the breadth and complexity of flavor in foods. There are big flavors, spicy flavors, fresh flavors—flavors from a world of diverse cultures that are rapidly changing American restaurant food.

American tastes—and the restaurant industry—are being reinvigorated by a shift in culinary basics from French to Asian. Exciting new flavors, cuisines, and preparation descriptions are emerging.[11]

Some chefs feel that fusion cuisine has run its course and that Americans want their food to taste familiar, with just a hint of a foreign influence—perhaps a predominant flavor, ingredient, or cooking method. Terms like *marinated* and *smoked* are being featured on more menus, indicating a trend to more flavorful foods.

Flavor is the sum of the sensory experiences people have when food enters their mouth. The total perception is a combination of aroma, taste, texture, sight, and sound, involving all senses.[12]

Wolfgang Puck, as chef and entrepreneur, guides the culinary paths of 38 restaurants—from the many locations of Spago to Chinois, Granita, Postrio, and the newest, Lupo, to the myriad Wolfgang Puck Cafés and Expresses—plus a sizable frozen food business and a nationally expanding soup line.

Among Puck's favorites are brioche-crusted sweetbreads with shallot marmalade, and black fig salad and fennel seed as an appetizer. "It excites every part of your mouth—it sweet, sour, crunchy, velvety, crispy," he says.[13]

Given the trend toward more flavorful food, it makes sense to promote flavor with menu descriptions such as aromatic, spicy, tangy, crisp, smoked, char-broiled, marinated, fresh, crunchy, wood-fired, sizzling, etc.

ACCURACY IN MENU

Most states have statutes stipulating that businesses (including restaurants) may not misrepresent what they are selling. Restaurants must be accurate and truthful when describing dishes on the menu. This means that if the trout on the menu comes from an Idaho trout farm, it cannot be described as coming from a more exotic sounding location. Similarly, if the beef is described as prime, then it must be prime, judged according to U.S. Department of Agriculture Standards; butter must be butter, not margarine; and fresh cream must be fresh. Some restaurants have been heavily fined for violations of accuracy in menu.

KIDS' MENUS

Restaurants that cater to families usually have a separate kids' menu—one using bold colors and catchy make-believe characters. Children like fun and humor. They come in various ages from toddlers to young teenagers; one size does not fit all. Children like tiny prizes to take home, and they like to be involved and treated as more grown up than they really are.

Many restaurants—McDonald's, for example—set aside play areas for children. Almost any restaurant can set aside a kids' corner (if only in self-defense). Some upscale restaurants would just as soon have parents leave the kids at home.

Most restaurants can provide fun placemats, color crayons, and small take-home prizes for kids. Someone on the staff who likes children and enjoys serving them should be the one to wait on them. Someone who is "cool," uses their vocabulary, and is bushy-tailed, lively, and laughs easily is best for the job. Restaurants serving pancakes can make a funny face on the top pancake with a few berries or colored forms.

Take a hint from McDonald's and come up with your own Godzilla, Monster Man, or just a funny hat and face with a bulbous nose that lights up. The character can be male or female. Kids also enjoy innocuous creatures like make-believe spiders, big bugs, and other crazy creatures.

Restaurant Hospitality magazine conducted a Best Kid's Menu in America contest and published the results, with comments, in its April 1999 issue.[14] Some of the ideas covered in that issue are:

- When families with kids appear, don't keep them waiting.

- Wait staff serving children should bend over and talk to them eye to eye. Don't patronize; use simple vocabulary.

- Include familiar items on kids' menus because children don't want to try unfamiliar foods. Before the entrées arrive, provide some snack or vegetables.

- 39% of children picked American foods as their favorite; 21% picked Italian, 20% Chinese, and 15% Mexican.

- Once kids are eight or nine, they eat a wider variety of adult foods. A junior menu means larger portions for older kids, including vegetables, tossed salad, ribs, steaks, fish, and a choice of potatoes.

French's mustard put together a "Little Squirts" program that makes it easy to start a children's program. A promotional kit includes 100 Toddle Tots characters along with promotional materials. No doubt other companies have or will have similar programs.[15]

MENU ITEMS

Independent restaurant menus tend to be more creative and adventurous than chain restaurants. Chefs tend to have a more extensive culinary background and a flair for innovation. Chain restaurants appeal to a broader section of the market and therefore have menu offerings that reflect items popular with the mass market.

The menu items selected will depend on the type of restaurant. The number and range of items on the menu is critical to the overall success of the restaurant. If the menu offerings are too extensive, there will be problems in getting the food to the guests in a timely manner. A family restaurant, for example, is mainstream for all ethnic groups and needs to offer a range of popular menu items. A balance is achieved by offering a selection of hot and cold appetizers, soups, and salads. Entrées might include several types of meat, poultry, fish, pasta, and dessert. Soups might include a popular favorite like vegetable beef, plus a daily special. Salads, which could also be served as a main dish, would likely include house salad, chef's salad, an oriental chicken salad, fajita, or a Caesar salad. Entrée dishes reflect the basic American family-type meal, including char-broiled chicken, baked halibut or codfish, fried shrimp, steaks, burgers, and a variety of sandwiches. Desserts may include a selection of ice creams and cakes or pastries. A choice of salad dressings is usually offered.

Adding new items to the menu can be risky. The large chain restaurants with decisions made at headquarters must reduce risk, because the failure of menu items at several, even hundreds of restaurants can be extremely costly. The rational decision-making process relies on the brain rather than the heart and not all of the steps are appropriate to an independent restaurant; however, some are. Most chains use this system in one form or another:

1. Create an objective and a timetable.
2. Develop a list of possible menu ideas.
3. Narrow that list down.
4. Test those ideas with consumers.
5. Build prototypes.
6. Internally narrow the prototypes down.
7. Test and renew the prototypes in selected restaurants.
8. Put the prototypes on the menu.[16]

Independent restaurants can simply put on a new item as a special and, if it's popular, add it to the main menu.

A recent special report, "The New Tastemakers," in *Nations Restaurant News* profiled the 50 people considered the most progressive and influential in shaping the foodservice landscape into the 2000s. Interestingly, the list also included not only some high-profile independents and fine dining, but also large chain restaurants.[17]

Obviously, we are acquainted with the better-known star chefs like Emeril Lagasse, Wolfgang Puck, Charlie Trotter, Jean-Georges Vongerichten, Danny Meyer, Drew

Menu du Jour

*oysters poached with braised baby leeks and osetra caviar and
oysters raw with borsht, crème fraîche and osetra caviar*

or

Yellowfin tuna tartare with basil vinaigrette and sauce sofrito

or

sautéed filet of snapper with pine nut crust, sauce saffron

or

warm lobster salad with potatoes, crispy leeks, and truffle vinaigrette

—M—

roasted côtelette of quail with savoy cabbage and bacon, jus de gibier

or

foie gras sauté with Fuji apples de trois façon

or

sautéed langoustine salad with a chapeau of pecorino sardo

—M—

*roasted Maine lobster bordelaise with corn flan and vanilla
scented pommes frites ($ 7.00)*

or

Hawaiian swordfish with jus de bouillabaisse

or

lamb T-bones with pistou and tomato confit, sauce pinot noir

or

*Niman Ranch Angus mignon of beef with foie gras mousse and
autumn vegetables, sauce perigord*

or

roasted squab with wild rice and Serrano jamon risotto

—M—

dessert

—M—

coffee and petit fours

*prix fixe at $75.00
Tuesday, November 9, 1999
Dinner at Masa's*

■ **FIGURE 7–3**

*Masa's menu, San Francisco. The menu is unique each night and features dishes
displaying visual and flavor harmony. Masa's is consistently ranked among the top
French restaurants in the world. Courtesy Masa's*

Nieporent, and Alice Waters. However, who would have guessed that the 1999 Menu Masters Award for best single product rollout would go to Einstein/Noah Bagel Corporation for Roasted Portabello and Pepper Baguette Sandwich?[18]

APPETIZERS AND SOUPS

Six to eight appetizers are adequate for the majority of restaurants. Most of these can be cold or cooked ahead and zapped in the microwave for speed of service and to avoid use of equipment being used for the entrées.

To accommodate a variety of guest tastes, offer a balance in the appetizer list. This may be achieved by selecting an item from each generally accepted group of offerings. For example:

- Chilled fresh tiger prawns cooked in saffron lemon tea with couscous semolina, almonds, bell pepper, angel hair, and avocado
- Home-smoked duck breast served with baby corn and wild rice
- Ravioli of Pacific prawns served with fresh thyme cream sauce and diced bell pepper
- California potpourri salad served with almond raspberry vinaigrette and tender lettuce and oak leaves, and dressed with warm goat cheese and rosemary

The selection of appetizers should be interesting enough for the guest to want to try one but not so filling as to detract from the entrée. It is a good idea to ensure that at least some of the appetizers utilize kitchen equipment that is separate from the equipment used for the entrée. An examination of some family restaurant menus indicates heavy use of the fryer for such items as chicken strips, onion rings, fried zucchini, and fried mozzarella. Some of the nonfried or partially fried items include nachos supreme (crispy tortilla chips with spicy ground beef, Mexican-style beans, cheddar cheese, green onions, chopped tomatoes, black olives, guacamole, and sour cream, with salsa on the side).

Independent dinner restaurants tend to be more adventurous than chain restaurants. Typical appetizers might include shiitake mushrooms in a sherry herb garlic sauce with Indonesian spice; smoked salmon served with capers, lemon, grapes, fresh fruit, and cheddar cheese; baked Brie coated with almonds and served with fresh fruit; shrimp cocktail; Dungeness crab with sherry cream dressing; fresh oysters; and marinated artichokes. Presentation of the appetizer is important because it is generally the first item guests see and taste. Consider whether or not appetizers on the dinner menu will be the same as the luncheon menu.

The kind and number of soups to offer depends on the restaurant concept and the guests. Soups may be categorized as thick, thin, clear, cream, cold, or chowder. Some menus might include a popular favorite like chicken noodle and a daily special, or more exotic Louisiana clam chowder with Tabasco butter.

LUNCH AND DINNER MENUS

From the viewpoint of both guests and restaurant operators, the lunch menu is different from the dinner menu. Today, most lunch guests have about 45 minutes in which to order and enjoy a meal. This means that the menu needs to be easy to read and the kitchen capable of producing the food quickly. In most cities, a psychological price barrier keeps lunch menu prices under $10.00. At dinner, when guests have more time to enjoy a leisurely meal, both the portions and the prices tend to be a little larger.

Degustation Menus

A number of exclusive restaurants are offering their guests a degustation menu— meaning to taste with relish. A degustation menu is a sample of the chef's best dishes. Generally consisting of several courses that showcase the chef's talent for combining flavors and textures, degustation menus take much longer to serve than normal dining.[19]

At Charlie Trotter's, in Chicago, customers have been able to choose from several tasting menus for several years. Each menu, produced daily, highlights the freshest foodstuffs obtainable. The menus are presented in three formats, each offering a unique perspective. Additionally, the kitchen can customize the evening's menus to complement the guest's wine selections.

The Grand Menu offers a sumptuous variety that weaves together pristine seasonal products. This menu features seafood and meat selections supported by vegetable and grain elements. Conceived to be experienced with a progression from lighter white wine to fuller red wine, this menu demonstrates Trotter's ability to balance the intense individual flavors of each course against the attributes of the wine being served. An example of a Grand Menu is shown in Figure 7–4.

Trotter also has a Kitchen Table Degustation, which is served to guests who dine at the kitchen table. This menu best illustrates his command of balancing flavors and portion sizes. Although the menu comprises about 15 courses, it is still the perfect amount of food. Trotter's true genius is his sense of balance and harmony and his ability to layer together a diverse series of flavors, textures, and cultural influences, as evident throughout the menu.[20]

MENU TYPES

Restaurants in the French tradition offer menus that feature about the same number of items in each category and follow the classical sequence of dining: first the hors d'oeuvres, followed by soup, then seafood, entrées, grillades (grilled meat items), legumes (vegetables), salads, and, finally, desserts.

The really fancy restaurants serving "la grande cuisine française" are likely to offer several specialties of the house or chef. A separate table d'hôte may be offered—a complete meal including soup or appetizer, salad, entrée, and vegetable for a fixed price. The other items are typically à la carte (priced separately).

Dinner-house menus separate similar entrées: beef in one section, seafood another. House specialties may be offered as a group. Many menus have breakfast items, dessert items, and beverages grouped in separate sections.

Coffee shops usually offer a separate page of breakfast items even though they may be available around the clock. The typical table-service restaurant uses three or even four menus—for breakfast, luncheon, and supper. Separate children's menus with smaller portions and lower prices may also be provided.

À la carte menus offer individually priced items. Most restaurants use this type of menu.

CHARLIE TROTTER'S

October 1999
Grand Menu

Amuse Gueule

Salad of Pheasant Breast with Asian Pear, Matsutake Mushrooms, Hazelnuts
& Seared Canadian Foie Gras

European Loup de Mer with Roasted Eggplant,
Cucumber-Yogurt Sauce & Spicy Curry Sauce

Grilled New Zealand Amberjack with Sea Scallops, Grilled Salsify, Tiny Fennel
& Shellfish-Red Wine Emulsion

Crawford Farm Lamb Loin & Rack with Butternut Squash,
French Lentils & Horseradish-Infused Cauliflower Puree

Roasted Italian Prune Plums with Buttermilk Sorbet & Pluot Soup

Sage Corn Scone with Papaya & Passion Fruit Foam

Mignardises

FIGURE 7–4

The Grand Menu at Charlie Trotter's offers a sumptuous multicourse variety of
dishes. Courtesy Charlie Trotter

A table d'hôte menu offers a selection of several dishes from which patrons choose to make a complete meal at a fixed price. These may be a choice of items for appetizers, soups and salads, entrées, and desserts. The advantage of this type of menu for the guest is value. With the price fixed, the guest is assured of a meal at a guaranteed price. The advantage for the restaurateur is that the number of menu items is limited.

Some restaurants add a list of daily specials to an à la carte menu. These items take much of the pressure off the kitchen staff, especially on a busy night, because approximately 70% of guests may order from this "select" menu insert.

Other menu types include the du jour menu, which is a list of food items served only on a particular day. Du jour literally means "of the day," as in "soup du jour." Cyclical menus repeat every few days, normally 7, 10, 14, or 28 days. Cyclical menus are generally used in institutions rather than restaurants.[21]

The California menu is so named because, in many California restaurants, guests may order any item from the menu at any time of the day. Many restaurants have a separate menu for each meal—breakfast, lunch, dinner, and perhaps brunch.

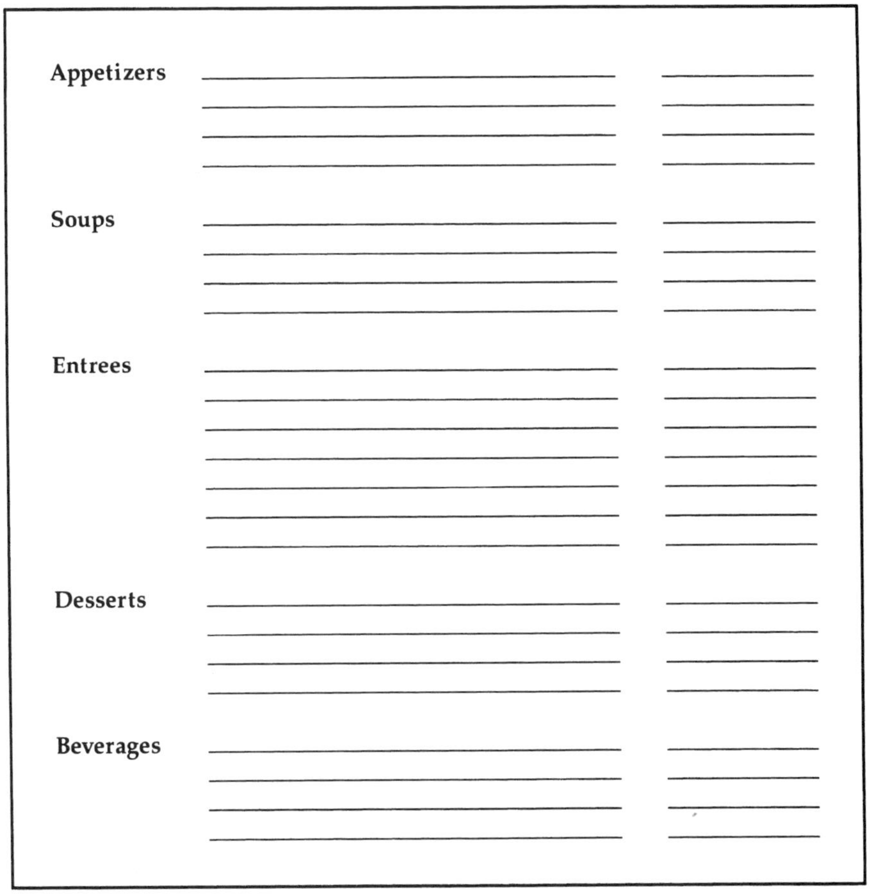

FIGURE 7–5

Sample of a menu format showing the sequencing of items

The tourist menu is occasionally used to attract tourists' attention to a particular restaurant. Generally, this kind of menu underlines value and acceptability to a guest who may be traveling in a foreign country where the food may be decidedly different.

SALADS

With the increase in the variety of salad items and their year-round availability, salads have become the preferred starter in a growing number of restaurants. Typically, salads are a light and healthy way to begin a meal, though more Americans are ordering them as main courses. More and more restaurants say that more women prefer salads as their main dish than men. The variety of ingredients that combine to make an attractive presentation is almost endless.[22]

Main-dish salads made with chicken, beef, seafood, fruits, and vegetables topped with a variety of exotic dressings are rising in popularity as consumers seek more ways to add fruits and vegetables to their diets. The traditional Caesar salad is the top main-dish salad choice on menus, with the traditional Cobb salad and salade Niçoise right behind it.[23]

ENTRÉES

Generally, in a table-service restaurant, there should be at least eight entrées. This allows for a minimum selection cooked in a variety of ways (baked, broiled, sautéed, fried, grilled, poached, and simmered). To maintain a balance, there should be an item or two from each of the major meat, pasta, poultry, seafood, and fish categories. One item, such as chicken, could be cooked in different ways: lemon herb chicken (broiled), grilled chicken breast marinated in ginger vinaigrette, chicken fajitas (sautéed), or chicken in the style of Burgundy (simmered).

DESSERTS

Desserts may include a selection of fruits, pies, cakes, ices, and pastries. When properly merchandised, they can boost the average check and profit of the operation.

Most restaurants cannot afford the luxury of a pastry chef. However, there are alternative ways of offering high-quality desserts to restaurant guests. They may be purchased from a local pastry shop or bakery. Another way is to purchase a tart base and add fruit and yogurt to it. Some restaurants have a sundae bar where guests may serve themselves ice cream and frozen yogurt and add a variety of toppings.

MATCHING/PAIRING[24]

In the past, food and wine pairings used to be classics, such as oysters with Chablis or a beef roast with claret or Beaune.

Today's menus take their inspirations not only from Europe but also from Asia, Latin America, and once-ignored corners of the United States, and the wines come from every continent except Antarctica.

The new classics couple a type of wine with a general class of food, with the recipe serving as an example. For instance, baked goat cheese frequently shows up on menus in salads, on a designer pizza, or incorporated into a baked melange. The accompanying wine is a sauvignon blanc. That works well when goat cheese is part of a fruit course, where a crisp dry wine such as sauvignon blanc fits better than it might with the cheese course at the end of the meal.

Another example is seared tuna. Its naturally purple-red meat turns grey when cooked, but it is juicy and jewel-like when raw. Taking a cue from sushi bars, which serve tuna raw, modern cooks not only serve uncooked tuna with Japanese seasonings as an appetizer but also have devised ways to impart a little more flair by seasoning and quickly flash-cooking the surface of a block of tuna. Slices from it frame the translucent red center with the black and gray of the cooked surface. A wine to complement this contemporary classic would be a chardonnay, whose spicy flavors from barrel fermentation and buttery undertone cozy up to the heady flavors and textures of the lightly cooked tuna.

With grilled salmon, nowadays, the wine of choice seems to be a pinot noir. The trend toward red wine with salmon appears to have started in the Pacific Northwest, where wine drinkers discovered that Oregon pinot noir has a naturally affinity for the fish.

Smoked tomatoes have appeared on menus recently, adding a distinctively sweet-and-smoky flavor to any dish that calls for fresh tomatoes. Pasta primavera is not the same any more. To match this new classic, try a modern-style Chianti with a tinge of smokiness from aging in small oak barrels. Combine it with the pasta and smoked tomatoes, and the flavors practically reverberate.

RESTAURANTS IN LAS VEGAS REPRESENT THE BEST COUNTRYWIDE

The best 25 restaurants in Las Vegas may be as good as the best 25 restaurants in any city in the world. Today, Las Vegas is probably the de facto capital of American cooking, the place where the nation's greatest chef's come together at the table.

Ten years ago, Benihana may have been the best restaurant in town. A few years ago, a California Pizza Kitchen opened and several people were delighted because they were able to get something other than buffet-line prime rib and 75-cent shrimp cocktails.

Then Wolfgang Puck opened a branch of his Spago in the Forum Shops next to Caesar's Palace and started posting numbers that made baccarat winnings look like penny-ante poker. Hotel owners started to lay huge bets on the drawing power of American cuisine. The MGM Grand had Santa Fe–cuisine Mark Miller open his popular Coyote Café and hired New Orleans chef Emeril "Bam!" Lagasse to replicate his salmon cheesecake and barbecued shrimp.[25]

When New York New York opened, it offered restaurants familiar to Manhattan-savvy diners: Chin Chin, Il Fornaio, and Gallagher's Steakhouse. Then Rio brought in Jean-Louis Palladin, dean of French chefs in America. Not to be outdone, Steve Wynn, Chairman and CEO of Mirage Resorts, has opened top restaurants and hired top chefs.

For steakhouses, you can choose between The Palm, Gallagher's, Morton's of Chicago, Emeril Lagasse's new Delmonico, and Smith and Wollensky. French chefs include Jean-Louis Palladin, Charles Palmer, Jean-Georges Vongerichten, Joachim Splichal, Jean Voho, and Eberhard Miller. There is a different Wolfgang Puck restaurant in Las Vegas for each day of the working week: Spago, Chinois, Trattoria del Lupo, Postrio, and the Wolfgang Puck Café.

MENU ANALYSIS

Over the years, several approaches to menu analysis have been recommended. No matter which is adopted, the important point to remember is that there should be a balance between a menu too high in food cost, which results in giving food away and too low in food cost, which rips off the customer. Expect some items on the menu to yield a higher margin than others.

Professor Jack Miller developed one of the earlier approaches to menu analysis. The winners were menu items that not only sold more but also were at a lower food-cost percentage. In 1982, professors Michael Kasavana and Donald Smith proposed "menu engineering." In this approach, the best menu items—the stars—are those that have the highest contribution margin per unit and the highest sales. In 1985, Professor David Pavesic proposed a combination of three variables: food cost percentage, contribution margin, and sales volume. Under this method, the best items are called primes—those with a low food-cost percentage and a high contribution margin weighted by sales volume.

More recently, professors Mohamed E. Bayou and Lee B. Bennett proposed an approach to menu analysis whereby each item at each meal is analyzed. Breakfast, lunch, and dinner items are analyzed to compute their measure of profitability. They recommend analysis by:

- Individual menu items
- Categories of menu offering (e.g., appetizers, entrées)
- Meal periods or business categories (e.g., the breakfast meal period, the banquet business)[26]

Pavesic recommends that restaurant operators first think of the psychological factors that influence customers' price perception. Some guidelines he suggests in menu pricing are:

1. Use odd-cents increments for digits to the right of the decimal point.
2. Do not write price increases over old prices.
3. Resist increases that raise the dollar amount of the item.
4. Give items that have been drastically increased in price a less noticeable spot on the menu.
5. Try reducing large portions before raising prices. Some restaurant operators suggest taking the items off the menu or changing the dish because regular guests might notice the smaller portions and feel that they were being cheated.
6. Never increase the price on all menu items.
7. Put "market-priced" on items that fluctuate wildly in price.
8. Do not list menu items according to cost, and make sure that menu prices appear after an item's description rather than in a straight column.[27]

Odd-cent menu pricing is widely used in fast-food restaurants. It may be that pricing an item using the 98-cent approach is not appropriate for unit-scale restaurants and it certainly should not be used for fine dining establishments. Many of these price items end in 95 cents. For example, lobster at $19.95 seems appropriate, while $19.98 does not.

MENU DESIGN AND LAYOUT

Menu design and layout have been called the silent salespersons of the restaurant. The overall menu design should reflect the ambiance of the restaurant. With the aid of graphic artists and designers, or the personal computer, menus can be designed to complement decor and ambiance.

The menu size may range from a single page up to several pages and be of a variety of shapes; however, menus are generally 9 × 12 inches or 11 × 17 inches. The printing may be elaborate or simple. Both the printing and the artwork should harmonize with the overall theme of the restaurant. The names of the dishes should be easy to read and understand. The menu cover is a symbol of the restaurant's identity.

For menus of more than one page, the outside cover may have the name of the restaurant and a picture appropriate to its style. The layout, typeface, illustrations, graphic design, paper color, and menu copy are a matter of personal choice. Several menu design–related sites on the World Wide Web feature menu borders and other graphics. Today, personal computers can easily create menus du jour using special software packages. The advantages of making your own menus are flexibility and the ability to recollect daily specials (that way, servers won't forget them!). Money is saved on expensive designers and print shops; records are easily kept and great graphics are just a mouse click away.

We tend to better remember the first and last things that we see or hear. When reading menus, people are also attracted to images, graphics, and icons that will increase sales of particular items—one hopes, those with the best contribution margins.

The layout and sequence of the menu may be a single page encased in plastic laminate. If the menu is more extensive, there is more space on the back for the desserts and beverages.

The focal point of a single-page menu is just above the center, an ideal place to list a special item that may be highlighted to increase sales. This item should also yield a good profit margin because of being a high-selling item. Figure 7–6 shows the focal point of a single-page menu and Figure 7–7 shows the focal point of a two- or four-page menu.

Menus with two or more pages may be laid out in an appealing way with a signature item or special dishes highlighted or boxed in the focal points. Beverages may appear on the back page or even as a suggestion to accompany a certain dish.

More elaborate menus include additional folds and more pages. Some menus have three panels while others have inserts for featured specials. Color photographs and graphic designs assist chain guests in making a selection. The Olive Garden has won awards for its picture menu. The Olive Garden and many other fine restaurants use photographs to depict menu dishes. Considering that many restaurant guests eat with their eyes, the picture menu is an effective merchandising tool.

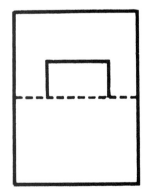

FIGURE 7–6

Focal point of a single-page menu

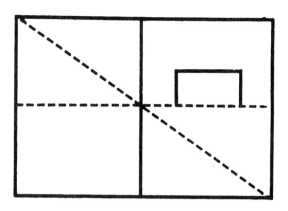

FIGURE 7–7

Focal point of a two- or four-page menu

■ *What Kind of Paper?*

The paper on which the menu is printed should reflect the atmosphere of the restaurant. In fine dining, use a low-key, expensive paper, and have an inexpensive reduced-size menu available for customers to take with them. A quick-service restaurant may rely completely on a lighted display menu located above the service center. Coffee-shop menus often use a heavy stock paper, enclosed in plastic, with color photos of menu items. The restaurant that changes menu items frequently, perhaps daily, may use a blackboard or a desktop computer to produce the menu.

When starting a new restaurant, it is more cost effective to print two or three menus in the first few weeks and months of operation as guests' choices determine which menu items are popular and which are not. If a restaurant operator prints an elaborate and expensive menu, it will cost even more when changes are required and new menus are printed.

STANDARDIZED RECIPES

Standardized recipes are used to maintain consistent food quality. A carefully developed recipe helps cooks because the portion size, ingredients, weights, and production steps, including cooking methods and time, are clearly indicated. Restaurant guests will be offered consistently high-quality food. The standard recipe also acts as a control device in that the same ingredients and in the same amounts are used over time.

FOOD-COST PERCENTAGE

Food cost is reflected in pricing. The cost of food varies with sales (a variable cost). When stated as a percentage of sales, food cost provides a simple target for the chef and management to aim for, becoming a barometer of the profitability of the restaurant.

Traditionally, menus were priced by using a fixed markup, or multiple, based on food cost. The system worked fairly well in that other costs tended to be fairly predictable in a well-managed restaurant with a steady market. If, for example, 33% of sales figure was used as a food-cost percentage target and other costs were steady, the main food items were multiplied by 3 to arrive at a sales price. A number of items, such as coffee, tea, cola, desserts, and soups, were sold at a much lower food-cost percentage.

░CHEZ░PANISSE░

DOWNSTAIRS DINNER MENUS: WEEK OF AUG. 30-SEPT. 4, 1999

MONDAY, AUGUST 30 $59
Prosciutto and figs with garden lettuces
Fresh ricotta soufflé with green bean and shell bean ragout
Bouillabaisse à la Panisse: Provençal-style stew of local fish and shellfish cooked in the fireplace
    with tomatoes, garlic, saffron, and rouille
Pink pearl apple tart with honey lavender ice cream

TUESDAY, AUGUST 31 $59
Tomato, basil, and Cantal cheese tart; with green beans and pearl onions
Grilled Monterey Bay squid with chanterelles, garden lettuces, and aïoli
Sicilian-style swordfish cooked two ways; with stuffed tomatoes, grilled eggplant, and
    summer squash *alla gremolata*
Lemon granita with summer berries and *crumiri*

WEDNESDAY, SEPTEMBER 1 $59
Marinated local sardines and roasted peppers with eggplant tapenade
Corn and shell bean soup with lobster, tomatoes, and fresh coriander seeds
Mixed grill of Cattail Creek lamb: loin, rack, and garlic sausage; with Chino Ranch lima beans,
    green beans, and potato fritters
Plum *jalousie* tart with cardamom ice cream

THURSDAY, SEPTEMBER 2 $59
Salt cod fritters and fried beets with frisée and basil oil
Tagliatelle with artichokes, sweet peppers, and anchovy
Paine Farm squab salad with giblets and bacon en brochette, new potatoes, cipollini onions,
    and sweet and sour figs
Warm chocolate fondant with raspberry ice cream and brandied raspberries

FRIDAY, SEPTEMBER 3 $69
An aperitif
Lobster salad with green beans and cherry tomatoes
Chino Ranch corn pudding soufflé with fresh lima beans and chervil
Grilled duck breast with roasted figs and pearl onions, garden lettuces, and straw potato cake
Almond crêpe with noyau ice cream and warm peaches

SATURDAY, SEPTEMBER 4 $69
An aperitif
Roasted pepper, chanterelle, hazelnut, and green bean salad
Steamed Atlantic cod with wild fennel and *poutargue*
Grilled Keene Summit lamb with Richard Olney's eggplant fans, Russian banana fingerling
    potatoes, and olive sauce
Fig *tarte en bande* with crème fraîche ice cream

Service charge: 15 percent	Corkage: $18	Sales tax: 8.25 percent
1517 Shattuck Avenue, Berkeley, California 94709		Reservations: (510) 548-5525

Most of our produce and meat comes from local farms and ranches that practice ecologically sound agriculture.
Other fish varieties may have to be substituted.

■   FIGURE 7–8

**At Chez Panisse, in Berkeley, California, only the finest fresh and organic ingredients
are used. Courtesy Alice Waters**

TO CELEBRATE OUR 28TH BIRTHDAY,
MONDAY DINNERS IN AUGUST AND SEPTEMBER WILL FEATURE
SPECIAL FOUR COURSE MENUS FOR $59.

♦♦♦

CHEZ PANISSE

DOWNSTAIRS MONDAY NIGHT DINNERS

♦♦♦

September 6
Closed for Labor Day

September 13
Capra con patate arrostite
Ligurian-style kid goat with little potatoes
roasted in the coals; with wild thyme and vermentino wine

September 20
Poisson grillé à la façon de Lulu
Lulu Peyraud's whole striped bass grilled in fig leaves
over a wood fire; with caper and herb sauce and roasted potatoes

September 27
Osso buco alla milanese
Range-fed veal shank and marrow bone braised
with tomatoes, garlic, and white wine; with saffron risotto

■   **FIGURE 7–8**

Continued

They balanced the higher-cost menu items and waste, which made it possible to achieve the target cost of 33%—provided the percentage of lower food-cost items sold was the higher.

Steakhouses came along, and their operators saw that the traditional factor markup did not apply. Steaks could be purchased pre-cut and sold at a price that would permit a 40% food cost, or higher, and still the operation was successful. The reason was that the labor cost in preparing and serving steak ran 15 to 20%, or even less, as a percentage of sales. The lower labor cost permitted a higher food cost.

Operators use food and labor costs as a combination known as "prime cost," which should be close to 55 to 60% of sales. This allows for a 15 to 20% operating profit.

The food-cost percentage is the most frequently quoted percentage in the restaurant business. It is generally calculated weekly or monthly.

The method of calculating a simple food-cost percentage is:

Opening inventory + Purchases − Closing inventory = Cost of food consumed
Food cost/Sales of food = Food-cost percentage

Opening inventory	$10,000
+ Purchases	$66,666 purchases + storeroom requisitions
Total food consumed	$76,660
− Closing inventory	$10,000
= Cost of food consumed	$66,666

If total sales were $200,000 for the month, the food cost of $66,666 divided into the $200,000 would produce a food cost of 33%. This is a basic calculation, which becomes more complex when transfers, returns, breakages, mistakes, customer returns, spillage, employee meals, promotional meals, and so on are factored into the equation.

The method of calculating a more complex food cost percentage is:

Opening inventory + Purchases = Total available for sale
− Returns to supplier
+ Cooking liquor
− Lounge and bar food (promotional and giveaway)
− Promotional food
= Cost of food

Taking a food inventory is time consuming and complicated. The storeroom and kitchen must be orderly to make the work of the auditor or inventory taker easier. One method requires that prices be marked on the food items or recorded in the inventory computer file or a book.

SUMMARY

The menu and menu planning are the most crucial elements of the restaurant. The many considerations in menu planning help us realize the scope and depth of general planning necessary for successful operation. The two main approaches to menu pricing strategies are comparative and individual dish costing. Contribution margins vary from item to item, with the higher food cost percentage items yielding the greater contribution margin.

The various types of menus and menu items are discussed together with menu design and layout.

KEY TERMS AND CONCEPTS

Considerations in menu planning	Nutritional value
Capability/Consistency	Contribution margin
Equipment	Accuracy in menu
Availability	Menu items
Price	Menu types

Food cost percentage   Menu analysis
Menu pricing strategies   Menu design and layout

REVIEW QUESTIONS

1. How would you prioritize the considerations in menu planning for your restaurant?
2. There is a tradeoff between a fully qualified chef and higher costs. How can a balance be achieved to leave a reasonable return for the owners?
3. To achieve maximum efficiency in your restaurant's kitchen, who should be involved? The menu?
4. Discuss how the equipment and menu must harmonize to create a smooth operation.
5. Ask several restaurant owners/managers how they arrived at their menu prices and compare their answers with the methods suggested in the text.
6. Use sample menus to analyze the following:

   How many items are in each course?

   What equipment will be required for each?

   Select a few items and determine what you would expect their food cost percentage to be.
7. How seriously should restaurant operators become involved with the nutritional content of foods chefs serve?
8. Describe the sources of the menu items that will be featured on your menu.
9. Describe how your menu will look when presented to guests.
10. What will your restaurant food cost percentage be? How will you achieve it?

ENDNOTES

[1] Jaqueline Dulen, "Quality," *Restaurants and Institutions*. 33, no. 7 (15 February 1999).

[2] Paula Disbrowe, "Plate Expectations," *Restaurant Business* 33, no. 15 (8 April 1999).

[3] Madrall Sanson, "Bright Lights Big City," *Restaurant Hospitality* 82, no. 1 (1998): 45.

[4] John Correll, "Pie R. Square," *Pizza Today* 15, no. 7 (July 1997).

[5] John Mariani, *American Eats Out* (New York: Morrow, 1991), 265–266.

[6] Anne Fletcher, "The Nutritional Goodness of Seafood," *Restaurant Hospitality* 74, no. 2 (February 1990): 162–714.

[7] Anonymous, "Healthy Option," *Restaurant Hospitality* 75, no. 2 (February 1991): 95, 98.

[8] Cecile Lamalle, "Vegetarian Fare," *Restaurant Hospitality* 75, no. 12 (December 1991): 106–119.

[9] Lendal H. Kotscherar, *Management by Menu* (New York: John Wiley and Sons, 1987), 50.

[10] Cathy Nash Holley, *Flavor and the Menu* (Tigard, Ore.: Media Unlimited, 1999).

[11] A. Elizabeth Sloan, "The Taste Of Tomorrow," *Flavor and the Menu* (Tigard, Ore.: Media Unlimited, 1999), 13.

[12] Helen Bauch, "Savoring Flavor: A Primer," *Flavor and the Menu* (Tigard, Ore.: Media Unlimited, 1999), 29.

[13] Tori Rogers, "What Inspires Flavor and How It Evolves," *Flavor and The Menu* (Tigard, Ore.: Media Unlimited, 1999), 60.

[14] Anonymous. "Contest winners," *Restaurant Hospitality* 83, no. 4 (April 1999): 46–52.

[15] French's Toddle Tot Promotion, P.O. Box 4403, Springfield, MO 65808-4403.

16 Mohamed E. Bayou and Lee B. Bennett, "Profitability Analysis for Table-Service Restaurants," *Cornell Hotel and Restaurant Administration Quarterly* 33, no. 2 (April 1992): 49–55.

17 Alan Gould, letter from the publisher, "The New Tastemakers," *Nations Restaurant News* 33, no. 4 (January 1999): 5.

18 David Pavesic, "Taking the Anxiety Out of Menu Pricing," *Restaurant Management* 2, no. 2 (February 1988): 56–57.

19 David Farkas, "Parker's Goes Casual, with Some Tasty Results," The Plain Dealer Publishing Company, July 24, 1998.

20 Information supplied by Charlie Trotter's Restaurant, Chicago, 22 November 1999.

21 Albin G. Seaberg, *Menu Design, Merchandising, and Marketing*, 4th ed. (New York: Van Nostrand Reinhold, 1991), 18.

22 National Restaurant Association, "Salads Soaring in Popularity, Study Finds," 10 August 1998.

23 *Ibid.*

24 This section draws on Harvey Steiman, "Made for Each Other," *Wine Spectator* 24, no. 11 (31 October 1999). pp 45–71.

25 "Table Service Restaurant Trends 1999." National Restaurant Association News Release, 15 August 1999.

26 Michael Sanson, "Will It Fly?" *Restaurant Hospitality.* 82, no. 183 (March 1998): 13.

27 Gould, "The New Tastemaker."

Chapter **8**

After reading and studying this chapter,
you should be able to:

Explain how to obtain an alcoholic beverage license.

Assist in the planning of a bar setup.

Suggest wines to accompany menu items.

Know the restaurant's liability under the law regarding the sale of alcoholic beverages.

*List ways in which bartenders and others can defraud the restaurant bar
and beverage operation.*

BAR AND BEVERAGES

Given today's social concerns about alcoholic beverage consumption and the high costs of litigation, creating and operating a restaurant bar and beverage operation presents challenges. By creating a convivial place for responsible alcoholic beverage service—one with a pleasant atmosphere that reflects the furnishings, decor, lighting, music, and service—restaurateurs can offer a place for relaxation, socialization, and entertainment. In some restaurants, bars are used as focal point or a centerpiece; TGI Friday's is an example. Others, like the Olive Garden, use the bar more as a holding area.

Beverage sales in restaurants can account for a significant portion of total sales. Today, a reasonable split is about 25 to 30% beverage sales and 70 to 75% food sales. A ratio any higher than this in favor of beverage sales will attract undue attention from the Department of Alcoholic Beverage Control (ABC)—as well as prosecuting attorneys in court during a "driving under the influence" (DUI) case!

The bar at Roy's New York City welcomes guests to a restaurant with a multiaward-winning wine list to match the Hawaiian-inspired Euro-Asian cuisine. Photo © Paul Warchol

Beverage sales yield more profit than food sales—a bottle of wine simply needs storage for a few days, then opening. A bottle of wine may be purchased for $6.00 and sold for $15.00–18.00. A measure of Scotch may cost 36 cents and sell for $3.50. The cost of production is much less in the bar than in the kitchen; consequently, the margins are greater.

ALCOHOLIC BEVERAGE LICENSES

Each state has a Department of Alcoholic Beverage Control. In California, for example, the department was created by constitutional amendment as an executive branch of the state government. The Director of Alcoholic Beverage Control heads the department and is appointed by the governor. The department has the exclusive power, in accordance with laws enacted, to license and regulate the manufacture, importation, and sale of all alcoholic beverages in the state.

A license issued under the ABC Act is a permit to do that which would otherwise be unlawful. Such a license is not a matter of right but is a privilege that can be suspended or revoked by administration because of violation of the act or department rule. The types of retail licenses are:

- *On-sale general.* Authorizes the sale of all types of alcoholic beverages—namely, beer, wine, and distilled spirits—for consumption on the premises.
- *Off-sale general.* Authorizes the sale of all types of alcoholic beverages for consumption off the premises in original, sealed containers.
- *On-sale beer and wine.* Authorizes the sale on the premises of all types of beer, wine, and malt liquor.
- *Off-sale beer and wine.* Authorizes the sale of all types of beer, wine, and malt beverages for consumption off the premises in original containers.
- *On-sale beer.* Authorizes the sale on the licensed premises of beer and other malt beverages with an alcoholic content of 4% or less by weight.

HOW TO APPLY FOR A LICENSE

For restaurants, there are two main kinds of alcoholic beverage licenses: a general liquor license and a beer and wine license. Both licenses must be applied for from the state liquor authority. The application process can be lengthy—up to several weeks—and may not always be a smooth ride. States have jurisdiction over the sale of alcohol and some are more stringent than others in granting licenses. For new licenses, states like New York, which is liberal when it comes to granting licenses, are quite different from neighboring New Jersey, which is stricter. In New Jersey, the number of new licenses is limited to the increase in population. In addition, new licenses must not only be approved by the state but also by city officials.

In order to be granted a license, certain regulations must be met. In California, for example, to obtain a general license, a person must find a licensed restaurant or an ABC license for sale and purchase it. When the restaurant is purchased, the license becomes part of the escrow. The current price of a license is $15,000 to $20,000. Licenses can be moved within but not outside the county. Once an application is filed, an investigation is conducted to ensure that the applicant is not a felon nor on probation.

Notices stating that a license has been applied for must be placed in the newspaper and in the window of the restaurant. This notice must be posted for a minimum of 30 days. After 45 days, providing there are no protests by residents, the police department, the sheriffs' department, or others, and assuming the zoning allows it, a conditional-use permit is issued.

Once a license is obtained, liquor may be purchased only from a wholesaler or manufacturer. Each state and county has its own regulations and prospective restaurateurs should consult with their respective ABC departments for relevant local information.

BAR LAYOUT AND DESIGN

Deciding on the bar layout and design can be intimidating for most people. Novices have made costly mistakes by overlooking important aspects. If you can afford to hire a specialist in restaurant design, then do so—but make sure the person has experience in planning bars. Alternatively, have a bartender look over the plans to double check the practicality of the proposed bar.

A number of factors affect bar location and the design of restaurant bars:

- The type of restaurant
- The overall design and layout of the restaurant
- The intended prominence of the bar
- The number of bartenders required to operate the bar and beverage service
- The volume of business expected
- The degree of self-sufficiency of the bar
- The electric and water supply

A restaurant front bar showing the well, where popular drinks are stored for quick service

A restaurant back bar displaying a selection of beverages

- The construction costs of providing electric and water supply
- The distance to the storeroom and the dispensing system
- The location of the beer kegs and cooling equipment

Restaurant operators have a constant dilemma of balancing the ideal bar setup with their particular situation. Should the bar be along a wall or in the center of the room? In most restaurants, it is less costly to set up the bar along a wall. Center bars may be suitable for some high-volume restaurants but, unless they are well planned and built with expensive cabinetry, can look unsightly to guests.

The bar setup is divided into three areas: the front bar, the back bar, and the under bar. The front bar is both the place where guests may belly up to the counter and where the bartender prepares drinks. The workstation has storage space for equipment, beverages, speed racks, ice, and glasses.

The back bar—usually the back wall of the bar—is for aesthetics and functions as a storage and display area. The lower part houses refrigerated storage cabinets and the upper part often has a mirror or other decor and a display of premium-brand liquors. The sales volume will determine the amount of refrigerated storage space required. One refrigerator may be required for wine and a separate one for beer. Most restaurants use the back bar to add atmosphere by displaying premium spirits and liqueurs. This display is a form of subliminal advertising.

The under bar is the part where the bartender prepares the drinks; it includes the part under the front counter. The main equipment in the under bar is the speed rack, which contains the well or pouring brands. It should be located in a convenient position to allow the bartender to work quickly and efficiently. The speed rack is generally centrally located at waist level. The speed rack holds several of the most popular pouring brands: Scotch whisky (2 bottles), bourbon, vodka (2 bottles), gin, (2 bottles) rum, tequila, vermouth (2 bottles), and cordials.

Shane Dudley demonstrating his skill at cocktail making

Only restaurants with very high volume have an ice machine at the bar; most have one in or near the kitchen. However, a sanitary ice bin is critical for a bar operation. The ice bin may require drainage; however, smaller restaurants manage with a bus pan lined with a plastic bag. Above the ice bin is an area where the bartender places glasses during the preparation of drinks. Kegs of draft beer may be located either under the bar or in a nearby storeroom. The name and logo of the beer is usually displayed on a pull handle supplied by the distributor and located in view of the guests on the bar counter or, occasionally, on the back bar counter. For draft beer to be at its best, the plastic lines from the keg need to be cleaned each week with a cleansing agent to remove any buildup of impurities.

PLACEMENT OF A BAR WITHIN A RESTAURANT

As so many things do, the location of a bar within the restaurant depends on the target market. Is it made up of the working class or some other demographic group? Is the bar to be featured by bright lighting or is it to be a service bar located out of public view? Is the bar seating made up of stools and is the bar stock of bottles to be prominently displayed? Will wine be displayed separately in a temperature-controlled glassed-in section? How many chairs will the bar have?

The floor plan of Roy's New York restaurant shows the bar as item 6, located so that it has easy access from the entrance (item 1). If the restaurant operator wants to highlight the bar, it is usually prominently lighted and placed near the restaurant entrance. At Roy's New York, the layout is such that display cooking (item is in the drawing) backs up the kitchen (item 8). Item 5 is a pizza oven. Some bars provide comfortable seating in which customers can relax. Most bars seat customers on small bar stools that almost require the customer to lean on the bar. The seats are placed close enough to encourage conversation.

THE SPEED GUN

The speed gun is used in bars as a pouring device that conveniently lets the bartender mix routine drinks. The speed gun can pour soda, juices, sweet and sour mix, and so on. The average gun contains two sodas (usually Coke and a clear soda like Sprite), a juice (cranberry juice, lemonade, or orange juice), soda water, ginger ale, and tonic. A speed gun is located at each drink-making station. The device enables bartenders to make

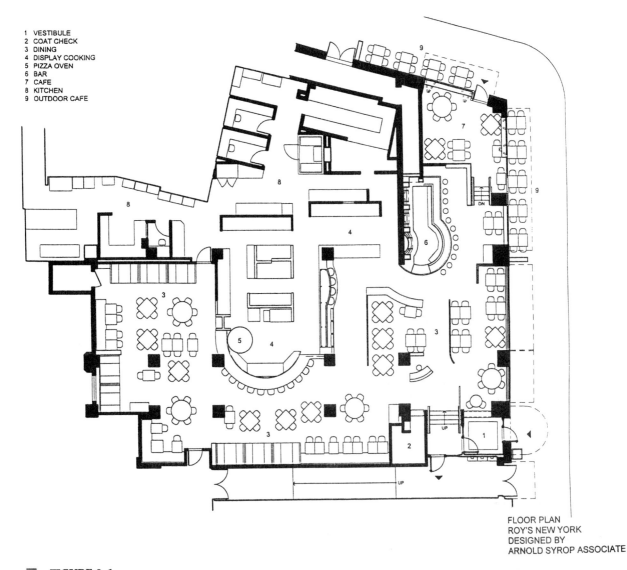

1 VESTIBULE
2 COAT CHECK
3 DINING
4 DISPLAY COOKING
5 PIZZA OVEN
6 BAR
7 CAFE
8 KITCHEN
9 OUTDOOR CAFE

FLOOR PLAN
ROY'S NEW YORK
DESIGNED BY
ARNOLD SYROP ASSOCIATE

FIGURE 8–1

Roy's New York floor plan

drinks quickly because all the mixers are in one dispenser, which allows the pouring of the alcohol and the mixer at the same time. This expedites the drink-making process.

GLASS WASHING

Glasses may be washed by a machine, which is normally housed under the bar counter, or in a three-compartment sink. In either case, a holding place is required to store glasses waiting to be washed. The reason for the three-compartment sink is sanitation. The first sink has a brush, is filled with hot water, and has a special cleansing agent for bar glassware. The middle sink has a clear, hot rinse, and the third sink has a sanitizing germicide agent. Finally, a space with a rubber mat is provided for glasses to drain on. Glasses are best air-dried.

BARTENDERS

The recruitment and selection of a great bartender is, obviously, critical to the success of the beverage operation of a restaurant. In addition to preparing and serving cocktails, maintaining good guest relations, and keeping the bar clean and well organized, bartenders are responsible for:

1. Always abiding by the state laws associated with operating a liquor license
2. Properly handling guest problems that arise at the bar
3. Maintaining an established liquor cost
4. Controlling the liquor inventory
5. Taking cash and operating a cash register
6. Seeing that all employees follow the house rules pertaining to the bar
7. Overseeing cocktail servers ordering and garnishing cocktails
8. Attending and giving responsible alcoholic beverage training courses[1]

During the morning shift, bartenders cut fruit, make mixes for drinks like piña coladas and margaritas, set up the bar, and prepare for service. They count the cash and place it in the till. The swing shift comes on duty at 4:00 P.M. and stays through the happy hour and evening rush. The closing shift comes on duty at 6:00 P.M. and continues the service of guests until closing. They also stock the bar and make out requisitions. Many restaurants require bartenders to first spend time on the floor of the restaurant as a food server in order to become familiar with the restaurant and its operational procedures.

Prerequisites for successful bartenders are possession of a positive attitude, the ability to talk to people, honesty, patience, maturity, integrity, and the ability to make guests come back.

Go to several restaurant bars and watch the bartender, noting how many steps they require and how easy or difficult it is for them to make the drinks. This should help you set up your restaurant's bar.

A BASIC BAR INVENTORY

The selection of a basic bar inventory depends on the type of restaurant. For example, a trendy upscale restaurant will carry several premium brands that a neighborhood Italian restaurant will not. The basic inventory given on the next page is for a contemporary upscale restaurant of 80 seats in the historic area of a major convention city.

Wine by the glass	Robert Mondavi Woodbridge Red/White
	Kendall Jackson Chardonnay
	Cabernet Sauvignon
	Merlot
Champagne	Moët & Chandon
	Korbel
Sherry	
Cognac	
Gin	Tanqueray, Gordon's
Vermouth	Martini & Rossi Red/White
Vodka	Smirnoff
	Absolut
	Golden Goose
Rum	Bacardi
	Mount Gay
	Captain Morgan
Tequila	Cuervo
	Sauza Hornitos
Scotch whiskey	House
	Johnnie Walker Red/Black
	Chivas Regal
Rye whiskey	
Cordials and liqueurs	Bailey's
	Grand Marnier
	Chambord
Draft beer	Budweiser
	Samuel Adams
Bottled beer	Budweiser
	Bud Light
	Samuel Adams
	Heineken
	Corona
Soda	Pepsi
	Diet Pepsi
	Sprite
	Dr. Pepper
Bottled water	Evian
	Perrier
Juice	Orange
	Cranberry
	Pineapple
	Tomato

A WINE LIST

Figure 8–2 illustrates the wine list of an upscale contemporary restaurant. The number of bottles offered in each category is perfect for this restaurant.

Wine List

Champagne and Sparkling Wine

	Glass	Bottle
Veuve Clicquot Ponsardin		75.00
Veuve Clicquot Ponsardin (1/2 bottle)	14.00	37.50
Tattinger "La Française" Brut		70.00
Roederer Estate "L'Ermitage" Brut '93		65.00
Moet & Chandon "White Star"		60.00
Iron Horse "Wedding Cuvee" '96		50.00
Jordan Vineyards "J" '94		45.00
Roederer Estate Brut	11.00	42.00
Domaine St. Michelle Brut	6.00	22.00

Chardonnay

	Glass	Bottle
Rutz Cellars "Dutton Ranch" '96		60.00
Chalk Hill Estate '97		60.00
Chalone, Monterey County '97		50.00
Jordan, Sonoma County, '97		50.00
Ferrari Carano, Alexander Valley '97		48.00
Stonestreet, Sonoma '96	12.00	46.00
ZD, Napa '97		45.00
Steele, California '97		46.00
Sonoma-Cutrer Russian River Ranches '98	10.00	38.00
La Crema, Sonoma '97		36.00
Silverado, Napa '97		36.00
Bernardus, Carmel Valley '97		36.00
Clos Pegase, Napa '97		34.00
Cambria, "Katherine's Vineyard", '98		32.00
J. Lohr, Monterrey '98	8.00	30.00
Benzinger Carneros, Sonoma '98		30.00
Chateau St. Jean, Sonoma '98	7.50	28.00
Beringer "Founders Estate" '98	7.50	26.00
Presidio, Santa Barbara '98		24.00
Flora Springs, Napa Valley '98	6.00	22.00

Sauvignon Blanc and Fume Blanc

	Glass	Bottle
Sauvignon Blanc, Cloudy Bay, New Zealand '99		39.00
Fume Blanc, Grgich Hills, Napa Valley '97		38.00
Sauvignon Blanc, Gainey, Santa Ynez Valley'97		36.00
Sauvignon Blanc, Matanzas Creek, Sonoma '98		33.00
Fume Blanc, Ferrari-Carano, Sonoma '98	8.50	32.00
Sauvignon Blanc, Villa Maria, New Zealand '99	7.00	26.00
Sauvignon Blanc, Markham, Napa '98		22.00

Selected White and Blush

	Glass	Bottle
Pinot Grigio, Santa Margherita, Italy '98		38.00
Pinot Blanc, Saddleback Cellars '98	9.50	36.00
Viogner, Cambria, Tepusquet Vineyard '98	9.00	34.00
Pinot Gris, Willamette, Oregon '97	8.50	32.00
Riesling, J. Lohr, Central Coast '98	6.00	22.00
White Zinfandel, Beringer, Napa '98	5.50	21.00

Vintages Subject To Change

Wine List

Cabernet Sauvignon

	Glass	Bottle
Jordan, Alexander Valley '95		75.00
Napa Valley Wine Company, Napa '96		60.00
St. Clement, Napa '96		53.00
Clos Pegase, Napa '97		50.00
Freemark Abbey, Napa '95		50.00
Pine Ridge Rutherford, Napa '96		48.00
Alexander Valley Vineyard "Wetzel Estate" '97	11.00	42.00
Beaulieu Vineyards, Rutherford, Napa '96		36.00
Lockwood, Monterey '96	9.00	34.00
Beringer "Founders Estate" '97	7.00	26.00
Beaulieu Vineyard "Coastal", Napa '97	6.50	24.00

Zinfandel

	Glass	Bottle
Edmeades " Ciapusci Vineyard", Mendocino '96		65.00
Kunde "Century Vines", Sonoma '96		45.00
Grgich Hills Cellar, Napa '96		38.00
Storybook Mountain "Mayacamas Range" Estate '97		33.00
Chateau Souverain, Dry Creek Valley '97	8.00	30.00

Merlot

	Glass	Bottle
Chalk Hill Estate '96		70.00
Clos Du Val, Napa '96		60.00
ZD, Napa Valley '97		55.00
St. Francis, Sonoma '97		50.00
Franciscan "Oakville Estate", Napa '97	12.00	46.00
Markham, Napa '97		40.00
Voss, Napa '97		38.00
Kunde, Sonoma '97		36.00
Chateau Ste. Michelle, Washington '97		34.00
Presidio, Santa Barbara '98	8.00	30.00
Camelot Vineyards, California '96		28.00
Kenwood "Yulupa" '97	6.50	26.00

Pinot Noir

	Glass	Bottle
Acacia, Carneros '98		48.00
Wild Horse, Central Coast '97	12.00	46.00
Sanford, Central Coast '97		45.00
Saintsbury, Carneros '98		42.00
La Crema, Sonoma '97		36.00
Presidio, Santa Barbara '97	9.00	34.00
Van Duzer, Oregon '97		32.00
Kenwood, Russian River Valley '98	8.00	30.00
Eola Hills, Oregon '97	7.50	28.00

Selected Red

	Glass	Bottle
Petite Syrah, Stags Leap, Napa '96		55.00
Sangiovese, Venge "Family Reserve", Napa '97		49.00

Vintages Subject To Change

FIGURE 8–2

A wine list from Blue Point Coastal Cuisine, San Diego. Courtesy The Cohn Restaurant Group

Proprietors Reserve List

Champagne
Louis Roederer Cristal '93	275.00
Perrier Jouet "Fleur de Champagne" Rose '88	225.00
Moet & Chandon "Dom Perignon" '92	200.00
Veuve Cliquot "La Grande Dame" '89	160.00
Salon "Blanc de Blancs" '88	150.00
Veuve Cliquot "Gold Label" '93	85.00

Chardonnay
Far Niente, Napa '97	80.00
Kistler, Sonoma Coast '98	80.00
Mer Soleil, Central Coast '96	78.00
Arrowood "Cuvee Michel Berthoud" '97	75.00
Silverado "Limited Reserve", Napa '96	75.00
Steele "Durell Vineyard" '96	70.00
Merryvale "Reserve", Napa '97	58.00
Plumpjack "Reserve", Napa '97	55.00
Sonoma-Cutrer "Les Pieres" '97	55.00

Pinot Noir
Ponzi "Reserve", Willamette Valley '96	80.00
Chalone, Monterey County '98	60.00
Bear Boat, Russian River '96	40.00

Cabernet Sauvignon
Lokoya, Mount Veeder '95	175.00
Caymus, Napa '96	130.00
Grgich Hills Cellars '91	125.00
Silver Oak, Napa Valley '94	125.00
Kenwood "Artist Series", Sonoma '94	125.00
Kenwood "Artist Series", Sonoma '95	120.00
Kenwood "Artist Series", Sonoma '93	115.00
Silverado "Limited Reserve", Napa '95	115.00
Silver Oak, Alexander Valley '95	100.00
Bell Cellars "Baritelle Vineyard", Napa '94	100.00
Grgich Hills Cellars '94	100.00
Heitz Cellars "Trailside", Napa '94	90.00
Girard Reserve, Napa Valley '94	90.00
Staglin, Napa Valley '96	85.00
Altamura, Napa Valley '95	80.00
Frazier "Lupine Hill Vineyard", Napa '95	75.00
Chateau Ste. Jean "Cinq Cépages", Sonoma '96	75.00
Saddleback, Napa '96	65.00

Meritage
Opus One, Napa '96	190.00
Stonestreet Legacy '96	150.00
Conn Creek, "Anthology" '94	140.00
Cain Five, Napa Valley '95	125.00
Merryvale "Profile" '96	110.00
Lancaster Reserve, Alexander Valley '95	115.00
Metisse, Napa Valley '95	90.00
Flora Springs "Trilogy", Napa '96	80.00
Spring Mountain, Napa '96	85.00
Bernardus "Marinus", Carmel Valley '95	70.00

Merlot
Chalk Hill Estate '95	75.00
Matanzas Creek '96	75.00
Jade Mountain "Caldwell Vineyards" '97	60.00
Fisher Vineyards "RCF" '95	60.00
Newlan "Reserve", Napa '94	50.00
Pride Mountain Vineyards '96	48.00

Vintages Subject To Change

After Dinner List

Port
Warre's '77	36.00
Dow "Silver Jubilee" '77	30.00
Dow "Quinta do Bonfim" '84	26.00
Dow '97	23.00
Dow '85	21.00
Warre's 97	20.00
Warre's '85	18.00
Warre's '68 Tawny	14.00
Fonseca 20 year Tawny	11.00
Sonoma Portworks Deco	9.00
Taylor LBV '94	8.00
Graham's Six Grapes	7.00
Sandeman Reserve N/V	7.00
Fonseca Bin 27	7.00

Dessert Wine
Dolce by Far Niente	21.00
Grgich Hills Violetta	17.00

Grappa
Ornellaia Grappa Di Merlot	14.00

Brandy and Calvados
Raynal VSOP Napoleon	5.75
Calvados, Busnel VSOP	8.00

Cognac and Armangnac
Louis XIII	125.00
Paradis	55.00
Hennessey XO	20.00
Martell Cordon Bleu	17.50
Delemain Pale & Dry	12.00
A. de Fussigny "Cigar Blend"	10.00
Janneau Reserve De La Maison	9.00
Hennessey VSOP	8.00
Remy Martin VSOP	8.00
Courvosier VS	6.00

Scotch
Johnnie Walker "Blue Label"	22.50
Macallan 18 Year	14.00
Lagavulin 16 Year	10.00
Glenmorangie Port Wood	10.00
Glenmorangie Madeira Wood	10.00
Glenmorangie Sherry Wood	10.00
Laphroig Islay Malt 15 Year	8.50
Talisker Skye Malt 10 Year	8.50
Oban 14 Year	8.00
Glenfiddich	8.00
Glenlivet	8.00

Bourbon
Bookers Small Batch	8.00
Bakers Small Batch 7 Year	8.00
Blanton's Single Barrell 12 Year	7.50
Basil Hayden's 8 Year	7.50
Crown Royal Reserve	7.50
Woodford Reserve	7.50
Knob Creek Small Batch 9 Year	7.00

Tequila
Herradura Seleccion Suprema	25.00
Jose Cuervo La Familia Reserva	10.00
Don Julio Anejo	8.50
Chinaco Anejo	8.00
Chinaco Anejo	8.00
Patron Anejo	8.00
Patron Silver	8.00
Sauza Tres Generaciones	7.50

■   **FIGURE 8–2**

Continued

WINES WITH FOOD

The combination of great food and wine is one of life's greatest pleasures. Today, anything goes, meaning that if a guest wants a red wine with a white meat, that's OK. Patrons should feel comfortable with any choice of wine with a meal. A restaurateur may want to be able to give advice as to what wine best complements a certain dish. Over the years, experience has shown that:

- White wine is best served with white meat—pork, turkey, chicken, veal, fish, and shellfish.
- Red wine is best served with red meat—beef, lamb, duck, and game.
- Champagne can be served throughout the meal.
- Port and red wine go well with cheese.
- Dessert wines, which tend to be sweeter than others, best complement desserts and fresh fruits that are not highly acidic.

Charlie Trotter offers an incredible selection of wine, including some 30 by the glass, to complement the dining experience. Courtesy Charlie Trotter

- When a dish is cooked in wine, it is best served with that wine.

- Regional food is best served with wine of the same region.

- Wines are best not served with salads with vinegar dressings, chocolate, or strong curries, all of which are too strong or acidic for it.

Food and wine are described by flavor and texture. Textures are the qualities in food and wine that we feel in the mouth, such as softness, smoothness, roundness, richness, thinness, creaminess, chewiness, oiliness, harshness, etc. Textures correspond to sensations of touch and temperature, which we can easily identify—for example, hot, cold, rough, smooth, thin, or thick. Regarding the marrying of food and wine, light food with light wine is always a reliable combination. Rich food with a full-bodied wine can be wonderful as long as the match is not too rich. The two most important qualities to consider when choosing the appropriate wine are richness and lightness.

Flavors are food and wine elements perceived by the olfactory nerves as fruity, minty, herbal, nutty, cheesy, smoky, flowery, earthy, and so on. A person determines flavors by using the nose as well as the tongue. The combination of texture and flavor is what makes food and wine a pleasure to enjoy; a good match between the food and wine can make special occasions even more memorable. Some restaurants offer wine tastings as special promotional events.

RESPONSIBLE ALCOHOLIC BEVERAGE SERVICE

Managing alcohol risks by practicing responsible alcoholic beverage service is vital to ensuring guest safety and the bottom line. Creating a responsible alcoholic beverage service program is in itself a powerful lawsuit defense. The following guidelines from the American Hotel and Motel Association's *Lodging* magazine focuses on safety and lawsuit preparedness.

1. Physically write a responsible alcohol serving mission statement outlining your position on drinking and safety. Once the mission is written down, the operator has a basis from which to complete the policy and plan.

2. Review local and state liquor laws.

3. Assess the operation's clientele.

4. Make a plan for developing and maintaining relationships with law enforcement officials and transportation organizations.

5. Establish a comprehensive program of ongoing staff training.

6. Create a schedule of management audits of policy and practice.

7. Create a system of actions that demonstrates support for responsible and enjoyable drinking.

Responsible alcoholic beverage service programs should also include responsible actions—for instance, having a trained person at the door to check IDs for proof of age, to discourage patrons from leaving with alcohol, and to prevent intoxicated patrons from driving. Restaurant and bar operators need to encourage a designated driver program, offering free or reduced-cost nonalcoholic drinks to a driver. Also, post taxi numbers next to the pay phone and provide them to servers for use with intoxicated guests. Another good practice is to encourage food consumption. Finally, record all incidents of concern to the server, noting the time of day, date, situation, management/server response, patron identity (if known), alternative transportation offered, and names and addresses of witnesses. The report helps form a defense strategy and provides a strong investigative tool.[2]

The National Restaurant Association's Barcode responsible for alcoholic beverage service program is highly recommended as a further method of training employees on the law and responsibilities of alcoholic beverage service, how alcohol affects the body, and techniques for responsible alcohol service and service in difficult situations.

THIRD-PARTY LIABILITY

Owners, managers, bartenders, and servers may be liable under the law if they serve alcohol to minors or to persons who are intoxicated. The penalty can be severe. The legislation that governs the sale of alcoholic beverages is called dram shop legislation. The dram shop laws, or civil damage acts, were enacted in the 1850s and dictated that owners of drinking establishments are liable for injuries caused by intoxicated customers.[3]

To combat underage drinking in restaurants and bars, a major brewery distributed to licensed establishments a booklet showing the authentic design and layout of each state's driver's license. Trade associations, like the National Restaurant Association and the American Hotel and Motel Association, have, together with other major corporations, produced a number of preventive measures and programs aimed at responsible alcohol beverage service. The major thrust of these initiatives is awareness programs and mandatory training programs like TIPS (Training for Intervention Procedures by Servers) that promote responsible alcohol service. TIPS, sponsored by the National Restaurant Association, is a certification program that teaches participants about alcohol and its effects on people, the common signs of intoxication, and how to help customers avoid drinking too much.

Responsible alcohol service programs offer a bonus to operators: a reduction in insurance premiums and legal fees, which have skyrocketed.[4]

CONTROLS

If the liquor inventory is not properly controlled, losses from spillage, theft, and honest mistakes can seriously affect the restaurant's bottom line, so think of a liquor bottle as a $100 bill and guard it accordingly. The loss or smuggling of liquor occurs in virtually all restaurants. It is safer to assume that, given a chance, people will steal it one way or another.

To avoid or solve liquor control problems, institute a weekly or biweekly audit. This may be done by an outside auditor, which is recommended for larger and higher-volume restaurants, or internally, with the correct equipment. For the large or high-volume restaurants, the audit begins with a physical count of all open and full bottles of liquor and wine, and beer kegs are weighed. Any other inventory, such as bottled beers and cordials, are counted. The sales and purchase figures are factored in, and the auditor is able to calculate the pouring-cost percentage. The source and volume of lost liquor may then be identified and a plan developed to investigate the losses and prevent reoccurrence.

Restaurants that use an external audit service receive a printout each week giving management/owners the information they need to target problem areas. Generally, the outcome is a reduction in smuggling and an increase in net savings. The cost of audits range from $150 to $250, depending on the site of the inventory and frequency of audits.

For operators who want to conduct their own audit and calculate liquor pouring cost, suppliers offer systems that use a PC, a portable scale, and a bar-code scanner. The cost for this is about $4,000 for the scale, $3,000 for the software, and $500 for installation. This may seem expensive for small restaurants; however, larger ones have reported recovering the initial cost of the system in six to nine months.[5]

Controlling Losses

Several other common sense measures can be incorporated into the control of the bar and beverage operation.

- Limit bar access to bartenders and make them accountable for the pouring-cost results.
- Give incentive bonuses for good results.
- Require that drink orders be rung into the register before the drinks are made.
- Use a remote system in which servers must ring up the order before it goes to the bartender.
- Install a video camera.
- Install an alarm on the bar door.
- Do not allow bags to be brought into the bar.
- Provide lockers in another area.
- If bartenders make mistakes, have them written off and signed for by management.
- Cushion bar floors to reduce breakage.
- Set up a system that allows employees to anonymously report incidents.
- Be careful in hiring employees for the beverage operation; check references and do background checks.

99 Ways to Steal in a Restaurant or Bar

In the food and beverage industry, it is estimated that 25% of employees steal regardless of the controls in place; 25% will not steal regardless of the controls in place; and 50% will steal if given the opportunity. The controls in place in a restaurant determine whether 25% are stealing or 75% are. The *Practitioners Publishing Company's Guide to Restaurants and Bars*, which may be accessed via the Web at http://www.profitable. com/results/articles/011.html, suggests 99 ways to steal in a restaurant or bar. The imagination shown in stealing from bar operations is exceeded only by some lawyers when billing clients.

Cash Register

The Restaurant Owner Is the Victim

1. Serve the drinks and/or food and collect the money while the register is being closed out at the end of a shift or at night or when the ribbon or tape is being changed.

2. Phony walkout—keep the cash and claim that the customer left without paying.

3. Short ring—charge the customer the actual price, under-ring the sale on the cash register, and pocket the difference.

4. No sale—charge the customer the actual price but don't ring up the sale. Bartenders often put the cash into their tip jar or their pocket, or leave it in the cash drawer.

5. Phantom cash register—put an extra cash register in the bar during specific times (for example, during happy hour). Because the sales are not recorded on the master cash register tape, they can be skimmed by the perpetrator.

6. Short tape—some old cash registers do not have cumulative cash register readings. In those cases, the cashier can total the cash register at a point before the end of the shift and use a new tape until it is time to close out. Then the cashier can keep the new tape and the cash generated during that period.

7. Voided sales—the cashier voids the check or some of the items on the check and keeps the proceeds.

8. Over rings—the cashier records an over-ring to reverse an actual sale.

9. Generate fictitious paid-outs (paid-outs are amounts taken from the till to pay for beer and food deliveries, light bulbs, and other miscellaneous charges).

10. Alter the breakout of tip and check amounts on credit card receipts to overstate the tips and understate the checks.

11. Cashier accumulates guest checks and rings them up after the customers leave (amounts can be altered or tickets may be destroyed).

12. Cashier steals cash and covers it up by falsifying the cumulative cash register readings and destroying the tape.

13. If the wait person acts as banker, he or she can provide the customer with an old guest check and not record the current sale.

14. Cashier records sales on the training key, which does not feed into the cash register's daily or cumulative sales total.

15. Cash a hot check for friends.

16. Steal customers' checks made payable to cash.

17. Charge the customer full price but ring up the sale at the discounted child or senior citizen price.

18. Jam the cash drawer during critical hours so that it must be left open.

The Customer Is the Victim

19. Shortchange the customer (for example, by giving change for $10 instead $20).

20. Have the customer sign the credit card slip in advance and overcharge for food or drinks.

21. Alter amounts on credit card slips.

22. Run the credit card through twice.

Bar

The Restaurant Owner Is the Victim

23. Bartender does not ring up the sale.

24. Wait person acts as bank and sometimes does not ring up the sales (this generally is detected if there is a pre-check system).

25. Returned drinks—bartender claims that a drink was returned when, in fact, it was sold.

26. Give away—if no internal controls exist, the bartender might give away free drinks to friends or in anticipation of larger tips.

27. Undercharge for drinks in anticipation of larger tips.

28. Pour higher-quality liquor than ordered and mention it to the customer in anticipation of a larger tip.

29. Mislead the manager as to how many drinks have been sold from a keg (generally, control over kegs is lax because of the level of waste involved and the difficulty of inventorying the amount on hand).

30. Phantom bottle—bartender brings his or her own bottle of liquor and pockets the cash earned from its sale. This scheme is much more devastating than merely stealing a bottle of liquor because even though the cost of a stolen bottle is nominal (for example, $10), the lost margin on sales from the bottle is significant (for example, $90).

31. The bartender and the cocktail server collude to overcome the dual inventory control system. In a pre-check system, the cocktail server inputs the drink order and the bartender releases the drinks based on the documentation system. The two systems provide independent totals, which can be reconciled. However, if there is collusion, the server does not enter the drinks into the system but the bartender makes and releases them.

32. Barter—bartender trades the cook free drinks for free dinners.

33. Kickbacks—a liquor distributor provides kickbacks. Kickback schemes can be difficult to detect. For example, if the distributor offers to sell the bartender ten cases of vodka for the price of nine, the bartender receives the value of one case as a commission. The distributor will charge the restaurant for ten cases and ten cases will be delivered and counted.

34. Complimentary cocktail or wine coupons are stolen by waiters and sold to bartenders, who turn in the coupons to justify missing inventory. For example, the wine server buys a coupon for $5 and sells a bottle of wine to a customer for $25, reaping a net profit of $20.

35. After-shift drinks provided to employees but not consumed by them are sold to customers. For example, the restaurant has 40 workers who are entitled to one drink at the end of each shift. If only 15 of the drinks are consumed, the bartender can sell an extra 25 drinks and pocket the proceeds.

36. Provide free drinks to visiting bartenders.

37. Cook requests a beverage for use in the kitchen (such as brandy, wine, vermouth, sherry, or other cooking spirits) but drinks it instead.

38. Bartender does not secure the draft beer system at closing, which makes it available to after-hours workers.

39. Bartender lines through (redlines) service orders without ringing up the sales and rings them up later for a lower amount.

40. Handwrite bar tabs and ring up amounts less than receipts.

41. Steal bottles of liquor.

42. If the entity sells both drinks and full bottles, claim missing bottles are to-go sales. Because the margin on to-go liquor is generally less than on individual shot sales, this distorts the accuracy of the beverage-cost percentage.

43. Reuse old drink receipts.

44. Under-ring drinks recorded on a computerized liquor dispenser tied into a point-of-sale system by using a magnet to throw off the scale.

45. Ring up cash liquor sales on the service dining room key.

46. Ring up food sold in the bar on the liquor key to help create additional drink sales and throw off beverage-cost percentages.

The Customer Is the Victim

47. Short-pour—bartender pours less than a shot to cover up drinks given away or sold on the side. Some bartenders do this by bringing in a shot glass that is one ounce instead of an ounce and a quarter. Therefore, it appears that they are pouring a full measure when, in fact, they are short-pouring.

48. Short-pouring can also be done on a computerized dispenser system—the bartender dispenses and the system registers one shot; however, the bartender pours the liquor into two glasses.

49. Charge the customer the regular price but ring up the happy-hour price. (Many bartenders cover up the cash register display with pictures of their dog, boat, or children to keep the customer from noticing how much has been rung up).

50. Charge for complimentary happy-hour hors d'oeuvres and bar snacks.

51. Omit most of the liquor from blended fruit drinks (especially if several drinks have been served to the customer).

52. Pour a lower-quality liquor after the first few drinks and charge for the more expensive brand.

53. Charge the customer for more drinks than actually served.

54. Resell returned beverages. (If the customer leaves an expensive liqueur, the bartender may stack it in the back and resell it to the next customer.)

55. Steal the customer's change left on the bar. (Some employees wet the bottom of their drink trays and set them down on top of the customer's change. The cash sticks to the bottom of the tray.)

56. Add two customers' drinks together, charge both customers, and (if caught) claim to have misunderstood who was purchasing the round.

Food Service

The Restaurant Owner Is the Victim

57. Server collects directly from the customer without providing a guest check and pockets the cash.

58. Reuse old guest checks for similar orders and do not ring up the sale.

59. Collusion between the server and the cooks—server does not record order on the pre-check system, but the cooks make and issue the food without proper authorization.

60. Wait staff claims a meal was returned when, in fact, it was served and paid for.

61. Add items by hand to pre-checked guest checks. (When installing pre-check systems, some restaurants only pre-check entrées. Therefore, the wait staff can issue salads, appetizers, desserts, or wine and manually record the item on the bottom of the customer's check. The wait person collects the full amount and remits only the pre-checked amount.

62. Steal food or liquor (walk-in freezers and liquor storage areas are especially vulnerable to theft). Employees sometimes claim that missing inventory was returned to the vendor or spoiled.

63. Take home trim food products.

64. Produce surplus food so that it can be taken home.

65. Many cash registers are set up to record food sold to go. This happens often in restaurants situated in hotels; for example, coffee and a roll are sold to a customer who chooses to take them out. The wait person does not record the sale and pockets the cash.

66. Wrap food and drop it into a box in the back or a trash can for later retrieval.

67. Kickbacks from vendors—generally, the chef takes a commission and accepts a lower quality of meat or produce.

68. Accept lower weights—for example, the produce box is weighed when received; however, if the boxes are not opened regularly by receiving personnel, the box might include a chunk of ice.

69. Feed friends for free.

70. Chef purchases specific items not on the inventory for employee or personal consumption.

71. Mobile catering truck driver or hot dog vendors purchase and sell their own inventory.

72. Chef obtains and submits falsified invoices that transfer food purchases to supplies, therefore affecting the manager's ability to perform an accurate ratio analysis.

73. Chef demands personal gifts from suppliers in exchange for business for the purveyor. The price of the gift is passed on the restaurant in higher prices or reduced quality.

74. Wine steward claims sold bottle was broken or returned.

75. Employee steals and uses gift certificates—for example, attach a two-for-one coupon to a guest check for which the customer paid cash and take the cash.

76. The person receiving food or beverage deliveries and the truck driver collude to provide short weights. In some reported cases, half the delivery was diverted and sold on the street. (A perpetual inventory system backed up by

frequent inventory counts by someone other than the person receiving the items can detect these thefts.)

The Customer Is the Victim

77. Wait person adds extra items to customer's check. This is often aided by a confusing guest check that is difficult to understand or is faint.

78. Overcharge customers for banquet sales—for example, charge customer for ten pots of coffee when only six were served.

Bookkeeper

79. Bookkeeper steals cash and records it as cash short.

80. Bookkeeper steals cash and records a bad debt expense for an improperly written check, NSF (bounced) check, or incorrect credit card transaction.

81. Bookkeeper writes and cashes checks to self but records them in the check register as FICA taxes (or some other frequently paid but rarely reviewed account, like utilities expense).

82. Bookkeeper/manager creates fictitious vendors.

83. Bookkeeper holds the daily bank deposit for some number of days and uses the cash for personal benefit.

84. Bookkeeper adds a "less cash" line to the deposit slip and receives cash at the bank.

Payroll

85. Phantom employees—manager adds phantom employees to the payroll and cashes their pay checks.

86. Manager adds fictitious hours to the employees' paychecks and splits the difference with the employee.

87. Employees overstate their hours—for example, employees who work the lunch shift go home for a few hours and come back for the dinner shift but do not sign out when they leave.

Other

88. Use the phone for long-distance calls.

89. Keep funds from the vending machine.

90. Keep funds from the grease-barrel pickup.

91. Steal silverware, glassware, napkins, tablecloths, etc.

92. Fake a burglary.

93. Give away or sell artifacts from the restaurant (such as pictures or statuary).

94. Keep cover-charge receipts.

95. Steal bar supplies such as jiggers, detergent, linens, and shakers.

96. Steal cigarettes that are intended to be sold at the bar.

97. Revisit the restaurant during closed hours and steal whatever is available.

98. When obtaining change from another cash register, don't reimburse it fully and pocket the difference.

99. Borrow the manager's keys and duplicate the void key, then void out entire or partial sales. (It has been reported that, at one restaurant, a ring of 17 employees engaged in this practice.)[6]

SUMMARY

Restaurant bar and beverage operations present operators with challenges and opportunities. The challenges begin with training or transferring a liquor license and operating with strict controls. Establishing and maintaining a program is critical not only to the restaurant's success but is also socially responsible. Opportunities exist for creating exciting cocktails and for the combination of wine with food.

KEY TERMS AND CONCEPTS

Holding area

Alcoholic beverage license

Responsible alcoholic beverage service

Department of Alcoholic Beverage Control

Front bar

Back bar

Premium-brand liquors

Well brands

Pull handle

Speed gun

Third-party liability

Controls

REVIEW QUESTIONS

1. Outline the steps involved in obtaining a liquor license.

2. Draw a rough sketch of a bar layout.

3. Write a mission and prepare a responsible alcoholic beverage service program.

4. Suggest six entrées and wines to accompany them.

5. List the ways that your restaurant bartender might try to steal from you and explain what preventive measures you will install to ensure 100% control of your beverages.

ENDNOTES

[1] Philip Moore, *Total Bar and Beverage Management* (New York: Lebhar-Friedman Books, 1981), 185.

[2] Carroll Conway, "Managing the Alcohol Risk," *Lodging* 19, no. 1 (September 1993): 43–44.

[3] Gerald D. Robin, "Alcohol Service Liability: What the Courts Are Saying," *Cornell Hotel and Restaurant Administration Quarterly* 31, no. 1 (February 1991): 102.

[4] John R. Walker, *Introduction to Hospitality*, 2nd ed. (Upper Saddle River, N.J.: Prentice Hall, 1999), 321–322.

[5] Jacquelyn Lynn, "Don't Let Bar Profits Go Down the Drain," *Restaurants USA* 18, no. 4 (April 1998): 34–35.

[6] Troy Brackett and Producing Profitable Results, November 11, 1999, http://www.profitable. com/results/articles/011.html

Chapter **9**

After reading and studying this chapter,
you should be able to:

Establish standards for purchasing restaurant food items.

Determine how to set up a basic restaurant purchasing system.

Establish par stocks and reordering points.

Operate a basic restaurant purchasing system.

FOOD PURCHASING

This chapter covers the basic elements of food purchasing. When setting up a food purchasing system, think in terms of:

- Establishing standards for each food item used (product specification)
- Establishing a system that minimizes effort and losses, and maximizes control of theft
- Establishing the amount of each item that should be on hand (par stocks and reorder points)
- Identifying who will do the buying and keeping the food-purchasing system in motion
- Identifying who will do the receiving, storage, and issuing of items

The National Restaurant Association's Foodservice Purchasing Managers Executive Study Group offers useful purchasing recommendations: a reduction in the number of suppliers and a move to partnering with them. This increases information on markets and aids in forecasting future supply availability and price movements. This is one strategy to beat the market; however, it is still crucial to accurately define market prices. The best tactic to accomplish this objective is to negotiate a long-term contract (annual, if possible) at a fixed cost with downside protection, where you can get it.[1] Suppliers for some perishable items may be invited to bid on a range of items for a week or month. This allows the restaurateur to control the process.

Written standards for food (food specifications) are set, preferably in writing, before a restaurant opens. The amounts to purchase are based on a forecast of sales, which admittedly, without a sales history, is a guesstimate. Here, previous experience with a similar kind of restaurant is most valuable. The same procedures are followed for buying other supplies—paper goods, cleaning materials, glassware, and so on. Purveyors are contacted, credit established, and the food received and stored. When in operation, par stocks (the reasonable amount to have on hand) and reorder points (the stock point that indicates more should be ordered) are established.

A FOOD PURCHASING SYSTEM

Purchasing can be thought of as a subsystem within the total restaurant system, which once installed can be set in motion, repeating itself. The following are steps in putting a purchasing system together.

1. Based on the menu, determine the food standard(s) required to serve the market. Will vegetables be canned, fresh, or frozen? What cut and grade of meat is appropriate for each meat item on the menu? Will fish be fresh or frozen, or some of both?

2. Develop product specifications—detailed descriptions of what is wanted based on consultation and best information available—and place responsibility for product consistency and quality on the supplier.

3. Gather product availability information and select supplier(s) based on reliability of service, price, and honesty. Obtain samples of the food and test them in order to select the best.

4. Have alternate suppliers in mind for comparison.

PRODUCT NAME: Shrimp, Cooked, Shell-on,   CONCEPT: RL
                    Headless, USA

DRI PRODUCT CODE: 1063   REVISION DATE: 9/16/99

1. PRODUCT DEFINITION

IQF (Individually Quick Frozen), clean, wholesome, shell-on shrimp, of the acceptable commercial species. The finished cooked, shell-on product shall be produced from first quality raw material. The raw material shall be treated with a solution of 92% chilled water, 4% Carnal 659S and 4% salt for one hour.

Product shall be in compliance with all aspects of the United States Food and Drug Administration Seafood HACCP (Hazard Analysis Critical Control Points) regulation 21 Code of Federal Regulations 123.

This product shall be of food grade and in all respects, including labeling, in compliance with the Federal Food, Drug and Cosmetic Act of 1938, as amended, and all applicable regulations thereunder.

This product shall be processed and packed under strict sanitary conditions and shall be free from all forms of foreign and extraneous matter, in accordance with FDA current Good Manufacturing Practices.

2. SENSORY ATTRIBUTES

The appearance, odor, and flavor shall be that of freshly caught and processed shrimp. The texture of the shrimp shall be moist, firm, and tender. There shall be no objectionable flavors (Muddy, Geosmin, Earthy, etc.) in the product. The product shall have no extraneous or off odors, flavors or colors.

3. PHYSICAL REQUIREMENTS

A. <u>Net Weight:</u> The net weight shall not be less than the declared net weight when inspected in the U.S.

B. <u>Count per pound:</u> The average count per pound shall fall within the declared count range. The finished count range shall be 40–80 with an average of 63 per lot/shipment. No individual sample shall exceed 67.

C. <u>Sulfiting Agents:</u> There shall be less than 100 parts per million residual sodium bisulfite in the shrimp meat as tested by an official procedure recognized by the U.S. States Food and Drug Administration.

D. <u>Cooked Evaluation Process:</u>

   D.1. <u>Methodology:</u> Take 10 pieces of randomly selected shrimp per sample bag and place them in a bag with a small amount of water. Seal the bag and place the bag in boiling water to warm the cooked shrimp.

   D.2. <u>Sensory Evaluation:</u>

      D.2.1 Smell: When opening the product, smell the bag and the individual shrimp for the following extraneous or off odors and flavors:

         D.2.1.1 Moderate to strong Geosmin, i.e. muddy/grassy

         D.2.1.2 sour, ammonia

         D.2.1.3 Fecal, putrid

         D.2.1.4 petroleum, diesel

         D.2.1.5 chemical

      D.2.2 Taste: for all of the above objectionable flavors

      D.2.3 Texture: The texture shall not be mushy (powdery), rubbery (crunchy), stringy (stale).

E. <u>Uniformity of Size:</u> The uniformity of size shall range from 1.4–2.4.

$$\text{Uniformity Ratio} = \frac{\text{Weight of 15 largest shrimp}}{\text{Weight of 15 smallest shrimp}}$$

■ **FIGURE 9–1**

An example of a food product specification. Courtesy Red Lobster

F. <u>Defects:</u> Total defects are the total amount of major and minor defects in each lot, not to exceed 15%. It is further understood that there is to be no intentional packaging of defective product.

<u>Critical Defects:</u> There is no tolerance for Critical Defects. The three types of Critical Defects are:

<u>Sensory Attributes:</u> Any of the defects listed in sections 3.D.2.1 through 3.D.2.3 constitutes a Critical Defect.

<u>Foreign Material:</u> The product shall be free from processing debris and all forms of foreign material that can pose a food hazard or safety issue, i.e., metal fragments, glass, insects).

<u>Microbiological Results</u> (See Microbiological requirements (Section 4)

<u>Major Defects:</u> Any major defect should not exceed 3%. Rejection of the production code will occur if the sum of the major defects or the only major defect exceeds 5%. Examples:

1. Melanosis—black spot on the meat
2. Brown Meat—Due to disease or enzymatic reaction around the neck meat.
3. Unusable Shrimp—Unusable (pieces and broken) shrimp

<u>Minor Defects:</u> Any minor defect should not exceed 5% by weight of the shrimp, except chipped tails, missing tails, and black spot on shell. The amount of chipped tails and shrimp with missing tails (boat run only) should not exceed 10% by weight provided the chipped tails are not shorter than the middle dorsal ridge. The amount of black spot on the shell should not exceed 8% by weight. Examples:

1. Throat meat—Throat meat should be no longer than one-half of the length of the first segment. Rejection occurs at the length of the 1st segment.
2. Tail rot and black tail—When two tail panels are affected and/or two-thirds of the panels are black.
3. Black spot on shell—melanosis on the shell
4. Soft tail—Any tail that is too soft to maintain its integrity through the production cycle in U.S.
5. Chipped tails/Missing Tails (boat run only)—The product is Individually Quick Frozen (IQF), and during freezing, the tail is fragile and is susceptible to breakage.

A. <u>Dehydration:</u> There shall be no dehydration in the product.
B. <u>Decomposition:</u> There shall be no decomposition in the product.

■ **FIGURE 9–1**

Continued

5. Select person(s) to order and receive supplies and give them authority to reject delivery of individual items. Make sure that the person ordering is different from the person receiving and that management authorizes or places each order, even for meat and other perishables.

6. Set up storage spaces for maximum utilization.

7. Establish the amount needed to be stocked (par stock) for each item.

8. Set up an inventory control system.

9. Decide on optimal delivery size to reduce cost of delivery and handling.

10. Check all deliveries for quality and quantity or weight.

11. Tie inventory control and cost control systems together.

The Purchasing Cycle

A purchasing cycle can be set up that rolls along efficiently, a system that repeats itself day after day with minimal demands on the operator (Figure 9–2). Even though under constant review, each part of the cycle is changed slowly, only as customers and menu change and as new products and purveyors are considered.

Product specification need only be reviewed, not reset, each time food is ordered. Par stock and reorder points are relatively fixed and changed only as sales volume changes appreciably or as the menu changes. (Product specifications and par stock are explained in detail later.) Major suppliers are changed infrequently. Receiving, issuing, and recording are carried out systematically, and the information becomes the basic data for the cost control system.

Who Sets Up the System? Who Operates It?

In the usual restaurant, the manager, in consultation with the chef and other key people, decides on product specification, selects purveyors, and has a rough figure in mind for par stock and reorder point. It is recommended that one person, and one person only, who has a clear understanding of food cost control and of the restaurant market, set up and operate the food purchasing system. That person is usually the manager. Too often it is a nonowner chef who has purveyor friends who get the orders and charge high prices. Experienced restaurant operators do not let a purveyor "par up" the restaurant. Remember, the purveyors are in the business of selling food, beverages, and related items to restaurants and will likely attempt to sell whatever they have on hand.

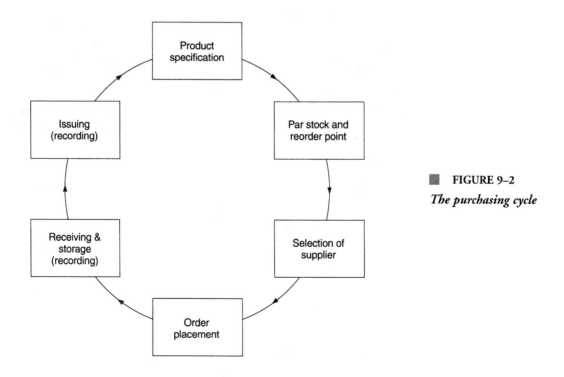

FIGURE 9–2
The purchasing cycle

Food Quality Standards

Standards for food quality are set to serve a particular market. Some operators serve fresh fish only, never frozen. If fresh fish is unavailable, no fish is served at all. Some restaurants use only fresh vegetables. Others use all frozen. Others use canned vegetables.

A chain of highly successful dinner houses specifies that all items be breaded to order and deep fried at once. No frozen breaded items are used. The quality of frozen items is believed to be lower than items breaded by hand and cooked immediately.

Buying by Specification

While many restaurants do not spell out in detail a specification for each food item purchased, the specification is usually well outlined in the operator's mind. Each operation needs a quality of food that fits its market. The quality needed varies with the market and also with the food item being produced. Canned vegetables used in a made-up dish need not be of fancy grade. Meat for grinding into hamburger may well come from U.S. good or even lower-graded meat and still be satisfactory. Canned beef may be satisfactory for deli- (thinly) sliced sandwiches. Apples for use in apple pie need not be of the same quality as those to be eaten out of hand, where appearance is important.

It might be expected that buying by grade alone would be sufficient to assure the quality desired. Not so. Canned vegetables, for example, vary considerably within a grade because of different growing conditions experienced in one part of the country as compared with another. Most large food service operations conduct can-cutting tests annually, after the fruit and vegetable crops have been harvested and canned. The oper-

A restaurant operator and a supplier discussing an order. Establishing a good working relationship with suppliers is beneficial to the operation.

COMMODITY SPECIFICATIONS

NAME: Beets, Quartered
TYPE: Quartered
PACK: (6) #10 cans/case
YIELD: 70 oz minimum drained weight

Grade: Grade A quartered beets

Color: Uniform bright deep red color, not off-brown, oxidized, or bright pink

Flavor: No objectionable taste or aftertaste, root or earthy taste

Size: Cut in even quarters from beets not over 2¼" in diameter

Defects: No woodiness, coarse texture, or excessive softness, poor trimming, peel, or black spots. Not too many first cuts (slabs), frayed edges, deep knife marks, or other injuries.

◼ FIGURE 9–3

Beet specifications

ator wants not only to know the unit cost but to compare the color, texture, taste, and uniformity of products.

Very often, a lower-cost fruit or vegetable is the best quality for a particular purpose. In such a case, it is smart to have written specifications. Clifton's Cafeterias, for example, located in Southern California, have studied their fruit and vegetable needs and drawn up specifications for each product. The one for quartered beets is seen in Figure 9–3. In this case, the company wishes to have at least 70 ounces of drained-weight beets (minus the liquid) from a number 10 can. They want a bright, deep-red color with no objectionable taste or aftertaste, and the beet should be not larger than 2.25 inches in diameter. The beet should have no woodiness nor should it be too coarse or too soft. Similar specifications are drawn up for julienned beets and pickled beets.

◼ How Much Inventory?

Every food item has a shelf life—the length of time it can be stored without appreciable loss in quality or weight. Nearly every food that contains a large amount of water shrinks with storage. Even under ideal refrigeration of 20 degrees below zero, ice cream shrinks. Consider also the dollars tied up in inventory, which represents money that draws no interest and does no work for the enterprise. There should be no more inventory than what is actually needed to cover the operation from one delivery date to another.

This target cannot be realized if the operation has delivery problems or is some distance from a source of food materials.

The temptation is to buy a large quantity when a price reduction is available—which may be fine for liquor, where little is affected by storage—but this requires extra handling space and time for most items. Some storerooms have been seen to hold as much as a year's supply of canned fruit merely because a salesman convinced the food buyer that the fruit was a good buy or that the buyer would receive a prize or gift certificate for the purchase.

■ **Par Stock and Reorder Point.**   A food purchasing system calls for a par stock and a reorder point for each food item. These are based on quantities used, storage space available, and availability of the product. A steak house may have a policy of ordering meat once a week and base the order size on forecasted sales for the upcoming week. Milk may be delivered twice a week and a standing order placed for it. Fresh produce may be delivered every other day.

When it comes to the par stock for canned foods, the amount that is considered a safe inventory may be ordered only when the supply is down to a specified amount, such as one case—the reorder point. Management may wish never to have more than one case of a certain wine on hand and will order only when down to the last two bottles. A fast-moving item may require ten cases as par stock.

■ **Par Stock Based on Pre-Prepared Foods.**   The operator with a fixed menu has an advantage in buying. Pre-preparation of entrées can be done in terms of prepared items—so many trays stored under refrigeration. At the Pump Room in Chicago, which has been an institution since 1938, the entrance is lined with hundreds of photos of celebrities who have dined there over the years. The restaurant serves fine American cuisine and is noted for its prime rib and roasted duck. Par stock calculations are based on the previous quarter's numbers. One beef rib is pre-prepared for each 60 expected guests and 10 ducks for each 100 guests. The figure fluctuates on holidays and in winter.

In a restaurant where several items are pre-prepared and stored, purchasing can be based on the par stock of pre-prepared and stored items, not on raw food in the refrigeration or freezer where inventory control is tighter. The savvy restaurant operator will call vendors frequently, even daily, because prices vary considerably. Fresh vegetables, meat, and fish are good examples of items on which to get frequent price quotations, especially in a high-volume restaurant.

■

The Mechanics of Ordering

Opinions vary as to the best way to place orders for food and supplies. Some experts recommend calling for competitive prices before ordering anything. This is time-consuming. It may also pit the supplier against the operator, and the supplier eventually passes on the excessive costs of making small deliveries to the operator. Other operators deal only with the one or two trusted suppliers. Still others get much of their food at local supermarkets.

A restaurant operator, in many instances, pays as much or more than does the casual shopper. The supplier has the cost of delivery to the door and, usually, the cost of providing credit and other service, which must be recouped if the supplier is to stay in business.

The standing order is a predetermined order that is filled regularly—so much milk per day, so much bread, and so on. The standing order can vary with the day of the week. On Monday, so much milk is delivered; on Tuesday, so much additional milk; and so on.

Large restaurants have a more formal purchasing system that includes a purchase order. This is a form with three or four copies; one or two copies go to the supplier, one of which accompanies the delivery. The buyer keeps a copy for company files. A fourth copy may be kept by the person doing the receiving in the restaurant.

Storage at the Prado restaurant marking the product with date and contents is important

Storage

Part of the purchasing system is to store food and other supplies so that they fit into the overall system. This means storage arranged for easy receiving, easy issuing, and easy inventory control. In the dry-goods storeroom, canned, packed, and bulk dry foods are stored according to usage. The most-used foods are stored closest to the door; the least-used foods in the less accessible corners and shelves.

Once a system of storage has been arranged and the items stored according to usage, a form can be made up listing the items in the sequence in which they are stored. The spreadsheet is then used in taking a physical inventory.

As foods are received, they are stored at the backs of shelves, the older items moved forward to be used first. This rotational system helps assure that items are not allowed to become too old.

The rotation of goods has no relation to any system of costing foods or other merchandise. In costing an inventory, the last-in, first-out (LIFO) system costs the item at the price paid for the merchandise purchased last. The first-in, first-out (FIFO) system uses the price actually paid for the item. During a period of inflation, the two costs could be quite different. Whichever method is selected, it must be used consistently. Changing methods requires the approval of the IRS.

Convenience foods usually come in a form that makes it possible for them to be stored in a minimal amount of space. Other items are received in a form that should be immediately processed to reduce the amount of storage needed. Lettuce is a good example. Crated lettuce can be uncrated, trimmed, cored, and placed core-side up under ice in less space.

Many operators buy only salad greens that have already been washed and cut. Both time and space are saved, but the quality is lower than if the greens were prepared on the premises.

TYPES OF PURCHASING

Buying from Full-Line Purveyors

Most of the populated areas of the United States have food distributors who carry a large line of the supplies and foods needed by a restaurateur, which makes for one-stop shopping. The full-line distributor can offer more than product in the usual sense, providing merchandise and promotional material and training in the use of certain products and preparation of some foods. Buying from a full-line distributor saves the operator time in placing and receiving orders. Most of the larger distributors use computers and simplified billing procedures. The large full-line distributors specify certain amounts for orders, which a specialized distributor may not require. One-stop buying eliminates the need for daily shopping but does not completely eliminate the need for price comparison. Dealing with only one distributor may be more costly than dealing with several, or dealing with another one-stop distributor.

Co-op Buying

Another type of distribution that can be found in many areas is co-op buying. The co-op management agrees to supply products at cost plus enough of a markup to cover the cooperative's cost. A co-op is a nonprofit institution that is able to provide restaurant food and supplies at lower cost than the profit-oriented purveyors.

Beware

Specialty foods are often produced by newcomers to food processing who are not aware of the dangers of food contamination and the real possibility of transmitting serious diseases via food. All food processors in this country are subject to health regulations, including periodic health inspections. However, the quality and frequency, however, of such inspections varies widely from one state to another, and a small meat packer or processor of specialty foods such as tofu may be in violation for months or even years before discrepancies are found and corrected. For example, raw peanuts are subject to a fungus growth called aflatoxin that can permanently damage the liver. Without proper inspection of equipment, peanuts and peanut butter can reach the market contaminated in one form or another without anyone knowing it.

One small food-processing plant that we visited—a tofu plant—used old diapers in place of fresh cheesecloth and mouse droppings were casually brushed off a strainer that was then used without further sanitizing. A visit to any small food processor soliciting your trade may pay for itself.

BUYING MEAT

Because meat is the most costly food item in most restaurants, it deserves the most thought in drawing up food specifications. Fortunately, the federal government, through the Department of Agriculture (USDA), provides a great deal of information about all commonly purchased meat. Other useful information is available from the National Livestock and Meat Board, headquartered in Chicago.

Principal factors in meat buying are the cut of the meat (what part of the animal), the USDA grade of the meat (its fat content, tenderness, and cost), and the style (its form: carcass, wholesale cut, or ready-to-serve portion). The patrons of the restaurant (the market), through the menu and price, mostly determine the best kind of beef to buy. A high style of beef house may need loins from which to cut and age prime steaks. A hamburger house may need grass-fed beef. Both operators must satisfy their patrons.

The Chicken versus Turkey Choice

For many dishes such as chicken chow mein, chicken or turkey à la king, and chicken or turkey pot pie, either chicken or turkey can be used. Which is the better buy?

Suppose that fryers are on sale at 69 cents a pound while 10- to 12-pound turkeys are available at 89 cents a pound. Very often, the turkey is the better buy because it provides a higher yield of meat and is easier to handle. Frying chickens have a lower yield, something like 35 to 40%, depending on whether or not the skin is counted. In other words, if you start off with a pound of chicken you will end up with about two-fifths of a pound that is edible after shrinkage and boning. Turkey yields anywhere from 45 to 50%, depending on the weight of the bird. Turkeys have been raised weighing as much as 100 pounds. Generally, the larger the animal, the greater the yield (higher percentage of edible product).

Serving half of a chicken as a portion means buying individual birds, even though the edible amount of meat is much less than meets the eye. Fat hens provide more flavor than fryers and are often used for chicken pot pie. Another alternative is to use less expensive fryer and add chicken fat that is purchased separately.

Recipes call for different parts of the chicken or turkey. Chicken Kiev calls for a breast to be pounded and used as an envelope filled with butter, for example. The question of whether to buy chicken at one price or turkey at another must often be resolved by the recipe, not the price. In other cases, expense and ease of handling determine the choice. In the past, menus have listed chicken when turkey was used. Truth-in-menu regulations prohibit this practice.

PURCHASING EGGS

Purchasing eggs presents another problem. For baked goods, frozen eggs are usually the best buy. Because there is an oversupply of eggs during the spring months, the extra eggs are frozen and can usually be purchased at lower cost per unit than fresh ones. For serving on a breakfast plate at a coffee shop, extra-large or jumbo eggs, although they may cost a few cents more per egg, may be worth the extra cost because of the value as seen on the plate by the customer. In buying fresh eggs for use in scrambled eggs (or for home use), break down the egg purchasing problem into cost per ounce. Eggs are a commodity; therefore, the price tends to fluctuate slightly. Which of the sizes of eggs listed below presents the best buy?

- Medium eggs (21 ounces per dozen) @ $0.66/dozen
- Large eggs (24 ounces per dozen) @ $0.71/dozen
- Extra-large eggs (27 ounces per dozen) @ $0.72/dozen
- Jumbo eggs (30 ounces per dozen) @ $0.80/dozen

The problem is quickly solved by calculating the cost per ounce. The medium eggs cost $0.031 per ounce; the large eggs cost $0.029 per ounce; the extra large eggs cost $0.026 per ounce; the jumbo eggs cost $0.026 per ounce.

If the eggs are going to be used for scrambling, jumbos would be the best buy because there would be less labor involved in cracking them (fewer would have to be handled). In most situations, a definite price advantage appears for one size, and if hundreds of eggs are purchased each week, large amounts of money can be saved by selecting the egg at the least cost per ounce.

BUYING FRESH FRUITS AND VEGETABLES

Many operators, especially those with higher-priced menus, feature fresh fruits and vegetables. If these are really fresh and cooked minimally, they taste better than frozen or canned fruit. The cost of purchase and preparation is also higher. The name restaurateurs, even since Lorenzo Delmonico, have made a point of ferreting out the finest produce possible, often visiting the wholesale market at an early hour or buying from a small farmer who specializes in certain fruits or vegetables. The proprietor of one French restaurant features tiny zucchini fresh daily when in season. Many operators, including a few chain operators, feature fresh strawberries the year around, even though they must be imported from such places as Mexico, New Zealand, and Chile.

Restaurants with lower-priced menus are likely to feature fruit that is in season. The most popular fruits—apples, bananas, and oranges—are available year round. Figure 9–4, prepared by the USDA, shows the months when seasonal fruits and vegetables are likely to be in greatest supply and, consequently, least expensive.

When one is selecting fruit and vegetables personally, these guidelines apply:

- Select freshly picked, mature items and use them as quickly as possible. This especially applies to such items as sweet corn, which begins losing its sugars (they change to other carbohydrates) once it is picked. Vitamin loss also begins with picking. Some fruits are picked early and ripened only later, such as avocados and bananas. Other fruits, such as pineapple, do not ripen after they are picked.

- Handle fruits and vegetables as little as possible to avoid injury.
- Distinguish between blemishes that affect only appearance and those that affect eating quality.
- Check on maturity of items.
- Avoid vegetables and fruits that are overripe or show decay.
- Be conscious of size and count. Use off sizes when possible; they may be better buys.
- Know sizes of containers and check on their contents. Watch for loose or short packs or packs with one quality on top and another on the bottom.

Most operators are unable to visit wholesale markets personally and rely on distributors for delivery. Grade standards can be used. The USDA maintains inspection services at principal shipping points and terminal markets and has developed these standards. They are helpful but, because of rapid perishability of produce, it is difficult to rely on grades alone. The buyer specifies grade, size, count, container size, and degree of ripeness.

■
USDA Wholesale Produce Grades

Grade standards are necessarily broad. Fruits and vegetables differ widely in quality according to type and growing conditions. Federal standards must have broad tolerances to encompass all the variations. A set of fruit and vegetable grade standards is available from the Fruit and Vegetable Division, U.S. Department of Agriculture, Washington, DC 20250. The grades and standards are as follows:

- *U.S. Fancy.* This grade applies to highly specialized produce, a very small percentage of the total crop. This grade is rarely used on most commodities because it is too costly to pack.
- *U.S. No. 1.* This grade is the most widely used grade in trading produce from farm to market and indicates good average quality.
- *U.S. Commercial.* This grade applies to produce inferior to U.S. No. 1 but superior to U.S. No. 2.
- *U.S. Combination.* This grade applies to produce that combines percentages of U.S. No. 1 and U.S. No. 2.
- *U.S. No. 2.* This grade applies to what is usually considered the lowest quality practical to ship. Produce of this grade usually has much poorer appearance and more waste than U.S. No. 1.
- *U.S. No. 3.* This grade applies to produce used for highly specialized products.

Examples of what to look for in fresh vegetables and purchase units for each are seen in Figure 9–4.

Small supermarket chains may offer produce at prices below vendor prices because their buyers pick and choose relatively small lots of produce in which the large chains

ASPARAGUS

Purchase Units:

Cartons		15-16 pounds
Pyramid Crates		30-32 pounds

Select firm, crisp, smooth, and clean spears with compact tips and good green color extending down near the base. Spears which are ridged, crooked, or have spread tips or excessive amounts of white at base are likely to be tough.

Watch For: Wilted, flabby spears or mushy condition of tips which indicate age and have objectionable flavor.

AVOCADOS

Purchase Units:

Cartons and Flats	12-15 pounds

Select avocados having a fresh, bright appearance, heavy, medium-size, fairly firm or just beginning to soften. Irregular light brown markings on the skin have no effect on the flesh.

Watch For: Dark, sunken spots may merge and form irregular patches. If the surface is deeply cracked or broken, this is an indication of decay.

BEANS, GREEN OR WAX

Purchase Units:

Baskets	bushel	28-30 pounds
	½ bushel	14-15 pounds
Crates	bushel	28-30 pounds
Cartons		28-30 pounds

Select young, tender, well-formed beans which are free from blemishes and are fresh and crisp. Look for bright color in either green or yellow podded varieties. Beans should snap or break in two pieces before bending double.

Watch For: Wilted and dry beans which are signs of aging after picking, resulting in poor flavor. Older beans with enlarged seeds which are likely to be tough and fibrous.

BROCCOLI

Purchase Units:

Crates	4/5 bushel	15-20 pounds
Crates, Wirebound		20 pounds
Baskets	8 quarts	6 pounds
Cartons	14 bunches	20-23 pounds

Select bunches having a deep green color, compact firm surface with small individual buds, and fresh appearance.

Watch For: Soft, slippery, watersoaked spots or irregular brown spots which are signs of decay. Heads which are spreading, wilted, turning yellow or have many enlarged flower buds are old and probably will have an off-flavor.

BRUSSELS SPROUTS

Purchase Units:

Wooden Drums		25 pounds
Flats	12 10-ounce cups	7½ to 8 ounces per cup
Cartons		25 pounds

Select sprouts having fresh, bright green color, tight fitting and firm outer leaves.

Watch For: Sprouts with yellow or otherwise discolored leaves or sprouts which are soft, open or wilted. Small holes or ragged leaves may indicate worm damage.

CABBAGE

Purchase Units:

Crates	1 3/5 bushels	50-55 pounds
Cartons		45-50 pounds
Mesh Sacks		50-60 pounds

Select well-trimmed heads having green, fresh outer leaves and heads which are firm and heavy for their size, free from signs of insects and bad blemishes. Stock out of storage is usually lacking in green color, but may be otherwise satisfactory.

FIGURE 9–4

What to look for in fresh vegetables

are not interested. Produce sold as loss leaders in supermarkets can also be featured by restaurants. The quality of fruit that is to be chopped up in a fresh fruit cup need not be the same as that offered on a fresh fruit plate. Premium-sized produce need not be purchased when it is to be cut up. Celery for soup or watermelon for fresh fruit cup are examples.

Some soup bases contain more salt than anything else; salt is cheaper bought by the pound. Salt (sodium chloride), the most widely used flavor additive to food in the world, has many values—when used in moderation. Americans, however, generally use too much. Less than $1/2$ teaspoon a day satisfies the daily current salt requirement. Yet Americans typically consume $3^{1}/_2$ teaspoons each day. If a little is needed, why use a lot? Overuse can damage the kidneys, interfere with nutrient absorption, and contribute to high blood pressure. Excessive salt intake sets up people with heart disease for congestive heart failure. Most canned and bottled products contain too much salt. For example, a 10-ounce can of chicken broth contains almost 1,000 milligrams of salt.

■ Canned Fruits and Vegetables

A great deal of information is available about canned fruits and vegetables, much of it developed by the USDA and by the Food and Drug Administration (FDA). Quality standards and the standard of fill of container are concerns of the FDA. The FDA also requires labeling on most food items containing several ingredients. The common or usual names of all ingredients, listed in descending order of their presence by weight, must be on the container. Some products turn out mostly to be filler. All foods shipped interstate come under the jurisdiction of the FDA. State and city laws regulate items produced and sold within the states, but most of these laws resemble the federal laws.

■ **Can-Cutting Tests.**   Operators who frequently use canned fruits or vegetables perform can-cutting tests, usually in the late fall, after the picking season. Cans from various vendors have their labels covered and the contents are graded for taste, texture, color, uniformity, price, and size. They can also be compared as to how well the contents hold up on a steam table. An important comparative measure is drained weight. The results of these tests are often surprising: The less expensive products may turn out to be superior.

SELECTING THE RIGHT COFFEE

Like everything else on the menu, the coffee must fit the clientele. The operator's choice may not be that of the market being served. Preferences vary around the country, and people tend to like the coffee with which they grew up. Widely traveled people often move toward a stronger coffee with a heavier roast.

Coffee served in restaurants is a blend, with mountain-grown coffees predominating. Probably the best way to select coffee is to serve it to a taste panel of typical patrons and use the one they choose.

Generally speaking, coffees are divided between the robust, heavy-flavored coffees and the lighter, milder mountain-grown coffees. Two separate coffees from a small country may differ widely. The degree of roast and the manner in which the coffee is brewed have a marked effect on the final flavor. It is not enough merely to buy the most expensive coffee, for that particular blend may not suit the market being served.

Some coffee vendors offer to train restaurant employees in coffee brewing and may clean the coffee brewing machine periodically at no charge. Aficionados of coffee are legion and many agree that the holding temperature of brew should be 185°F, held no longer than 30 minutes.

■ Coffee Brewing Machines

Coffee vendors often supply the restaurant operator with a coffee-making machine at a no-cost lease basis provided the operator agrees to buy all of his or her coffee from the vendor. Sometimes the vendor charges a few cents more per pound of coffee—which, over time, pays for the machine. For a beginning restauranter who is short of capital, such offers are welcomed. (Ice cream cabinets are often provided on a similar basis.)

SUMMARY

Successful foodservice operators establish standards of food quality that please the clientele served. They also establish a purchasing system that helps assure that the food is purchased, stored, and accounted for so that theft, waste, and overproduction are minimized.

Basic to such a system is the establishment of food standards appropriate to the kinds of customers served and the prices that can be charged to achieve a profit. The percentage of fat in the hamburger, the size of the fried egg, the ingredients in the milkshake, the grade of meat in the steak are examples of the information needed to establish food standards. The standards are expressed in terms of food specifications used in ordering and monitoring food purchases.

In independent restaurants, the responsibility for food purchasing usually rests with the manager. Standards and specifications are set at headquarters for chain operations. Purchasing controls are necessarily tight because theft is a strong possibility. Collusion between vendors, managers, and employees happens. Storeroom keys are tightly controlled by issuing them to one or a few people.

Receiving and storage practices are spelled out. Canned and dried goods can be stored so that the most frequently used items are easiest to get.

Items that must be refrigerated or frozen are kept in separate locations.

Government standards for such items as meat, fish, and poultry can be used in establishing the standards used by the restaurant. For restaurants that use a lot of canned goods, annual can-cutting tests that compare brands of canned goods for quality and price are useful. Several examples of food specifications are given.

Inventory control—the amount of food to be ordered and stocked—can be built into the purchasing system by reference to past records. Excessive inventories tie up capital and space and lead to food waste. Establishing reorder points (when to reorder specific items) and par stocks (amounts normally stocked) are part of a purchasing system.

The number of vendors used in a policy matter based on the reliability, prices, and trustworthiness of the vendor(s). In larger towns and cities, reliance on full-line purveyors may save time and money. Some vendors offer training for restaurant personnel in dish machine use and coffee brewing.

A food purchasing system includes periodic review of current buying practices and customer preferences and a readiness to change any part of the system as necessary.

KEY TERMS AND CONCEPTS

Food purchasing system
Par stock
Quality food purchase specification
  standards
Inventory
Purchasing

USDA wholesale produce grades
Perishable foods
Market quotation list
Standing orders
Reorder point

REVIEW QUESTIONS

1. Explain the statement "The quality of food served must fit the clientele of the restaurant."
2. Define *par stock* and *reorder point.*
3. How will you select the coffee to be served in your restaurant?
4. What is a can-cutting test?
5. What form of eggs would you buy for use in baked goods?
6. Hamburger used in most fast-food restaurants probably is of what USDA grade?
7. What are two disadvantages in using USDA prime beef?
8. Who should be in charge of food purchasing?
9. How is the food-purchasing system related to the food and beverage cost-control system?

ENDNOTES

[1] Doug Patterson, "Purchasing Managers Group Continues to Grow Stronger," *Nations Restaurant News*, 15 June 1992, 64.

Chapter **10**

After reading and studying this chapter,
you should be able to:

Plan a basic kitchen layout.

Determine what kitchen equipment is appropriate for your restaurant.

Prepare for a health department inspection.

PLANNING AND EQUIPPING
THE KITCHEN

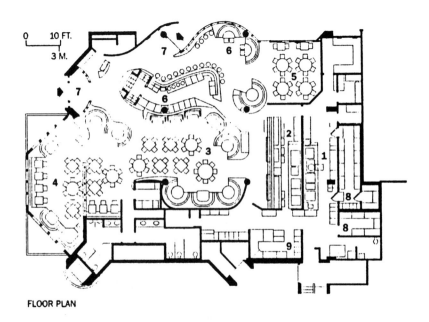

FLOOR PLAN

This chapter states principles of kitchen planning and the selection of kitchen equipment. Kitchen planning involves the allocation of space within the kitchen based on equipment needs, spatial relationships within the kitchen, and the need to keep traffic flows within the kitchen to a minimum. Food is received, processed (prepared) before cooking, and cooked food is moved to a serving station.

The second part of the chapter presents examples of the most commonly used kitchen equipment, their use, and their performance characteristics.

When an existing restaurant is bought, the buyers are often too concerned with survival to think much about changing the layout or the equipment. If they have the capital, they may ask a restaurant equipment dealer to evaluate the present equipment and suggest kitchen layout changes. Some restaurant equipment dealers are quite knowledgeable about layout planning. Others are not.

In large, complicated kitchens, restaurant companies and institutions such as hospitals usually turn to experienced, professional planners to draw up plans for building a new or modifying an existing kitchen configuration.

An overall objective of layout planning is to minimize the number of steps taken by wait staff and kitchen personnel. In quick-service restaurants, equipment is placed so that servers take only a few steps. The same principle applies in fine-dining restaurants, even though a particular dish may pass through five hands before being picked up by wait staff.

Full-service restaurants are usually laid out so that the kitchen flow is from the receiving area to the cold and dry storage spaces to the pre-prep area, where bulk ingredients are measured and cans opened, to the prep area, where vegetables are washed and peeled, and fish, meat, and poultry cut. The flow continues to the cooking area, where soups and stocks are prepared and other cooking takes place. The last station is where final prep takes place (cooking is finished, plated, and readied for pickup by staff).

Baking and pantry areas (desserts and sandwiches) may be set off by themselves. If feasible, dishwashing and the pots and pans are best kept off to one side, out of the traffic flow. The restaurant configuration and limitations often require special layout and design. Ventilation and necessary airflow and building codes may pose special problems.

In complicated kitchens, arriving at the best layout is a highly sophisticated skill that requires art. John C. Cini, President and CEO of Cini Little, an international food-service and hospitality business and also a design consulting firm headquartered in Rockville, Maryland, comments, "Great thought is put into every one of our designs, taking into consideration the activities that actually occur during the food preparation, cooking, and serving processes."[1] A designer with experience in operations has the advantage of being able to relate and anticipate the behaviors of the personnel intended

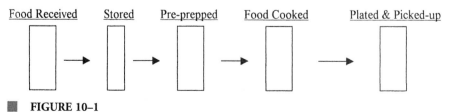

■ **FIGURE 10–1**

Kitchen flow. Courtesy The American Gas Association, Washington, D.C.

to utilize the facility. For example, one cannot assume that staff members will understand or obey the design intent of a facility. The designer must realize that servers will typically take the shortest and most convenient route from any one place to another. Chefs want their work organized in a manner that minimizes excess activity and unnecessary steps. If these concepts are not incorporated into a design, the workers may implement their own makeshift accommodations to satisfy their needs. This diminishes the value of the design and decreases the efficiency of the operation. The efficiency and comfort of the staff is important to the operation. Recent trends, such as ergonomics, (the applied science of equipment design intended to reduce staff fatigue and discomfort) influence foodservice facility design. This may include lowering counter heights to make the task of slicing deli meats easier or providing a floor covering that does not tire the body as quickly.

Outside pressures in the form of legislation and public policy also affect foodservice design. For example, compliance with the provisions of government plays a major role in maintaining standards to accommodate the needs of workers and customers who are disabled. These influences are responsible for widening aisles and making equipment more readily accessible. Sanitation is another large factor in foodservice equipment. Designers must understand National Sanitation Foundation standards and apply them to the actions of the workers. By providing a safe work environment, the restaurant benefits by limiting injuries, maintaining morale, and reducing employee turnover. Customers benefit from a decrease in food-borne illness, better service, and an overall higher-quality dining experience.

Cini lists trends in kitchen equipment and their use:

- New equipment combines refrigerated bases with kitchen ranges and grill tops. This enables chefs to have raw foods at hand, so that they need not turn around to open a refrigerator.

- Self-cleaning hoods and ventilators that trap odors and fumes can be automatically controlled by pumps that spray hot water and detergent on the hoods during off hours, thereby limiting grease buildup.

- Combination oven/steamers allow cooks to use either moist or dry heat, or a combination of both. Vegetables can be steamed, cookies can be baked, and meat can be braised with one piece of equipment.

- Induction heating, which has been used in the past for exhibition cooking and in cafeterias, allows chefs to prepare food in full view of customers while eliminating wild heat, excess grease, and noisy ventilators.

- Kitchen equipment now includes computers that automatically control ovens. The worker in a bakeshop can program the oven to bake different breads at different temperatures and levels of humidity for specific times. Desired oven temperatures can be saved in the computer's memory.[2]

The American Gas Association has published examples of kitchen plans to show the work flow within a typical kitchen layout (Figure 10–2). The plans show the movement of food from delivery through the various workstations and on to the customer. The work flow diagram shows how circular work flow patterns are not efficient. Square designs also waste space in the center of the service area. The preferred kitchen plan is rectangular in shape, providing the shortest paths when not all stations within the kitchen are contacted.

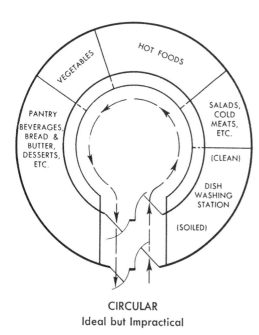

CIRCULAR
Ideal but Impractical

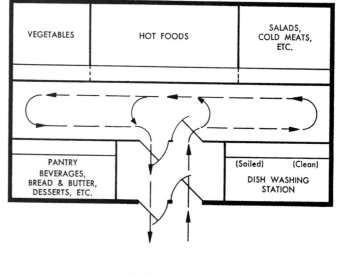

RECTANGULAR
Kitchen Entrance on Long Side

This is usually the preferred layout of the serving area of a restaurant kitchen. The shortened paths indicate the travel if all stations need not be contacted.

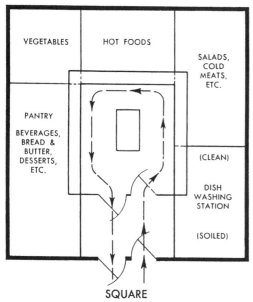

SQUARE
Approximates a Circle
But Usually Wastes
Space in the Center
of the Serving Area

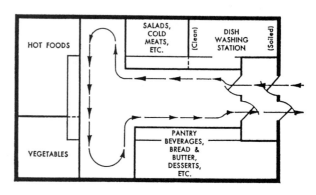

RECTANGULAR
Kitchen Entrance on Short Side

Hot foods must be carried considerable distances and waiters at the various stations may be obstructing traffic to and from the dining area.

FIGURE 10–2

Serving area. Courtesy American Gas Association

Dr. Arthur C. Avery, professor emeritus at Purdue University, has studied kitchen efficiency. He shows the arrangements of work centers in a typical service restaurant that has a fairly limited menu. A flowchart traces the movement of food from storage and preparation areas to the center of the kitchen where the food is cooked. From the cooking area, the food goes to the service area and from there into the dining room. System elements are interdependent; meat preparation is dependent on meat preparation, meat prep on refrigeration, refrigeration on receiving (Figure 10–3).

Avery suggests several methods of increasing kitchen efficiency:

- Use purveyors that have a wide base of supply so that fewer deliveries are needed.

- Use conveyors to take food to service areas.

- Place service stations throughout the dining room. Locate silver, beverages, soups, and other items there to reduce back-and-forth traffic to the kitchen.

- Use automatic conveyors to take racks from the dining room through the dishwasher and then back to the dining room.[3]

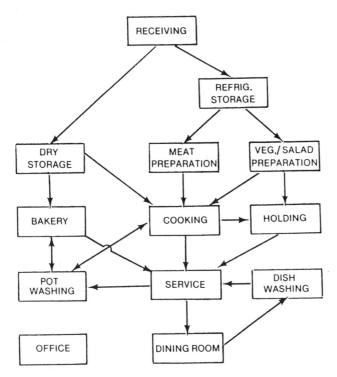

Arrangements of Work Centers

■ **FIGURE 10–3**

Arrangement of work centers. Courtesy of Dr. Arthur C. Avery, Professor Emeritus, Purdue University

THE OPEN KITCHEN

Open kitchens (also called exhibition kitchens) have their own equipment and are growing in popularity. Elaine Martin Petrowski offers guidelines and floor plans of open kitchens in her article "The Open Kitchen as Theater."[4] Drawing on the expertise of several kitchen designers, she points out that the open design highlights the kitchen and, sometimes, a piece of equipment. A steakhouse focuses on the cooking of meat, an Italian restaurant on pizza, by lighting the dining room slightly less than the kitchen. Place standard kitchen equipment, such as refrigerators, in other parts of the kitchen. Standard food preparation is not usually featured. The open kitchen is reserved for what is glamorous: bright, shiny ladles, stainless steel and copper utensils—perhaps a

THE CALIFORNIA CAFÉ BAR & GRILL IN SCHAUMBURG, ILLINOIS, by Engstrom Design Group, serves California cuisine. The open kitchen, visible from all 200 seats in the restaurant, directs views away from the adjacent Woodfield Mall and its huge parking area. The kitchen is divided with a granite-topped pass shelf that is clad in wood veneer on the restaurant side. Work counters are maple butcher block or stainless steel. The back wall of the open kitchen is covered in ceramic tile and stainless steel, and acid-etched copper panels hide the exhaust hood. The floors are quarry tile. Actual cooking ingredients are set on metal shelves on the wall behind the pantry. Noise is mitigated in the dining room with a combination of drop-in acoustical ceiling tiles, carpeting, fully upholstered booths, and heavy draperies dividing open, private, and semi-private dining areas.

1. Kitchen
2. Open kitchen
3. Dining area
4. Semiprivate dining
5. Private dining
6. Bar
7. Entry
8. Refrigeration
9. Dishwasher

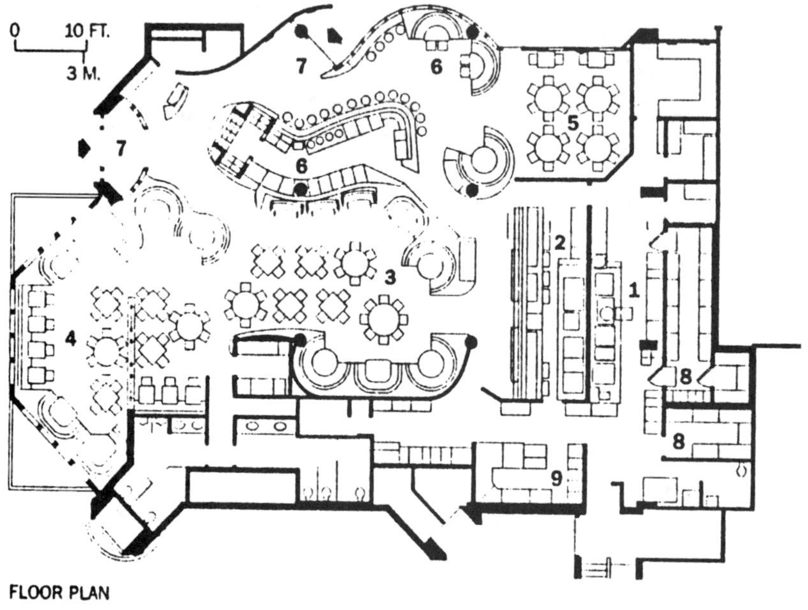

FLOOR PLAN

■ **FIGURE 10–4**

Floor plan courtesy of the California Café Bar and Grill in Schaumburg, Illinois

■ TABLE 10–1
Dimensions for Commercial Foodservice Kitchens

Type of Service	Kitchen Square Footage per Dining Room Seat	Total Square Footage in the Back of the House per Seat
Cafeteria/commercial	6–8	10–12
Coffee shop	4–6	8–10
Table service restaurant	5–7	10–12

Source: Robert A. Modlin, ed., Commercial Kitchens, 7th ed. (Arlington, Va.: American Gas Association, 1989).

stainless-steel counter where food is picked up by staff. A hole in the counter can be used for dropping garbage into a container. A few exhibition kitchens cook by induction coils. Some open kitchens use under-the-counter refrigeration units to conserve space and expedite work. The area set aside for open kitchens costs about 25% more than in a standard kitchen. A floor plan of an open kitchen is shown in Figure 10–4.

The noise level of a completely open kitchen must be reduced with washable acoustic tile in the ceiling. The dining room and banquet rooms must feature carpet, upholstered chairs, and washable window drapes, plus acoustic ceilings. A few visually open kitchens are enclosed in glass, which eliminates the noise problem.

Costas Katsigris and Chris Thomas, in their book *Design and Equipment for Restaurants and Foodservice: A Management View*, assembled a number of tables that show the range in space needed for various restaurant activities.[5] The tables can be used as reference when buying, building, or modifying a restaurant. In general—there are many exceptions, depending on the restaurant service—kitchens are about half the size of the dining room, and the space needed for seating varies:

Deluxe—15 to 20 square feet per seat
Medium—12 to 18 square feet per seat
Banquet—10 to 15 square feet per seat

The space needed in the back of the house varies as well:

Deluxe—7 to 10 square feet per seat
Medium—5 to 9 square feet per seat
Banquet—3 to 5 square feet per seat[6]

■ TABLE 10–2
Dimensions for School Foodservice Kitchens

Meals per Day	Total Facility Square Footage	Main Kitchen Square Footage
200	730–1015	400–500
400	1215–1620	700–900
600	1825–2250	1100–1300

Source: Robert A. Modlin, ed., Commercial Kitchens, 7th ed. (Arlington, Va.: American Gas Association, 1989).

■ **TABLE 10–3**

Space Dimensions for Receiving Areas

Meals Served per Day	Receiving Area Square Footage
200–300	50–60
300–500	60–90
500–1000	90–130

Source: Carl Scriven and James Stevens, *Food Equipment Facts* (New York: John Wiley and Sons, 1989).

■ **TABLE 10–4**

Space Dimensions for Dry Storage

Meals Served per Day	Dry Storage Square Footage
100–200	120–200
200–350	200–250
350–500	250–400

Source: Carl Scriven and James Stevens, *Food Equipment Facts* (New York: John Wiley and Sons, 1989).

KITCHEN FLOOR COVERINGS

Kitchen floors are usually covered with quarry tile, marble, terrazzo, asphalt tile, or sealed concrete—materials that are nonabsorbent, easy to clean, and resistant to the abrasive action of cleaning chemicals. In areas where water is likely to accumulate (for example, near the dishwasher), neoprene matting provides traction, making walking and standing less stressful than it is on hard surfaces. In all kitchen areas, the surfaces should be covered with nonskid material. The number-one cause of restaurant accidents is slipping and falling. Older employees who fall, may break bones or suffer a concussion. The same rule applies in dining rooms with even more urgency. Large lawsuits against restaurants have been won by plaintiffs who have fallen and broken bones.

Carpeting in kitchens is not permitted by building codes. Coving, the curved, sealed edge on kitchen perimeters that eliminates sharp corners and gaps, is essential.

Perhaps the most effective way to prevent slips and falls in kitchens and elsewhere in a restaurant is to enforce a rigid rule that anything spilled, including water, be wiped up at once.

KITCHEN EQUIPMENT

Selection of kitchen equipment may seem simple or complex, depending on your level of experience. Independent restaurants may be copies of existing restaurants, more or less duplicating kitchen layout and equipment. Operators taking over an existing restaurant are likely to continue using the equipment already there. Equipment dealers are ready to make recommendations. Restaurant shows, where dozens of equipment manufacturers display their wares, are staged each year; the largest is one managed by the National Restaurant Association in Chicago. A similar one is held in New York City and

■ **TABLE 10–5**

Full-Door Reach-Ins

Number of Doors	Height (inches)	Width (inches)	Depth (inches)	Cubic Feet
1	78	28	32	22
2	78	56	32	50
3	78	84	32	70–80

Source: Carl Scrivner and James Stevens, *Food Equipment Facts*, (New York: John Wiley and Sons, 1989).

■ **TABLE 10–6**

Walk-Ins (All 7′6″ Height)

Size of Unit	Square Footage	Cubic Feet
5′9″ × 7′8″	35.7	259.9
6′8″ × 8′7″	47.4	331.8
7′8″ × 7′8″	49.0	340.2
8′7″ × 11′6″	86.4	604.8

Source: Carl Scriven and James Stevens, *Food Equipment Facts* (New York: John Wiley and Sons, 1989).

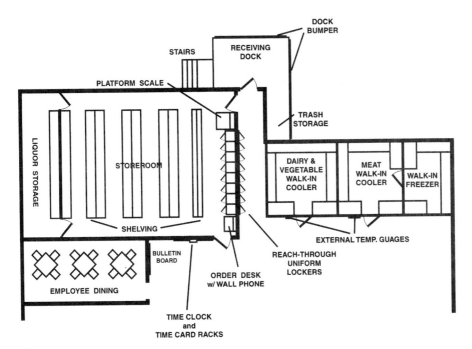

■ **FIGURE 10–5**

The Back of the House: A layout for a receiving and storage area that includes a separate employee break room. **Source:** *Costas Katsigris and Chris Thomas,* **Design and Equipment for Restaurants and Foodservice** *(New York: John Wiley and Sons, 1999), 39.*

another in California each year. Tens of thousands of foodservice operators attend these shows to see new developments in food and equipment.

As previously discussed, professional restaurant planners are available for a fee to plan, lay out, and recommend restaurant equipment. They can also help in developing, changing, or modifying concepts.

■ *Categories of Kitchen Equipment*

The standard equipment needed in restaurant kitchens can be divided into those needed to:

- Receive and store food
- Fabricate and prepare food.
- Prepare and process food.
- Assemble, hold, and serve food.
- Clean up and sanitize the kitchen and kitchenware.

■ *Select the Right Equipment*

Anyone selecting kitchen equipment, beginner or veteran, faces some common questions:

- Of the equipment available, which will be the most efficient for the menu, item by item, and for menu items contemplated in the future?

STORAGE

Cold storage reach-in-units   Cold storage walk-in units

FABRICATION and PRE-PREPARATION

Breading machines	Cutters and slicers	Mixers
Can openers	Knife sharpeners	Peelers

PREPARATION and PROCESSING

Broilers	Hot dog cooking equipment	Revolving tray ovens
Cheese melters	Hot plates	Steamers
Convection ovens	Microwave ovens	Steam-jacketed kettles
Display cooking equipment	Mobile mini-kitchens	Steam boilers
Egg cookers	Ovens	Tilting fry pans
Frying equipment	Proof cabinets	Ventilators
Griddles and grills	Ranges	Waffle bakers

ASSEMBLY, HOLDING, and SERVING

Beverage equipment	Dispensing equipment	Mobile buffet and banquet
Coffee brewers	Food reconstitutors	equipment
Coffee ranges	Hot serving equipment	Shake and soft-serve
Cold serving equipment	Infrared warmers	equipment
Dish-dispensing equipment		Toasters

CLEANUP and SANITATION

Cleaning and sanitizing	Dishwashing equipment	Glass washers
Compactors	Disposers	Water-heating equipment

FIGURE 10–6

Electric equipment found in restaurants

- What is the equipment's purchase cost and the operating cost?
- Should the equipment be gas fired or electric?
- Will the equipment produce the food fast enough to meet demand?
- Is it better to buy a large unit or two or more smaller units?
- Are replacement parts and service readily available?
- Is reliable used equipment available?

■

Match Equipment with Menu and Production Schedule

The menu determines the equipment. Look at the menu, item by item. What equipment is needed to prepare each item? Other variables include:

- *The projected volume of sales for each menu item.* What size of equipment or how many pieces of equipment will be needed? Do not overequip. Market conditions may force menu changes.

- *Fixed or changing menu.* A fixed menu needs fewer kinds of equipment.

- *Menu size.* Large menus may call for a greater variety of equipment.
- *Speed of service desired.* Fast service may call for equipment of larger capacity. Reduced cooking time translates into higher seat turnover in the dining room.
- *Nutritional awareness and equipment selected.* Interest in nutrition brings an increased interest in the method of food preparation used. Frying is avoided to cut down on consumption of fats. Baking, broiling, and steaming are more healthful ways to prepare meat, fish, and fowl.

Multiple uses for equipment means less kitchen space must be allocated to equipment. Slow cooking with ovens can be done during the night, freeing up oven space for daytime use. Small-quantity, staggered cooking for vegetables can be done with a relatively small piece of steam-pressure equipment.

Total Cost versus Original Cost

The initial cost of equipment is but one factor in the cost equation. What about life expectancy and parts replacement? How often must the magnetrons in a microwave be replaced? How long do the infrared lamps last? The thermostatic controls in the fryer?

Even more important is the cost of energy each piece of equipment consumes. In most locations, gas is much less expensive than electricity, sometimes dramatically so. Electric equipment requires warm-up time. Gas heat is immediate. Cost of warm-up time is considerable on equipment that is used intermittently. Over the period of a year, the operational cost differential becomes an important factor in the choice of equipment.

Select the Most Efficient Equipment for the People and Skills Available

Too often a kitchen is loaded with equipment seldom or never used. Select only those pieces of equipment that are most efficient and necessary for the menu. Many European kitchens and small restaurant kitchens in the United States prepare outstanding food using only a stovetop burner, pots and pans, a few knives, and other small equipment. A few seafood restaurants produce a high volume of food using only deep fryers. McDonald's restaurants are built around a griddle and deep fryers.

Burger Chef restaurants and several other large hamburger chains revolve around a conveyor-type broiler.

De-skilling the Job with Equipment

Much of the new kitchen equipment is planned to reduce or eliminate cooking skills. One of the best examples of this type of equipment is the conveyor broiler used by several fast-food hamburger chains. The employee only needs to place frozen patties of hamburger on the conveyor belt, which carries the patties through flames directed from above and below. The movement of the conveyor belt is timed so that when the patties drop out at the other end of the broiler, they are done. There is no need for the employee to know when to turn the patties, how to control the griddle temperature, or to clean the griddle. The same is true of the new conveyor pizza ovens.

Automatic crêpe-making machines are controlled so that a perfect crêpe is produced automatically, without timing or turning.

The grooved griddle de-skills broiling. The griddle maintains a constant temperature and meat is merely placed on it. There is no need to raise or lower a rack to control temperature, as must be done with traditional broilers.

The quartz-fired griddle produces heat from above as well as from below and eliminates the need for turning the food.

Cook-chill and sous vide are two techniques that have gained in popularity. Cook-chill is a process that makes it possible to safely and efficiently prepare large quantities of food for long-term storage in a refrigerated environment.[7] Food is prepared and rapidly chilled to prevent bacterial growth and is available in portions of various sizes and can provide consistent quality and substantial reduction in labor cost and stress levels in the kitchen. Food is prepared to restock inventory rather than to order. One of the best applications of cook-chill is when cooking batches of food in a centralized kitchen for later use in a satellite facility.

Sous vide is popular in Europe, especially in France, where it was developed. With this technique, food is prepared in the restaurant kitchen, often during slack times. It is then individually vacuum packed and refrigerated for future use. Perhaps the best application of sous vide is for à la carte menu restaurants and for a group of restaurants that share a centralized production kitchen. Sous vide requires refrigeration equipment and a vacuum-packing machine, but these costs may be recovered by labor savings and more effective portion control.

EQUIPMENT STARS

The principal pieces of cooking equipment—the stars—are selected to best prepare the principal menu items. The other equipment is arranged around the stars and constitutes the supporting cast.

The stars of a hamburger restaurant are the griddle (or broiler) and the deep-fat fryers. The same is true for the coffee shop and pancake restaurants. In a full-service restaurant, stovetops, ovens, and broilers dominate the scene. In a Chinese restaurant, the star is the wok, a large basinlike pan around which the supporting equipment is arranged.

In planning a kitchen and selecting equipment, think of the dominant menu items, those expected to have the highest volume of sales. Cooking equipment for these items is placed to support the cooking stations. Preparation of these foods can take place elsewhere, but preferably close by.

The Stove/Oven

Probably the most prominent piece of equipment in the full-service kitchen is the traditional range, the combination stove and oven, fired by gas or electricity (Figure 10–7). The kitchen is often planned around the stove/oven. With the availability of convection ovens, steam-jacketed kettles, and tilting skillets, some kitchen planners deliberately eliminate the range, regarding it as cumbersome and inefficient. Newer equipment that transfers heat more efficiently than the old space-consuming range is preferred. Important pieces of cooking equipment are the oven, tilting skillet, combination convection and microwave oven, convection steam cooker, the microwave oven, and the deep fryer. The rangetop stove, however, is still probably the workhouse of a full-service restaurant kitchen.

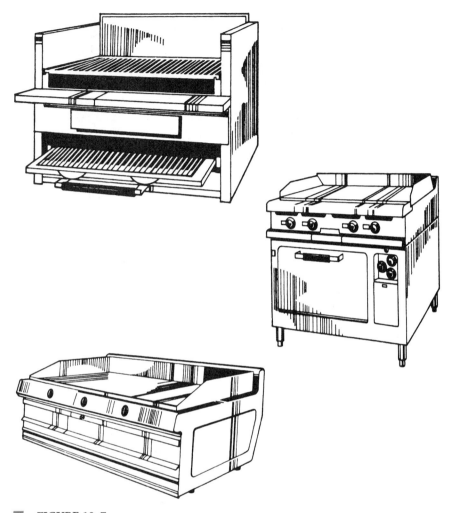

■ FIGURE 10–7

Broilers: *Charbroilers have briquettes, that when heated, give off heat for broiling food. Ceramic broilers use ceramic chips that are heated to high temperatures and give off heat. Open-hearth broilers produce heat from gas flames or electric rods that focus heat directly onto meats from below. Oven-fired broilers produce heat from over the racks holding the meat. Infrared models produce infrared rays once temperatures of 160°F and more are reached. The time it takes to preheat a broiler is a consideration; infrared broilers require heat from above and below simultaneously. Salamander or back-shelf broilers are usually used in conjunction with an oven to hold or finish cooking food. They are sometimes used to create a crust on food or to apply quick heat to a sauced food.*

Griddles: *Griddles, the heated flat surfaces used for fast-cooking such items as hamburgers, eggs, and pancakes, are a principal cooking device for fast-food restaurants. Some can be heated by section.*

The sectionalized griddle, whose surface has sections separately controlled for temperature, can cook different foods at different temperatures at the same time: 300°F for eggs, 350°F for sausages, and 400°F for small steaks. The sectionalized griddle provides flexibility. If only hamburgers are to be cooked, all sections can be set at the same temperature, or one section can be set at a lower temperature for slower cooling in case customer demand is unpredictable.

Griddle tops are usually made of steel boilerplate, ½ to 1 inch thick. The thicker ones are less likely to warp. Some tops are made of sheet aluminum, and one brand is made of steel with a chromium surface. The griddle surface itself can be on a stand, mounted on a table, or set as part of a rangetop. To achieve even temperature across the griddle surface, a heat pipe has been introduced.

To determine the size of griddle needed, planners project the volume of food to be cooked during peak periods and the time required for each item to cook. If a hamburger requires four minutes to cook and 100 are needed during the peak hour, 25 hamburgers must be cooked at one time. One griddle is needed. Suppose that eggs, pancakes, and other foods will also be ordered during the peak period. Two griddles are called for. Two griddles, placed side by side, enable two cooks to work simultaneously. Two griddles also permit a trainee cook to watch, work, and learn alongside an experienced cook. Most coffee shops install two griddles side by side, even though both may be needed at the same time only an hour or two each day. Alternatively, a sectionalized griddle with separate controls for each griddle may do the job.

To maximize the griddle during peak periods, some foods may be precooked in a steamer, then finished quickly on the griddle during mealtime.

Griddles require adjacent worktables for holding and getting food ready. Arthur Avery, restaurant consultant, suggests that 60% of a griddle operator's time is spent at a table working on the next batch of food. Because of this, he recommends placing a worktable or worktop conveniently to the left of the griddle. To the right of the griddle, he places a pan with overhead infrared lamps to keep the cooked food hot and to dry out moisture that migrates to the food surface and softens the crust.[8]

In purchasing a griddle, Avery recommends buying only those that preheat to 350°F or 400°F in 7 to 12 minutes. To conserve energy, he recommends covering a griddle not in use with a metal or, preferably, a pressed-foam cover.

Griddles serve multiple purposes. They can substitute for a solid-top range; perhaps one part is used as a griddle, the other as a stovetop. Griddles are used for browning and cooking meat, cooking pancakes and eggs, and toasting buns and sandwiches.

More recently, the grooved griddle has been widely used for cooking steaks and, in many fast-food restaurants, it has replaced the broiler. The ridges in the griddle produce marks on a steak similar to a broiler and the grooves allow fat and juices to drain off, avoiding most of the smoke created by the conventional broiler. Another consideration: The grooved griddle uses less fuel than a broiler. The grooved griddle is popular with chain operators because much less skill is required to cook meat. Hamburgers cooked by grooved griddle are less likely to be burned. With a hot broiler, if the cook looks away for a minute or two and the hamburger becomes a charburger.

■

Deep-Frying Equipment

Manufacturers produce fryers designed for water boiling with thermostats that go up to 212°F (as opposed to 390°F for deep-fat fryers). Operators use these fryers to boil seafood, vegetables, and pasta products (Figure 10–8).

Pressure fryers are fryers whose lids, when closed, act to create pressure within the fry kettle. Increased pressure reduces the cooking time by as much as one half, mainly because less evaporative cooling occurs. Some pressure fryers include moisture injection systems. The water injected turns to steam.

Deep-fat fryers can act as cooking pots; filled with water they can be used for quick-cooking vegetables, cooking hams or frankfurters, reheating foods, hard-boiling eggs, cooking macaroni or spaghetti, or holding canned or containerized foods. (Electric fryers cannot be so used; water will affect the heating element.)

A number of restaurants that serve fresh vegetables blanch them in a deep fryer, remove them, and immediately cover them with ice to stop the cooking process. Blanched vegetables can be held in a refrigerator for later service. Final preparation is done by sautéing the vegetables and serving them immediately.

■ FIGURE 10–8

Deep-frying equipment. Electric or gas-fired kettle for holding fat or oil in which baskets can be immersed for frying food. Temperature usually can be controlled in a range of 325° to 400°F.

■ *Tilting Skillets*

Tilting skillets are mounted on pivots, allowing them to tilt and dispense food that has been cooked in them.

Because of the temperature control that is possible, when fired by gas, tilting skillets can be used to braise or roast meat, cook pancakes, scramble or fry eggs, simmer, cook roux, and fry chicken. They serve as grills, hot tops, ranges, and ovens; with a lid, they become steamers. The tilting skillet has been called "a pot that thinks; it's a griddle and a griddle that acts like a pot."

The tilting skillet is most versatile (Figure 10–9). It is used as a fry pan, kettle, griddle, steamer, and poacher. With a little ingenuity, it can also be used as a proof box and bake oven. Filled with about four inches of water and set at 175°F, it becomes a steam

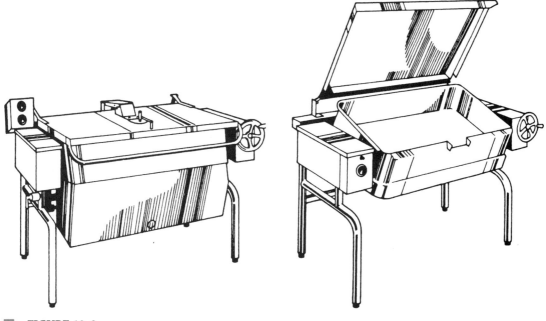

■ FIGURE 10–9

Tilting skillets

table—a large pan with hot water for holding hot foods. In an emergency, it can be used to sanitize dishes.

Different manufacturers call tilting skillets by different names: tilting skillet, braising pan, and sauté pan. With its four sides and flat bottom, it could be called a flat-bottomed frying pan.

Insulated sides make for less energy consumption and a cooler kitchen. Tilting skillets with insulation can be purchased.

A major advantage of the tilting skillet is its fast startup and controls that permit low temperature settings—so low that it can be used, cover down, for holding food, or for low-temperature roasting at 200°F.

Low-Temperature Ovens

Low-temperature ovens that permit low-temperature roasting and baking are widely used in the restaurant business to reduce shrinkage of meat and to hold meat so that it can be served to order from the oven. One such oven, the Auto Sham, an electric-fired oven, is popular for roasting beef. A large coffee shop chain buys two- to three-pound tips (meat cut in chunks near the sirloin). The tips are cooked for four hours at 250°F and held at 140° to 150°F. All of the meat is cooked to the rare stage or a little above. If medium beef is called for, the ends are used. When well-done is ordered, a hot "au jus" is poured over the meat to bring it to the well-done stage.

Forced-Air Convection Ovens

This type of oven is similar to a conventional oven except that a fan or rotor, usually located in the back, makes for rapid circulation of the air and quicker heating of the food, and preheating and cooking times are considerably less than with the conventional oven. Directions for baking with a convection oven must be followed exactly, otherwise some foods, such as sheet cakes, will dry out excessively on top. A pan of water is placed in the oven when baking some foods to humidify the oven air and reduce moisture loss in the food.

Microwave Ovens

The cooking chamber of the microwave oven is usually small and lesser capacity than that of larger conventional or other types of ovens (Figure 10–11). Magnetrons in the top of the oven emit microwaves. These electromagnetic waves of 915 megacycles or 2,450 megacycles penetrate foods in the chamber and are absorbed by food materials containing water, agitating the water and fat molecules to produce heat, which is conducted to other kinds of molecules surrounding them. Cooking by microwave relies completely on radiated energy to penetrate food materials and set up intermolecular friction, which heats the food.

There is no preheating time, because once the microwaves are produced they travel at the speed of light and enter the food material almost instantaneously. Microwave ovens produce relatively small quantities of cooked food as compared to standard ovens. However, they are excellent for reheating small quantities of food.

Strangely, some materials are transparent to the waves and are not heated by them. Glass, china, and paper containers do not absorb the waves. Metal reflects the waves, so metal containers are not used in microwave ovens.

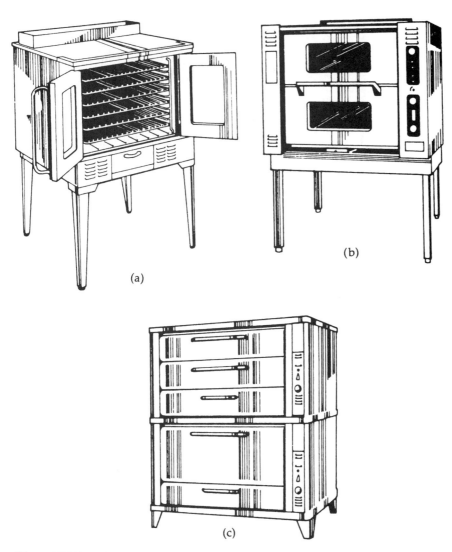

(a)

(b)

(c)

◼ FIGURE 10–10

Kinds of ovens: (a) Conventional ovens. Standard or range ovens heat food by heating the air in a chamber. This air surrounds food and cooks it. (b) Deck ovens. Same as conventional ovens, except that the chambers are long, deep, and usually rectangular. Constructed in sections, each deck is stacked on top of another. Each section can be operated separately and at a different temperature. (c) Slow roasting ovens. These ovens permit steady, low temperatures to be used, primarily for roasting meats. Some of them can be preset to roast for two or three hours, say 300°F, then turn themselves down to 140°F and maintain that temperature until the meat is needed. A cook can place a roast in such an oven at 11:00 P.M., allow it to cook for three hours at 250°F and then remain at 140°F until needed for the next day's lunch. Shrinkage of 10% or less is common when using these ovens for roasting beef.

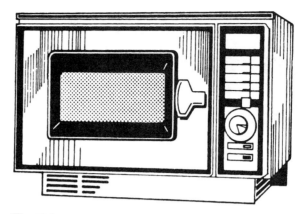

■ **FIGURE 10–11**
Microwave oven

Because microwaves are absorbed preferentially by water, cooking is not uniform. Instead of heat being applied to the surface of the food, then being conducted slowly into the interior of the food, microwave energy heats the food under the surface as well. The surface is left uncooked and relatively cool, unless the oven contains a special browning unit with infrared heating elements.

■ **Advantages and Disadvantages of Microwave Cooking.** Microwave cooking has several advantages over conventional methods of cooking. The energy can be directed; there is no heat loss to the kitchen from the oven, and the speed of cooking is amazingly fast for small quantities of food.

Without a browning unit and used correctly, there is no spillage or sputtering, which makes for easy cleaning. There is little fire hazard.

The principal disadvantage of the microwave oven for commercial kitchen use is its relatively low capacity. It is usually the fastest-cooking device available for heating, defrosting, or cooking one or a few small items like a single casserole, hot dog sandwich, lobster tail, or trout. All of these are high-moisture items. As additional items are placed in the oven, heating or cooking time may increase by 75% or more per item. A microwave oven can bake a single Idaho potato in a little over 5 to 7 minutes, compared to an hour for a conventional oven. Two potatoes almost double the baking time in the microwave oven. The conventional oven bakes 2, or perhaps 50 potatoes in the same one-hour period.

The second major disadvantage of the microwave oven is a result of its very advantage—its speed. A few seconds short or long, and the food is under- or overdone. Different food materials heat at different rates. For example, bread in a frozen sandwich heats faster and is overheated before the filling is thawed; fat and water heat faster than muscle. Also, microwaves do not evenly distribute in a food, which results in uneven heating and cooking. Other variables are involved, making microwave ovens the most complex to use of all cooking equipment in the present-day kitchen. In restaurants, microwave ovens are mostly used to heat finished food items. When a quantity of food over 8 pounds is to be cooked, the microwave oven cooks no faster than a conventional oven. Some practical uses for microwave ovens are:

- Reheating previously cooked foods
- Quickly heating desserts
- Defrosting
- Special-request orders
- Precooking

Its principal use is probably for reheating frozen foods that have already been cooked. The microwave oven has little value for producing baked-dough items or any food that involves a leavening action.

Infrared Cooking Equipment

Like microwave energy, infrared waves, transmitted at the speed of light, can penetrate the vapor blanket that surrounds moist food when heated. Infrared wavelengths used for cooking are only microns in length. Wavelengths of about 1.4 to 5 microns are said to be the most effective for cooking foods. Several specialized infrared ovens are marketed for the purpose of reheating frozen foods. Infrared broilers and ovens, which reduce cooking time, are also being produced.

Relatively new equipment on the market uses infrared emitters above and below a conveyor belt or in compartments resembling a standard oven. Electrically fired, the emitters can be temperature controlled separately, depending on the product being cooked. An 8-ounce filet mignon, for example, can be cooked in ten minutes using 700°F temperature on both the top and bottom deck. A 9-inch deep-dish pizza takes 14 minutes using 575°F on the lower deck and 650°F on the upper deck. A 12-ounce soufflé is done in 12 minutes using 530°F for both decks. Cookies are done in seven minutes using 500°F.

Steam Cooking Equipment

The convection steamer is different from other steamers in that it operates at atmospheric pressure. Most steam equipment relies on steam pressure to move the steam about the food or pan to speed heat transfer. With equipment under pressure, there is some danger. Gaskets must be replaced frequently and sometimes the door jams so that it is difficult to open. The convection steamer, on the other hand, moves the steam around, creating convection currents (hence the name). Cooking time is longer than steam under pressure because the temperature is lower, about 212°F, than the higher temperatures created as pressure is increased.

Steam-jacketed kettles ranging in capacity from about 1 gallon to 500 gallons are surrounded by an enclosed shell into which steam is introduced. The steam does not come into contact with the food in the kettle but, as it condenses, it gives up its latent energy (the heat absorbed or released by a substance undergoing a change of state from water to steam). The heat passes through the shell into the food inside the kettle. If the steam is under pressure, its temperature increases above 212°F.

Steam-jacketed kettles should have covers for energy conservation. Keeping the cover closed during the heating of kettle contents reduces energy usage 5 to 10% and when the contents reach boiling temperature, the energy reduction is 23 to 33%. Cooks have resisted covers on steam-jacketed kettles because of the cloud of steam released

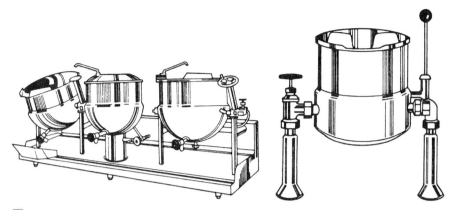

■ **FIGURE 10–12**

Steam-jacketed kettles

when the cover is raised. This can be avoided by placing the cover hinge halfway between the back and the side away from the cook. A scraper-type mixer can be inserted into the kettles, which speeds heat transfer and reduces cooking time.

Another advantage of steam-jacketed cooking is that the steam can be replaced by cold water, which quickly cools food that need such treatment, such as puddings, gelatins, and desserts.

Rather than boiling food in a kettle, many products call for simmering, which is not done at 212°F but at 185°F. Kettles can be used to heat canned or precooked vegetables quickly and readily by stacking these products criss-cross fashion with a small amount of water in the bottom (Figure 10–12). These products are heated only to serving temperature: 160°F.

■

Hot-Food Holding Tables

Food being held almost always loses quality, but in many restaurants there is little choice but to hold some of it prior to service. Hot tables constitute the serving containers in cafeteria service. Here, warming tables patterned after the old bain marie (water bath) are needed. The bain marie is simply a tank holding heated water in which hot foods in pots or crocks are placed to keep food warm and to avoid cooking. The modern steam table is heated by gas, electric, or steam elements controlled by a thermostat.

The more sophisticated warming tables are sectionalized to permit specific temperatures for particular foods: soup at 180°F, meats at 145° to 150°F, and vegetables at 140°F. Those tables containing heated water keep the foods moist and delay their drying out. The typical hot-food table holds a number of steam table pans 12 by 12 inches in size.

It should be remembered that although hot tables are not cooking appliances, foods held above 140°F are still cooking. Foods to be held any length of time should, therefore, be slightly undercooked.

Refrigerators and Freezers

A refrigerator or freezer can be thought of as two boxes, one inside the other, separated by insulation. Heat is withdrawn from the inside box by a cooling system. The insulating material is usually polyurethane foam. The cooling system consists of a compressed gas that is allowed to expand within the cooled interior. An expansion valve permits the gas to expand into an evaporator. As it expands, the gas absorbs heat and is returned to the compressor where, under pressure, it becomes a liquid.

Refrigerators require a minimum of 2 inches of polyurethane insulation; freezers require 3 inches.

Large restaurants need considerable refrigerator and freezer space, usually large enough for a person to walk into; such coolers are called walk-in boxes. Refrigerator drawers and under-counter refrigerators permit storage at point of use. Reach-in refrigerators conserve energy.

Multiple-rack units on wheels permit maximum storage and save energy in moving food in and out of refrigerators. See-through glass or Plexiglas doors reduce the need for opening. Kitchen planners recommend the following amount of refrigerator space on a per-meal basis for a luxury restaurant:

Meat/poultry	.030 cubic feet
Dairy products	.015 cubic feet
Produce	.040 cubic feet

Walk-in boxes are often placed adjacent to food-receiving areas. Doors can be installed on two sides, one on the receiving side and one on the exit side toward the preparation area. Food can then be received at one side of the box and taken out on the other when needed.

Compressors should be located away from the kitchen or in the basement so that heat generated by their use is not dumped into the kitchen itself and so that the noise of the compressors is unobtrusive.

For efficient functioning, coils within the refrigerator must be kept defrosted and free of ice. If the coils are icy, the cooling system cannot pick up heat within the box and transport it away.

Ice Machines

Restaurants need at least one ice machine for producing ice for ice water and for such beverages as soft drinks, iced tea, and—if liquor is served—a variety of alcoholic drinks. Machines are available for producing small-sized cubes ideal for tall drinks, which make a tall drink look even taller.

Ice cubes are good for beverages served at banquets. The larger size melts more slowly and lasts longer.

Crushed ice drops the temperature of a beverage quickly and is also used as part of a salad bar, oyster bar, or juice display.

The hotter the climate, the more ice capacity is needed. A bar often has its own ice machine. A 100-seat restaurant with a bar probably needs an ice machine capable of producing 400 pounds of ice during the hours of operation and having a storage capacity of 540 pounds (see Table 10–7).

■ **TABLE 10–7**
Ice-Sizing Guide Suggested for Temperate Climate

Restaurant Type	Realistic Average	Production/Storage Recommendations
Informal (with soft drinks)	0.5–1# Person	400#/540# for 125–200 seats
Formal (no liquor)	0.5# Person	300#/540# for 100–125 seats
Formal (with liquor)	1.5# Person	800#/750# for 200 seats
Drive-ins	0.5# Person	—
Fast food	0.25# Person	800#/750# per $1 million of sales
Cafeterias	0.5# Person	—
(iced salad bar)	10/sq. ft. display	200#/400# crushed ice
Cocktail lounges		
(with restaurant)	1# Person	400#/540# for 125 seats
Bar (no food)	0.5# Person	200#/170# Avg. or 300#/235#
Taverns (mostly beer with limited food)	Small 100#/day	100#/65# (for possible underbar application)
	Medium 200#/day	200#/170#
	Large 300#/day	300#/235#

Some experts advise against buying one central machine, which, if broken, leaves the restaurant without ice. Rather, purchasing two or more smaller machines and locating them near their points of use is recommended.

■
Pasta-Making Machines

A number of restaurants that feature pasta have purchased their own pasta-making machines and each week produce various types of pasta: macaroni, vermicelli, fettuccine, and the like. With the low cost of flour, and if volume of sales warrants, the purchase of such a machine pays for itself in a short time. Operation of the machine is fairly simple. Different pasta products are produced by simply changing an extruder head through which the dough is forced.

■
Other Specialty Cooking Equipment

As might be expected, special foodservice equipment has been developed for special menus. Hot food items on a Mexican menu, for example, are best served at higher than average temperatures. Some Mexican restaurant operators use convection ovens. Characteristically, a chili sauce or a cheese sauce covers the entrées, and these are placed under a cheese melter for a short time just prior to service. A cheese melter is an overhead, broiler-type piece of equipment, usually several feet long and just wide enough to hold a plate. It is used for toasting, browning, and finishing. It is recommended for preparation of lobster, garlic bread, and au gratin potatoes.

Restaurants that feature salads may have a spin drier in which centrifugal force whips off excess moisture from salad greens. Places that use frozen entrées may use a special quartz-fired oven for quick reheating.

Special spaghetti cookers, dough mixers, pasta-making machines, pizza ovens, and an array of other special cooking equipment are available. Adaptations of old equipment are constantly being made.

New forms of energy are being developed. Stovetops that use magnetic induction coils for energy are a novelty at this time but could be commonplace in the future.

Several chains have developed special equipment for producing featured items in front of the patron. Crêpe-making machines are a good example; the machines are located near the restaurant entrance or other focal point, where patrons can watch the crêpes being made.

None of the heavy-duty electrical equipment operates on the standard 110/120 volts installed for residential use. A revolving brush glass washer may operate on 110-volt wiring, but equipment calling for large amperage needs the heavy-duty wiring carrying 208, 240, or 480 volts. Heavy-duty motors may call for 208/240-60, one-phase current; others call for 440/480-60 three-phase current. Booster heaters call for as much as 550 volts. Rewiring a kitchen to fit a particular piece of equipment can be costly.

Natural gas requires a different size jet and different settings from that for LP (low-pressure) gas. The heating qualities of the two are quite different.

■ **Evaporative Coolers.**   Evaporative coolers installed in kitchens reduce the cost of cooling considerably where humidity in the outside air is low, as in desert areas. The coolers take in outside dry air and pass it through loosely woven pads. Water from the regular water supply is either dripped or pumped over the pads. As the fresh air is drawn by a blower through the pads, it is cooled and filtered. Water in the wetted pads evaporates and as it does so, absorbs the heat as it changes from water to vapor. This is evaporative cooling, known as the heat of fusion-energy involved when matter changes from one form to another.

Evaporative cooling, although inexpensive, is not usually satisfactory for the dining room because the air brought in from the outside absorbs moisture. On muggy days or in climates with high humidity, moisture accumulates in the dining room. The kitchen, however, is a different matter. There, air movement to the outside is usually rapid, air being pulled up the exhaust ducts to rid the kitchen of noxious fumes, odors, and accumulated heat from the cooking equipment. Evaporative coolers are used even in St. Louis, known for its high humidity.

Because evaporative coolers have no need of compressors, they operate at approximately 25% of the cost of operating a refrigerated air-conditioning unit of similar cooling capacity.

Evaporative coolers can be used in combination with refrigerated air-conditioning, relying on evaporative cooling except on the hottest, most humid days. Evaporative cooling is a relatively inexpensive way of making the kitchen a much more pleasant and efficient place to work, provided outside humidity is low.

■

Other Equipment

Numerous other small kitchen items are available that may be useful for a particular menu. Such items include ice cream holding units, display cases, cream dispensers, meat patty–making machines, garbage disposals, infrared heating lamps, drink dispensers, dough dividers, and bakers' stoves.

■ **Used Equipment.**   Because so many restaurants go out of business, used equipment is almost always available from equipment dealers. Few items fall more drastically in value after purchase. Once bought, restaurant equipment may drop as much as 80% in value. Restaurant equipment auctions may offer excellent used equipment.

Used items without moving parts are about as good used as new. Examples are sinks, wire shelving, worktables, steam tables, cutting boards, kitchen utensils, and cooling racks. Refrigeration units may need only compressor replacement. Old mechanical equipment, however, may not be a bargain, because of the difficulty of locating replacement parts.

MAINTAINING KITCHEN EQUIPMENT[9]

Maintenance of equipment is a little like preventive medicine. By following certain practices, major problems can be avoided. Moving parts, when properly oiled, last longer. Removing grease and dirt from compressors helps ensure that they are not overworked. Clean griddles operate better than those with grease deposits on their surfaces. Gas burners adjusted for gas-air mixtures provide more heat. Checking electric wires for loose connections or frayed insulation can avert fires and equipment breakdown.

Restaurant equipment is generally thought to have a life expectancy of about ten years. Yet, properly cared for, equipment can last much longer. For best maintenance information, consult the instructions provided by the manufacturer. The old quip "When everything else fails, read the instructions" is just too true. Restaurant operators are likely to be more people-oriented, sales-oriented, and food-oriented than mechanically inclined. A schedule of maintenance helps and is one of those details that makes a good restaurant both a work of art and a nuts-and-bolts business.

The usual restaurant operators give little thought to regular maintenance of kitchen equipment. They are too involved in other problems and in keeping up with the demands of the day-to-day operation—purchasing and receiving food, replacing personnel, handling complaints, and seeing to it that the operation moves smoothly. Knowing this, chain operators often employ a full-time mechanic who moves from restaurant to restaurant performing maintenance checks or who can be called to handle breakdowns of equipment. Because every piece of equipment eventually breaks down or deteriorates, especially if it has moving parts, it pays to establish and follow a system of maintenance that forestalls breakdowns or emergency situations.

Dishwashing Equipment

The place where most equipment headaches occur is in the dish machine.[10] It is not uncommon for the hot-water booster heater, used to raise the temperature to the 180°F needed for dish sanitation, to break down. As a result, thousands of dishes are washed without the benefit of sanitization. As water is heated in the booster, minerals in the water tend to precipitate out and deposit on the walls and in the pipes of the heater. These deposits can be removed by periodic flushing; open the drain valve and drain two to five gallons of water from the tank, then run the water until it flows clear. If the local water contains a high percentage of lime or other minerals, the heater may need to be drained monthly.

Repair of dish machines is usually beyond the capacity of the manager or kitchen personnel. This means that a mechanic must be brought in. In the time that it takes to repair the machine, the dish machine room can become bedlam. Inevitably, dishware breakage is high.

If the dish machine water is heated by steam, there is usually a steam trap through which the condensate flows. The condensate, which is in the form of water, then flows back into the boiler, where it is reheated and converted to steam again. The steam trap is intended to permit the condensate—but not the steam—to pass out of the heater. The trap blocks the steam and frees it to condense into water before it leaves the heater. The trap can jam shut or open. If it jams open, the steam blows through the trap, wasting energy and causing problems in other parts of the system. If it jams shut, neither steam nor condensate can pass through, and no water will be heated. Many installations include a test valve that can be operated to see if the trap is working. Follow the instruction sheet provided by the manufacturer.

Because the steam trap prevents steam from passing out into the heater, one way to determine if it is operating is to put on canvas-type work gloves and simultaneously grasp the pipe leading into the trap and the one leading out. If the trap is working, there will be a marked temperature difference. The trap should allow only condensation, and the steam that has condensed, to flow back to the heater. If steam is blowing through the trap, both the entering pipe and the exit pipe will be at the same temperature. The trap is probably stuck open, wasting steam.

When the dish machine breaks down or there is no hot water, dishes can be washed in cold water and sanitized by using diluted Clorox or other compounds used for cold-water sanitization. (Bar glassware is usually sanitized in cold water.)

The spray nozzles inside the dish machine are there to provide a forceful spray onto the ware being washed. Lime deposits build up in the nozzles, which must be cleaned periodically by inserting a wire in the openings.

Low-temperature dishwashing machines may be leased. This way, the leasing company assumes responsibility for maintenance and operation. The lessor may also offer to train new dish machine operators. In the traditional dish machines, wash water is raised to 140°F, rinse water to 180°F—a considerable expense. The low-temperature machines operate with water temperatures as low as 100°F. Germicidal chemicals, rather than heat, are used to kill the germs. Some restaurant chains that have shifted to low-temperature dishwashing have cut ware-washing costs in half.

MEETING WITH THE HEALTH INSPECTOR

Before a restaurant can officially operate, it must pass a rigorous examination by a public health official. Public health officials and planning boards, quite rightly, want to assure the public that eating in restaurants under their jurisdiction is safe. To this end, local health officers draw up extensive requirements for floor covering, number of toilets, foodservice equipment, lighting, fire exits, and other factors that bear on the hazards associated with restaurant operation. Requirements vary from place to place. One community may insist on toilet stalls for the handicapped and impermeable floor covering in toilet stalls and in kitchens; another jurisdiction may not. Floor drainage systems, exhaust ductwork, distances between dining room tables, number of seats permitted, number of parking spaces required, number of entrances and exits to the parking area and to the restaurant—all must meet safety requirements.

Even if a building has been used as a restaurant for years, a new owner must pass the health and building inspector's close scrutiny. A new owner or lessee may find that a number of changes are required. All proposed building modifications must be approved. The eager operator is often astonished and frustrated to learn that the linoleum floor installed in the rest rooms must be taken up and replaced. The delays can be extremely costly because a number of people may already be on the payroll, interest expenses continue, and the cash flow expected is delayed. There is no way the restaurant can open until it passes the health inspection and the building inspection. Approval for building equipment and modifications must be secured beforehand. Assuming that approvals will be forthcoming can be hazardous.

SUMMARY

Kitchen planning precedes equipment purchasing. Some restaurant equipment dealers also assist in laying out a kitchen and selecting equipment. The kitchen plan helps assure an easy flow of food in and out of the kitchen. The idea is to place the equipment such that the distance between it and the staff who uses it is minimized. Professional planners, assisted by drafters, are available for a fee. Planners may also recommend equipment that fits the menu and the restaurant's clientele and make sure that the chef and kitchen crew have the knowledge and skills to operate the kitchen. The purposes, uses, limitations, and prices of restaurant equipment are discussed. Decreasing energy use is another result of good kitchen planning and equipment selection.

KEY TERMS AND CONCEPTS

Work centers	Kitchen work flow
Space allocation	Exhibition kitchen
Conduction heating	Equipment selection
Deep-frying equipment	Matching equipment to menu
Low-temperature ovens	Low-temperature dishwasher
Categories of kitchen equipment	Slow-roasting oven
Cook-chill	Deck oven
Broilers	Forced-air convection oven
Tilting skillets	Steam cooking equipment
Combination oven and microwave	Refrigerator
Freezer	

REVIEW QUESTIONS

1. Before equipment selection takes place, what are the factors you must evaluate? Use at least three examples of equipment in your discussion.

2. What are the advantages of microwave ovens? Why are they not more widely used in restaurant kitchens?

3. Why are low-temperature dishwashing machines growing in popularity?

4. Why is it important that service persons stack tableware according to size on a soiled dish table?

5. What conditions favor purchasing a tilting skillet for your kitchen? a vertical cutter/mixer? a convection oven?

6. In starting a restaurant, what used equipment would you consider buying? What equipment would you want completely new?

7. Will you install gas or electric kitchen equipment, or both? What factors will affect your decision?

8. Kitchens are generally becoming smaller in relation to dining areas. Why?

9. You forecast your restaurant to gross $1 million per year in sales. Will you include a bakery section in your kitchen? Explain.

10. What are these pieces of kitchen equipment used for?
    a. Bain marie
    b. Ridged griddle
    c. Salamander
    d. Infared broiler
    e. Charbroiler
    f. Reel oven
    g. Convection oven

11. What are two advantages of reach-in refrigerators and under-shelf refrigerators over the bigger walk-in boxes?

12. Explain the statement "The menu determines the kitchen equipment."

ENDNOTES

[1] One kitchen layout consulting organization is Foodservice Consultant Society, Louisville, KY. Phone: (502) 583-3783.

[2] Courtesy of John C. Cini, President and CEO of Cini Little.

[3] Arthur C. Avery, "Up the Productivity," in *Commercial Kitchen* (Baltimore, Md.: American Gas Association, 1989), 205–214.

[4] Elaine Martin Petrowski, "The Open Kitchen as Theater," *Architectural Record* 187, no. 9 (September 1999): 171–176.

[5] Costas Katsigris and Chris Thomas, *Design and Equipment for Restaurant and Foodservice: A Management View* (New York: John Wiley and Sons, 1999), 93–100. This is by far the best book available on the subject. Costas Katsigris is director of the Food and Hospitality Service Program at El Centro College in Dallas, Texas. Chris Thomas is a professional writer specializing in food and wine topics.

[6] Ibid, p. 88.

[7] Joseph Durocher, "Cook-Chill Systems," *Restaurant Business* 91, no. 11 (20 July 1992): 154.

[8] Personal conversation with Arthur Avery, 22 February 1997.

[9] For detailed information, see "Equipment Maintenance," National Restaurant Association Technical Bulletin, 1978.

[10] For a detailed discussion of this subject, see "Equipment Maintaining Programs," National Restaurant Association Technical Bulletin, 1978.

Chapter **11**

After reading and studying this chapter,
you should be able to:

Forecast sales.

Prepare an income statement.

Prepare a financial budget for your income.

Establish a cash flow budget.

Identify requirements as a basis for determining the appropriate computer system for a restaurant.

BUDGETING AND CONTROLLING COSTS

BUDGETING

The purpose of budgeting is to "do the numbers" and, more accurately, forecast if the restaurant will be viable. Sales must cover all costs, including interest on loans, and allow for reasonable profit, greater than if the money were successfully invested in stocks, bonds, or real estate. Financial lenders require budget forecasts as a part of the overall business plan. The first step in the budget process is to forecast sales. The next is to allocate costs to the forecasted sales, allowing for a fair profit margin. This must all be done in relation to the competitive price-value-quality equation.

In establishing an accounting format to project sales and operational costs of a restaurant, the following basic categories are useful:

- Sales
- Cost of sales
- Gross profit
- Budgeted costs
- Labor costs
- Operating costs
- Fixed costs

FORECASTING SALES

Sales forecasting for a restaurant is, at best, calculated guesswork. Many factors beyond the control of the restaurant, such as unexpected economic factors and weather, influence the eventual outcome. Without a fairly accurate forecast of sales, however, it is impossible to predict the success or failure of the restaurant because all expenses, fixed and variable, are dependent on sales for payment. Predicting sales volume, while not easy, can be done with a high degree of accuracy if a budget forecast is completed.

Sales volume has two components: the average guest check and guest counts. The average guest check is the total sales divided by the number of guests. Menu prices plus beverage sales partly determine the amount of the average check. The guest count is simply the total number of guests patronizing the restaurant over a particular period.

A Method for Forecasting Sales

The first step is to estimate the year's projected guest count. This is done by dividing the year into one 29-day and twelve 28-day accounting periods, then breaking these down into four 7-day weeks. It is better to keep separate records for each meal, because the sales and therefore staffing levels will need to be compatible. Keeping a sales history from day one is recommended.

After the four weekly forecasts are complete, they are totaled on the period-one sheet. The remaining twelve accounting period sheets are then completed, giving total sales forecast for the year (Figure 11–1).

The totals from each of the accounting periods sum to a yearly total sales forecast. The results may be checked by discussing with other restaurant personnel and credit card representatives to gain an estimate of sales at a similar restaurant. With experience, the margin of error in estimating a restaurant's total sales generally decreases.

Budget Forecast of Restaurant Sales, Period _____ – 28 Days, Week _____ 19XX

Period	Forecast No. of Guests	Actual No. of Guests	% for (–)	Forecast Amount of Average Check	Actual Amount of Average Check	% for (–)	Forecast Amount of Food Sales	Actual Amount of Food Sales	% for (–)	Forecast Amount of Beverage Sales	Actual Amount of Beverage Sales	% for (–)	B	L	D	Total Forecast Sales	Total Actual Sales	% for (–)
1																		
2																		
3																		
4																		
5																		
6																		
7																		
8																		
9																		
10																		
11																		
12																		
13																		
Annual Total																		

Note: B = Breakfast; L = Lunch; D = Dinner.

■ FIGURE 11–1

Sales forecast for the year

281

The sales forecast for the first few months should consider the fact that it takes time for people to realize that the restaurant is open or that a large number of people are usually attracted to a new restaurant.

Once weekly, monthly, and yearly sales figures are estimated, the cost of sales is determined. It is then possible to allocate fixed and variable costs to reveal a predicted profit (or loss) figure.

INCOME STATEMENT

The purpose of the income statement (Table 11–1) is to provide information to management and ownership about the financial performance (profitability) of the restaurant over a given period of time. Information on sales and costs is provided in a systematic way that allows for analysis and comparison. The net income (or loss) is shown after expenses are deducted from sales.

TABLE 11–1
Sample Income Statement

	Amount	Percentage
Sales		
Food		
Beverage		
Others		
Total sales	_____	100.00
Cost of Sales		
Food		
Beverage		
Others		
Total cost of sales	_____	
Gross profit	_____	
Other income	_____	
Total income	_____	
Controllable Expenses	_____	
Salaries and wages		
Employee benefits		
Direct operating expenses[a]		
Music and entertainment		
Marketing		
Energy and utility		
Administrative and general		
Repairs and maintenance		
Total controllable expenses	_____	
Rent and other occupation costs		
Income before interest, depreciation, and taxes		
Interest		
Depreciation		
Net income before taxes		
Income taxes	_____	
Net income	======	

Source: Adapted from Raymond S. Schmidgall, *Hospitality Industry Managerial Accounting*, 2nd ed. (East Lansing, Mich.: Educational Institute of the American Hotel and Motel Association, 1990), 94.
[a]Telephone, insurance, accounting/legal office supplies; paper, china, glass, silvers, menus, landscaping, detergent/cleaning supplies, and so on.

The income statement begins with sales of food, beverage, and other sales (which could be take-out, catering, cigars, cigarettes, tobacco, telephone, etc.). The cost of goods sold is deducted from total sales. This leaves a gross profit, which is sales minus cost of goods sold.

From the gross profit, the remaining controllable variable and fixed costs must be deducted before taxes are paid and profits distributed.

BUDGETING COSTS

Costs may be budgeted according to two main categories: fixed and variable.

Fixed costs are normally unaffected by changes in sales volume—that is, they do not change significantly with changes in business performance. Whereas fixed costs may change over time, such changes are not normally related to business volume. Examples of fixed costs are real estate taxes, depreciation on equipment, and insurance premiums.

Variable costs, on the other hand, change proportionately according to sales. Food and beverage costs belong to this category. Thus, a restaurant that incurs a $30,000 food and beverage cost when sales are at $100,000 is expected to register a $45,000 food and beverage cost when sales rise to $150,000.

The following simple income statement illustrates the point:

	Week 1	*Week 2*
Sales	100,000	150,000
Cost of food	30,000	45,000
Gross profit	70,000	105,000

GROSS PROFIT

Sales minus cost of sales equals gross profits is a standard accounting entry. While it may be standard for the accountant, the concept is not always clearly understood by the restaurant manager. Gross profit is the amount of money left from sales after subtracting the cost of sales and must provide for all other operating costs and still leave enough dollars for a satisfactory profit. Some of those operating costs are fixed. Some are variable, meaning management has some control over them and they vary according to sales volume. All costs must be covered by gross profit dollars. When gross profit is insufficient to cover the remaining operating costs and provide a satisfactory profit, the sales and cost mix must be replanned. If this cannot be accomplished, the business venture is not viable.

CONTROLLABLE EXPENSES

Controllable expenses is the term used to describe the expenses that can be changed in the short term. Variable costs are normally controllable. Other controllable costs include salaries and wages (payroll) and related benefits; direct operating expenses, such as music and entertainment; marketing (including sales, advertising, public relations, and promotions); heat, light, and power; administration; and general repairs and mainte-

■   **TABLE 11–2**

Projected Income Statement Showing Controllable Expenses

	Amount (Thousands)	Percentages
Projected Income Statement Period _____		
Sales		
Food (Schedule D-1)	750.0	75.0
Beverage (Schedule D-2)	250.0	25.0
Total sales	1,000.0	100.0
Cost of Sales		
Food	232.5	31.0
Beverage	55.0	22.0
Total cost of sales	287.5	28.8
Gross profit	712.5	71.2
Other income (Schedule D-3)	4.5	0.5
Total income	717.0	71.7
Controllable Expenses		
Salaries and wages (Schedule D-4)	240.0	24.0
Employee benefits (Schedule D-5)	40.0	4.0
Direct operating expense[a] (Schedule D-6)	60.0	6.0
Music and entertainment (Schedule D-7)	10.0	1.0
Marketing (Schedule D-8)	40.0	4.0
Energy and utility (Schedule D-9)	30.0	3.0
Administrative and general (Schedule D-10)	40.0	4.0
Repairs and maintenance (Schedule D-11)	20.0	2.0
Total controllable expenses	480.0	48.0
Rent and other occupation costs (Schedule D-12)	50.0	5.0
Income before interest, depreciation, and taxes	187.0	18.7
Interest	15.0	1.5
Depreciation	23.0	2.3
Total	38.0	3.8
Net income before taxes	149.0	14.9
Income taxes	50.0	5.0
Net Income	99.0	10.7

Source: Adapted from Raymond S. Schmidgall, *Hospitality Industry Managerial Accounting*, 2nd ed. (East Lansing, Mich.: Educational Institute of the American Hotel and Motel Association, 1990), 94.
[a]Telephone, insurance, accounting/legal office supplies; paper, china, glass, silvers, menus, landscaping, detergent/cleaning supplies, and on.

nance. The total of all controllable expenses is deducted from the gross profit. Rent and other occupation costs are then deducted to arrive at the income before interest, depreciation, and taxes. Once these are deducted, the net profit remains.

LABOR COSTS

In most full-service restaurants, the largest variable cost is labor. Depending on the type of restaurant and the degree of service provided, labor costs may range from approximately 16% of sales in a quick-service restaurant to 24% in a family operation and up to about 35% in an upscale continental restaurant.

JOB TITLE	RATE	HOURS PLANNED							WEEKLY TOTAL		SUMMARY	
		SAT.	SUN.	MON.	TUES.	WED.	THURS.	FRI.	HOURS	AMOUNT		
											PROJECTED SALES	
											ESTIMATED PAYROLL	
											PAYROLL RELATED	
											TOTAL PAYROLL	
											% TO SALES	
											DATE PREPARED	
											PREPARED BY	
TOTAL HOURS												
PROJ. CUST. COUNT											APPROVAL	
PROJ. CHECK AVER.												
ESTIMATED SALES		$	$	$	$	$	$	$	$			

UNIT NAME   UNIT NUMBER

■ **FIGURE 11–2**

Form for projecting expected payroll amounts

Projecting payroll costs requires the preparation of staffing schedules and establishing wage rates. Staffing patterns may vary during different periods of the year, with changes occurring seasonally or when there are other sales variations. These changes are identified and categorized on a schedule form used to project any single week's payroll activities and to compare them to customer count/sales projections. A form such as Figure 11–2 can be used both for projecting expected payroll amounts for any future period and for comparing these projections at a later time for cost control purposes.

In some cases, it may be desirable to complete this effort for each of the 52 weeks in the coming year. More often, some standardizing can accommodate expected variations, and three or four standard weeks can be established and used as a basis for shorter calculations. (Many weeks develop a pattern and can be duplicated.) The more accurate the breakdown, the more precise the result.

Table 11–3 illustrates a summary of expected staffing and resulting payroll costs utilizing a breakdown into four categories of restaurant staffing: management and administration, production, service and cashiers, and sanitation. The breakdown allows for planning by activity as well as for control of both employee hours and payroll dollars.

Payroll and related costs fall into two categories: variable (percentage ratio to payroll) and fixed (dollar amount per employee on the payroll). Variable items include those mandated by law: Social Security (FICA), unemployment insurance (state and

■ **TABLE 11–3**

Projected Payroll Costs for a Hypothetical Casual Restaurant of 175 Seats with Sales Volume of $2.75 Million

The average check for lunch is $9.00 and dinner $16.00

I. Management and Administration			
1	General Manager		$ 50,000 + Bonus
2	Assistant Managers (open & close)		48,000
1	Office Clerical		20,000
			118,000
II. Production			
1	Kitchen Manager		35,000 + Bonus
7	Line Cooks	@ Avg. 9.50 per hour	138,320
3	Dishwashers	@ 6.00 per hour	37,440
4	Prep Cooks	@ 7.00 per hour	58,240
			$269,000
III. Service			
3	Hosts @ 6.00 per hour		37,440
20	Servers and Bussers @ 6.00 per hour		249,600
3	Bartenders @ 6.00 per hour		37,440
3	Cashiers @ 6.00 per hour		37,440
			$360,920
IV. 1	Sanitation	@ 6.25	$ 13,000

Recapitulation

I	Management and Administration	118,000
II	Production	269,000
III	Service	360,920
IV	Sanitation	13,000
	TOTAL	$760,920

federal), workers compensation insurance, and state disability insurance. The fixed items usually mean employee benefits and include health insurance (an amount per employee per month), union welfare insurance (also an amount per employee per month), life insurance, and other employee benefits.

Employee meals can be treated as payroll costs or as part of food cost and wages. It is more common to find employee meals treated as food cost for a restaurant operation. Operators need to establish a value for employee meals, but they are treated as a non-taxable benefit by the IRS.

Wendy's, in a recent cost-cutting mode, trimmed unit payrolls by 30 hours per week. This was achieved by finding a different way to pan meat and by weighing cash on scales so no one has to count it. Another labor-saving method is using a Jacuzzi-like power washer to scrub pots, pans, and condiment pumps.

Streamlining was attained by reducing the average time for drive-through service from 160 to 100 seconds. That jump in efficiency enabled stores to crank another 30–40 cars through the line at peak periods. Window sales increased from 56 to 63% of sales.

Source: Peter Romeo, "Less Is More: Wendy's Initiatives Cut Labor, Boost Sales," *Restaurant Business* 98, no. 21 (1 November 1999): 13–14.

RENT

The amount of rent paid is dependent on the length and type of lease negotiated. Leases, generally, approximate 5 to 10% of sales, triple net lease cost, depending on location.

A triple net lease means that the lessee is responsible for making the lease payments, all improvements or alterations to the property, and insurance. Lease costs are normally calculated on a square foot basis, with charges ranging from about $2.00 to $7.00 per square foot per month, depending upon location.

UNIFORM SYSTEM OF ACCOUNTS FOR RESTAURANTS

The income statement recommended for commercial food service operations is prescribed in the Uniform System of Accounts for Restaurants (USAR) published by the National Restaurant Association.

The benefits of the USAR are that:

■ It outlines a uniform classification and presentation of operating results.

■ It allows for easier comparisons to foodservice industry statistics.

■ It provides a turnkey accounting system.

■ It is a time-tested system.[1]

Accounting principals advocate the use of an income statement that clearly shows sales and costs for an accounting period, which is normally one month or one year. See Table 11–2 for an income statement prepared in accordance with USAR.

PRE-OPENING EXPENSES

A new facility must consider pre-opening expenses. While these are not present in an ongoing facility and probably not in the purchase of an existing facility, they *are* a consideration in the construction and opening of a new facility. Such costs as pre-opening offices; the initial purchase of all equipment, including china, cutlery, and glassware; the hiring and training of personnel; and pre-opening advertising costs are encountered. A budget forecast should be allocated for this classification.

Fixed Costs (If Restaurant Building Is Owned)

■ Depreciation

■ Insurance

■ Property taxes

■ Debt service

Variable costs change in direct proportion to the level of sales: food, beverage, labor, heat, light, power, telephone, and other supply costs.

Learn from the mistake that a friend of one of the authors made. Jim successfully opened one restaurant with a term loan from a bank. He was negotiating with another bank to obtain financial backing to open a second when the first bank called in his loan. Jim had to borrow from relatives he hardly knew in order to pay off the first bank before continuing on to successfully open several more units with the second bank.

CASH FLOW BUDGETING[2]

Having available cash is necessary for any business. If McDonald's, with all its potential for profit, had no cash with which to purchase necessary food and beverage items, it, like any other restaurant business, would be in trouble. In fact, the bigger the business, the greater the need for cash. Net income means nothing if bills can't be paid. Managing cash is crucial to a restaurant, especially during the first few months of operation. It is unwise to spend all your time managing the restaurant to the exclusion of maintaining an efficient cash management system.

Positive cash flow is enhanced by either increasing sales while containing costs or by decreasing costs while maintaining sales. To manage a restaurant's cash flow, the Bank of America recommends "a cash management system that can speed up the availability of incoming funds, slow down the disbursement of outgoing funds, and accurately monitor the amount of funds going in either direction."[3]

This can be achieved by:

- Keeping a cash receipts journal and a cash disbursements journal for day-to-day transactions
- Preparing period cash flow budgets to track cash flows and balance books
- Collecting cash and accounts receivable as quickly as possible
- Disbursing cash and paying accounts as slowly as possible
- Improving inventory turnover
- Consolidating cash reserves to use the money more efficiently and profitably

Fortunately, nearly all restaurant guests pay by cash or credit card, and some credit card companies have a direct debit from the guest's account to the restaurant in two days. Otherwise, the average time for credit card companies to pay restaurants for the charges that cardholders incur is about two weeks.

These days, unless a credit arrangement is made in advance, many suppliers insist that beginning restaurants pay on delivery. Good inventory management can assist positive cash flow. Restaurants generally turn over their inventory between four and eight times a month.

PRODUCTIVITY ANALYSIS AND COST CONTROL

Various measures of productivity have been developed—meals produced per employee per day, meals produced per employee per hour, guests served per wait person per shift, labor costs per meal based on sales. Probably the simplest employee productivity measure is sales generated per employee per year (divide the number of full-time equivalent employees into the gross sales for the year). An easy and meaningful measure is to divide the number of employees into income per hour. Some restaurants achieve a $70 per hour productivity rate. When labor costs get out of line, the manager can analyze costs per shift or even productivity per hour to pinpoint the problem.

Without knowing what each expense item should be as a ratio of gross sales, the manager is at a distinct disadvantage. He or she should know, for example, that utilities ordinarily do not run more than 4% of sales in most restaurants, that the cost of bever-

	Month 1		Month 2		Month 3		Month 4		Month 5		Month 6	
	Budget	Actual	Budget	Actual	Budget	Actual	Budget	Actual	Budget	Actual	Budget	Actual
Cash Opening Balance												
Cash Sales												
Credit Sales												
0–30 Days												
31–60 Days												
Total Cash Receipts												
Cash Disbursement												
Purchase Cash												
Purchase Credit												
0–30 Days												
31–60 Days												
Payroll												
Benefits												
Payroll Tax												
Benefits												
Advertising												
Telephone												
Insurance												
Accounting/ Legal												
Repairs/ Maintenance												
Office Supplies												
Utilities												
Taxes												
Miscellaneous												
Total Cash Disbursements												
Net Cash Surplus (Deficit)												

FIGURE 11–3

Six-month cash flow budget for a hypothetical restaurant

TABLE 11–4
Operating Ratios[a]

Sales	100%
Cost of sales	33.0%–43.0%
Gross profit	57.0%–67.0%
Operating expenses	
Controllable Expenses	
Payroll (including manager)	23.0%–33.0%
Employee benefits	3.0%– 5.0%
Direct operating expenses	3.5%– 9.0%
Music and entertainment	0.1%– 1.3%
Advertising and promotion	0.8%– 3.0%
Utilities	3.0%– 5.0%
Administrative and general	3.0%– 6.0%
Repairs and maintenance	1.0%– 2.0%
Occupation Expenses	
Rent, property tax, and insurance	6.0%–11.0%
Interest	0.3%– 1.0%
Franchise royalties (if any)	3.0%– 7.0%
Income before depreciation	12.0%–19.0%
Depreciation	0.7%– 5.0%
Net profit before income tax	5.0%–15.0%

[a]These figures represent typical ranges for operating ratios in California restaurants. The data cannot be added vertically. Operators who want to balance their budgets will find that a high expense ratio for one item, such as payroll, will have to be offset by low ratios in other areas, such as direct operating expenses. Figures were developed by the *Small Business Reporter* in California.

ages for a dinner house ordinarily should not exceed 25% of sales and could be much less, and that occupancy cost should not exceed 8% of gross sales, in most cases. Ratio analysis must be in terms of what is appropriate for a particular style of restaurant: coffee shop, fast-food place, or dinner house (Table 11–4).

Moreover, the ratios must be appropriate for the region. Restaurant labor costs, for example, are usually low in the South as compared to the North.

SEAT TURNOVER

Some restaurant operators consider the number of times a seat turns over in an hour the most critical number in the entire operation. This number roughly indicates volume of sales and is also an index of efficiency for the entire operation.

What should seat turnover be per hour? This figure varies with the style of operation and what the operator is trying to accomplish. Restaurants featuring bar sales may wish to slow down seat turnover, making it possible for the patron to indulge in several drinks rather than none or a few. At the other end of the spectrum, the restaurant where people line up to wait for lunch is concerned with as rapid a turnover as possible.

Some restaurants have set a turnover rate as high as seven in an hour; others have one turnover every two hours. The rapid-turnover style of restaurant generally has a low-check average, which produces high sales volume. The fast-turnover restaurant features rapid-production menu items—those that are already prepared or those that can be prepared quickly.

A dinner house on Friday or Saturday night—the busy periods—may want to feature roast beef, which is already prepared. The cooks merely slice it and place it on the plate. The concept is known as stored labor, preparing as much as possible during slow periods for use during rush periods.

Restaurants that depend on fast turnover have a number of techniques for speeding service. Servers are instructed to clear the tableware as soon as possible. One technique is to ask the guests if they would care for anything else.

Customers who are due back at work may not mind such rush treatment, whereas the same person eating in a dinner house would resent it.

Servers and the entire staff can be tuned to rapid service. A clumsy or slow wait person is a liability in an operation that depends on turnover for sales volume. The rush period may last only an hour or an hour and a half. Maximum sales must be achieved in that period. Rapid seat turnover may be critical not only for the operator but also for the patron who needs and wants fast service. The menu, the kitchen production, the service, the style of operation all affect seat turnover and help determine the appropriate target figure for seat turnover.

Seating customers who cannot be served quickly can be a problem. The customers expect service that does not appear and might be happier sitting in the bar. On the other hand, operators have been known to ask patrons to wait in the bar in order to increase bar sales. The customer, however, seeing empty tables, may become infuriated and leave.

Any new restaurant that relies heavily on a lunch business must do it right, from the start. Guests will expect that lunch can be completed within about 45 minutes.

CONTROLLING THEFT AND ACCIDENTAL LOSS

Accountability helps in guest check writing—that is, in pricing and in extensions—and helps reduce losses that show up in food costs. Unrung checks, often the result of favors for friends, are a part of check accountability and can reduce sales. Managers as well as servers are guilty of serving sundaes, salads, beverages, or whole meals without making a check. Auditing checks for pricing, extension, and addition should be done on a limited but regular basis. Randomly selecting one food server's guest checks per shift gives a good indication of what is being done, right and wrong.

A number of systems may be installed to reduce theft:

- *Supply control.* Storerooms are kept under lock and key and supplies issued to each station only at the beginning of a shift, according to a par stock needed for the day.

- *Tight key control.* All keys are signed out by name and must be returned by name. When a manager leaves, all locks, safe combinations, and codes are changed.

- *Shopping reports.* An independent shopping company is employed to investigate the restaurant and to observe and report on every employee at regular intervals. Among the factors observed are whether or not all sales are recorded on sales slips. At the cash register, items such as candy bars are purchased to see if the sale is rung up. Questions such as the following are completed by the shopper:

- Was your guest check added correctly?
- As you approached the cash stand,
  a. How many patrons were there ahead of you?
  b. Was payment taken in a reasonable length of time? How long?
- Was the cashier working with the cash drawer opened?
- Were numerals on the cash register window plainly visible?
- Did cashier call back
  a. Amount of sale?
  b. Amount tendered?
- Was correct change given?

A number of factors contribute to employee theft, including:

- The easy distribution and sale of stolen merchandise, mainly through flea markets
- The affluence that makes people less protective of their possessions and merchandise
- The attitude of many employees that whatever they take is owed to them
- A general tolerance of nonviolent criminal behavior by the public and by some employers (insurance can cover such losses)
- Dissatisfaction with the job, pay received, or general working conditions, or a feeling that the position is not permanent
- Low morale, a feeling of lack of appreciation or recognition, or an imagined wrong
- Lack of respect for supervision
- A feeling that the job is just a paycheck and that the employee should grab what he or she can
- Debts built up from drug use, gambling, extended credit, or drinking problems
- Perhaps most important, the perception that, if caught, the worst that can happen is to be fired

Theft of food and other items must always be viewed in the context of attitude and enforcement policy. When a well-publicized or obvious policy concerning the taking of small items and the eating of food or taking it home is lacking, there is little wonder that theft becomes "okay" and commonplace.

Many restaurants have a policy of permitting leftover food to be taken home by the employees. Oddly enough, there always seems to be plenty of extra food. The reason is simple: The employees see to it that a little extra is produced, enough to take home. To counteract this, many restaurants have a policy of destroying all leftover food when it cannot be reworked or served later. This may seem a callous type of behavior on the part of management, but it does tend to reduce leftovers. Some deem it better to give it to relief organizations such as the Salvation Army.

Food theft is often accomplished by wrapping steaks or other food in foil or a napkin and placing it in a garbage can to be picked up later, either by a confederate or by the employee who put it there. Some consternation may be caused by the restaurant operator picking through a garbage can and looking for such wrapped food. (The operator could be estimating the amount of overproduction or of uneaten food not liked by customers.)

Food is also placed on the outside of a windowsill or handed to someone on the outside. Another way of carrying out stolen steaks: Strap them to thighs or under blouses.

Undercharging favorite customers or giving food to friends who are customers is common and can be controlled only by insisting on a policy of no ticket, no food, and following the duplicate check system whereby no food is given by a cook to a server without a guest check.

GUEST CHECK CONTROL

If not controlled, guest checks are like blank checks that the operator has already signed. Without check control, a server can give food and beverages away or sell them and keep the income. Without guest check audits, the checks can be padded in favor of the server or the guest.

Numbered guest checks are issued to servers. Each check must be accounted for and at least a spot check of the additions and correct prices made.

A great temptation for servers exists if guest checks are not strictly accounted for. The server may bring in his or her own checks, present them to the customer, and pocket the payment. Guest checks can be altered and substitutions made if the checks are not numbered.

To avoid such temptations, most restaurants require that the server sign for checks as received and return those not used at the end of the shift.

Checks can be issued by book, 150 to a book. For tight control, every guest check is audited, additions checked, and every check accounted for by number. Guest check auditing may be done in a central office, in the case of a restaurant chain, or in someone's home for an independent restaurant. Most restaurants use the duplicate check system to maintain tight control. The second copy of the check is handed to the cook in return for the food. No check, no food. Every food item is recorded on a guest check, even a cup of coffee.

Some operators control restaurant income by having servers act as their own cashiers. Servers are, in effect, set up in business for themselves. They bring their own banks of $50.00 in change; they do not operate from a cash register but out of their own pockets; they deposit their income in a night box at the bank.

No food can be taken from the kitchen or liquor from the bar without being "paid for" by a duplicate check. If, indeed, no food is issued from the kitchen to anyone without the duplicate check, the checks provide an adequate record of sales. Much more responsibility is placed on the server. A cashier need not be employed with this system, but the servers must be able to add and subtract and perform the same functions as the cashier.

A bookkeeper totals all of the checks of each server and this amount is compared with the amount deposited to the restaurant account by the server at the end of the shift. It is often said that being a server is like being in business for oneself. This plan carries the analogy one step farther.

One restaurant that we stumbled on in London may have the answer: The servers have to pay the cooks *cash* for each dish they take out of the kitchen. Now that's an interesting twist!

Few restaurants employ a full-time bookkeeper, especially one on the premises. Restaurant Adventures, a small chain of restaurants in California, has a different idea. Each of these restaurants grosses more than $1 million in sales annually and each has a full-time bookkeeper, or auditor, who comes on duty in the afternoon and audits all transactions by 2:00 A.M. The day's business is completely recorded and analyzed by the next morning. Labor, food, and other percentage ratios are computed daily.

The smaller restaurant is likely to employ a part-time person in his or her home who does the restaurant bookkeeping on a day-by-day basis. An accounting firm is employed to prepare monthly statements and help with income taxes. Chain operations ordinarily do most of the bookkeeping and operating analysis at the home office. Recordkeeping at the unit level is minimal.

COMPUTER SYSTEMS

More chains are using computers routinely. The Jerrico Company, parent company of the Long John Silver's chain, centralizes bookkeeping by computer in its Lexington, Kentucky, office. All data from the day's operation in each store is sent over phone lines to a central computer during the night, when long-distance rates are inexpensive. Their system, "Computer Talking to Computer," is highly sophisticated. The computer in the store feeds the daily data of the store's operation to the central computer, where the information is analyzed and printed out for operating executives of the company. Top management knows each day what the food costs, labor costs, and other statistics were for the entire chain for the previous day.

A computer is a general-purpose machine that processes data according to a set of instructions that are stored internally, either temporarily or permanently. The computer and the equipment attached to it are called hardware. The instructions that tell it what to do are called software. A set of instructions that perform a particular task is called a program or software package.

A mainframe computer has a large amount of information storage capacity and a fast central processing unit. Restaurant chains may interconnect (network) all of their stores' computers using a mainframe.

Computers have three parts: a central processing unit (CPU), an electronic memory, and a means of entering and displaying the processed information (an input-output device, such as a keyboard for entering information and a video screen). The CPU contains the circuitry for storing and processing the information. The computer functions only at the direction of an operator and a program. If hard copy is needed, the output must come through a printer. By definition, a computer can be anything from a $10 wristwatch with date and time output to a mainframe computer that processes data from dozens of input terminals.

Now that computer costs have come down, personal computers (PCs) are being used widely in restaurants. Point-of-sale (POS) minicomputers record each order and can be programmed to provide a variety of data on demand. Servers use nearby computer terminals to enter meal orders and beverages. A printer in the kitchen prints the order on a small tape for the cook to read. The bar receives the bar order on another printer. Information entered in the terminals, which also serve as cash registers, can be called up at any time. How many steaks were served? How many martinis? How much money was received between 6:00 and 7:00 P.M.? The computer can also be used to maintain a running inventory. At any given time, the amount of all food and beverage items on hand can be read from the computer. (This does not remove the need to take periodic physical inventories.)

In deciding which system is best suited to particular restaurant's needs, an operator should consider the following:

1. How will you organize and use the data? How will you summarize it and disseminate it to your competitive advantage?

2. What kinds of data do you need? For one operator, the ability to break the table into individual seats may be vital. For another, sales forecasting, customer tracking, tip reporting, or labor scheduling may be more important.

3. Be aware that some systems provide too much information. The trick is to extract the information required for decision-making purposes.

4. The result of a cost-benefit assessment of a data system sometimes hinges on the efficiencies a company can realize compared with more labor-intensive methods of data management.

5. What are you selling? Who is buying it at what hour of the day and in how much volume?

6. Set goals that you want the system to meet. For example, trimming labor and food costs by 1% can save thousands of dollars that go straight to the bottom line.

7. Remember that customers do not come to restaurants because of fancy POS systems.[4]

An example of how a computer system can help management keep a tight control of the labor costs is taken from a 280-seat casual fine dining restaurant.

The labor distribution summary (Figure 11–4), which is a summary of one week, lists the lunch and dinner sales forecast and actual sales, together with the number of customers. The labor hours and labor dollars are then broken down by department. This is also available in more detail (Figure 11–5). Here, the hours worked by each person in the department are listed, including the amount of overtime hours worked.

The labor distribution summary is also available for one day (Figure 11–6). However, one day may be slightly up and another slightly down, so the weekly summary gives more interesting and comprehensive information.

■

How Much Computer Assistance?

In starting a new restaurant or changing a concept, most owners or managers are familiar with at least one computer application for the restaurant business. The POS cash register and the electronic draft system for credit card approval and processing are needed in almost every restaurant. To begin with, these may be sufficient and are relatively inexpensive.

In purchasing computer equipment, the restaurant buyer is cautioned to buy reliable equipment that the vendor will service. Replacement parts may be difficult to get and many computer vendors have gone out of business making it difficult to get information or replacement parts. Reliability is of the greatest importance. Some vendors offer a service contract. Investigate this thoroughly before you buy.

Computers can be particularly efficient when used to link multiunit restaurant chains. For example, in the 600-unit Mrs. Field's cookie chain, the unit manager turns

LABOR DISTRIBUTION SUMMARY
For 8/17/92–8/30/92

Page 1
RUN 8/31/92

Operations	Sales	Actual	Forecast	Customers	Actual	Forecast
	Lunch	54,936.50	56,000.00	Lunch	4,539	4,505
	Dinner	38,160.50	40,400.00	Dinner	2,093	2,080
	TOTAL	93,097.00	96,400.00	TOTAL	6,632	6,585

Department	Labor Hours			Labor Dollars			Labor $/Sales		Customers/ Labor Hr	
	Actual	Budget	DIFF	Actual	Budget	Diff	Actual	Sched	Actual	Sched
Server										
Dept Total	1,115.12	1,403.00	287.88–	4,879.30	6,161.44	1,282.14–	5.24%	6.39%	5.95	4.69
Busser										
Dept Total	490.76	524.00	33.24–	2,111.57	2,255.69	144.12–	2.27%	2.34%	13.51	12.57
Kitchen										
Dept Total	1,059.55	1,165.50	105.95–	7,567.95	8,227.50	659.55–	8.13%	8.53%	6.26	5.65
Disher										
Dept Total	436.94	344.50	92.44+	2,110.99	1,591.50	519.49+	2.27%	1.65%	15.18	19.11
Bar										
Dept Total	185.56	200.00	14.44–	1,018.39	1,099.38	80.99–	1.09%	1.14%	35.74	32.93
Cocktail										
Dept Total	144.27	150.00	5.73–	646.58	690.63	44.05–	.69%	.72%	45.97	43.90
Host										
Dept Total	204.72	237.75	33.03–	1,167.70	1,346.75	179.05–	1.25%	1.40%	32.40	27.70
Operations	Total All Departments									
TOTAL	3,636.92	4,024.75	387.83–	19,502.48	21.372.89	1,870.41–	20.95%	22.17%	1.82	1.64

FIGURE 11–4

Labor distribution summary—two weeks

on the computer before warming up the oven. Next, he or she enters a few facts into the computer, such as weather conditions, whether the schools are in session, and other information that affects cookie sales. The computer shows the numbers of customers per hour last year, the same day, and predicts cookie sales for the current day. The computer program indicates how much cookie dough to mix and when, and may even suggest giving away free samples if sales do not keep pace with production. As hourly sales are entered throughout the day, the computer updates the forecast.

Mrs. Field's also owns La Petite Boulangerie, a bakery/restaurant chain. When the company acquired the 119 bakery outlets from Pepsico in 1988, 53 people were employed at headquarters. Four weeks later, Mrs. Field's software reduced that number to three. It will come as no surprise that Randall Fields, Mrs. Fields husband, is a former computer programmer.[5]

Persons unfamiliar with computer uses are cautioned against buying computer hardware without assistance. A small restaurant may need nothing more than an electronic cash register with add, subtract, and divide capabilities. Hourly, daily, and weekly sales totals can be looked up. Spreadsheet analysis and more sophisticated programs can be added later, if needed. If a new, well-capitalized restaurant chain is being established, computer capability to network the units may be justified as part of the concept and start-up costs.

P-T-D LABOR REPORT (DETAIL)
Department #30 thru 40   From 8/28/92 to 8/30/92

Employee Name	Employee Number	Work Date	Time In	Time Out	Reg Hours	O/T Hours	Job Code	Tips Claimed
Albear, Magdaleno	25600000	8/28/92	8:00 AM	4:00 PM	8.00	.00	4003	.00
		8/29/92	8:00 AM	3:59 PM	7.98	.00	4003	.00
		8/30/92	8:00 AM	4:00 PM	8.00	.00	4003	.00
		Employee Totals			23.98	.00		.00
Allsworth, Eugene	46500000	8/30/92	11:40 AM*	6:43 PM	7.05	.00	3001*	.00
		Employee Totals			7.05	.00		.00
Brancely, Marina	39800000	8/28/92	6:00 AM*	12:30 PM*	6.50	.00	3004*	.00
		8/29/92	6:00 AM*	12:30 PM*	6.50	.00	3004*	.00
		8/30/92	7:15 AM	12:16 PM	5.02	.00	3004	.00
		Employee Totals			18.02	.00		.00
De La Cruz, Estaban	35400000	8/28/92	8:00 AM	4:00 PM*	8.00	.00	4004	.00
		8/29/92	8:00 AM	2:00 PM*	4.60	1.40	3011	.00
		Employee Totals			12.60	1.40		.00
Figueroa, Juan A	43800000	8/29/92	3:30 PM	11:39 PM	8.00	.15	4003	.00
		8/30/92	10:00 AM	3:25 PM	5.42	.00	4003	.00
		Employee Totals			13.42	.15		.00
Gonzalez, Rolando	33400000	8/28/92	6:00 AM*	3:30 PM	8.00	1.50	3011*	.00
		8/29/92	6:30 AM*	1:37 PM	7.12	.00	3011*	.00
		8/30/92	7:00 AM*	3:17 PM	.88	7.40	3011*	.00
		Employee Totals			16.00	8.90		.00
London, Terry	44300000	8/28/92	8:30 AM	4:00 PM*	7.50	.00	3001	.00
		8/29/92	8:30 AM	4:00 PM	7.50	.00	3001	.00
		8/30/92	8:30 AM	4:00 PM	7.50	.00	3001	.00
		Employee Totals			22.50	.00		.00
Long, George	07600000	8/28/92	2:00 PM	10:58 PM	8.00	.97	3016	.00
		8/29/92	2:15 PM	11:30 PM*	8.00	1.25	3016	.00
		8/30/92	2:00 PM	10:14 PM	8.00	.23	3016	.00
		Employee Totals			24.00	2.45		.00
McLeod, Paul	12300000	8/30/92	8:30 AM	3:28 PM	6.97	.00	3001	.00
		Employee Totals			6.97	.00		.00
Mendez, Juan	34600000	8/28/92	8:30 AM	4:00 PM	7.50	.00	3011	.00
		8/29/92	8:30 AM	4:30 PM*	8.00	.00	3011	.00
		8/30/92	9:00 AM	5:00 PM*	8.00	.00	3011	.00
		Employee Totals			23.50	.00		.00

■ **FIGURE 11–5**

Detailed labor distribution summary

| LABOR DISTRIBUTION SUMMARY | | | | | | | Page 1 |
| For 8/30/92–8/30/92 | | | | | | | RUN 8/31/92 |

Operations	Sales	Actual	Forecast	Customers	Actual	Forecast
	Lunch	4,177.00	4,300.00	Lunch	361	350
	Dinner	1,436.04	2,300.00	Dinner	92	120
	TOTAL	5,613.04	6,600.00	TOTAL	453	470

| Department | Labor Hours | | | Labor Dollars | | | Labor $/Sales | | Customers/ Labor Hr | |
	Actual	Budget	DIFF	Actual	Budget	Diff	Actual	Sched	Actual	Sched
Server										
Dept Total	65.34	95.50	30.16–	277.70	425.53	147.83–	4.95%	6.45%	6.93	4.92
Busser										
Dept Total	29.56	33.50	3.94–	136.96	142.38	5.42–	2.44%	2.16%	15.32	14.03
Kitchen										
Dept Total	75.50	86.00	10.50–	544.55	635.63	91.08–	9.70%	9.63%	6.00	5.47
Disher										
Dept Total	21.42	21.50	0.08–	115.39	100.50	14.89+	2.06%	1.52%	21.15	21.86
Bar										
Dept Total	12.65	16.00	3.35–	73.27	96.88	23.61–	1.31%	1.47%	35.81	29.38
Cocktail										
Dept Total	9.86	15.00	5.14–	47.45	76.50	29.05–	.85%	1.16%	45.94	31.33
Host										
Dept Total	15.67	18.00	2.33–	91.39	103.00	11.61–	1.63%	1.56%	28.91	26.11
Operations	Total All Departments									
TOTAL	230.00	285.50	55.50–	1,286.71	1,580.42	293.71–	22.92%	23.95%	1.97	1.65

FIGURE 11–6

Labor distribution summary—one day

After the electronic cash register, the most widely used computer equipment in restaurants is POS equipment. Requiring that all orders be entered into the POS system helps reduce the number of food items prepared by mistake, but the big advantage is that the server remains on the floor and need not run back and forth to the kitchen nor deal face-to-face with the cooks. (In some instances, this may be a disadvantage.) POS equipment is also valuable as a cost control device. Servers enter orders by using preset keys or price look-up keys. The preset keys are programmed with frequently ordered menu items. Modifier keys allow servers to relay information such as portion size, cooking times, and accompaniments to cooks.

POS terminals and electronic cash registers can produce the guest check. The most popular approach seems to be a softcopy check that can be printed at any time.

A final caution: Before buying any computer hardware, be sure a computer programer is available that will enable it to function and that maintenance and repair service is readily available. Also, be sure that users are adequately trained to use the equipment.

■

POS Systems

Micros systems has packages for table-service and quick-service restaurants. Integrated into its widely used POS software, Guest Service Solutions, are models for running a frequent-diner reward program, surveying guests, and learning more about customers who call for deliveries.

Several types of POS systems are available, ranging from the basic Casio QT 200, with a keyboard interface, to high-end systems such as the Squirrel Restaurant Management System, the Micros 3700, and Ibertech's Aloha Table Service, all of which utilize touch-screen user interfaces and options. Squirrel runs on a Microsoft Windows NT software platform and has standard features to accommodate most restaurant operations. Many systems allow for screens to be customized to suit individual needs.

POS systems, says the manufacturers, help improve efficiency and provide controls for cash handling. For instance, the touch screen is quicker to operate than keystroke machines; this allows service staff to spend more time attending the guests. Additionally, on-screen prompts lead servers to the next step. The rapid turnover of restaurant employees means that the look of the POS screen should be easy to understand and use with minimal training.

Handheld POS remote terminals are the next wave in restaurant technology, but they may not be for everyone. An article in *Nightclub and Bar* lists the pros and cons of handheld terminals.

Pros

1. Servers can place orders directly from the table.

2. They are slightly less expensive than fixed terminals.

3. They are excellent for remote situations, such as banquets rooms and poolside bars.

4. They deliver reliable performance and functionality.

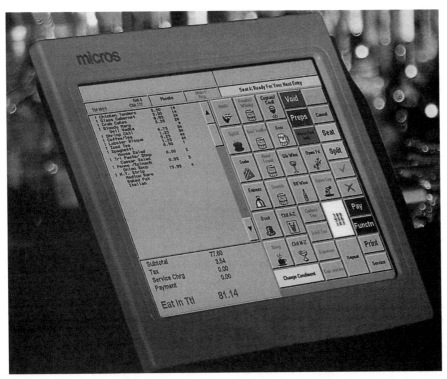

POS systems facilitate prompt service and control. Courtesy Micros Systems

Cons

1. They need at least one unit per server.
2. Units get dropped and can be easily damaged.[6]

Today, POS systems are able to handle inventory control, accounting, employee records, profit calculations, and all operational paperwork. They can inform operators when items are running short, who supplies them, and then place an order—all without human intervention.

FINANCIAL MANAGEMENT

The old-time restaurant owner managed finances by the cigar box method. Each day, money received from customers for meals went into the box. Money for food purchases came out of the box. At the end of the day, whatever was left in the box went into the owner's pocket and was taken home—a kind of cash accounting financial system. With time, a manual cash register was installed. Cash sales were rung up and the money went into the cash drawers. A tape on the cash register recorded sales and could be added at the end of a work shift or at the close of business.

Eventually, the owner realized he needed help in keeping financial records. A local bookkeeper was hired to set up the books and to prepare a monthly profit and loss (income and expense) statement. At the end of the year, the bookkeeper assembled a balance sheet showing the assets and liabilities of the business.

The bookkeeper pointed out that the key figures in the profit and loss (P&L) statement were food and labor costs, variable costs that go up and down with sales and must be tightly controlled.

Other costs were seen as fixed costs, which vary little and which little can be done to control. Actually all costs, fixed or not, can be reviewed periodically, and some variable costs are more or less fixed. The manager's salary is fixed in the sense that it is paid regardless of fluctuation in sales volume. Parts of expenses are also fixed—the monthly basic cost of phone service, for example.

More employees were hired; income and others taxes were imposed. The owner needed to borrow money for expansion. Financial management became more complicated. The owner found he could buy a car and charge the cost to the business. He could buy his restaurant building and depreciate its book value each year. If the IRS approved, he could accelerate the depreciation taken on the building during the first few years of ownership. He could keep the amount depreciated and forget about it until he sold the building. Financial management got more complicated.

To be competitive, the restaurateur had to install air conditioning in the dining room. He learned that the air-conditioning equipment could either be purchased or leased. If purchased, depreciation could be taken each year and be income-tax deductible. Which was the better choice? Buy or lease?

A new son-in-law worked in the restaurant and urged the owner to buy a failing restaurant in a nearby town. Should the entire operation, including the building, be bought, or should only the equipment be bought and leased? More levels of complexity were added.

Financial management is much more complicated than striving to achieve a high bottom line or high income per share of stock. It is quite possible, and often desirable, to keep income per share or net profit low to reduce taxes. Another way was to reduce taxes and build cash flow by maximizing the depreciation allowed by the IRS and to take advantage of any tax concessions allowed for making a new investment in a business (investment credit).

Ratio Analysis

Financial and operational analyses rely heavily on the comparison of several relationships that are telltale signs of restaurant performance, numbers that reveal significant information about operational effectiveness and financial health.

When two experienced foodservice operators get together, one is likely to ask the other, "What is your food cost? your labor cost?" The question really addresses the ratio of your cost of food to your sales income, a key figure in controlling the major cost in a restaurant. The ratio varies with the style of operation. For fast food, it can range from about 28% (some ethnic fast food) to 45% (some full-service steakhouses). All restaurant food cost ratios are best considered in conjunction with the cost of labor as a ratio to sales income. The two costs are closely related. Self-service restaurants with low labor costs—say, 20%—often have high food costs, perhaps 40% or more. The reason: The restaurant business is highly competitive. Self-service customers expect to get their food at a lower price, which translates into higher food costs for the operator.

Labor costs vary around the country—very high in Alaska, low in Alabama; high where the union is strong, lower where cheap labor is available. Where labor costs are low, competition usually forces food costs up. Appropriate food and labor costs depend partly on the prevailing food and labor costs of the competition. One cost is a function of the other. When it is possible for one to be low, the other is likely to be high. Together, they can seldom exceed 55 to 60% and still permit a reasonable profit. The reason: Costs other than food and labor are likely to total 25 to 30%.

The most familiar financial ratio, one used by lenders to interpret financial health, is the current ratio. This is derived by dividing current assets (cash, accounts receivable, inventory) by current liabilities (debt due within a year). The equity (the unencumbered value of a business) is what counts. Well-managed restaurants, experts say, should have a current ratio of 1 or greater.

The current ratio can be made to look better by borrowing long-term and paying off the short-term debt. If a restaurant has current assets of $100,000 and current liabilities of $125,000, the current ratio is:

$$\frac{100,000}{125,000} = 80 \text{ (not good in the eyes of a lender)}$$

By borrowing $25,000 long term, the current ratio could be

$$\frac{100,000}{100,000} = \text{(acceptable)}$$

An even more important ratio, closely related to the current ratio, is the quick ratio. The quick ratio determines whether you have quick access to money to pay off current liabilities. Because it is so important, from a liquidity viewpoint, the quick ratio is also known as the acid-test ratio.

Cash management is that part of management that arranges for the finances to stay liquid enough to cover current liabilities without keeping excess funds from earning income. One way to avoid being caught short of cash is to maintain a line of credit with a bank—an agreement that a specified amount of money can be borrowed on short notice, that amount having already been approved for a loan.

Another aspect of cash management is making certain that money is not idle, placing it with a bank or other financial institution that pays interest on any balance in an account. The days of placing money in a low- or no-interest checking account are over. Where considerable sums are in cash, management means moving funds into whatever pays the highest interest with little or no risk.

Some businesses have a policy of holding off vendors as long as possible—in some cases, 90 days. If the cash being held is drawing interest or being used to produce other income, the effect is a free loan from the vendor. The vendor may accept the policy to retain the business relationship. Be aware, however, that the vendor may add the cost to future charges or look for other ways to cover the free loan cost. You rarely get something for nothing!

SUMMARY

Budgeting sales is particularly important because costs are paid by sales and profit is derived from sales. The more accurate the sales projections, the easier it is for restaurant operators to manage costs and make a reasonable profit. The income statement gives the owner/manager a clear picture of the restaurant's performance over a specified period of time. The information gained from the income statement is valuable in decision making. The Uniform System of Accounts for Restaurants provides a standard approach to restaurant accounting. This system has several advantages to owner/operators. Costs are categorized as fixed or variable. Control of food and beverage costs and other expenses is imperative if the owner is to maximize potential profit.

Computers, especially the electronic cash register, can expedite service and accounting. In table-service restaurants with high sales volume, point-of-sale equipment makes it possible to electronically link foodservers to cooks and lessen the need for personnel to walk to the kitchen to transmit guest orders. Computer use is increasing in restaurants, especially large ones and chain units.

KEY TERMS AND CONCEPTS

Budget	Cash flow budgeting
Forecast	Breakeven point
Business plan	Controllable expenses
Gross profit	Income statement
Labor costs	Payroll-related costs
Operating costs	Food cost
Fixed costs	Productivity analysis
Uniform system of accounts	Computer assistance
Operating profit	

REVIEW QUESTIONS

1. In drawing up a sales budget for a casual Italian restaurant, what percentage of weekly sales should be forecasted for Friday and Saturday evenings?

2. A family restaurant with a $1 million annual sales volume would have about how many employees?

3. If a restaurant has close to the usual cost percentages, what would be its forecasted labor cost in dollars? its food cost? its occupancy cost?

4. Aside from its value in planning, why is it essential to produce a budget (forecast) of sales, cost, and profits?

5. The budgeted operating statement cannot be made unless a menu is developed. Is it possible for two restaurants to have the same menu and same total sales, but widely different food and labor costs? Explain.

6. In projecting sales figures for a restaurant, it is necessary to take into consideration daily and seasonal (monthly) variations. Draw up a projected sales curve showing daily variations and another one showing monthly variations.

7. What factors will determine your food and liquor sales mix?

8. Suppose that after forecasting sales, costs, and expenses, you arrive at an operating profit of 3% of sales before interest expenses and taxes. What should you do?

9. What ratios are important to a restaurant manager?

10. What operating control system will you have in your restaurant? How much will it cost to run it?

11. List three costs ordinarily considered fixed and three considered variable.

12. In deciding to purchase a POS system, what must be kept in mind?

13. In planning a restaurant, what profit, as a percentage of sales, can reasonably be expected?

ENDNOTES

[1] Raymond S. Schmidgall, *Hospitality Industry Managerial Accounting*, 2nd ed. (East Lansing, Mich.: Educational Institute of the American Hotel and Motel Association, 1990), 94.

[2] This section draws on *Small Business Reporter* (San Francisco: Bank of America, 1991).

[3] Ibid.

[4] Milford Prewitt, "Dinner Houses Seek Competitive Edge Advantages Through Cutting-Edge Computer Upgrades," *Nations Restaurant News* 30, no. 13 (1 April 1996): 53–54.

[5] Linda Grant, "Recipe for Survival," *Los Angeles Times*, 31 May 1992, D1.

[6] "Register with a Difference Nightclub and Bar," *Nightclub and Bar* vol. 14, Issue 4. (April 1998, Oxford Publishing Inc.), 72–74.

Chapter **12**

After reading and studying this chapter,
you should be able to:

Draw up task and job analyses for each position in a restaurant.

Develop job descriptions for each position in a restaurant.

Know which interview questions are appropriate and which are not.

ORGANIZATION, RECRUITING,
AND STAFFING

Presumably, we have our concept, our location, our menu, health and fire department approval, liquor licenses, and other local permits. We have found finances and taken care of legal matters. Now we think of setting up the jobs and organizing the restaurant so that it fulfills its function—to serve patrons and produce a profit. In an existing restaurant, improvements in job content and organization may be possible. In a new concept restaurant, tasks have to be defined to form jobs, and the jobs have to be related to each other. This chapter discusses how to analyze jobs and relate them to each other to form an organization chart. We first look at task and job analysis.

TASK AND JOB ANALYSIS

A task is a related sequence of work. A series of related tasks constitutes a responsibility. A job, then, is a series of related responsibilities. When these are written down in an organized form, they constitute a job description.

Fundamental to the entire human resource function is task and job analysis, the examination in detail of the tasks and jobs to be performed. From these analyses come job descriptions, which are essential for selection and training of staff and for setting performance standards. Job specifications identify the qualifications and skills needed to perform the job. Job instructions provide the step-by-step details needed for training. Performance standards identify the outcome of the work.

There are two main approaches to task and job analysis. The bottom-up method is most frequently used when the organization already exists and the work behavior of the existing employees is the basis for analysis. The bottom-up method has some merit in that experienced workers often find shortcuts to save their legs. For example, an experienced server will never enter or leave the dining area empty-handed.

The top-down method is utilized when opening new restaurants because there are no existing employees whose work can be analyzed. The restaurant's mission, goals, and objectives are examined to determine what tasks must be performed to achieve them.[1] There is nothing to stop operators analyzing jobs in similar organizations and, indeed, reanalyzing the jobs in relation to the mission goals and objectives of the restaurant after it has been open for a year or two. From these analyses come job descriptions that are essential for training and for developing job specifications.

Once the jobs are broken down into their various steps and the tasks detailed, it is possible to develop training programs based on this information. This same information may then be used to evaluate or appraise job performance. Figure 12–1 shows the sequence from task and job analysis to appraisal.

If the employee's performance meets or exceeds the standards, the employee may receive not only praise but also a pay raise. If the employee's performance does not meet the standards, coaching to improve performance is the next step—followed by termination, if performance fails to improve. Depending on the severity of the situation, the employee could be given a verbal or written warning, or even be dismissed.

In technical terms, jobs, positions, responsibilities, and tasks are quite separate and distinct. The job of server may have a number of server positions—one job but several positions. Each person fills a position.

A server's job may involve performing the following tasks:

- Setting up tables prior to food service
- Taking orders/suggestive selling

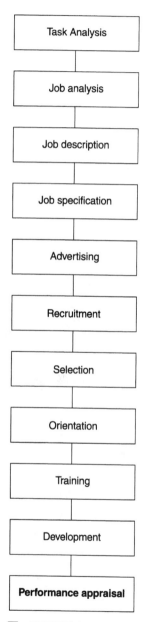

FIGURE 12–1

The sequence of a job from task to performance appraisal

Task Analysis

Job analysis

Job description

Job specification

Advertising

Recruitment

Selection

Orientation

Training

Development

Performance appraisal

- Waiting on and serving customers
- Making coffee
- Preparing simple salads or desserts
- Performing side work (cleaning salt and pepper shakers, folding napkins, cleaning ketchup bottles, cleaning ashtrays)

As one server puts it, "You may have to perform tasks that generally are someone else's responsibility, such as seating or bussing tables. This happens when the restaurant is busy. You also may have to prepare entrées with wines and other beverages, make sure stations are stocked, keep coffeepots filled, make sure trays and silverware are available at all stations."[2]

Preparing employees to work successfully in the restaurant requires constant ongoing training to keep them up-to-date and well-informed.

The job description is the basis for identifying the employee qualifications needed to perform the job. These qualifications form the job specifications—or more accurately, the person specifications.

The kind of person recruited and what is taught in training are based on task and job analysis. Selecting the right person for each job—based on its analysis—is critical for successful job performance. No amount of training can produce a sincere, friendly welcome if it is not in the person's character when hired. Most training is based on what is carried in the heads of supervisory personnel. This is excellent information, no doubt, but probably not well organized or in a form that can be systematically presented for effective training. Chain organizations have detailed training processes and manuals. Owners of small chains making the transition to large chains employ human resource directors and training directors to organize and present the training in a systematic manner. Necessarily, they must perform job and task analysis to obtain basic information.

Technical Tasks Vary with the Establishment

In breaking down a job into its various tasks, the analyst tries to determine logical work sequences or elements that can be pulled out as separate tasks and taught as a logical sequence of duties, practices, and skills. Each establishment will have somewhat different jobs and tasks within jobs. Tasks that might be broken out of a broiler cook job are:

- Care of broiler
- Broiling seafood exactly as ordered
- Broiling steaks exactly as ordered
- Broiling chicken to specification
- Cleaning the broiler

In analyzing tasks and jobs, emphasize the job objective. For example, a person can be thought of as a clean-up person, but a better description would be "a person who expedites seat turnover." In the description for a busser, the purpose of the job might be spelled out like this: "The general objective of a bus person is to speed seat turnover by setting up and clearing tables rapidly and as efficiently as possible without interfering with the comfort of the patron. By speeding seat turnover, customer satisfaction (due to shorter waits) is increased, along with volume of sales and tips."

The tendency is to analyze the entire job, rather than its parts, the tasks—but it is easier to examine the tasks separately, describe them, and use the analysis as a basis for

In recent years, job descriptions have become important documents in law cases dealing with employee-employer problems. For example, employees may sue the employer for wrongful dismissal, alleging they were not properly informed of the duties they were expected to perform.

A preservice briefing, at which managers describe the specials of the day and other service-related information

training. Figure 12–2 shows a task breakdown for the preparation of a green salad. It could be part of a job of salad person, or part of a cook's job, depending on the restaurant.

A number of tasks are common to more than one job within a restaurant—for example using good telephone manners, giving first aid, dealing with special requests and complaints, acting in emergencies, and cleaning. Running through restaurant operations are other common denominators such as courtesy, cooperation, dexterity, and friendliness.

JOB DESCRIPTIONS

A well-organized restaurant has written job descriptions and specifications. Few independent restaurants bother to perform job analysis but rely on the owner's or manager's knowledge of the job. Chain operators usually have documented job descriptions and specifications for use by both manager and employees (Figure 12–3). Often, the description and specification are combined for convenience. The importance of good job descriptions cannot be overemphasized. They have been used as evidence in a number of lawsuits and Equal Employment Opportunity Commission (EEOC) cases. More importantly, they help in creating a clean and common understanding of the purpose and expected outcomes of each job. Every restaurant should have one for every position.

Guidelines for Writing a Job Description

- Describe the job, not the person in the job.
- Do not describe in fine detail such as would be the result of a time and motion study.

JOB TITLE: _Salad person_   LOCATION: _Pre-prep Area_

OBJECTIVE:

To prepare and serve a quality, elegant-looking tossed green salad with crisp greens.

(Standard of performance: One salad in three minutes)

EQUIPMENT AND SUPPLIES:

Large salad bowl; peeler	Parsley sprigs	Red tomato
Paring knife, grater	Head of lettuce	Carrot
Shredder	Head of red cabbage	

"WHAT TO DO"	"HOW TO DO IT"	"REMARKS" (important information)
I. Preparing the vegetables		
A. Lettuce	1. Lay aside outer leaves. 2. Pull apart leaves and shred into portion size.	Make sure leaves are clean, crisp, and not deteriorated.
B. Red cabbage	1. Pull off outer leaves. 2. Shred cabbage with shredder.	Be sure to shake off excess water same as above. Make sure not to get it too fine and be careful of fingers when shredding.
C. Carrots	1. Wash carrots thoroughly. 2. Peel carrots. 3. Grate carrots into very small pieces.	Grate to small pieces.
D. Tomatoes	1. Wash thoroughly. 2. Cut into 8 sectional wedges.	Leave skin on to make a uniform looking tomato.
II. Arranging the salad	1. Place large outer lettuce leaves inside bowl. 2. Toss lettuce, cabbage, and carrots together. 3. Place tomato wedges on top of green salad.	It is very important not to toss the tomato with the rest of the salad.
III. Garnishing the salad	1. Garnish salad with parsley leaves — or/and — 2. Place a scalloped edge tomato in center also with above.	Be careful not to "overdo" the garnish. People want the salad—not the garnish.
IV. Serving the salad	1. Serve at once or keep it in a refrigerated area.	The crispness of the salad will deteriorate if left in a warm area too long.

FIGURE 12–2

Task breakdown: preparation of tossed green salad

POSITION: Assistant Manager

REPORTS TO: Manager

POSITION OVERVIEW: Under the general supervision of the manager, subject to the Service Policy and Procedure Manual, assures constantly and consistently the creation of maximal guest satisfaction and dining pleasure.

RESPONSIBILITIES AND DUTIES:

A. Planning and organizing
1. Studies past sales experience records, confers with manager, keeps alert to holidays and special events, and so on; forecasts loads and prepares work schedules for service employees in advance to meet requirements.
2. Observes guest reactions and confers frequently with waiters and waitresses to determine guest satisfactions, dissatisfactions, relative popularity of menu items, and so on, and reports such information with recommendations to the manager.
3. Observes daily the condition of all physical facilities and equipment in the dining room, making recommendations to the manager for correction and improvements needed.
4. Anticipates all material needs and supplies, and assures availability of same.
5. Inspects, plans, and assures that all personnel, facilities and materials are in complete readiness for excellent service before each meal period.
6. Anticipates employment needs, recommending to the manager plans for recruitment and selection to meet needs as they arise.
7. Discusses in advance menu changes with waiters and waitresses to assure full understanding of new items.
8. Conducts meetings of service employees at appropriate times.
9. Defines and explains clearly for waiters, waitresses, and buspersons their responsibilities for relationships:
   - with each other
   - with guest
   - with the hostess/host
   - with the manager
   - with the cashier
   - with the kitchen personnel

B. Coordinating
1. Assures that waiters and waitresses are fully informed as to all menu items—how they are prepared, what they contain, ounce per portion.
2. Periodically discusses and reviews with employees company objectives, guest and personnel policies.
3. Keeps manager informed at all times as to service activities, progress, and major problems.

C. Supervising
1. Actively participates in employment of new waiters, waitresses, and buspersons; suggests recruitment sources; studies applications; checks references; and conducts interview.
2. Following an orientation outline, introduces new employees to the restaurant, restaurant policies, fellow employees.
3. Using a training plan, trains new employees, also current employees in need of training.
4. Corrects promptly any deviations from established service standards.
5. Counsels with employees on job and personal problems.

■ **FIGURE 12–3**

Job description

6. Follows established policy in making station assignments for waiters and waitresses.
7. Establishes, with approval of manager, standards of conduct, grooming, personal hygiene, and dress.
8. Prepares, in consultation and with approval of the manager, applied standards of performance for waiters, waitresses, and buspersons.
9. Recommends deserving employees for promotion and outstanding performers for special recognition and award.
10. Strives at all times through the practice of good human relations and leadership to establish esprit de corps—teamwork, unity of effort, and individual and group pride.
11. Has a responsibility to maintain and keep a keen and constant alertness to the entire dining room situation—a sensitivity to any deviation or problem, and to assist quickly and quietly in its correction, adjusting guest complaints.
12. Greets and seats guests cordially and courteously, to assure a sincere welcome and genuine interest in their dining pleasure.

D. Controlling
1. Controls according to established policies, standards, and procedures employees—performance, conduct, dress, hygiene, sanitation, personal appearance.
2. Studies all evidence of waste—time, materials, making recommendations for prevention.

E. Other
1. On emergency occasions may serve guests, act as cashier, or perform specifically assigned duties of the manager.
2. Personifies graciousness and hospitality to guests and employees on the basis of "We're glad you're here" and "We're proud to serve you."

FIGURE 12–3

Continued

- Sentences should be short, simple, and to the point. Only words and phrases that really contribute to the description should be used.
- If technical jargon is used, explain it.
- The description should be detailed enough to include all aspects of the job.
- Include the essential functions of the job and the outcomes expected from performing the job.[3]

The Job Specification

A job specification lists the education, and technical/conceptual skills a person needs to satisfactorily perform the requirements of the job. Once the tasks performed in a job are described, a separate section of the job description form can be developed. Remember, no job requires all the faculties of an individual, which means that many jobs can be performed by people who lack several abilities or who are physically unable to perform certain tasks. Many jobs can be done by mentally or emotionally handicapped people. For example, at the Olive Garden restaurants, such workers make salads and do the dishwashing.

The Job Instruction Sheet

Task analysis can be converted into job instructions, which can serve not only as a guide to new employees but also as a quality assurance measure for the maintenance of work

Position: Hostess/Host

1. Maturity—capable of relating effectively to elder and younger patrons and employees. Observable personal competence and stability.
2. Education—minimum of a high school education required, some college desired.
3. Experience—prior positions as a waitress/waiter required, experience as a hostess/host desired. Possess ability to perform as cashier and assist in table clearings. Prior supervisory experience desired. Basic understanding of food, service skills, sanitation, and dining room equipment mandatory.
4. Physical requirements—appropriate physical stature, excellent hearing and vision. Observable strength to be able to walk and stand for long periods without noticeable fatigue.
5. Mental requirements—observable average intelligence, ability to retain sense of order and balance of patron seating placements. Ability to relate to several persons concurrently in a pleasing and prompt manner.
6. General character—observable conscientiousness, good grooming, basically pleasant, and exudes an attitude of willing cooperation. Possess a "taking charge" demeanor of personal authority. Speaks clearly and with acceptable volume and intonation. Possesses personal confidence.

FIGURE 12–4

Job specification

standards. Job instructions comprise a list of the work steps performed, arranged in sequential order if there is a natural cycle to the work. It is a short step from job description to job instruction sheet. If the job description is well done, the information can be reorganized, some information added, and some omitted, to form a job instruction sheet. This is used both by trainer and trainee.

ORGANIZING PEOPLE AND JOBS

In one way or another, every restaurant is organized so that the following restaurant functions are performed:

- Human resources management and supervision
- Food and beverage purchasing
- Receiving, storing, and issuing
- Food preparation
- Foodservice
- Food cleaning; dish and utensil washing
- Marketing/sales
- Promotion, advertising, and public relations
- Accounting and auditing
- Bar service

All of the functions can be performed by one person, as in a one-person pizza parlor, or thousands of people can be involved, as in a large foodservice chain.

RESTAURANT MANAGER—Coordinates and directs the entire operation to assure efficient quality, courteous foodserivce. Works through supervisory personnel, but in smaller restaurants may directly supervise kitchen and dining room staffs. Must know all of the details involved in every restaurant job.

ASSISTANT MANAGER—Performs specific supervisory duties under the manager's direction. Generally takes over in the manager's absence.Must be thoroughly familiar with the entire operation and have good management skills.

BOOKKEEPER—Audits guests checks. May compute daily cash intake, operating ratios, deposits money in bank, and maintain financial records.

PURCHASING AGENT AND STOREROOM SUPERVISOR—Orders, receives, inspects, and stores all food for distribution to the different food departments. Must be capable of managing an inventory and keeping track of current market prices. This job is sometimes the responsibility of the manager or chef.

FOOD PRODUCTION MANAGER—Responsible for all food preparation and supervision of kitchen staff. Must have thorough knowledge of food preparation and good food standards. Should know how to work with and supervise people

DINING ROOM MANAGER—Coordinates dining room activities, trains and supervises host/hostess, waiters, waitresses, busboys, and busgirls. Should possess leadership qualities, objectivity, and fairness.

CASHIER—Receives payment for food and beverages sold. May total checks. Must be personable, quick at mental arithmetic, and completely honest.

PANTRY SUPERVISOR—Supervises salad, sandwich, and beverage workers. Should be able to create attractive food arrangements. May be in charge of requisitioning supplies and supervising cleaning crew.

BEVERAGE WORKER—Prepare hot beverages such as coffee, tea, or hot chocolate. May assist in the pantry and help others in the kitchen during rush hours. It is a good beginning position.

SANDWICH MAKER—Does basically what the name implies, but also is involved in preparing fillings and dressings. This position is an opportunity for a quick, careful worker who may find the job has a touch of creativity. Skills acquired here will help the individual to move to a better paying position.

CHEF AND COOK—Prepares and portions all foods served. In large restaurant operations, job can be highly specialized with individual cooks or chefs responsible for a single produce category such as vegetables, cold meats, soups, sauces, and short orders.

KITCHEN HELPER—Assists the cooks, chefs, and bakers by performing supervised tasks. It's a good entry job for the individual who wants to learn food preparation because the kitchen helper is busy measuring, mixing, washing, and chopping vegetables and salad ingredients.

SANITATION/MAINTENANCE WORKER—Maintains clean cooking utensils, equipment, walls, and floors. In most modern restaurants, dishwashers and other machines simplify part of the job. This behind-the-scenes position allows the individual to study the various kitchen duties before choosing a particular job or direction for the future. This category includes porters, dishwashers, and potwashers.

PASTRY CHEF AND BAKER—Bakes cakes, cookies, pies, and other desserts. Bakes bread, rolls, quick breads. In some restaurants, must also be skilled in cake decorating.

HOST/HOSTESS—Takes reservations. Keeps informed on current and upcoming table reservations. May present menu and introduce waitperson. Should be attractive, friendly, able to maintain composure when restaurant is busy.

WAITER-CAPTAIN—Supervises and coordinates activities of dining room employees, performing in a formal atmosphere. May be responsible for scheduling hours and shifts and keeping employees' time records and assigning work stations.

WAIT PERSON—Takes food orders and serves the foods to customers. These key employees must like people, be poised and have good self-control, be able to coordinate and respond to many requests made at almost the same time. The individual must move quickly and accurately. Many people make this a career position.

BUS PERSON—Clears the table, re-sets it with fresh linen and eating utensils, fills water glasses, and helps in other housekeeping chores in the dining area. A fine way to start learning the business.

FIGURE 12–5

Unit restaurant

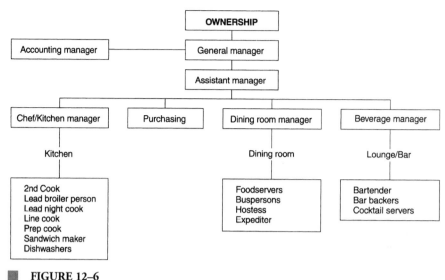

■ **FIGURE 12–6**

A hypothetical dinner house/restaurant organization chart

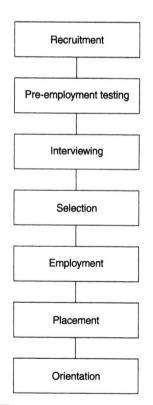

■ **FIGURE 12–7**

The steps in staffing the restaurant

An organization chart lays out the lines of communication and relationships between jobs. It also suggests lines of authority, responsibility, and accountability, which means that the jobs themselves must be structured and defined. Who is responsible for what? Who reports to whom? Who has authority for making what decisions? Who is accountable for what? Organization charts are shown in Figures 12–6 and 12–7.

As the restaurant grows, specialization of function becomes necessary. The owner/manager must delegate most or all of the restaurant functions, except management, retaining responsibility for planning, overseeing, motivating, and making major decisions—especially financial decisions. People are added and specialists take on responsibilities for purchasing, for food preparation, and for service.

STAFFING THE RESTAURANT

The restaurant continues to grow and finally reaches the maximum capacity of sales that can be generated in the location. The owner adds another restaurant by taking over a failed place or perhaps constructing a new restaurant.

Recruitment, interviewing, selection, preemployment testing, employment, placement, orientation, and training are key words in finding the right people and preparing them to work successfully in the restaurant. Figure 12–8 shows the steps involved in staffing the restaurant.

CIVIL RIGHTS LAWS

Civil rights laws state that employers may not discriminate in employment on the basis of an individual's race, religion, color, sex, national origin, marital status, age, veteran status, family relationship, disabilities, or juvenile record that has been expunged. Neither may employers retaliate in any way or discharge employees who report, complain about, or oppose discriminatory practices or file or participate in the complaint process.

Federal and state laws on discrimination are similar. The state may be charged with the enforcement of federal civil rights legislation. Different state agencies are charged with enforcing various aspects of the law. For example, in Oregon, the Bureau of Labor processes federal complaints for the EEOC, while the U.S. Department of Labor (DOL), Wage and Hour Division, deals with sex and age discrimination. Other aspects of the law are enforced directly by the DOL, the Office of Federal Contract Compliance, and the U.S. Department of Health and Welfare. As you might guess, when more than one agency is involved, they do not necessarily agree on the interpretation of the law.

■

Equal Employment Opportunity

Equal employment opportunity (EEO) is the legal right of all individuals to be considered for employment and promotion on the basis of their ability and merit.[4]

Providing equal employment opportunity is required by law and applies to discrimination based on race, sex, religion, color, national origin, veteran status, age and non-job-related mental or physical disabilities. The intention of this legislation is to

Selection

They don't necessarily look for experience. When I applied at the Olive Garden, I was applying to be a hostess, but they wanted me to work as a server, and it didn't matter that I had no prior experience because they had a good training program.

Source: Topaz Walker and Andrea Jenson, personal conversation, 22 November 1999.

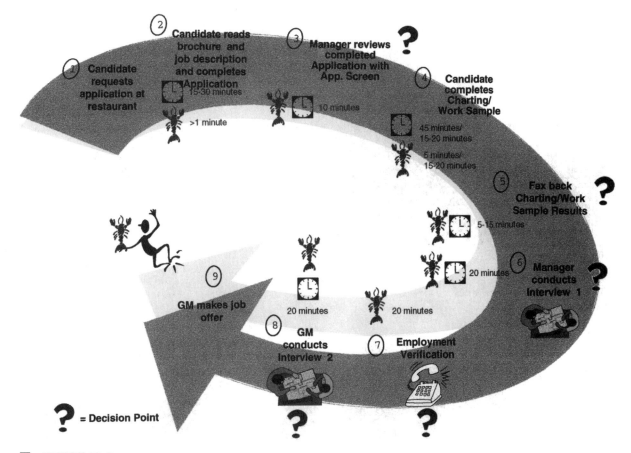

■ **FIGURE 12–8**

Red Lobster recruitment process. Courtesy Red Lobster Restaurants

An employment interview allows the prospective employee and the employer to get to know one another. Photo credit: Ann Jenson

prohibit discrimination against job applicants or employees for promotion for one or more of the above reasons.

The EEOC is the organization to which employees or job applicants may appeal if they feel they have been discriminated against. If the EEOC agrees, this agency files charges against an individual and/or the organization.

The Immigration Reform and Control Act of 1986 outlaws discrimination against legal immigrants to the United States. It covers all employees, and someone with permanent work authorization cannot be favored over someone with temporary status. Fines and even imprisonment of offending employers have increased in recent years.[5]

The Age Discrimination Act was passed in 1967 to protect people over the age of 40 from discrimination.

The Americans with Disabilities Act

The Americans with Disabilities Act (ADA) prohibits discrimination against employees who are disabled and requires making "readily achievable" modifications in work practices and working conditions that enable them to work.

A sweeping new federal law, the ADA, provides comprehensive civil rights protection for people with disabilities in the areas of:

- Employment (Title I)
- All aspects of state and local government operations (Title II)
- Public accommodation, private business serving the public (Title III)

- Transportation (included under both Titles II and III)
- Telecommunication (Title IV)

The law specifically requires that restaurants welcome customers with disabilities by removing barriers that interfere with access to the facilities and services provided.

Today, there are 43 million people with disabilities in the United States and, as the population ages, the number will increase steadily over the next several decades.

■ **Who Is a Person with a Disability?**   One out of five Americans is considered disabled, according to the Census Bureau, and the ADA protects any employee who has a mental or physical disability that substantially limits a major life activity, such as working.[6] The ADA defines a person with a disability to be an individual who falls within one of the following three categories:

1. An individual with a physical or mental impairment that substantially limits one or more major life activities, such as walking, seeing, or hearing

2. Someone with a history of such an impairment—for example, a history of heart disease or cancer

3. Someone who is perceived as having a disability, such as an individual who is severely scarred or someone who is believed to have tested HIV positive

■ **How Does the ADA Affect Your Restaurant?**   All areas in a restaurant used by the public are places of public accommodation under the ADA and thus are subject to the requirements of Title III, which regulates access to both a restaurant's physical facilities and to the services it offers. In terms of access to physical facilities, new construction designed for first occupancy after 26 January 1993 is required to meet the ADA Accessibility Guidelines (ADAAG). ADAAG provides technical design requirements to assure that newly constructed facilities are accessible to individuals with disabilities. Alterations undertaken later must also meet the guidelines. However, barrier removal that is readily achievable, defined as easily accomplishable without significant difficulty or expense, is required in all existing buildings. The factors for determining what is readily achievable in removing barriers are listed in *Americans with Disabilities Act: Answers for Foodservice Operators*, published by the National Restaurant Association.[7]

■

Hiring People Who Are Physically or Mentally Challenged

Sources of employees usually overlooked are the seriously disadvantaged emotionally, mentally, or physically. Hundreds of restaurant operators state categorically they hire such workers because they are more loyal, try harder, and are more appreciative of having a job than the average employee. Numerous studies support this view.

Ask yourself which restaurant position is the most demanding, least satisfying, most confining, and, usually, at the bottom of the pay scale. The answer is the dishwasher, pot and pan person, or clean-up person. These are the jobs with the greatest turnover. In many restaurants, the dishwashing section is humid and noisy, and sometimes the only people doing the dog work of the kitchen are emotionally disturbed or addicted people. In many restaurants, the dish room has automatic dishwashers, good ventilation, lighting, and protective gloves, which make the job more acceptable.

A person with physical limitations may be able to do the job given a high-legged chair on which to rest periodically. Indeed, these assists may be helpful for all employees, not only persons with physical limitations. The chair can be on large wheels that enable the person to move about easily. A sit/lean backrest may help. A thick rubber or vinyl mat helps prevent slipping and the development of varicose veins in the legs.

Employers should keep in mind that they are selecting personnel for the facilities they have that are used in the tasks to be performed. High intelligence is not needed for most routine jobs and the unchallenged person will probably soon leave. Avoid hiring those at obvious risk for work at hand. A person with a history of epilepsy may do extremely well as a receiving clerk or bookkeeper. As a line cook, he or she is at risk for self-injury and injury to others. Alcohol addicts are not good candidates as bartenders but may do well in other jobs.

Some restaurant chains actively support hiring the handicapped. Bob Evans Farm has, since 1991, hired 185 people with disabilities, including blindness. McDonald's, Pizza Hut, and the Olive Garden seek the physically and mentally challenged. The human resource vice president of the Olive Garden notes that the Olive Garden works with vocational training groups and hires candidates who are already well trained. Some operators employ obviously retarded people who may require six months to be able to perform well but who remain on the job for years. Besides providing jobs to citizens in the community, hiring people of varying abilities is good from a public relations viewpoint.[8]

Restaurant jobs are often divided into front of the house and back of the house. Server and host positions put a premium on appearance and a desire to please. As one operator put it, "To hire a server, I ask only one question: Are you happy?" Happiness is not requisite for back-of-the-house people, but it helps. The chef's job is the most critical, requiring someone who is a teetotaler or who can control his or her temper and alcohol consumption. A sense of humor is divine.

Most of us are handicapped in one way or another, or will be under stress. Excessive work hours destroy efficiency.

AIDS[9]

Acquired Immune Deficiency Syndrome (AIDS) cannot be transmitted through the air, water, or food. The only medically documented ways in which AIDS can be contracted are by sexual contact, by shared needles (usually associated with drug addiction), by infusion of contaminated blood, and through the placenta from mother to fetus.

AIDS is not passed through the daily routines that occur in restaurants. You cannot catch the disease by working with someone who has AIDS or by eating food prepared by someone who has AIDS.

The Centers for Disease Control states:

> All epidemiological and laboratory evidence indicates that bloodborne and sexually transmitted infections are not transmitted during the preparation or serving of food or beverages, and no instances of HBV or HTV-III/LAV [the viruses that cause AIDS] transmission have been documented in this setting.

The statement of the Surgeon General is less technical but equally emphatic:

> Nor has AIDS been contracted from . . . eating in restaurants (even if a restaurant worker has AIDS or carries the AIDS virus).

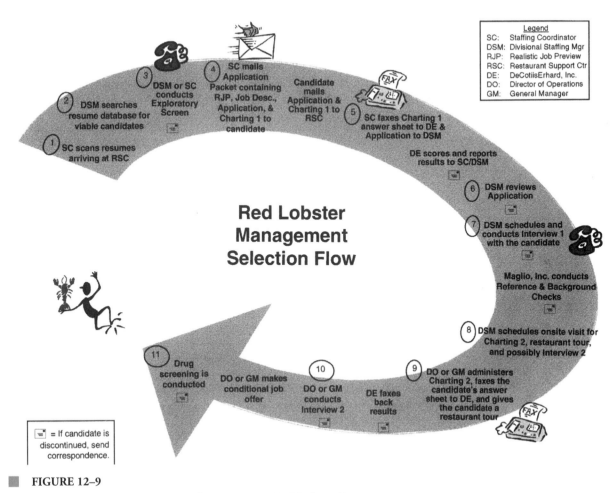

Legend

SC:	Staffing Coordinator
DSM:	Divisional Staffing Mgr
RJP:	Realistic Job Preview
RSC:	Restaurant Support Ctr
DE:	DeCotiisErhard, Inc.
DO:	Director of Operations
GM:	General Manager

Red Lobster Management Selection Flow

1. SC scans resumes arriving at RSC
2. DSM searches resume database for viable candidates
3. DSM or SC conducts Exploratory Screen
4. SC mails Application Packet containing RJP, Job Desc., Application, & Charting 1 to candidate
   Candidate mails Application & Charting 1 to RSC
5. SC faxes Charting 1 answer sheet to DE & Application to DSM
   DE scores and reports results to SC/DSM
6. DSM reviews Application
7. DSM schedules and conducts Interview 1 with the candidate
   Maglio, Inc. conducts Reference & Background Checks
8. DSM schedules onsite visit for Charting 2, restaurant tour, and possibly Interview 2
9. DO or GM administers Charting 2, faxes the candidate's answer sheet to DE, and gives the candidate a restaurant tour
   DE faxes back results
10. DO or GM conducts Interview 2
11. Drug screening is conducted
    DO or GM makes conditional job offer

= If candidate is discontinued, send correspondence.

FIGURE 12–9

Red Lobster management selection flow. Courtesy Red Lobster Restaurants

RECRUITMENT

Recruitment is the process by which prospective employees are attracted to the restaurant in order that a suitable applicant may be selected for employment. Recruitment must be carried out in accordance with existing federal and state employment laws and regulations and with civil rights regulations.

SELECTION

Selection is the process of determining the eligibility and suitability of a prospective employee—not only how well a person can cook or serve but also how he or she will fit in with the team. Personal appearance, grooming, and hygiene are also important.

The purpose of the selection process is to hire an employee who will be a team player, a person who will exceed the performance expectations of guests and management.

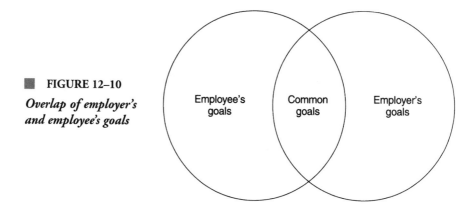

■ **FIGURE 12–10**

*Overlap of employer's
and employee's goals*

INTERVIEWING

Making a hiring decision based on a job interview is not easy because interviewees are on their best behavior. We are looking for a caring, skilled, outgoing, conscientious, loyal person with good work ethics. How do we determine if a person has all these qualities in the short time an interview allows?

Interviews seek to identify certain behavioral characteristics that may determine successful employment practices.

The purposes of the interview are to:

■ Gain sufficient information from the candidate to enable the interviewer or a member of management to determine that the applicant is capable of doing the job for which he or she is applying.

■ Give information about the company and the job to help the applicant determine if both are right for him or her.

■ Ask appropriate legal but leading questions that will weed out undesirable workers.

First impressions are important both ways—in other words, the restaurant also needs to make a good first impression. An interview takes careful planning. The setting should put the applicant at ease; it should be comfortable yet businesslike and without interruptions.

Once the applicant has been made to feel welcome, the completed application form is a good starting point for discussion. If the applicant has had nine jobs in ten years, it would appear that he or she is not a stable employee who, if hired, would stay a long time. If there are gaps in the employment record, be sure to check them thoroughly.

The majority of applicants want to be placed in positions that will allow them to be challenged, to grow and develop. Other applicants may be happy to do the same job year in, year out. A win-win situation is achieved when the goals of the employee and employer overlap—the more overlap, the better. The overlapping circles in Figure 12–10 depicts this. If either the employee or the employer has too strong a personal agenda, problems will occur.

CALIFORNIA CAFE BAR & GRILL
APPLICANT INTERVIEW AND RATING FORM
(FILL OUT AFTER INTERVIEW AND ATTACH TO APPLICATION)
(DO NOT WRITE ON APPLICATION)

Date Of First Interview __/__/__/   Manager:_____

Call For Second Interview: 1st try: __/__/__/   2nd try: __/__/__/   3rd try: __/__/__/

Date Of Second Interview: __/__/__/ Time:_____   Manager:_____

Approved For Hire GM's Initial:_____

Department:_____   Salary Requirements:_____

RATE EACH CATEGORY 1 THROUGH 5:

APPEARANCE & ATTITUDE:_____

KNOWLEDGE:_____

EXPERIENCE:_____

SOCIAL SKILLS:_____   (PERSONAL TRAITS)

STABILITY:_____

       TOTAL:_____
COMMENTS:

_____

_____

_____

REFERENCES CHECKED BY:_____ PERSON(S) CONTACTED:_____

DATE:__/__/__/COMMENTS:_____

_____

_____

Date Of Hire:__/__/__/   Rate Of Pay:_____

Checked For Citizenship:_____   Managers Initial:_____
(Or Work Permits)

Foodhandler Card:_____   Review Date:__/__/__/
(If Applicable)

Employee Folder Completed:__/__/__/   MGR/BKPR Initial:_____

Employee folder must contain: Send To Datamasters:
Photocopies of: Drivers Licence & Social Security Card   Copy of W4
            Other Documentation For Proof Of Work Elegibility   Datamaster New Hire Sheet
            Signed Parking Policy Sheet etc.
            19 Immigration Form
            W4 Tax Form
            Application & Ratings Sheet
            Signed Manual Receipt Pages
            Datamaster New Hire Sheet

FIGURE 12–11

Applicant interview and rating form

■
Ideal Employee Profiles

Because employees constitute such a large part of restaurant ambiance, spirit, and effi-ciency, management decides what type of personnel will fit best with the restaurant's style. Outgoing personalities fit well in the front of house, where staff must be clean-cut, optimistic, healthy, and outgoing. The kitchen can use those who are not so extroverted.

Apparent health and goodwill are obvious assets to all foodservice personnel, adding to the atmosphere, helping to create the eating-out experience.

Obviously, the ideal cook would probably not make an ideal server, nor would the ideal bartender be the ideal assistant manager, and so on.

The temptation is to think of a kitchen with a highly trained chef at its head. However, only about one-third of all restaurants employ anyone with the title *chef*. Sometimes the terms *kitchen manager* or *head cook* are used. Large hotels generally have chefs. Full-service restaurants are more likely to have chefs than other restaurants, and about half of foodservice operations have someone with the title of chef. Quick-service restaurants may call someone chef, but the title is more name than reality, as few of the skills required of a chef are needed. The highly profitable restaurants are those with rel-atively fixed menus that require few skills in the kitchen; here, the ideal employees may be teenagers rather than experienced cooks. The dining room may be staffed almost completely by students.

For restaurant service jobs, attitude is more important than ability and, in a plen-tiful job market, the operator can afford to take the time to be highly selective. Prestige restaurants may select only 1 out of 20 applicants. Because of the low wages offered in most restaurants, the operator does not have such a wide choice and must rely on con-tinuous training to meet high service standards.

A problem in hiring is determining whether the candidate is underqualified or overqualified, and whether he or she will be satisfied with the job. Another big problem in selecting restaurant personnel is determining the candidate's degree of honesty and responsibility. Cost controls diminish the need for absolute honesty, and productivity standards help ensure responsibility.

California Café uses an applicant interview and rating form (Figure 12–11) that managers fill out immediately after the interview and attach to the application form. It is not permitted to write on the application form.

EMPLOYMENT OF MINORS

The National Restaurant Association and many state restaurant associations have taken a positive approach to improving the industry's reputation as a youth employer. The threatening legislative climate has conscientious restaurateurs considering the larger social issues surrounding the development of the nation's youth.[10]

A concerted effort has been mounted by a cooperative task force made up of offi-cials from the DOL, the U.S. Congress, and the National Restaurant Association to go beyond what is merely required by law to provide a high-quality work experience.

The specifics of programs for students are:

1. Education comes first.

2. Participating restaurants gather parental permission slips before hiring young workers.

Protected Class	Inappropriate Inquiries	Comments
Marital status	Are you married? Divorced? Separated?	Since it is illegal to discriminate on the basis of marital status, all these inquiries are inappropriate. One's marital status has nothing to do with his or her ability to perform the job, nor is this an effective means of discerning one's "character."
Age	Birth date? How old are you?	If it is necessary to know that someone is over a certain age for legal reasons, this question could better be stated, "Are you 21 or over?"
National origin	Are you native-born or naturalized? Have you proof of your citizenship? What was your birthplace? Where were your parents born?	If it is necessary to know if someone is a U.S. citizen for a job, this question could be asked directly without asking further which might reveal national origin. If it is necessary to require proof of citizenship immigrant status, employment can be offered on the condition that proof be supplied.
Family relationship	Do you have any relatives currently employed here?	A job cannot be legally refused to someone who has a relative already working for the employer unless either relative would have supervisor or grievance adjustment authority over the other family member.
Mental or physical handicap	Do you have, or have you ever had cancer? epilepsy? drugs, alcohol? an on-the-job injury? Have your ever been treated for a mental condition?	A job cannot be refused because of a mental or physical handicap that would not prevent the person from performing the functions of the addiction to any job. If there is a question about someone's physical or mental ability to the job can be offered on the condition that a physician's opinion be furnished indicating the person is able to do the job with the probability that the person would not harm himself or pose danger for others.
Race, sex	What is your race, sex? Furnish a photograph. What is your hair and eye color?	If it is necessary to ask for this information for Affirmative Action purposes, these inquiries should be accompanied by a statement indicating that the information is needed for affirmative action reporting purposes and will not be used to discriminate. A photograph should not be required: how someone looks has nothing to do with how he or she performs the job.

■ **FIGURE 12–12**

Questions to avoid

Sex	Are you pregnant?	Some state laws clearly state that discrimination on the basis of pregnancy is sex discrimination. In order to legally refuse employment because of pregnancy, an employer would have to show there was strong reason to believe the woman couldn't do the job (such as a physician's opinion to that effect) or that the nature of the position would not allow the employer to grant maternity leave without undue hardship. Pregnancy must be treated as other physical conditions under the law.
Injured Worker	Have you ever applied for workers' compensation?	It is illegal to refuse to hire because a person has applied for workers' compensation. If it is necessary to know about someone's physical condition to perform a job, it is better to ask for this information directly.
Religion	What is your religious affiliation? What clubs/ associations are you a member of? Can you work Saturdays? Sundays?	The first two questions are inappropriate. Religious affiliation is no indication of work ability. Asking for membership information may reveal religious affiliation; club membership is not an indicator of work ability. It may be necessary for an employer to know if an applicant cannot work Saturdays or Sundays because of religious beliefs. However, an employer has an obligation to accommodate those beliefs unless it would cause undue hardship to the business.
Race	Have you been arrested? Have you been convicted of crimes other than minor traffic violations?	Since minority group members are arrested and convicted of crimes at a significantly higher rate than non-minority people, these inquiries could be used to exclude minorities from job opportunities disproportionately more than non-minorities. Asking for *arrest* records is highly questionable, since being arrested is not a true indicator of guilt. Courts have held that conviction records can be used to deny employment if the crime for which the person is convicted is related to the type of job. For example, an employer could refuse employment to someone convicted of theft and receipt of stolen goods for a job as bellhop where personal belongings of customers would be handled.
	Do you own your own home?	This question may also tend to exclude people from minority groups because they do not own homes at the same proportion as non-minority people. Home ownership is not an indicator of someone's ability to do the job.

FIGURE 12–12

Continued

3. Restaurants send notices of employment to the worker's school.

4. Employers pledge to schedule work hours flexibly to better accommodate students' school workload.

5. Some programs encourage job-site visits by parents.[11]

Several leading restaurant chains have found that teenagers, beginning at age 16, are excellent candidates for almost every restaurant job, from bussing and dishwashing to cooking and order taking. Some restaurants have teenage shift managers, lead people, and assistants.

All of the quick-service chains in this country and a number of table-service restaurants have built outstanding operations around teenagers. The biggest success story of them all, McDonald's, employs a high percentage of teenagers—if possible, part-time only, so that they can perform at peak efficiency during the hours worked. A tired, dispirited employee destroys the character of a restaurant almost as fast as poor food.

■

Restrictions on Employing Minors

A number of federal regulations control the kind of work permissible for minors (under age 16). State laws also apply and may be different from the regulations laid down by the federal government. Where state laws are more restrictive, they take precedence over the federal regulations. The regulations change from time to time, as do their interpretations. The National Restaurant Association spells out the work that may not be done by minors under 16 years of age:

- Work on connection with maintenance or repair of machines or equipment
- Outside window washing that involves working from windowsills, and all work requiring the use of ladders, scaffolds, or their substitutes
- Cooking (except at soda fountains, lunch counters, snack bars, or cafeteria serving counters) and baking
- Work in freezers and meat coolers and all work in preparation of meats for sale (except wrapping, sealing, labeling, weighing, pricing, and stacking.
- Loading and unloading goods to and from trucks, railroad cars, and conveyors
- Work around cars and trucks involving the use of pits, racks, or lifting apparatus or involving inflation of tires mounted on a rim equipped with a movable retaining ring
- Work as a motor vehicle driver or outside helper
- Work in warehouses, except office and clerical work, and at any occupations found and declared to be hazardous by the DOL.[12]

Minors between 16 and 18 years of age cannot:

- Operate elevators or power-driven hoists
- Operate power-driven shaving machines or bakery machinery
- Operate circular saws, power-driven slices, bandsaws, and guillotine shears

There are exceptions for students engaged as apprentices or in student-learner programs. Of course, federal and state laws set the absolute standard and may specify additional requirements for employing minors.

At age 18, teenagers may legally work at any job. If in doubt, call your local DOL office for an interpretation of the law or regulations.

Children under 16 may be employed by their parents in occupations other than those declared hazardous for minors under 18.

Maximum Work Hours

- *Ages 14 and 15.* On school days, three hours per day, 18 hours per week; on nonschool days, 8 hours per day, 40 hours per week

- *Age 16 and over.* No restrictions on working hours even during school hours. However, if a state law is stricter, it must be followed.

Night Work Restrictions

- *Ages 14 and 15.* Not before 7 A.M. or after 7 P.M. on school days; from June 1 through Labor Day, until 9 P.M.

Because of the restrictions, some employers refuse even to consider minors under age 16.

Federal laws are enforced by the DOL, Employment Standards Administration, Wage and Hour Division, Washington, DC 20210. The U.S. Child Labor Requirements provide for a criminal fine for willful violators.

EMPLOYMENT OF UNDOCUMENTED ALIENS

The Immigration Reform and Control Act of 1986 makes it illegal for employers to employ undocumented aliens. It is the employer's responsibility to verify the prospective employees' legal immigration status and right to work in the United States. Fortunately, employers are not required to verify the authenticity of documents presented. However, human resources directors are required to do their best to ensure the authenticity of all documents and, in case of doubt, may refer to the Immigration and Naturalization Service (INS). Keep copies of all documents presented in case of a government audit. The I-9 form is proof of having inspected the employees' documentation. Failure to keep appropriate records may result in fines and, potentially, the loss of employees just before opening for Friday night business. The following documents may be used to determine the status of a prospective employee:

- U.S. passport
- Certificate of U.S. citizenship
- Alien card
- Foreign passport with INS stamp authorizing the individual to work
- Certificate of naturalization
- U.S. birth certificate with picture identification

EMPLOYEE SOURCES

The most useful source of employees is referrals by reliable present employees. Other sources depend on the area and the employment situation at the time. Possible sources include:

- Present employees via promotion (the first place to look)
- State employment service
- Classified ads
- Schools—high school co-ops, culinary technical schools, colleges, regional occupation programs
- Vendors
- Customers
- Youth groups (e.g., Boy Scouts, Girl Scouts)
- Fraternities, sororities
- Walk-ins
- The Internet
- Minority sources
- Church groups
- Bus ads
- Radio
- Veterans organizations
- Retiree organizations (a valuable resource that goes untapped)
- TV (often available on local cable stations at reasonable rates)
- Community bulletin boards
- Job fairs
- Local partnerships

QUESTIONS TO AVOID ON THE APPLICATION FORM AND DURING THE INTERVIEW

The civil rights laws do not prohibit specific questions, but they do forbid discriminatory use of information in selecting employees. The burden is on the employer to show the need for the information requested and how it is used in the hiring decision. If it is necessary to identify applicants by race and sex, the employer should include a statement informing the applicant that the questions are being asked for affirmative action purposes and that the information will not be used in a discriminatory way. Questions to avoid are shown in Figure 12–12.

- Name and address
  - What is your full name?
  - What is your address?
  - What is your telephone number?
- Age and citizenship
  - Do you meet the minimum age requirement for work in this state?
  - If hired, can you show proof of age?
  - Are you over 18 years of age?

■ *Religion.* What is acceptable here is a statement by the employer of regular days, hours of shifts to be worked, and the expectations of regular attendance.

■ *Physical condition handicap.* It is acceptable to say, "Are you able to perform the essential functions of this job with or without reasonable accommodations?"[13]

Some questions are appropriate only if asked of all candidates—for example, "Do you know any reason why you might not be able to come to work on time every day?" You may ask if a person has ever been convicted of committing a felony. If the answer is yes, then it's legal to ask what for. You would then need to make a determination about the suitability of placement in the available position. You wouldn't want a person convicted of stealing as a bartender.[14]

■

Questions You Can Ask

General Opener

■ Tell me a little about yourself.

■ What is the most important factor in the success of a restaurant?

Experience

■ What is your favorite restaurant and why?

■ What is your (foodservice, cooking) experience?

■ What are your present duties and responsibilities?

■ How well do you think you succeed in meeting those?

■ Describe your ideal job.

■ How do you see this restaurant helping with your future?[15]

Transportation

■ Can you get to and from work reliably for the shifts?

Availability

■ What are your available working hours?

■ Is there any time you cannot work?

■ Are you available to work overtime when necessary?

■ Do you have limitations on what shifts you can work?

Hobbies/Interests

■ What are your hobbies and interests? (This is a general question that may encourage an applicant to open up.)

Goals/Ambitions

■ What are your goals and ambitions? (The restaurant owner may be able to provide assistance, counseling, and overall encouragement to a person who has identified goals.)

- What goals have you established for yourself that are not work-related for the next few years and why?
- Where do you see yourself three years from now?

Sports

- Which sports do you play or follow?

Languages

- Do you speak more than one language?

Work Experience

- How would your previous employer describe your work?
- What did you like most and least about your former job?
- How did you handle problems such as a drunken or obstreperous customer?

Skills and Specific Job-Related Questions

- Describe how you would prepare an item on the menu (for a cook's position) or the way to serve a particular food item (for a foodserver).
- What skills do you possess that make you think you should be employed here? What do you think this job and our organization can do for you?
- How long do you think you will be able to work for us?

Other Interview Questions

How do you plan to achieve your career goals?

What do you consider to be your greatest strengths and weaknesses?

How do you think your last employer will describe you when we call to check references?

How do your coworkers describe you? your subordinates?

What motivates you to put forth your greatest effort?

Why should I hire you?

What qualifications do you have that make you think you will be successful in the restaurant business?

What qualities should a successful manager possess?

Describe the relationship that should exist between a supervisor and those reporting to him or her.

What two or three accomplishments have given you the most satisfaction? Why?

What led you to choose the restaurant industry?

Do you have plans for additional education? What have you done to implement those plans?

Do you think your grades in school are a successful indicator of your abilities?

In what type of work environment are you most comfortable?

How do you work under pressure? Give me an example.

Why did you decide to seek a job with us?

What do you know about our restaurant?

What criteria are you using to evaluate the company for which you hope to work?

What major problem have you encountered and how did you deal with it?

Tell me about an unusual request or demand from a guest and how you handled it.

Give me an example of a situation in which you solved a problem of an angry guest.

What two or three things are important to you in your job?

The Multiple Interview Approach

When plenty of applicants are available, the multiple interview is probably more effective than a single interview by a single person. A first interview may be given and the candidate rated from 1 to 5 on whatever factors are considered relevant to successful job performance. Only those candidates receiving a rating of 5 are given an additional appointment with a second interviewer.

Telephone References

Following up references by phone is much more effective than sending a written request, if the caller is adroit in asking questions. The phone call should be directed toward finding out the applicant's strengths and weaknesses. Reference checks are also useful in verifying what the applicant has said about previous wage or salary, job title, and length of employment.

The caller should state his or her name, title, and restaurant, and request to speak to a past supervisor. Then he or she should explain that the applicant has applied for employment and has given the person being called as a reference. "Would you mind answering a few questions?" The caller can review what the applicant said he or she earned and did.

Few people voluntarily make adverse comments about applicants. The tone of voice and what is not said may be more important than the words. With "right to know" legislation and our litigious society, it is wise to ask only questions relating to the applicant's attendance, such as "How long has *x* been with you?" the dates work began and ended, and work capability and rate of pay. An important question might be, "Is the person eligible for reemployment?" (Conversely, restaurateurs should not volunteer opinions about former employees, no matter how factual they may be. A former employee could have a friend call and record the conversation. The former employee could then sue for slander.)

Research-minded operators can rate applicants on a scale of 1 to 5 and use the rating as a prediction of success or failure on the job. A follow-up of worker performance can be correlated with the original ratings. Over time, an operator can see how effective his or her judgment has been in predicting employee performance and can change the interviewing process to sharpen the predictions.

CAREFUL SELECTION OF PERSONNEL

Taking time and care in selecting personnel is one of the best investments possible. Aside from the several positive reasons already mentioned, there is the need to take a defensive posture in trying to make sure that disruptive, dishonest people are not hired. Lawsuits brought by employees can be disastrous in cost and mental anguish. Some trials go on for years, with lawyers the only winners. Wrongful discharge alleged to involve race, color, creed, marital status, age, handicap, political affiliation, and so on are juicy complaints for lawyers. Lawsuits can be brought for such things as defamation of character, intentional infliction of emotional stress, and sexual harassment. Cases going to a

---

Do not write comments on the application form, because they may be used against you in legal proceedings.

Bill Nordhem, an experienced Chicago restaurateur, says that, over the years, he has developed a sixth sense about which servers will succeed and which will not. He looks for applicants with a positive mental attitude and willingness to participate in a team effort. "I don't believe in hiring the wrong person. I know in five minutes or less if someone is going to work out. I've learned to trust my gut. Every time I haven't, I've paid the price."

Source: Nancy Backas, "Training and Personality," *Cheers* 9, no. 2 (March 1998): 58.

jury trial often result in huge settlements unrelated to much of anything except the skills of the plaintiff's lawyer, who pockets much of the award as legal fees.

The Three Main Hiring Objectives

1. Hire people who project an image and attitude appropriate for your restaurant.

2. Hire people who will work with you rather than spend all their time fighting your rules, procedures, and systems.

3. Hire people whose personal and financial requirements are a good fit with the hours and positions you are hiring for.[16]

Attitude and appearance are critical, say many human resources directors. Employers can teach the job skills, not the human and interpersonal skills.

Five Tips for Better Interviewing

A key in recruiting and training the best-qualified managers is effective interviewing techniques and procedures. Here's a checklist of important tips that can help make you a better interviewer.

1. *Use a job profile based on the job description*, a list of duties, responsibilities, and the personal characteristics the ideal candidate has. This will also help evaluate each candidate's potential once the interview is over.

   If your organization's human resources department has job descriptions for each position in your department on file, review them periodically to make sure that they are up to date and truly reflect each position's responsibilities and necessary qualifications of potential candidates.

2. *Describe the job in reasonable detail at the start of the interview.* Let the candidate know what his or her day-to-day responsibilities will be, what opportunities there are for growth, how the rest of the management team is structured, and what is expected of the candidate in the larger organizational structure.

3. *Ask the right questions.* Knowing the right questions to ask is a critical part of effective interviewing, so prepare a list of questions in advance and think about how you will ask each. Avoid questions that require a yes/no answer, which discourage the candidate from elaborating. Instead, ask open-ended, focused questions like, "Think back to a difficult situation you had with an employee under your supervision and tell me how you handled it." Identifying how a candidate handled past conflicts or situations is a good way to assess how he or she will handle that problem if faced with it again.

   Tom Cooley, director of nutrition services at St. Luke's Hospital in Bethlehem, Pennsylvania, asks hires several behaviors-based questions to help determine their work habits. "I ask candidates if they like to work and if they like to work on their own. This helps me determine whether or not a person is a self-starter. I prefer a go-getter who requires steering to someone who needs prompting."

   Gene Reed, director of foodservice at Ohio University in Athens, Ohio, asks potential management candidates which day is their favorite, Monday or Friday. "I'm looking for a Monday person," Reed says. "People who like Fridays generally like them because they look forward to having two days off. Monday people typically look to the start of the week as a chance to work toward accomplishing their goals."

4. *Get specific.* A good question to ask a job candidate is "What specific things did you do in your last job to improve your effectiveness or to improve productivity in your department?" The answer gives you a sense of a candidate's motivation and willingness to surpass the basic job requirements. Candidates who went that extra mile in a former job will probably do the same in your operation.

   Peter Cayan, director of food and nutrition at the University of Rochester (New York) Strong Memorial Hospital, looks for candidates who describe past problems and solutions using teamwork-related words. "If they say, 'We did this to correct the situation,' that tells me that this person has team player attributes and is a problem solver."[18]

5. *Take notes.* Hiring decisions are too important to rely on your memory about every candidate you interview, so take good notes during each interview so you can review them later.

The ADA poses a number of questions. If there are two equally qualified candidates, one of whom is disabled, must the disabled applicant be given hiring preference, even though some modification investment will be required? The most qualified person would get the job. If questioned or challenged, an operator would have to prove how the person who got the position was the most qualified person.

Make a bad choice and it will cost you; some experts estimate a poor hiring decision typically costs between $4,000 and $5,000.[17]

Thousands of people with disabilities work in the restaurant industry as dishwashers, kitchen helpers, foodservers, cooks, and pot and pan washers. Many were first trained by a job coach funded by state or federal grants. Totally blind persons can be proficient dishwashers. A number of other jobs require only travel vision—enough sight to move about and generally see what is going on. Defective hearing does not disqualify applicants for some jobs.

EMPLOYMENT TESTING

Federal and state laws and regulations restrict the use of employment tests if they are not valid or reliable. The validity of an employment test relates to whether it measures what it is supposed to measure and whether test scores predict successful job performance. A test is said to be reliable if essentially the same results are seen on repeated testing. A test cannot be valid unless it is also reliable.

There is a range of tests for employers to select from: intelligence tests, aptitude tests, and achievement tests. These may or may not be considered necessary for a restaurant, depending on the position available and the desire of the owner or management to utilize a test as a step in the selection of staff.

Some restaurant companies check for substance abuse and honesty, and some use psychological tests in order to select the best possible employees. For example, a cashier position may require a police check. First, however, a prospective employee would have to sign a waiver. Cooks may also be tested on their culinary skills before employing them.

SCREENING OUT THE SUBSTANCE ABUSER

Alcohol abuse is a big problem for restaurant managers; it is magnified by the sale of liquor and the high-pressure atmosphere in many restaurants. More recently, cocaine, marijuana, speed, and other drugs used by employees have added to management concerns.

Substance abuse impairs performance. More importantly, the addict frequently steals to support the habit.

Screening out drug abusers in the employment process is step one. Applicants who are habitual users show signs of health deterioration. Reference checks usually do not elicit explicit statements about drug abuse. The employment record can provide indicators: absenteeism, compensation claims, high number of sick days, accidents, late arrivals, and early departures. If the applicant has a history of arguments or fights with other employees or supervisors, substance abuse may have been involved. Tremors, excessive perspiration, slurred speech, and unsteady gait are physical indicators of substance abuse.

PREEMPLOYMENT PHYSICAL AND DRUG EXAMINATIONS

Preemployment drug and physical exams are being considered or used by many restaurants as a means of avoiding future personnel problems. Physical exams, as long as they pertain to the job, are permissible (for example, lifting a tray or a stack of dishes). However, the ADA regulations must be conformed with. Drug testing may be required in order to provide a safe and secure working environment for both guests and staff.

SUMMARY

Staffing the restaurant is extremely important because effective screening not only selects the best employees but also screens out undesirable ones. Effective recruitment selects people with the most positive service spirit and professionalism. Compliance with existing employment legislation is a must.

The human resource cycle begins with defining jobs and organizing the restaurant. A task is a related sequence of work and a job is a series of related tasks. Task and job analyses examine the details of the work performed and form the basis of the job description. The job specification identifies the qualifications and skills necessary to perform the job. The two main approaches to task and job analysis are bottom up, which is used when the organization already exists, and top down, which is used when opening new restaurants.

KEY TERMS AND CONCEPTS

Task and job analysis

Job specification

Job, position, task

Organizing the restaurant

Job description

Recruitment

Training

Interviewing

Civil rights laws

Selection

Equal Employment Opportunity
   Commission (EEOC)

Preemployment testing

Immigration Reform and Control Act

Placement

Orientation

Age Discrimination

AIDS

The Americans with Disabilities Act
   (ADA)

REVIEW QUESTIONS

1. How long before opening would you employ your chef? your servers? your hostess?

2. Describe the ideal server, the ideal hostess, the ideal cook. How do they deliver on the experience you intend to provide to your customers?

3. Will you employ undocumented aliens in your restaurant? Give your reasons for your decision.

4. List five employee sources other than newspaper classified ads.

5. In some locations, job vacancy notices bring literally hundreds of job applicants. If this happens to you, what methods will you use to select the best of them?

6. In checking employee references, how can you improve your chances of getting valid information on the applicant's past performance?

7. Will you use psychological tests in selecting employees?

8. Many people have a drug or alcohol problem. Would you hire such people? How would you avoid hiring such people?

9. Suppose you want to employ only women for your dining room and bar service. Will you be violating the Equal Employment Opportunity laws?

10. How will you prepare for interviewing a chef? What questions will you ask?

11. What is the difference between a job and a position? Between a task and a job?

12. Give at least three reasons for performing job analysis.

13. In your restaurant, will your host be a "greeter and seater" or a dining room manager? What factors bear on your decision?

14. Will you bother to draw an organization chart for your restaurant? Justify your decision.

15. In your restaurant, will the sanitation/maintenance employees report to the chef or to you, the owner/operator? What factors bear on this choice? Is there an advantage in having these employees report to someone other than you or the chef?

16. What elements will you include in the job description for a food server? a line cook?

17. What elements will you include in the job specifications for a food server? a line cook?

18. Is a restaurant that performs task and job analysis and writes job descriptions and specifications likely to be more successful than one that does not? Why?

19. What is the value of training a person for working more than one job?

ENDNOTES

[1] Personal conversation with Wayne Johnson, S&A Restaurant Corporation, June 26, 1997.

[1] Mary L. Tanke, *Human Resources Management for the Hospitality Industry* (Albany, N.Y.: Del Mar, 1990), 60.

[2] Personal conversation with Topaz Pritchard and Andrea Jenson, 22 November 1999.

[3] Philip M. Perry, "Recruiting Employees to Play on Your Team," *Restaurants USA* 19, no. 19 (November 1999): 32.

[4] Tanke, *Human Resources Management*, 60.

[5] *Food Service Management: Professional Review Notebook* (Chicago: National Restaurant Association Educational Foundation, 1991), 11–12.

[6] Phillip M. Perry, "Gray Matters: The Do's and Don'ts of Dealing with Disabilities," *Restaurant USA* 18, no. 10 (November 1998): 35.

[7] Ibid.

[8] Michael Adams, "Access Denied," *Restaurant Business* 98, no. 2 (15 January 1999): 37.

[9] This section draws on *Basic Facts about AIDS*. Pamphlet prepared by The National Restaurant Association. 1997.

[10] Linda Way, *Restaurants USA* (September 1991): 8.

[11] Ibid.

[12] National Restaurant Association booklet, "Employing Minors," 1994.

[13] Personal conversation with Joan Mitchell, La Jolla Mariott, April 19, 2000.

[14] Personal Interview with Topaz Pritchard, Olive Garden Restaurants, 23 November 1999.

[15] http://www.primenet.com/~armsco/sertrn, 5 November 1999.

[16] Stephen Michaellides and Carolyn Watkins, "The Big Talent Search," *Foodservice Solutions* 32, no. 13 (March 1997): 24.

[17] Personal conversation with Dick Rivera, Red Lobster Restaurants, May 20, 2000.

[18] Personal conversations, July 14, 1999, and October 7, 1999.

Chapter **13**

After reading and studying this chapter,
you should be able to:

Plan and conduct an orientation.

Develop a training program.

EMPLOYEE TRAINING AND DEVELOPMENT

Experience has shown that the most practical and immediately beneficial way of training restaurant employees is the time-tested hands-on method (showing and telling the trainee, then having the trainee do the task). The method prompts immediate rewards and shows where further instruction is needed.

The assumption, however, is that the trainer knows the skill being taught and at least some of the principles of learning. It also assumes that the trainer has laid out the steps needed in order to attain competence.

This chapter gives an overview of employee training and the related subjects of employee orientation and development.

ORIENTATION

A well-planned orientation program helps new employees become acquainted with the restaurant and feel a part of it. Because much of labor turnover occurs in the first few weeks of employment, it is important to establish a bond between the new employee and the restaurant. As with any other program, it is necessary to establish the goals to be accomplished. The goals for an orientation program are:

1. To explain the company history, philosophy, mission, goals, and objectives

2. To make employees feel welcome

3. To let employees know why they have been selected

4. To ensure that employees know what to do and who to ask when unsure

5. To explain and show what is expected of employees

Orientation allows new employees to get acquainted with the restaurant and to learn the procedures to be followed. Courtesy The Prado, San Diego, California

6. To have employees explain and then demonstrate each task so that supervisors can be sure they understand their full job

7. To explain the various programs and social activities available

8. To show where everything is kept (tour of restaurant storerooms, refrigerators, etc.)

Help employees become familiar with the restaurant and the food. For example, at the Olive Garden, everyday training of new employees involves sampling the food. This makes servers better equipped to answer customers' questions and helps build employee confidence.[1]

TRAINING

Most training programs have common characteristics: ease of comprehension, step-by-step job learning, emphasis on sales incentives, use of job checklists, and management control.[2]

To train, the trainer needs to know what should be learned—the tasks that make up a job. Much restaurant training is accomplished by absorption—watching someone and somehow learning the job: "Follow George!" or "Watch Mary." Training by observation has its place. It is much better and more efficient to approach training systematically by analyzing a job, breaking it down into the tasks performed, and teaching the tasks in the sequence in which they are normally performed.

Management decides how extensive written job instructions should be. Brevity is an asset, and if the job tasks can be printed in brief form on a pocket-sized card, the employee has a handy reference. Guidelines for a job can be put together and given to the new employee to augment more comprehensive, detailed job instructions. Both can become part of a training manual. Here is TGI Friday's training schedule for new employees:

Day 1

Orientation
Lunch
Station tour and observation
Study alcohol awareness
Employee handbook review
Study first third of recipe references
Read training manual

Day 2

On-the-job training shift
Alcohol awareness test (open book)
Employee handbook review due
Recipe review; study second third of recipe references
Study for introduction to kitchen and sanitation tests

Day 3

On-the-job training shift
Introduction to kitchen and sanitation tests
Recipe review; study final third of recipe references

Training for jobs and careers in restaurant is offered in high schools, community colleges, and specialized culinary courses. The Culinary Institute of America is an example. It has campuses in Hyde Park, New York, and in the Napa Valley in California. Courses offered range from basic culinary skills to a four-year bachelor's degree program.

Lettuce Entertainment training program lasts five days, for eight hours daily. Each new hire studies the company's training guides in the morning on site and trails a server in the afternoon.

Day 4

On-the-job training shift
Recipe review; study all recipe references

Day 5

On-the-job training shift
Recipe review; study all recipe references

Day 6

On-the-job training shift
Review with the manager
Final test

Performance is evaluated on each shift. If necessary, additional training shifts can be scheduled to successfully meet requirements.[3]

Personnel training is the key to keeping satisfied, capable, confident, and competent employees. Training can give employees a feeling of confidence. At one restaurant in Deburne, Texas, the owner wanted to increase sales at his restaurants by $0.25 per guest. That goal was reached one week after the servers participated in a sales training program. An increase of $1.10 was obtained at dinner and $0.91 at lunch. These increases were credited to a script that was developed for the servers to use. Sales prior to the training as well as after were monitored and employees were able to share a percentage of the profit above their individual sales goals.[4]

Without enthusiasm in training, learning suffers. How many well-informed professors offer dull classes attended by only a handful of students? The best speakers are

Training is a critical link to consistent service. Courtesy The Prado, San Diego, California

also entertainers who appeal to the emotions as well as the brain. Professional speakers use gimmicks to gain attention. Humor is carefully put into the presentation. Concepts are condensed into models and slogans. A catchy training slogan that appears on the blackboards in some kitchens reads: "We forgive all mistakes except what you serve to our customers."

PART-TIME EMPLOYEES INCREASE THE NEED FOR TRAINING

Part-time employees are both a benefit and a drawback. One of the benefits to the operator is in not having to pay benefits (which may be up to 28% of payroll). One of the drawbacks is the possible lack of continuity.

The Bureau of Labor Statistics reports that well over half of all persons employed in foodservice occupations work part time. In the quick-service segment, the proportion of part-timers is higher. Part-time employees are good for the industry because they can be scheduled to fit the peaks and valleys in sales. Moreover, the overwhelming majority, reports the Bureau, want to or can only work part time. Using part-timers means giving more training; most part-timers do not think of foodservice as a permanent career. The result: more people to train, more people who are not particularly motivated to learn their job.

TRAINING AND DEVELOPMENT

The objective in training and developing employees is to produce desired behavior—attitudes and skills appropriate for producing food and service that pleases the restaurant's clientele. Much of learning can be programmed; employees are trained to follow a sequence of behavior. Behavior can be taught by role playing—smile, pour coffee, present the menu, ask about wine. The routine is critiqued by other employees and by managers.

Employee development, usually thought of as training for management, is partly programmed, but it is also based on knowledge that provides background for flexible responses to problem situations. What do I do when all the restaurant seats are filled, when I spill spaghetti, when a customer is angry, when the refrigeration or the ice machine cuts out?

Employee development promotes problem-solving ability and provides analytical skills, new perceptions, and methodologies. Development deals with principles; training, with procedure and process. Both types of learning are needed in any business. Learning for management and supervision emphasizes development; on-the-job training is closer to programming. One is more conceptual than the other.

Training can produce robotlike behavior: smile, say "thank you," and say "goodbye, come again." Training produces skills quickly by breaking them down into segments and piecing them together into sequences:

Turn the hamburger when the juices rise to the top.
Cut the steak ¾-inch thick and weigh each piece on a portions scale.
Make fresh coffee every hour.

In management development, we learn rules or follow models such as:

> When criticizing an employee, use the plus-minus-plus model: Start with praise, bring in the criticism, end with praise.
> Never criticize in public.
> Every day, everyone needs praise.

Though these rules of supervision are in the nature of principles and are on a conceptual level, they can be programmed and memorized for use as appropriate.

Training suggests doing something to others, teaching people skills they do not have today. "We will train new hires to serve food to and from the left, beverages to and from the right." But what about the exceptions to the program—for example, guests sitting against the wall where service from the left is awkward or impossible?

Employee development programs deal with perspectives, with attitudes, and with feelings about the restaurant, the job, the customers, and the boss. Can attitudes be programmed? Every coach tries to program the team to have a winning attitude. The restaurant owner also wants spirit and optimism. The old McDonald's slogan "food, folks, and fun" sums it up neatly.

Here, leadership and training merge. Management works to help employees understand that their needs—for praise, for achievement, for dignity and approval—are congruent with the success of the restaurant. If managers believe it and live it, employees are likely to absorb some of the same spirit. The coach shows the players how to win; in a restaurant, that translates to how to keep dishes and stations clean, how to broil a steak to a medium-done steak, how to filet a fish, stuff a pork chop, make a Mornay sauce, or set a table.

To a certain extent, problem solving can be programmed. What should be done when something happens that is not taken care of by the system, when the unexpected happens or a crisis occurs? Just about every crisis that will happen in a restaurant can be considered beforehand and behavior suggested:

- A robbery
- A dishwasher breakdown
- A customer fainting
- An electricity outage
- A fistfight in the dining room
- A drunk spilling his food
- Coffee spilled on the customer
- Toilets backing up
- An argument over the check
- A customer without funds

Planning for contingencies is part of development. What should be done when there is a mistake in scheduling employees? What should be done when employees fail to show up for work? What about theft of tips? Definite solutions that cover all cases are probably not possible, but the steps to be taken in problem situations can be learned: Keep cool. Think. What are the alternatives?

The broad solutions can be programmed; the exact solutions often cannot.

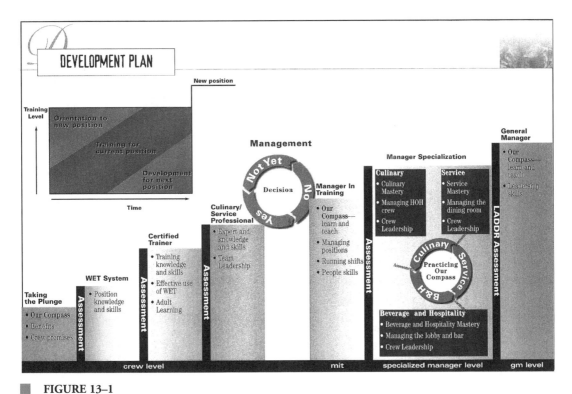

▪ FIGURE 13–1

Red Lobster's development plan. Courtesy Red Lobster Restaurants

---

▪
Combine Training with Development

Probably every job calls for some training and some development. Programming (training) servers provides the base. What should be said when approaching a customer? When do you hand the menu to the person? When is water served? Each job also calls for adaptability—some jobs more than others. Cutting meat calls for little adaptability; supervision calls for a lot.

Should a server be encouraged to make small talk? Small talk is difficult to program. Guidelines would suggest avoiding subjects like politics and religion. Never argue with a guest. Never upstage a guest. What should a server do when propositioned? Be tactful. But where tact is difficult to program, principles can be suggested: Keep your cool. Quickly divert attention to another subject.

Should servers joke with customers? House policy may encourage it or prohibit it, depending on the character of the restaurant. If encouraged, some guidelines may help: stay impersonal. Stay away from touchy subjects. Keep conversations brief and friendly.

▪
Slogans Help

Most of us like "thought packages," as put together in slogans:

Plan Your Work, Work Your Plan.
Use Your Head to Save Your Feet.

Be Firm, Fair, and Follow Through.
KISS—Keep It Simple, Stupid!
Protect Your Employees with Controls.

■

Step-by-Step Training

It is essential to explain not only how to do something but why it is important. Server training can be broken down and taught step by step. It can also be summarized on a card small enough to be carried around in a pocket for easy reference.

TGI Friday's new employees must be validated (checked off) by a back- or front-of-the-house trainer. There may be up to 30 trainers in a TGI Friday's restaurant. The trainer who is certified gives small group and individual training in the mornings. New employees must pass a written test and demonstrate competence in both the health card and alcohol awareness test. In addition, they must pass an individual department test.

For hosts, TGI Friday's has developed a checklist that represents a typical day and is used as a guideline for training.

A typical day for a host working at TGI Friday's is similar to hosting your own party.

Think of guests as friends of yours and treat them in the same manner you would treat honored guests visiting your home.

You are the host of a party on each shift. Greet guests on their arrival, ensure that their dining experience is better than expected, and bid them farewell as they leave.

1. Be in proper uniform.

2. Obtain your time card and clock in at scheduled time.

3. The manager will sign your time card and check your uniform.

The first impression a restaurant makes is with the greeting from the host.
Courtesy Cohn Restaurant Group

4. Review the cleanliness and organization of the station. Check for restocking of necessary supplies. Bring all areas up to standard. Discuss problems with your manager.

5. Ensure that all menus are clean.

6. Fill out requisition (if applicable).

7. Check restrooms to ensure cleanliness standards (continue to check every 15 minutes).

8. Shift responsibilities:
   a. Open the door for each guest.
   b. Greet guests upon entering.
   c. Properly check identification after 8:00 P.M.
   d. Maintain a cheerful, courteous disposition (*smile*).
   e. Maintain a neat, clean, professional image.
   f. "Read" guests and seat them as soon as possible at an appropriate table. Be alert for:
      - Elderly guests
      - Guests with children
      - Handicapped guests
      - Smoking/nonsmoking guests
   g. Present only *clean* menus to guests. Open each menu to the appetizer page and offer assistance if necessary.
   h. Inform guest of your name.
   i. Notify a manager if you perceive that *any* guest is the least bit unhappy.
   j. Properly assist guests when on a waiting list.
   k. Work with bussers to ensure that tables are bussed and reseated within one minute.
   l. Bid farewell to each departing guest. Ensure that everything was satisfactory and invite them to return.
   m. Answer the telephone within two rings.
   n. Assist in properly setting and aligning tables.
   o. Perform shift change and/or closing duties.

9. Meet with the manager on duty to check out your station and sign your time card.[5]

■
Training Theory

Dozens of books have been written on theories of learning and their application to training. Here are proven guidelines for a trainer:

- All of us react to discipline and punishment. Examples of discipline: absence of approval, reprimands, lack of apparent progress. Reward might include: praise, smile, recognition.

- Reward (reinforce) desired learning; allow undesired behavior to extinguish itself by not rewarding it.

- Reward or punish immediately after the observed behavior.

- Spaced training is more effective than a long period of training. Spacing allows the learning to be absorbed and avoids fatigue.

- Expect learning to proceed irregularly. There may be periods when no apparent learning is seen but changes are taking place.

- Expect wide differences in the ability to learn. Many restaurant employees are not rapid learners, but once they have learned, they do excellent work. Slower learners are often not bored as quickly as rapid learners.

Much of the theory of learning is incorporated in the following trainer test. Try it out and see how your answers compare with the discussion that follows.

Test Yourself as a Trainer

Answer true or false.

General

1. The restaurant has an obligation to provide employees with the skills necessary to perform the job.

2. Employee turnover is often related to training or the lack of it.

3. Learning by on-the-job training is not the only way to provide necessary learning for new employees.

4. Training low-skilled employees may be just as important as training highly skilled workers.

5. Prior to training, explain the rules and regulations of the company to the new employee.

6. Prior to training, answer the unspoken question in every trainee's mind: "What's in it for me?"

7. Popular persons are certain to make good trainers.

8. Before actual training begins, explain the position as it relates to the total restaurant.

9. A person who performs well on the job is qualified to teach others the skills needed for the job.

10. The ability to train can be developed, to a large extent.

11. A trainer should always be available for social activities with trainees.

12. A trainer should spend as much or more time in preparation to train as in actual instruction.

13. The trainer should have written task instructions before beginning to teach and should list the key points around which instructions are built.

14. The trainer should learn what the employee already knows about the job before starting to train.

15. The trainer should have a timetable with a schedule of instruction for each day and the amount of learning that is expected daily.

Points to Remember While Training

16. In setting instructional goals, give trainees more work than they can accomplish so that they will work toward high standards.

17. When a trainee performs correctly, reward the person with praise, something like "That's good" or "You're doing fine."

18. A trainer must never admit past or present errors or not knowing an answer to a question.

19. The best way to handle a cocky trainee is to embarrass the person in front of others.

20. In training new employees, concentrate on speed rather than form.

21. A trainer must continuously be aware of the attitudes and feelings of the trainees.

22. Surprise quizzes and examinations are good ways to ensure performance at a high level.

23. Expect that there will be periods during the training when no observable progress is made.

24. Expect some employees to learn two or three times as fast as others.

25. Both tell and show the trainee how to do the skill involved.

26. When an employee performs incorrectly, say, "No, not that way!"

27. After a task is learned, ask trainees for suggestions on how to improve the task.

In the above quiz, the first six statements, according to the experts, are true. To create learner interest, explain the benefits to the person and explain the rules and regulations of the company. Answer such obvious questions as location of the employee dining area and the locker room, if there is one. All of the benefits and the requirements should be explained and gotten out of the way before skill training is started.

Number 7 is false. Popularity does not necessarily correlate highly with being a good trainer. The desire to train is needed, and the ability to train can be developed, to a large extent. Number 8 is true; it is important to see the particular job as a part of the whole. Number 9 is false and Number 10 is true.

Numbers 12, 13, 14, and 15 have to do with getting ready for instruction before actually doing it. All of these statements are true.

Number 16 is false. Training is an occasion when success at every step is important. Standards should be set that are achievable and avoid the experience of failure. Number 17 is true. Number 18 is false; no one expects a perfect trainer.

Number 19 is false. Even when a trainee is out of line, it does no good to embarrass the person. Rather, talk to the person privately.

Number 20 is false. Form comes first; speed comes later.

Number 21 is true; 22 is false. Surprises are not considered good in training.

Number 23 is true. There are times when consolidation of skills takes place and no observable progress is made. Number 24 refers to a vast range of individual differences found in the general population.

Numbers 24 and 25 are true.

Number 26 represents a negative way of teaching—far better to emphasize the positive.

The last item is true. Every task can be improved by new techniques, new methods, new equipment, new skills—or it may be completely eliminated as unnecessary.

BEHAVIOR MODELING

Closely related to role playing, which has been around a long time, behavior modeling is a technique that depicts the right way to handle personnel problems, shows how to interview and evaluate applicants, and demonstrates decision making. Emphasis on interpersonal skills—"people handling"—has always been of great important in the restaurant or in any management position, but the move to deemphasize theory and emphasize "how to do" is new.

Everyone has had behavior models: parents, schoolteachers, athletic coaches, friends, and others. Which model should one follow?

Systematic exposure to models favored by an organization constitutes the training. Audiovisual materials in which an actor or company executive demonstrates the correct or approved techniques for dealing with problems are used by several foodservice companies. Feedback from peers and videotapes of trainee performance give trainees the advantage of seeing how they look to others and how well they are progressing.

Host International holds training sessions at one-week intervals and asks trainees to take each new skill back to the work situation, where it can be practiced. At the end of each session, the trainee is asked to explain how the skill is put to use.

LEARNER-CONTROLLED INSTRUCTION

Learner-controlled instruction (LCI) is a program in which employees are given job standards to achieve and asked to reach the standards at their own pace. Many believe the LCI method is less costly than classroom instruction and reflects employees' different levels of motivation, energy, and ability. The learner is self-motivated and can proceed from unit to unit at a speed with which he or she is comfortable.

To be effective, LCI presumes the availability of learning resources. These can be in the form of books, written practices and policies, and the availability of knowledgeable people willing to pass along their skills and information. A manager's resources manual, assembled by C&C Services of Cucamonga, California, sets up performance criteria for management trainees that lead them through nine modules of learning: bartender, cook, prep, meat cutting, cocktail, cashier, waiter, hostess, and assistant manager. Each learning module is completed when the trainee passes a module test at an 80 to 90% score and completes the work experience prescribed for the module.

If done satisfactorily, the supervisor signs off on the module and the trainee can think about passing on to the next module.

The resources suggested for a section on attitude awareness include a book (with discussions of it with a trainer). In learning the bar operation, the trainee is scheduled to work the bar one day per week until competence in bartending is achieved. The bartender written test includes items on glasses used with each drink on the bar list, garnishes to use with various drinks, bar abbreviations used, and the ingredients for all of the drinks served. (Do you know what is in a Sex on the Beach or a Long Island Iced Tea?) The management trainees are urged to follow the 2½ times rule—2½ contacts with each patron or party in the restaurant during the course of a meal:

A hello when they come in equals ½ contact.
A contact during the meal to obtain feedback equals 1 contact.
A contact when the meal is over equals 1 contact.

The trainee checks a certain number of tables every 20 to 30 minutes. It takes only five minutes, says the manual, to check four to five tables. If this is done every 15 to 20 minutes, most tables can be covered in an hour.

The proficiency test for the cook module is detailed enough to cover such points as:

How do you tell when chicken is done?
How do you put out a butter fire?

How do you tell whether the ovens are at the correct temperatures?

How often should you turn a steak?

How many carrots go onto a plate?

How do you cook swordfish?

What should you do if you:

    a. Drop an order of crab on the floor?

    b. Drop half a pan of potatoes?

How can you tell when zucchini is done?

What is a sign of old mushrooms?

How long do potatoes keep in a warmer?

How many lemons do you serve on a side dish?

Standards are set up for nearly everything that is done by a manager, who is expected to know about and be able to perform every task in the restaurant.

Putting together such a comprehensive LCI program is a large task that can take months. The material is best assembled in loose-leaf form to allow easy insertion and deletion.

Much of the success of an LCI program depends on the cooperation of all concerned. Trainees are scheduled into the various jobs and must learn from incumbent employees as well as from supervisors, who are the main resource to whom trainees turn for information and instruction.

RESPONSIBLE ALCOHOL BEVERAGE SERVICE

Dram shop laws enacted by state legislators bring alcohol awareness training to the forefront because, without it, the restaurant risks losing its liquor license. More importantly, in most states, commercial servers of alcoholic beverages can be held accountable for drunk-driving accidents under state statutes or under common-law liability evolving in state courts.[6] Serving liquor to an intoxicated person is a criminal act in some states. Judgments against places serving alcohol can be so large as to wipe them out of business. With an oversupply of lawyers looking for lawsuits, cocktail lounges and bars are ready targets. Publicity about the number of deaths caused by drunk driving has focused attention on the problem and made alcohol awareness training a must where liquor is served to the public.

Many people serving liquors—bartenders, servers, and managers—are first concerned with sales volume. Concern about drunkenness comes only after a customer causes a problem. Happy hours and two-for-ones do increase liquor consumption and move the drinker toward drunkenness.

The absolute necessity of requesting proof of age from suspected minors is stressed in bartender training.

Many restaurants cut off any person who appears to have had a little too much liquor, especially those who become belligerent. Judging the level of alcohol intoxication, however, is difficult. In carefully controlled tests conducted at the Rutgers Center of Alcohol Studies, social drinkers, bartenders, and police officers were able to judge levels of intoxication of subjects accurately only 25% of the time. The three groups were able to tell when subjects were sober but underestimated the intoxication level of the subjects who had been drinking.

S&A Restaurant Corporation (Steak and Ale, Benningan's, and JJ Muggs) has turned away customers under 21 years of age after 9 P.M. in many of its restaurants regardless of whether the state law permits drinking at a younger age. The company policy is to see to it that inebriated patrons get into a taxicab rather than drive their own cars.[7]

A PROFESSIONAL TRAINING AND DEVELOPMENT PROGRAM

A professional training and development program creates a situation in which all concerned win; the customer and the employee enjoy better product, better service, and greater professional satisfaction. "Winning," said Vince Lombardi, the famous football coach, "isn't everything; it's the only thing." In the training experience, there should be no losers, only winners. The training effort is geared so that winning begins with day one. Everyone needs a series of successes; learning favors the success experience.

The Educational Foundation of the National Restaurant Association (NRA) has developed informative videotapes. Five topic areas are currently available: Wait Staff, Back-of-the-House Training, Wine Training, Profits from Produce, and How to Implement Video Training. In addition, individual tapes focus on current foodservice concerns, such as tip reporting, the immigration law, the AIDS issue, and alcohol awareness training.

Several practical guides have been written to meet a variety of operational needs as well. Contact the NRA Educational Foundation, 250 South Wacker Drive, Suite 1400, Chicago, Illinois 60606-5834, (800) 424-5156.

The Educational Foundation of the NRA has developed a Foodservice Management Professional Credential (FMP). This credential has minimum requirements and a certification examination with five sections that must be passed before the certification is awarded. The examination covers the five major areas of competence for foodservice managers: accounting and finance, administration, human resources, marketing, and operations.

THE MANAGER AS COACH

A restaurant staff is similar to a football team. It has a coach, a manager, and personnel to train and motivate. The operation calls for timing, coordination, signals, and a will to win. Deadlines must be met, morning, noon, and night. Hundreds of expectations must be met on time. Hundreds of variables are involved in the personalities, the food products, the equipment, and skills of the players. Any one or many of the variables can go wrong. When there is a full house, action is at a fever pitch. Tension is high. The manager must be on the premises, calling the signals. The coach coaches. He or she shows people how to perform. Criticism is given if needed. More importantly, the right way is stressed. Everyone, including the pot and pan person, needs positive feedback, reinforcement of the right way, and information on how the game is going.

> A smart manager will leverage concept strengths against well-defined employee needs better than the competition. If not, restaurant operators might drive away their employees faster than their customers.[8]

The goal is to please the customer at a profit. The coach is constantly motivating, triggering the will to win. The coach controls the game in a restaurant more so than in most businesses. Training regimens, systems of play and pull the team together into an operating whole.

Like football teams, restaurants rise and fall. The talent changes as players come and go. There is always another restaurant down the street ready to move up in restaurant popularity. Coach X may be more knowledgeable than Coach Y, but may not be able to instill the winning spirit into his team. Teamwork is critical to the success of any restaurant.

Coach Y may have been a winning coach, but he has lost his enthusiasm and drive, or he has lost some of his key players and can't seem to get it together without them. He may have lost interest in the team and prefers concentrating on his evenings off. Or he may have made the big time too soon and cannot handle the prestige and the money that goes with success. Coach Y, who formerly was out on the floor for every meal, now sits in his office and reads the *Wall Street Journal* during the heavy meal periods. Coach X is on the floor greeting the guests, speaking to the employees, instructing, checking details, and lending a life force to the restaurant.

The word *manage* implies purpose and the mobilization of resources for given goals. A restaurant manager has resources with which to accomplish the purpose of a restaurant: to satisfy patrons at a profit. The resources at the manager's disposal are the restaurant itself, its personnel, its supplies, and its operating capital. Managers have a variety of skills, such as knowing how to motivate, train, delegate, forecast business, plan the menu, and to market what is produced. Systems or programs are set up and, once in place, administered by the manager.

Teamwork is essential to success in the restaurant business. Courtesy Red Lobster

LEADERSHIP

Leadership transforms problems into challenges, excites the imagination, calls on pride, develops a sense of accomplishment and achievement, and provides opportunities to overcome obstacles.

How the manager or supervisor looks at a problem determines, to a large extent, if it is seen as a roadblock or an avenue to achievement. The level of resistance to frustration, ambition, and energy relate to whether a situation is seen as a challenge or a crisis. When a manager is confronted by two new servers who are obviously upset by what they think is poor scheduling, the manager can sympathize, jump in, and help. The situation can become a challenge if the servers feel they can handle the situation. The problem is transmuted to a game. Winning is seen in the form of extra tips as well as meeting the personal challenge.

Putting problems into the form of challenges is part of leadership:

Can you correct the backed-up sewer?
Can you get by without electricity for the next hour?
Do you think we can get through the evening without calling an electrician?

Such problems can be viewed as challenges a few times. Constant crises breed resentment and frustration.

Better Management Behavior

Theory aside, most management experts agree that certain types of management behavior beget superior results. Ask yourself whether or not you can answer yes to the following statements. Do you:

- Discuss sales, cost control, and other goals with employees?
- Try to see merit in the ideas of employees, even if they conflict with your own?
- Expect superior performance and give credit for it?
- Take time to coach employees who need to know more about the job?
- Accept mistakes as long as the employees can learn from them?
- Help employees who seek to get ahead in the restaurant?
- Apply the same high standards consistently to all employees?
- Regularly tell employees how "we" are meeting goals and budget?
- Feel good when employees share their job or personal problems?
- Leave your personal problems at home?

Characteristics of Effective Managers

Management observers delineate characteristics of effective managers, the high performers. Stated in various ways, here are behavior characteristics of effective managers:

- They continuously try to better past performance and to compete with other restaurants.
- Rather than resting on past laurels, they never let themselves become too comfortable in their job.

- They are problem solvers and enjoy challenge.

- They are flexible and adapt to change.

- They anticipate future problems, rehearsing coming events in their minds. As the U.S. Navy preaches to its officers, "Be forehanded." They tend to be future oriented.

- They do not cry over spilled milk or hold trials to place blame for what went wrong.

- Contrary to behaving like a good bureaucrat and dodging responsibility, they seek responsibility.

- They handle rejection or temporary failure without becoming unduly discouraged.

- They are not perfectionists; however, they can act in the absence of complete information and allow others the latitude to reach common goals in their own way. In other words, good managers build others by delegating and team building.

- They perceive people as ends, not means.

- They take responsibility for employees.

- They build employee independence and initiative.

- They communicate confidence in themselves and the enterprise.

- They remember that they are the role models and that employees quickly pick their habits, values, concern for others, and determination to get things done.

- They have concern and compassion for employee well-being.

- They lead by example, with consistency and fairness.

- They aim to motivate employees.[9]

Subtleties of Supervision

Management experts urge that employees be informed of what is important to the manager, the things the manager feels will make for the success of the department and, particularly, for the manager's and employee's success. The explanation of what the manager thinks is important is basic to the employee's motivation. The employee must know what must be done to spell out success in the manager's mind.

Similarly, what does the individual employee feel are the factors that will be important for his or her success? Congruence of the two lists of expectations sets the stage for working together.

Nearly all motivation theories stress reinforcing desirable behavior. Behavioral scientists urge that specific behavior be emphasized rather than general praise. The "great job you did" makes the employee feel good, but it is too general to reinforce the specific behavior that is expected. Better to say:

You did a great job in cleaning the floor and the dishwasher last night.
Your report was letter perfect.
Thanks for cleaning the carpet—it was spotless.
I like the way you handled that customer.
You did a nice job in keeping calm when things really got hectic this morning.

When praised for a specific behavior, an employee is likely to repeat that behavior. Design jobs with a sense of satisfaction built in. "The best managers communicate the importance of a job well done," says Trudy Cooper, vice president of training and development for Outback Steakhouse.[10]

Undesirable behavior, say the experts, is treated in somewhat the same way: Name what is undesirable, tell the employee why it is undesirable, and, if possible, get the employee to face up to the fact that it is undesirable.

The tardy employee is a good example to consider:

The fact that you were five minutes late made Mary and Carolyn set up part of your station.

You have been late three times running and you are throwing the dining room out of kilter. It makes things difficult for me and for the others here.

Confrontation may be necessary: "We cannot go on this way. Do you still want to work here?"

Should the employee be told that the employer is irritated and unhappy about certain behavior? Experts say yes. Individuals vary widely in reacting to the displeasure of bosses. Some become rebellious, others passive, and others antagonistic. Some employees, figuratively, must be hit over the head to react. Others can be upset with a frown. It is up to the manager to sense the approach that will be most effective with the individual.

In developing a caring culture, a mission statement of long-term goals is essential. Each employee needs to read, understand, and believe in it. By using this method, employees are able to improve their performance and be rewarded. A financial reward, a bonus, is the number one way to show appreciation. Public recognition by naming a worker Employee of the Month is the second most popular way.[11]

There is much to be said for the reward-and-discipline approach to motivation. It works well in animal training and has reappeared in the guise of behavior modification theory. The punishment aspect can be played down or removed. Behavior modification theory urges an immediate reward for whatever behavior is desired. The person who is trying to break a chain-smoking habit rewards himself whenever the urge to smoke is resisted. The cook is rewarded with a "That is good" when the omelet comes out right; the busperson gets a nod of approval for clearing a table quickly and quietly; the hostess receives a "You handled that well" after calming down an irate customer.

Behavior modification is based on animal studies showing that behavior is modified when a particular act is reinforced. The behavior is gradually extinguished, or fades, if it is not rewarded or is punished. Punishment is used in the broad sense of anything perceived as being unpleasant or unrewarding. The manager saying "Good morning" to an employee is a reward. Saying nothing can be construed as a punishment. The notion is almost too simple, yet it is effective and has proved so in a number of business situations. When a waitress sets up a table quickly, efficiently, and in the right way, the supervisor says, "That's good." The "That's good" reinforces correct behavior and is a form of reward. Look for the good things you want to happen. Then praise them.

When the utility worker cleans a floor, the supervisor notes it at once and says, for example, "That's very clean"—again, a reinforcement. The key is to continue reinforcement time after time until the individual does the correct procedure automatically. Critics may say that the technique is too obvious, too unsophisticated, but it works on all levels.

Nearly everyone wants praise, wants approval, and wants it now, not sometime in the future. Praise that immediately follows an act has an immediacy effect. The same

The Plus-Minus-Plus Model

Psychologists tell us that inserting a constructive criticism between two favorable comments softens the criticism while at the same time working the criticism. The plus (or beginning statement) is favorable, such as "You deliver especially good service." The next statement is the minus part: "but you seem not to be doing your part of the side work." End with a plus, such as "I'm glad you show you care by giving such quick service."

technique is applicable in any situation. Develop the wanted behavior, explain it, and reinforce it time after time.

> Say this, don't say that.
> You put the knife on the right side of the plate—that's good.
> You put the tip of the wedge of the pie toward the guest. That's good.
> You use a deodorant every day before coming to work. That's good.
> Good morning. You look sharp today. You left those big earrings at home.
> Wow, what a bright smile you have.
> You loaded that tray just right—not too many dishes.

MOTIVATION THROUGH PART OWNERSHIP

A piece of the action is the term used by some restaurants in encouraging unit managers to acquire through purchase a percentage of the store they manage. The incentive of ownership probably attracts a different level of management talent, persons who want to see a direct relationship between their efforts and their personal income. Such a plan makes every unit manager a capitalist, a part owner, without the high risks of independent entrepreneurship. The plan allows persons with the enterprise spirit to enjoy it with a minimum of investment and a maximum of protection from failure.

A TIPPING POLICY

Restaurants must not only report an appropriate amount of tip income to the IRS but also they must establish a tipping policy that is seen as equitable by employees. Tip income, who gets it, and its perception by the staff has a history dating from European experience. The word *tip*, according to the Oxford English Dictionary, was used as early as 1755 to mean a gratuity given by a superior to an inferior. The implication bothers tippers and tippees. Social scientists report that the amount of a tip given relates to the tip giver's opinion of guests as much as it has to do with the self-esteem of the person tipped. The social class of the person being tipped figures into the amount of the tip. Seniors or favored servers get better table assignments, where larger tips are expected. Servers in fast-food restaurants are seldom tipped, one reason for quick-service popularity with customers.

Policies vary. Many restaurant owners decide that some tip income should be distributed among kitchen staff and host personnel following an established plan. In many restaurants, only bus persons share in the server's tip income.

The percentage of the bill left as tips varies among individuals. Tips are higher in large cities and in expensive restaurants. Tips are lower in small towns and in rural areas. Patrons in groups tend to tip less.

Tipping in New York City is probably as high or higher than most American cities, close to 20%, as compared to the 15% typical in other American cities.

As practiced in Europe, tip income is put into a pool and divided by management according to an established system—so much for the person receiving the tip, a percent for bus personnel, something for the host, an amount for key kitchen personnel. The pool system is widely used in this country.[12]

SUMMARY

Restaurants employ teenagers and other people under 30, many of them working part-time and on their first job. Many or most do not expect to make a career in the restaurant field. Wages are low and employee turnover high. For these and other reasons, training and management development is important.

Training can be broken down into orientation training and job training. The purpose of training is to teach specific ways of doing things.

Management development deals with principles and policies that managers use in relating to employees and customers. Behavior modeling assumes that employees will copy supervisors' attitudes and job performance. Learner-controlled instruction provides learning material that can be studied and learned by individuals at their own pace.

Restaurant managers act like coaches. They are engaged in informal training much of the time—showing, telling, correcting, praising, and providing direction.

KEY TERMS AND CONCEPTS

Orientation

Training and development

Training schedule

Development

Management

Behavior modeling

Learner-controlled instruction

Responsible beverage alcohol service

Leadership

REVIEW QUESTIONS

1. In programming first-day employee training, what kind of information should be given priority?

2. What is the difference between employee development and training?

3. Explain the plus-minus-plus model as it relates to criticizing an employee.

4. How are you, as an owner/manager, involved in behavior modeling?

5. What are some advantages of learner-controlled instruction? What is the big disadvantage?

6. Traditionally, employee training in restaurants has been unstructured—that is, there are no formal classes, formal instructional materials, or a particular trainer. How will you set up your training program, if any?

7. What kind of orientation training will you give new employees?

8. Does it follow that your chef, who is highly experienced and skilled, will be effective in passing along knowledge and skills? If he or she is not motivated to do so, what can you do?

9. How will you get across your do's and don'ts—your policies about stealing, courtesy to patrons, parking rules, eating on the job, and so on?

10. Suppose you employ a number of people who do not speak English, a situation not uncommon in American restaurants. How will you communicate with them?

11. In what way is a restaurant manager like a football coach?

ENDNOTES

[1] Personal Interview with Topaz Walker, Olive Garden Restaurant, 22 November 1999.

[2] Nancy E. Combs, "Training for Profit," *Restaurant Management* 1, no. 2 (November 1987): 28–29.

[3] TGI Friday's training manual.

[4] Lagreca, Gen. "Training for Profit," *Restaurant Business* 90, no. 7 (1 May 1991): 110.

[5] TGI Friday's training manual.

[6] Riggs, Silvia. "Drunk Driving," *Restaurants and Institutions* 86, no. 10 (July 1984): 101.

[7] Personal conversation with Wayne Johnson, S & A Restaurant Corporation, June 26, 1997.

[8] Jennifer Waters, "Catering to Employees," *Restaurants and Institutions* 102, no. 15 (15 October 1998): 27.

[9] Personal Interview with Topaz Walker, Olive Garden Restaurant, 22 November 1999.

[10] Paul Hertenky, "Gotta Job," *Restaurant Hospitality* 83, no. 1 (January 1999): 50.

[11] "Restaurant Industry Forecast Management Trends," *National Restaurant Association* 103, no. 13 (15 September 1999).

[12] William Grimes, "Tips: Check Your Insecurity at the Door," *New York Times*, 3 February 1999, B1.

Chapter **14**

After reading and studying this chapter,
you should be able to:

Establish restaurant foodservice policies and procedures.

Know how to take guest food and beverage orders.

Set up procedures for dealing with various situations.

SERVICE AND
CUSTOMER RELATIONS

It is generally accepted that servers contribute as much to the dining experience, or perhaps more, than the décor, appointments, background music, lighting, and even the food served.

Customer service, including customer recognition, is important for all restaurants, but particularly so for dinner houses and fine dining restaurants because they offer more service.

Service is often ranked as the most important factor in restaurant selection by patrons. Similarly, service quality is often the most frequent complaint made by restaurant patrons.

Customer relations is an aspect of marketing and sales. James Bitt has illustrated this at Blazers, located in Greenwood, South Carolina. He managed to make Blazers profitable within four months of taking over the restaurant. Instead of spending a great deal of money on media advertising, he developed a signature shrimp dip, a complimentary appetizer that is delivered to the table as soon as guests are seated.[1]

The psychology of foodservice as practiced by the server varies tremendously with the type of establishment, from the hot dog emporium to the deluxe dinner house. The teenager in McDonald's is probably thrilled with working as a part of a team of other teenagers in an air-conditioned, well-lighted, well-appointed, and fast-paced establishment. The skills required are minimal: assembly of food orders, a few simple cooking skills, making change. Most important, though, is the customer contact and the pleasure in working with one's peers. Supervision is minimal; most of the motivation comes from the necessity of keeping up with customer demand.

Consider the more complex relationships and skills required in a dinner house. The dining area is usually broken into tables and booths. Each booth forms a separate environment and protects the territorial imperative, the walls visually blocking some stimuli and providing social distance from other patrons, facilitating social interaction among those seated within the booth. The booth can be thought of as providing social and psychological security while accentuating the need for group interaction. Group participants are physically forced to look at each other and focus attention on those sitting within the confines of the booth. Its very design establishes intimacy and makes for a more relaxed atmosphere.

The server standing at the head of the booth commands the attention of those seated and tends to interact with them as a group more than as individuals. Everyone hears what everyone else is saying, including what each orders. The server need not repeat answers to questions and can establish a rapport with the individuals as a group, answering questions, explaining the menu, and making suggestions.

Individuals entering a restaurant alone feel like an outsider, compared to the couples and parties. If seated at an exposed table, they may feel even more isolated and uncomfortable. On the other hand, the hostess or maitre d' is reluctant to tie up a booth with a single. If the individual is noticeably shy or ill at ease, the decision should be for the booth. One study found that solos appreciated and were made comfortable by fast, friendly service. They did not like sharing a table, nor did they want to be seated in a special section for singles. Men seemed to prefer more attention from servers, while added service disturbed some women. Wine by the glass was appreciated. More women than men said they liked eating alone.

Servers can expect more problems from people seated in open spaces—more complaints about noisy people at neighboring tables, uneasiness, concern over speed of service, and defensive behavior.

Banquet rooms can be expected to produce the same sort of customer behavior.

Very often, the customer is seated next to someone he knows only casually, or not at all. It usually takes an aggressive, self-assured person to break the ice of separateness.

Low lighting is favorable for the dinner house, encouraging people to relax and breaking down social distance. In the fast-food establishment and in the coffee shop, the lighting is brighter, in keeping with the mood of the customer who wants to eat quickly and move on. In a darkened room, people are encouraged to speak and eat more intimately and to focus on those in the party rather than on the distractions of people entering, leaving, or moving around.

THE SERVICE ENCOUNTER

Many servers are skilled performers in the service encounter. The dinner house, and especially the lounge, is the stage. Two shows daily—lunch and dinner—deliver the same great performance every time. The server and the customer are both actors in the play. Both knowingly engage in the drama. The payoff for the customer is a feeling of warmth, friendship, and ego enhancement. The reward for the server is the big tip and the excitement of the drama.

Danny Myer, an owner of Union Square Café, says, "A great restaurant doesn't distinguish itself by how few mistakes it makes, but by how well they handle those mistakes."[2]

For some servers, the play is the thing. They know they are acting and love it. They may also "love" their customers. The customers feed back similar feelings to generate a staged love affair. All smiles and attention, the server hangs on the customer's every word and gesture, radiating goodwill and the desire to please.

Once the meal is finished, the play is over, the customer leaves, and the server moves on to the next stage. Should the customer and server meet in the supermarket the next morning, they may scarcely acknowledge each other. (The same thing may happen on a plane trip, the flight attendant dispensing love and warmth in-flight. Off the plane, the play is over. Should a passenger and the flight attendant pass in the terminal, they scarcely nod in recognition.)

If the dinner house adds liquor to the environment, guests may experience loosening inhibitions, clouded perceptions, and a reduction in anxiety and hostility. Voices rise, suppressed needs surface, conversations become animated, ego guards are lowered, jokes are funnier. This increases the need for restaurant owners, managers, and servers to become aware of and practice responsible alcoholic beverage service.

The traveling person eating alone is uneasy, especially in a dinner house where couples and groups are out having fun. Alienated and self-conscious, he or she wonders about the price of the meal and may order something more expensive than usual to let anyone who might be interested know that he or she can afford it. The traveler may want more rapid service, eating quickly and leaving as soon as possible.

The same person in a group, exhilarated by the presence of friends, can take on a completely different personality. Instead of being impersonal with the server, he or she is now friendly.

If the group is large and made of relative strangers, as in a banquet setting, servers may become nonpersons. Customers may refer to them in the third person even though they are nearby and can overhear the comments. No one likes to be treated this way. Servers may set themselves up sometimes for such treatment by displaying a lack of self-confidence, excessive deference, or overeagerness. Something in human nature, at least in some people, causes them to treat such people as inferiors and even to humiliate them.

Alex von Bidder, co-owner of Four Seasons Restaurant, sometimes makes personal phone calls to his closest customers when their patronage drops. His intention is to show that he cares and to inquire about the customer's welfare. Those phone calls give customers an opportunity to discuss any service failure they may have experienced. By making the calls, von Bidder personalizes his service as well as gathers relevant information.

Source: Beth G. Chung and K. Douglas Hoffman, "Critical Incidents: Service Failures That Matter Most," *Cornell Hotel and Restaurant Administration Quarterly* 39, no. 3 (June 1998): 71.

What Makes a Good Server?

There is a lot of agreement as to what makes a good server. Here's a list of attributes that restaurateurs look for.

- *Personality.* It's fine to know the technical aspects of service, but the customer puts more emphasis on the attitude and personality of the server. These are the most important elements of good service.

- *Team orientation.* Servers must be willing to participate in a team effort. They have to be willing to contribute to the guest's satisfaction, whether or not he or she is in their section.

- *Knowledge of product.* Servers must have thorough knowledge of both the food and the wine. They need to have confidence at tableside. A customer can pick up on lack of knowledge very quickly.

Source: Nancy Backas, "Training and Personality," *Cheers* 9, no. 2 (March 1998): 58.

Visitors to this country are surprised by the service, especially that given by college students. Many times, the financial and educational level of the server is higher than the customers'.

Veteran Chicago restaurateur Doug Roth once said, "Good service can save a bad meal. A good meal cannot save bad service." It's well known that people who experience bad service often won't complain to management; they simply won't return.[3]

GAMESMANSHIP

In restaurants with snob appeal, a little game may be played between customer and server: one puts the other down. Customers unaccustomed to frequenting such establishments may be impressed by the aloofness of the maitre d', the captain, and the server and may hasten to overtip, more in fear than for service rendered. Many servers look on the customer-server relationship as a battle of wits. The customer is the opponent. The object of the game is to extract the maximum tip possible. At the end of each evening, word is passed as to who received the most in tips. "Mary made $90 tonight." "Don took in only $45 in tips." If servers are pitted against each other and the prizes are for who gets the most tips, it is easy for a dining room to degenerate into a game with the customer as secondary participant. Sometimes it seems as if supper clubs were designed more for the servers than for the diner. Perhaps the diner likes it that way. Certainly the server becomes a star, receiving $100 or more in tips in an evening (which may not set well with the hardworking kitchen crew and bussers, whose compensation is considerably less).

One way to ensure harmony among all of the restaurant's personnel is to insist that all tips be pooled and everyone share. Customarily, servers decide on the amounts distributed from the tip pool to bussers. Usually the kitchen crew is excluded. In other establishments, all share on a fixed-ratio basis, a practice common in Europe and the Middle East; this is called the TRONC (trunk or box) system. Union contracts usually prohibit the pooling of tips.

GREETERS

The host is the first and last person the guest meets at a restaurant, so naturally, the impression he or she makes is important. A smiling, well-groomed, friendly person is an asset to the restaurant, but the position calls for more. Hosts who know the restaurant add luster and are able to answer a variety of specific and general questions. The main part of the host's job is to represent the restaurant by offering a friendly greeting and facilitating the seating of guests, even if it means politely asking them to wait a while in the lounge or holding area. Being a great host is an art and takes practice. Another key aspect of the job is knowing how to seat guests so as not to overload a server or the kitchen. That is where experience comes in.

Hosts keep a sheet for reservations, whether they are called in or walk-ins. The sheet has several columns, each representing a table size or "top," as it is called in the restaurant business—one column for two-tops or "deuces," one for four-tops, one for six-tops, and one for larger parties. Names of parties are entered under the respective table size. Over time, restaurants gauge their turn time. For example, the deuce waiting time will be faster than the four- or six-top. Full-service restaurants normally allow about 1½ hours for a deuce, 2 hours for a four-top, and 2½ hours for a six-top.

In order to avoid calling out names—and thus annoying other guests—some restaurants give guests a beeper device that lets them know when their table is ready. Hosts know when the table is ready by receiving a signal from the server.

If waiting guests have opened a bar tab, it is preferable to transfer that over to the food server to avoid inconveniencing the guests having to pay the closeout bar tab when being seated. Any beverages from the lounge/holding area should be carried on a tray to the dining area by the hostess. Here, the service calls for a way to remember who was drinking what so as to place the correct beverage in front of each guest.

On arrival at the table, the host might pull out the best seat, perhaps a window view. This seat is normally offered to and occupied by the senior woman of the party. The hostess then assists others in being seated and offers their menus.

THE SERVER AS AN INDEPENDENT BUSINESSPERSON

It is too easy to set servers up as private businesspersons, each doing his or her own thing—in effect, operating an independent business on premises leased for nothing. Such a situation can foster competition rather than cooperation. If any situation calls for teamwork, it is a fast-paced dining room, which requires working in harmony, goodwill, and trust. It is much easier and faster for two service people to serve a party of six than it is for one, and more fun. Normally, a server cannot carry more than four plates, and if it is necessary to make two trips to the kitchen to serve six people, two of the plates will get cold. A party of six or eight usually starts each course together, and then they have to wait for all to receive the salad, then all to receive the entrée and, finally, the dessert, the delays become troublesome.

FOODSERVICE TEAMS

Various kinds of dining room service organization exist, the server/busperson combination being the most common. Some restaurants operate with servers working two to a team so that at least one of the team members is on the floor most of the time dealing with the patrons rather than off the floor.

The team system differs from the usual server-busperson relationship in that buspersons ordinarily confine their work to cleaning and setting up tables.

From the moment the phone is answered to their last step out the door, customers judge a restaurant not on great food at good prices but on those intangibles that define customer service.

Source: Jennifer Waters, "Eye on Service," *Restaurants and Institutions* 108, no. 28 (1 December 1988): 46.

Experienced servers learn to read guests and react accordingly. Some guests are in a hurry, some want advice on what to order, etc. Good service means subtle, unobtrusive service. For example, there is no need to the server to arrive at the table with a handful of plates asking who's having what.

Comeback Kids

There's a story of a group of diners at a restaurant. Everyone's ordering a number of items to pass round, but one customer wants to mix and match an appetizer with an entrée. "Oh, we can't do special orders," apologizes the waitress. "Why not?" asks the customer. "The chefs really get mad at me," the waitress responds. "They won't do it even one time because if you should ever come back, you might want it again."

Source: Jennifer Waters, "Eye on Service," *Restaurants and Institutions* 108, no. 28 (1 December 1988): 46.

In other situations, the entire serving crew works as a team. Anyone entering the kitchen picks up any order and delivers it, and if a table needs more than one server to flame a dish or to perform other duties, the servers in the general area will pitch in, even though it removes them from their assigned station. A slogan—"Full Hands In, Full Hands Out"—helps everyone work to help each other.

The team system has one major advantage: Hot food is served hot. Whoever is nearest the setup counter picks up the food and serves it. The check accompanies the order; the number of the table is written on the check. Seats at each table are numbered clockwise, starting at the seat closest to an agreed-upon anchor point.

Food service teamwork at Le Bec Fin, in Philadelphia, makes for a memorable experience. Courtesy Le Bec Fin

Stations where two servers rotate tables encourages teamwork because each is paying attention to the customers to see when the next table will be leaving, trying to get them out the door. "I might help the other server's table because the sooner they leave, the sooner I get my next table!"[4]

HARD SELL VERSUS SOFT SELL

Restaurant literature and educational programs uniformly urge service personnel to promote and sell as part of the service job. The rationale is that sales and tips will increase— and, if the sales job is done correctly, customers will have a better dining experience. Discussions with servers bear out the thesis, but there are some qualifications. Undoubtedly, some patrons have a fixed idea of how much they will spend on a particular meal and such people may resent a hard sell: "Would you like a cocktail?" "Will you have dessert?" "Will you have an after-dinner liqueur?" People may feel pressured and sometimes say so, especially if the server's approach is the hard sell. Those who receive a higher check than expected may avoid the restaurant in the future.

The kind of clientele may determine the best approach, hard or soft sell. Low-key, complete service may be what is expected. Other patrons, wanting to live it up, may welcome the hard sell and purposely run up the tab as a kind of self-indulgence. "Nothing is too good for our anniversary"—or business client, or prospective buyer. The expense account tab, using the company's money, is the excuse to have the best there is.

> Food is the number-one reason why customers choose a restaurant. Whether or not they come back is related to customer service.[5]

Servers characteristically compete with each other in the amount of tips received in the course of a work shift. Some servers make 50 or even 100% more than others. The service rendered has been perceived by the diner as superior or the server has manipulated the diner into increasing the check or the tip percentage or both. Tip and tab go together. Management mostly pushes the thought, "When in doubt, promote."

Aside from selling, service includes a number of other factors and practices, including showmanship, ritualization of wine service, paying attention to what is said by the diner, attention to detail, refilling water glasses, cleaning ashtrays, replacing soiled silver, and so on. The server is attempting to control the behavior of the diner. Call it manipulation, influencing attitude, making friends, maintaining rapport, or what have you, it is still selling.

A server who displays skill and confidence is desirable. In most situations, a harassed or timid server may elicit sympathy but can also arouse apprehension or uneasiness in the customer. No doubt, a number of customers want to be courted and wooed, buttered up, and even fawned upon. Others may resent this kind of behavior.

A research study of the ability of servers to control diner behavior compared an experimental group of diners who were not subject to the promote-and-sell treatment with another group who were given the hard-sell treatment. High-priced items were recommended to the experimental group; specifics concerning cocktails, appetizers, and main courses were suggested. Desserts and after-dinner drinks were promoted.

The control group of diners was treated to a non-manipulative type of service. When members of the dining party asked, "What is good?" they were politely reminded that everything was good. Two phrases used extensively for this group were, "Are you ready to order?" and "Would anyone care for anything else?" The server was as attentive and available as for the experimental group; however, the server's behavior was marked by lack of initiative. Diner groups were divided into three broad age categories: young (20–34), middle-aged (35–54), and senior (55 or older). The study took place at a leisure-dining restaurant with a high check average in a summer resort in the northeast United States.

The results of the study showed that young parties did spend and tip more than the senior group. Middle-aged foursomes ran up the highest tab, middle-aged singles the lowest. The experimental group, the ones subjected to manipulative control, had significantly higher tabs. The expected happened: The "promoting server not only maximizes his or her returns but, more importantly, he or she is able to exercise a measure of control over the reward structure governing the work."[6]

Seven Commandments of Customer Service

1. *Tell the truth.* When it comes to customer service, honesty is the best policy.

2. *Bend the rules.* Learn why a rule is a rule in the first place. Once you know the reason for the rule and its boundaries, go ahead and bend it, if that's what it takes to make the system better serve your customer.

3. *Listen actively, almost aggressively.* Customers are ready, willing, and able to tell you everything you need to know. All you need to do is listen.

4. *Put pen to paper.* A letter or e-mail after a conversation can be a terrific way to confirm facts and details or just to say thanks.

5. *Master the moments of truth.* If you pay attention to details—the promises made in your advertising, how long your phone rings before being answered, the look of your parking lot—customers will know and notice.

6. *Be a fantastic fixer.* An effective customer service recovery process includes these components: apologize, listen and empathize, fix the problem quickly and fairly, offer atonement, keep your promise, follow up.

7. *Never underestimate the value of a sincere thank-you.* It's easy to take regular and walk-in customers for granted. Don't. Customers have options every time they need a service or product. Thank them for choosing to do business with you.[7]

FORMALITY OR INFORMALITY

How formal should the relations between host and guest be? Should the server be seen and not heard? Does the customer want formality or informality?

The answers vary with the kind of experience you are trying to deliver.

Some restaurants thrive on informality. The servers may appear in tennis shoes and blue jeans, saying, "Hi, I'm Bob, I'll be your server tonight. Please call on me for anything that I can do to make your meal pleasant."

In another, more formal atmosphere, the server may speak only when spoken to. His conversation may be limited to, "Good evening, madam. Good evening, sir," "I hope you enjoy your meal, madam," etc.

Some general principles apply to all restaurants:

■ Restaurants, by their nature, are service oriented, and all personnel should accept this as a continuing challenge to give excellent service. Complaints should be accepted at face value, at least until proven to be without substance.

■ The customer's viewpoint is different from that of the employees or the manager. Most complaints are left unspoken. When a complaint *is* voiced, a public relations opportunity emerges. Food should be replaced at once with another of the same or of the customer's choice. A complimentary bottle of wine or an after-dinner liqueur adds a gracious note.

- Never try to explain why things go wrong. A customer is not interested in excuses.
- The general atmosphere at a restaurant should be friendly. A warm smile is almost never out of place.
- Teamwork is always appropriate.
- The little extras, like a birthday cake or a Polaroid portrait of the diners, are almost always appreciated.

The famous maître d' at the Waldorf Hotel in New York, Oscar, considered himself a stage manager and would often approach a table, examine the food, and, even if nothing was wrong, add some little touch or have it whisked away and replaced. Waiters were trained to focus on him. Hand signals let the waiters know what to do. His mien expressed grave concern for the customer's well-being. He was very polite, very formal, tuned in to the guest.

The outcome of great customer service is customer loyalty. Loyal customers feel great about visiting your restaurant. They're not just satisfied, they're ecstatic about your service, food, and atmosphere. They can't wait to return—and they'll urge others to try your restaurant as well.[8]

SETTING THE TABLE

The table setting should be pleasing and inviting to the guest. Guests notice clean cutlery and flatware that is free from watermarks, fingerprints, and food particles. Avoid watermarks by cloth-drying the flatware immediately as it comes out of the dishwasher. Remember—to avoid fingerprints, train staff and servers to hold the cutlery flatware by the center-middle part.

Experienced maître d's bend their knees to level themselves with the glassware and can spot a dirty one at a distance. All glassware, like cutlery, should be free of water spots and fingerprints. Dirty rinsewater causes spots; chemicals in the rinsewater can streak glassware. An improper mix of washing and sanitizing chemicals might lack the action that makes the water sheet off the glass without streaks or watermarks.

When the table setting is complete, it should look pleasing to the eye. This is accomplished by arranging everything symmetrically. Everything should be clean and free from fingerprints.

TAKING THE ORDER

If they have not already done so, servers introduce themselves and take the opportunity to suggest beverages. This is done by describing two or three drink items (depending on the guest). This might, for business convention guests, be a special martini—if the bartender is known for that—or a choice of wines. The main thing is to get people to make a selection from a variety of choices rather than a simple yes-no decision. At the initial guest contact moment, the server may also describe food specials, then depart to obtain the beverage while the guests decide on their food order.

Less Choice

Pare down the menu. People forget that service often relates to the time it takes to them to make a decision on what to order. Too many choices are too time-consuming to wade through.

Source: Jennifer Waters, "Hurry, Please," *Restaurants and Institutions* 108, no. 11 (1 May 1998): 119.

The table setting at Charlie Trotter's is a delight to the eye. Courtesy Charlie Trotter

The food order should be taken by asking the senior female for her order first, followed by the other women. (The server has to politely take control of the situation to prevent everyone from shouting his or her order.) Then the senior male's order is taken, and so on. The server's team takes the order by seat number from a vantage point (say, the entrance.) This allows each plate to be placed correctly in front of the person who ordered the dish. Some restaurants use the clockwise system.

Restaurants generally have a rule as to which side food is served to and cleared from. Beverages are both served and cleared from the right-hand side from and to a tray. Some restaurants clear plates as soon as a person has finished, while others wait until everyone has finished; it's a matter of personal preference and how soon you need the table.

MAGIC PHRASES

A coffee shop waitress leaves an indelible impression on the customer when she says, as the patron leaves, "I hope to see you tomorrow." Phrases recommended by the Nassau Beach Hotel (in the Bahamas) for use by guest contact employees include:

Welcome back.
We're happy you're here.
It's good to see you again.
I trust everything is to your liking.

How was your evening?
Sorry to have kept you waiting.
I am as close as the telephone.
I'm sorry; I'll put that right.
Have a nice trip home.

Other than the magic phrases, the following are the Top Seven Server Secrets that should be followed thoroughly (if appropriate, depending on the character and style of the restaurant concept).

1. Smile.

2. Introduce yourself.

3. Get down to eye level.

4. Try a casual touch.

5. Doodle on the check.

6. Use a tip tray with a credit-card insignia.

7. Write "thank you" on the back of the check.[10]

One chain recommends these replies in response to a complaint:

I apologize.
Thank you for letting us know about this.
I'd feel the same way if I were in your position.
You've certainly been patient. We appreciate your taking time to tell us about this.

Keep responses simple and sincere. Accept ownership for the problem, even though you personally may not be responsible.

When a guest orders "incorrectly," accept the responsibility. Avoid making the guest feel stupid. Tact is in order: "Perhaps next time you'd like to try a medium-done steak and be sure to let us know how it is."

One restaurant general manager puts customer relations in this framework: "Unless you are willing to give each customer a little bit of yourself, you shouldn't be in the hospitality field."

THE SERVERS' VIEWPOINT

Let the servers speak regarding restaurant customers and perhaps some curious information will surface.

The thing that bugs me the most is that some customers will eat almost all the food and then send a few crumbs back, complaining that it is inedible. I mean, sometimes they will send back a sandwich and only the bread will be left! Other customers will even count the number of noodles in a bowl of chicken soup and complain when the total isn't high enough—just as if we were violating a rule from the Bureau of Standards.

Older people are the worst offenders. They simply do not treat waitpersons like human beings. They have certain expectations about what a meal in a restaurant is supposed to be and, if they are not satisfied, they are mad and feel ripped off. They also talk to you as if you were a moron. "Get me water!" or "Where is the bathroom?" never "please" or "thank you." The next worst to deal with are the families with small children. They demand the most service, make the biggest messes, and leave the worst tips.

My biggest gripe is people who say "Smile"—customers who order you to grin. I mean, you could have left your husband that day or something terrible might have happened to your kid, or maybe you've been standing on your legs for hours . . . but people expect that, if they are buying a meal, they are also paying you to look happy. Hell, they don't expect the kid at the station who pumps gas to smile! Why do they expect it here?[11]

Some servers complain about the large parties who, after the meal has been put on one check, insist that the waitress make out separate checks. Another gripe is when a group is asked if they want coffee, only one says yes. Then, one by one, the rest of the party orders it later on.

"I hate it," say a number of servers, "when they snap their fingers to get my attention."

Then there are the customers who treat the servers as invisible, a kind of subperson or nonperson. Some customers come in for criticism because somehow, if the server is attractive, the women in the party take on a competitive stance.

One restaurant owner claims, "When a person walks in here, they are psychologically sitting in a high chair. Their attitude is one of the screaming child: "Look at me first, notice me first, feed me first, and make me the most important person in the world."

Then there is the comforting customer who sees the perpetual smile on the server's face and says, "You don't have to do that to yourself. I know you have feelings, you don't have to turn yourself into a Barbie doll." The server's retort, "I'd rather deal with a drunk than a shrink. They're easier to handle."

THE DIFFICULT CUSTOMER

Once in a while, the server is confronted by a difficult customer who is determined to prove his manhood or vent his hostility on other customers, the serving personnel, or on the manager personally. A large coffee shop chain encountering more than its share of such customers because its units are open around the clock insists on a "hands-in-the-pocket" policy, which means that no matter how obnoxious a patron becomes, a manager never considers being physical in handling the situation.

"Ninety-nine percent of complaint handling is in the employee's lap," says Wienerschnitzel's Lowry Hughes. "[Employees] have to know how to solve the problem right away."[12]

The approach is "What can I do to help?" which is, in itself, quite disarming. The fact that the manager has a pot of hot coffee in hand may also give the patron pause. It matters not how big the manager or whether male or female, the manager who speaks calmly and acts ready to mediate or settle a problem can usually calm the most disruptive person.

If the calm approach fails, the manager may have a system of hand signals for employees, one of which means "call the police." Suggesting that the police are on the way (even though that may not be the case) is also effective in emergency situations. If a problem customer is completely unreasonable, the best thing to do is insist that he or she leave. Any food served is on the house.

Bar operators say that an effective approach to anyone drinking excessively is to say, "If you leave, I'll pay for all of your drinks." If the patron is too inebriated to drive, it is often wise to insist on putting the person in a cab and, if necessary, paying the cab fare. The so-called third-party liability feature of the law can place the restaurant at fault for serving too much alcohol. Should the person become involved in an auto accident, the restaurant operator can be sued and, in some cases, held liable for damages, sometimes involving hundreds of thousands of dollars.

If it is necessary to get rid of a problem guest, call the police if unable to resolve the problem any other way—or if violence occurs.

No restaurant likes to hear customer complaints. According to Kay McCleery, director of training for Hobee's Franchising Corporation, a win-win result can be obtained by using these action tips:

- Act immediately on a complaint.
- Let the customer know you care.
- Calm the customer by acknowledging the problem and encouraging feedback.
- Tell the customer in an honest way how the problem will be addressed.
- Invite the customer to express his or her feelings.
- Never invalidate or make the customer wrong.
- Offer appropriate and reasonable amends.
- Nurture the relationship by smiling and thanking the customer again.[13]

Other strategies can also make the situation better. Although there are no specific steps to follow, operators and staff members can do the following to make irate customers feel better. These responses are critical to regaining diners' loyalty and encouraging repeat business.

- *Be diplomatic.* The issue is not whether or not the customer is justified in his or her complaint—as long as the diner feels justified, he is. A helpful initial response from you and your staff can go a long way toward salvaging the situation.

- *Remain calm.* Although you may feel that you are being personally attacked by the customer, try to remember that the person is mad at the situation and not at you. You must put your personal feelings aside and handle the situation in a professional, calm manner. Arguing with an already annoyed customer is a no-win situation.

- *Listen.* When customers become angry, they have to vent that anger in order to feel better. Listen to everything they have to say without interrupting. Just feeling that they are being heard can help ease customers' anger.

- *Empathize.* The best response you can make when handling complaints is to show empathy. Empathy is the ability to feel as another person feels. Your objective is to identify with the diner's feelings and to let him or her know that you understand. Whatever you do, don't offer excuses for the problem or complaint.

  You can show empathy by rephrasing both the contents of the problem and the customer's feelings about it. For example, you might say, "I realize that you are upset about your steak being undercooked, and I understand that it makes you feel angry." Be sure to tell the diner that you are sorry the incident occurred and that his or her feelings are important to the restaurant. Also tell the person that you will take care of the problem immediately.

■ *Control your voice.* The volume, speed, and tone of your voice can help defuse difficult situations. Your volume should never go up—even if the customer's does. Speaking in a calm, slow voice will show the customer that you are really concerned about the problem and are prepared to solve it. Sometimes speaking softer and softer helps too.

■ *Get the facts.* Some incidents, such as a lost coat or a charge-card error, may be difficult to resolve. Collect as much data as you can and write it all down. Writing down the details shows the customer you take the incident seriously and will also help you remember pertinent information.

■ *Take care of the problem immediately.* Whether it is an entrée that is not prepared properly or dirty glassware, remove the offending object from the customer's table immediately. If you are unsure what the response the customer wants, ask, for example, "Would you like me to take that and bring you the menu?" (or "another glass?").

■ If you do take back a diners' entrée, offer to keep the meals of the other diners in the party warm in the kitchen so that the group can eat together. An irate customer may become more so if he or she has to sit there and watch others enjoy their food while waiting for a replacement entrée.[14]

■ **TABLE 14–1**

Readers Tell How Restaurants Fare

USA Today received about 6,000 responses to a recent readers' survey on the quality of restaurant service. Here are some of the results:

	Percentage of Respondents Who Encounter These Problems Very/Somewhat Frequently
Slow service	82.5
Inattentive waiters	68.5
Forgetful waiters	56
Waiters who don't know the product	55.5
Unclean plates	40.5
Rushed waiters	38.5
Intrusive waiters	32
Rude waiters	30.5
Unwillingness to meet special needs	20
Incorrect billing	13.5
How satisfied are you with the overall quality of service at . . .	
Food-food restaurants	
Very/somewhat satisfied	70%
Not very/dissatisfied	29%
Do not frequent fast-food restaurants	1%
Casual dining restaurants	
Very/somewhat satisfied	91%
Not very satisfied/dissatisfied	9%
Fine dining restaurants	
Very/somewhat satisfied	93.5%
Not very satisfied/dissatisfied	6.5%

Source: USA Today/Penn State survey. "Serving Up Satisfaction," USA Today, 14 February 1997, 10D.

■
Teen Confrontations

Fast-food restaurants catering to the younger crowd can easily become hangouts and the scene of altercations of one kind or another. Ground rules must be laid down and, in some cases, a security person employed to maintain order. These guidelines for preventing volatile situations have been found effective:

- An experienced host is employed who quickly identifies the few troublemakers in a crowd and refuses them service. If the troublemaker insists on remaining in the restaurant, the police are called at once.

- When the troublemakers are enrolled in nearby schools, the host or manager works with school administrators to discipline the troublemakers. Young students who have squirted catsup on walls are required by the principal to clean it up, and a rule requiring them to avoid the restaurant is also enforced by the school administration.

- A host on the scene can readily identify incipient trouble and do what is necessary to avoid it. Students have been known to throw hamburgers at the serving personnel in a hamburger restaurant, spew condiments on the floor and the walls, fight among themselves, and use loud profanity, all of which must be curbed at once if the problem is not to get out of hand.

SERVICE PERSONNEL AS A FAMILY[16]

Many managers do whatever possible to create a family feeling among foodservice personnel. They encourage employees to eat and drink on the premises by reducing their price for meals and drinks by a third or even half. Employee parties are sponsored; liquor and sometimes food is provided. (Other operators do not permit their employees to come back even if off duty.)

The serving group, in many ways, is the elite within the restaurant, having the fun of working with the customer. In many restaurants, servers are selected, in large part, on the basis of appearance—the best-looking women and the handsomest men. If management is not careful and the waiters not equally so, the other personnel will resent them.

GREETER OR TRAFFIC COP

The greeter in the restaurant is supposed to be just that—a host welcoming the arriving customer, saying a few kind words, and really being pleased to have the person pay the restaurant a visit. As the first representative of the restaurant to interact with the visitor, the host sets the tone for the entire dining experience. His or her welcome, or lack of it, creates a feeling, positive or negative, that colors the entire meal experience.

It has been observed that the rookie who, for the first few weeks of being a host in a busy restaurant, is an outgoing, warm, friendly human being, can easily turn into a traffic cop who orders visitors, "Leave your name and we'll call you," or "Sit over there until a table opens up." It is quite understandable that, with fatigue, the big hello can become a little hello, or less. It is difficult to smile and act friendly when the individual feels anything but friendly or ready to cope with new problems.

As a new host, it does not take long to realize that the pay may be a fraction of that of the servers, yet the host may be working just as hard as the servers and may be contributing as much or more to the dining experience. With a few exceptions, hosts receive close to minimum wage, while servers may earn three times that amount. Little wonder the host loses some zest for doing an outstanding job. One solution is to give the host the option of becoming a server as the next vacancy occurs.

TACT: ALWAYS

How many times have you entered a restaurant to be greeted with the words "How many?" or by some comment such as, "The waiting time is 30 minutes," or "Please have a seat at the bar."

Don't say, "Just one?" or "Are you alone?" When tables are plentiful, the question could be, "Do you want a table or a booth?"

How much better to look at the patron full in the face, smile, and say, "May I help you with your coat?" To men, say, "May I take your hat?" The patron wants common courtesy, which means recognition, respect, and a friendly welcome. We all know that a principal reason people dine out is the desire for sociability. Failing to meet this basic need is an unnecessary form of deprivation foisted on the customer by an unthinking service person who has mixed up his or her priorities.

SUMMARY

Customer relations is one of the aspects of restaurant keeping that makes it so interesting—and so frustrating. It is a continuous challenge, a challenge that is not for the timid, the tired, or the malcontented. The perfectionist and the thin-skinned cannot win at the customer relations game—there are too many variables. A sense of humor, good health, and a lively intelligence are decided assets. A desire to please and to serve is even more valuable.

KEY TERMS AND CONCEPTS

Service encounter	Difficult customer
Social distance	Assertiveness
Team	Eye contact
Hard sell/soft sell	Tact
Formality or informality	Handling complainers

REVIEW QUESTIONS

1. Service personnel must be aware of the degree of social distance desired by their customers. Explain.
2. As a restaurant manager, your attention is called by a server to a booth of four men who are talking loudly, using profanity, and appear to be belligerent. How would you handle the situation?

3. Your restaurant is located near a high school. Recently, several of the students who are patrons have been throwing ice and wadded paper napkins at each other. What should you do?

4. Eye contact is particularly important in patron relations. Explain.

5. In seating a lone woman in a restaurant, what factors should be considered?

6. The degree of psychological tension desirable varies with the situation. How can a restaurant manager work to raise or lower the tension to make it appropriate for the situation?

7. What are three phrases suitable for use by a hostess in greeting patrons? What are three phrases for saying goodbye to them?

8. In taking reservations, what factors help determine how much time to allow between seatings?

9. Can you, in your mind, make a table setting for a dinner guest, mentally placing plate, cup and saucer, silverware, and glassware?

10. Have you decided to take lunch or dinner reservations? What are the pros and cons? Would you take them on Friday and Saturday evenings, your busiest nights?

11. What will be your policy in handling guest complaints about the food (the steak is too tough, my soup is cold)?

ENDNOTES

[1] Don Nichols, "Inexperience Pays Off in Restaurant Business," *Blazers* 90, no. 4 (1 March 1991): 112–114.

[2] Amanda Hesser, "Oops! Misadventures at the Table," *New York Times*, 4 April 1998, C1.

[3] Nancy Backas, "Training and Personality," *Cheers* 9, no. 2 (March 1998): 56.

[4] Personal conversation with Topaz Walker, Olive Garden Restaurants (14 November 1999).

[5] Linda Lipsky, as cited in Jennifer Waters, "Eye on Service," *Restaurants and Institutions* 108, no. 28 (1 December 1998): 46.

[6] S. R. Butler and W. E. Snizek, "The Waitress-Diner Relationship," *Sociology of Work and Occupations* 3, no. 2 (May 1976): 15.

[7] Ron Zemke and Kristin Anderson, Tales of Knock-Your-Socks-Off Service: Inspiring Stories of Outstanding Customer Service (AMACOM: December 1997). As cited in Michael Sanson, "Service Smarts," *Restaurant Hospitality*, 83, 3 (February 1998): 48.

[8] Carolyn Z. Lawrence, "Forget Customer Satisfaction?" *Quick Service Restaurants*, 12 November 1998, 29.

[9] Carl A. Litndes and Bruce H. Axler, *Restaurant Service: Beyond the Basics* (New York: John Wiley and Sons, 1994), 86.

[10] "A Night in Fine-Dining Hell," *Restaurants and Institutions* 106 (1 November 1996): 26.

[11] Rubin Carson, "It's a Good Thing Waiters Don't Tip Us," *Restaurant Guide* (Los Angeles, 1979).

[12] Carolyn Z. Lawrence, "Complaints Are Our Friends," *Quick Service Restaurants* (January–February 1999): 29.

[13] Kathy L. Indermill, "Calming Complainers," *Restaurant Hospitality* 74, no. 10 (October 1990): 70.

[14] Bob Losyk, "Placating Patrons: How to Satisfy Dissatisfied Customers," *National Restaurant Association* 16 (May 1996): 5.

[15] Some of the ideas for this section were taken from Greg W. Green, *The Psychological Necessities of a Successful Restaurant*, a Senior Project at California State Polytechnic University, 1976.

Chapter **15**

After reading and studying this chapter,
you should be able to:

Develop and maintain a food protection system.

Discuss the various types of food poisoning and how to prevent them.

FOOD PROTECTION
AND SANITATION

FOOD-BORNE ILLNESS

Posted in the kitchen of a large university is the aphorism "cleanliness is next to godliness."[1] Restaurant patrons may not believe in the religious implication of the statement, but they place a childlike trust in the integrity of restaurant operators, believing that food served will be clean, free of harmful germs and foreign materials.

The United States Public Health Service identifies more than 40 diseases that can be transferred through food. Many can cause serious illness; some are even deadly.[2] A food-borne illness is a disease that is carried or transmitted to human beings by food. There are three types of hazards to safe food: biological, chemical, and physical. Of these three, biological hazards cause the highest percentage of food-borne illness outbreaks. Disease-causing microorganisms, otherwise known as pathogens, such as bacteria, molds, and yeast, are considered biological hazards.

BIOLOGICAL HAZARDS—BACTERIA

The highest number of biological food-borne illness is caused by bacteria, single-celled microorganisms that are capable of reproducing in about 20 minutes. Under favorable conditions, one bacterium can become a colony of 72 million bacteria, more than enough to cause serious illness.[3] By understanding bacteria, we can destroy or control them and render them harmless. Bacteria, like all living organisms, need sustenance to function and multiply.

Bacteria can cause illness in two ways. The first is via disease-causing bacteria, known as *pathogens*, which feed on nutrients in hazardous foods and, given favorable conditions, multiply rapidly. Other bacteria, while not being harmful themselves, do, as they multiply, discharge toxins that poison humans when food containing them is eaten. Pathogenic bacteria can cause illness in humans in one of the three ways: by intoxication, infection, or toxin-mediated infection.[4]

The best known example of intoxication is botulism, a toxin produced by some bacteria; it cannot be smelled, seen, or tasted. Unlike many other bacteria, high temperatures do not destroy botulism, so special care is required in food handling to avoid illness.

The second type of bacterial illness is called infection, and salmonella is the best-known example. The bacteria live in the intestine of chickens, ducks, mice, and rats and, given favorable conditions, may cause illness to humans. Cooking foods to a temperature of 165°F or higher can kill them.

The third type of bacterial illness is toxin-mediated infection; it has characteristics of both intoxication and infection. Examples are *Clostridium perfringens* and *Escherichia coli* 0157:H7. (*E. coli*). After ingestion, these living organisms establish colonies in human or animal intestinal tracts, where they produce toxins. Young children and the elderly are vulnerable to these bacteria.

From time to time, the general public's faith in the safety of restaurant food is badly shaken by an outbreak of food-borne illness in a relatively few restaurants, cases that are widely publicized in the news and that frighten the public. A few such instances have resulted in death and caused serious financial damage not only to the restaurant where the outbreak occurred but to the restaurant industry in the region. On 11 January 1993, a two-year-old ate a dinnertime cheeseburger in a Tacoma, Washington, Jack-in-the-Box restaurant. The next night the boy, suffering with severe stomach cramps and bloody diarrhea, was taken to the hospital. Ten days later, he died of kidney and heart failure.

Health officials traced the boy's sickness to the presence of a pathogen called *E. Coli* 0157:H7, a bacterial strain often found in ground meat, especially in less developed countries. The officials found high levels of the coliform contaminating-animals feces or waste-in two of ten ground beef samples collected from Jack-in-the-Box units in King County, Washington. An epidemic of food poisoning struck more than 500 people in five western states.[5]

The fallout from the Jack-in-the-Box experience caused the stock of the parent company, San Diego–based Foodmaker, to fall from nearly $14 a share to $8.50. Sales dropped an estimated 30% and a number of lawsuits were initiated.[6]

All or most of the illness could have been prevented by a simple practice: cooking the hamburger to 165°F. Simple food protection practices are not simple to enforce and it must be assumed that all employees carry potentially dangerous bacteria and are shedding them in their feces and urine and from noses and mouths. An ill person passes about 10 to the 9th power bacterial cells per gram of fecal matter. If, when using the toilet, the toilet paper slips only slightly, there will be as many germs as 10 to the 7th power on the user's fingertips. To ensure clean hands and nails, double handwashing, using a fingertip brush, must be done. Proper handwashing includes using water as hot as the hands can comfortably stand, using a brush for the fingernails, and rubbing the hands together using friction for 20 seconds. The fingernail brush is not used during the second wash. Paper towels or heat should be used to dry hands.[7] Other food protection practices are discussed below.

CAUSES OF FOOD-BORNE ILLNESS

Any kind of food can be the vehicle for food-borne illness. However, generally, the high-protein foods that we eat regularly are responsible for most food-borne illnesses. These high-protein foods are classified as potentially hazardous by the U.S. Public Health Service and include any food that consists in whole or in part of milk or milk products, shell eggs, meats, poultry, fish, shellfish, edible crustacea (shrimp, lobster, crab, etc.) baked or boiled potatoes, tofu and other soy-protein foods, plant foods that have been heat treated, raw seed sprouts, or synthetic ingredients.[8]

Thousands of cases of stomach upset in the United States are traceable to restaurant food. The result of neglected food protection is seen more dramatically in some foreign countries. Many North American visitors who travel to developing countries come down with food-borne illness. The foodservice operator should consider the cultural backgrounds of employees and understand that food sanitation practice and attitudes toward cleanliness vary widely from one culture to another. The Japanese are known for their emphasis on sanitation. In Tokyo, persons with colds wear face masks to curb the spread of the cold to others. Other cultures place less emphasis on cleanliness and sanitation.

In developing countries, the germs most likely to cause intestinal upsets are strains of *E. Coli*, whose germs pass from bowel to hand to food. *E. Coli* causes a majority of the tourist symptoms commonly experienced in developing nations. Food protection problems increase in hot, humid climates where cockroaches are endemic, flies abound, and rodents are searing for food and shelter.

While sanitation rulers are straightforward and relatively simple, consistent implementation demands constant attention and concern. Habits are like giant flywheels— once learned and set in motion, they are difficult to change. Sanitarians are unanimous in their praise of the wonders of soap and water.

The NRA's *Sanitation Operations Manual* discusses a number of cases of food-borne illness in which the causes were tracked down.[9] Here is what typically happens in restaurants when food is not well prepared.

- In a large downtown restaurant, many patrons became ill after eating a Thanksgiving Day meal. Salmonella was allowed to grow in the turkey and gravy because the food was held between the noon and evening meal at a low temperature in the danger zone. A cook was identified as carrying a positive salmonella culture.

- At a sandwich shop, 22 cases of salmonella infection were traced to the owner and two employees. Barbecued pork was chopped by hand on a pine cutting board. The pork was not refrigerated for two hours.

- For a catered picnic, 100 pounds of potato salad was put in a tub while still warm, then placed in a walk-in refrigerator overnight. Salmonella was present and grew because the interior of the potato salad never cooked; the temperature was 50°F. Salmonella was found in the stool culture of the person who made the salad.

- Roast beef is sometimes infected with *clostridium perfringens*. Beef was sliced on a wooden cutting board and contaminated by the liquid from plastic bags enveloping the turkeys previously cut up on the board.

- Staphylococcus poisoning at a drive-in restaurant was caused by a high staph count in chocolate and other cream pies. The pies had been stored in a refrigerator at temperature between 52°F and 60°F.

The three disease-causing microorganisms most commonly associated with food-borne illness in the United States are *staphylococcus aureus*, salmonella, and *clostridium perfringens*. Staph bacteria live in our noses and on our skin and are concentrated in large numbers in boils, pimples, and other skin infections. Staphylococci present a special problem. In a favorable environment, they produce enterotoxins impervious to boiling water temperatures or the other temperatures commonly associated with food production. This means that you cannot destroy the staphylococci poisons. High-protein foods such as meats, poultry, fish, eggs, and dairy products that involve human handling are usually associated with staphylococci food poisoning. The microorganisms thrive and grow rapidly at temperatures above 44°F and survive to about 140°F or higher in certain circumstances.

Salmonella is the name of some 2,000 closely related bacteria that continually cycle through the environment in the intestinal tracts of people and animals.

First discovered in swine by Dr. Daniel E. Salmon in 1885, salmonella occurs in hundreds of different species, essentially as infections in animals and animal products such as eggs, meat, and milk. Researchers believe that only 1% of the infections caused by salmonella germs are reported.

Clostridium perfringens ranks third as a cause of food-borne illness. The bacteria are present in the soil, the intestines of animals, include humans, and in sewage. It has been called the cafeteria germ because it grows so well in food left standing at temperatures between 70°F and 170°F. A problem with *perfringens* is that while the vegetative cells of the germ are destroyed at normal cooking temperatures, the spores are not.

Perfringens is a natural contaminant of meat and is commonly found in the intestinal tract of healthy humans. It is around most of the time. Meat that has been cooked and then left out at room temperature for some time is almost certain to develop *perfringens* bacteria.

Streptococcus food infection, found in contaminated nasal or oral discharges, is spread by sneezing or poor food handling and can cause scarlet fever and strep throat. Foods contaminated with excreta by unclean hands also cause intestinal strep infections.

Bacillus cereus organisms are found in soil, water, and dust. Keeping hot foods hot, cold foods cold, and preventing cross-contamination controls this bacteria. Shigella dysenterial is another serious threat in foodservice. As few as ten germs of this kind in a salad can make healthy people ill.

Parasites also cause infections. Trichinosis, fish tapeworm, and some kinds of amoebas are the parasites that North America are most likely to encounter. Viral infections—the common cold and hepatitis—are other hazards found in the restaurant. Viruses are transmitted to food by humans. Luckily, viruses do not multiply in food. Unfortunately, heat does not kill them.

Raw or insufficiently cooked pork can support the parasite *trichinella spiralis*, which burrows into the muscles of the host. Fish tapeworms, alive and well in some fish taken from infected waters, are another hazard, and make the practice of serving any raw fish questionable. Tapeworms, also found in raw beef, attach themselves to the intestinal wall of the host and can grow to 30 feet in length.

Some food-borne diseases are parasites that have quite serious consequences. Amoebic dysentery, for example, is not a self-limiting diarrhea and can last for months. Bacillary dysentery, a self-limiting diarrhea, widespread in the tropics, may have an onset period of about two days and last about six days. Cholera is spread by ingesting food and liquids contaminated by sewage that contain the virus *vibrio comma*.

Infectious hepatitis is dangerous, often lethal. Unlike food poisoning, which usually runs its course in a few days, infectious hepatitis has a long incubation period, 10 to 50 days, before its symptoms of yellow discoloration, severe loss of appetite, weight loss, fever, and extreme tiredness set in. Caused by a virus, infectious hepatitis is found in feces and urine of infected persons and in raw shellfish harvested from infected waters.

The paradox of food-borne illness is that most of it can be avoided by clean hands and by following a few simple precautionary practices. Salmonella presents no problem if suspect foods are heated to 165°F (74°C) or higher. Make sure the hands do not brush the hair, fingers are not in the nose, and the hands are washed after changing money or after working with any potentially contaminated object, such as garbage.

How does one know which of the three principal pathogens is the cause of food-borne illness? One cannot be sure, but the symptoms manifested are a clue to the microorganisms at fault. All three types of bacteria cause vomiting and diarrhea. *Staphylococcus aureus* (staph) symptoms appear two to six hours after eating infected food and last a day or two. Salmonella symptoms normally show up later, 12 to 36 hours after eating, and last longer—two to seven days. *Perfringens* symptoms appear as diarrhea and pains 8 to 24 hours after consumption and often end within a day.

Microorganisms for causing food-borne illness are not visible to the naked eye. Staph germs are grapelike cells; salmonella are rod-shaped cells that cluster together. *Perfrongens* are also rod-shaped but not clustered together like salmonella.

The most frequently cited errors in food handling are:

1. Failure to properly cool food

2. Failure to thoroughly heat or cook food

3. Infected employees who practice poor personal hygiene at home and at the workplace

4. Foods prepared a day or more before they are served

5. Raw, contaminated ingredients incorporated into foods that receive no further cooking

6. Foods allowed remaining at bacteria-incubation temperatures

7. Failure to reheat cooked foods to temperatures that kill bacteria

8. Cross-contamination of cooked foods with raw foods, or by employees who mishandle foods, or through improperly cleaned equipment[10]

CONTROLLING OR DESTROYING BACTERIA

Bacteria, like other living things, have a comfort zone. In order to grow, bacteria require food and moisture, the proper pH, and time. The food on which bacteria thrive is called potentially hazardous. Among the potentially hazardous foods are those high in protein, like meat, milk and dairy products, and especially eggs, fish, and shellfish. Items like custard, mayonnaise, hollandaise sauce, and quiche are particularly susceptible to contamination.

Temperature is the most important element for bacteria survival and growth; it is also the easiest for restaurateurs to control. The temperature danger zone—between 40°F and 140°F—is the range in which bacteria can thrive and multiply most rapidly. Outside of these temperatures, bacteria become dormant, only to reactivate when more favorable conditions return.

It is critical for operators to heat the internal food temperature to a minimum of 140°F. Other safe practices include:

1. Hold foods at internal temperatures of at least 140°F.

2. Heat foods rapidly to avoid the danger zone.

3. Heat small quantities at a time.

4. Heat foods close to service time.

5. Do not use a steam table to reheat foods; instead, heat them rapidly to an internal temperature of 140°F, then transfer them to the steam table for holding.

6. When hot foods are required cool, chill them quickly in an ice bath or with running water.

7. Place cooked foods in the refrigerator above uncooked foods; this will help avoid cross-contamination.

8. Do not thaw foods at room temperature.

9. Thaw foods gradually in the refrigerator. Put them in a container to prevent them dripping onto other foods.

The golden rule in restaurant operations is to keep hot foods hot and cold foods cold. By controlling the environment in which bacteria may grow and thrive, restaurant operators can prevent outbreaks of food-borne illness.

ACIDITY AND BACTERIAL GROWTH

Bacteria thrive on protein foods that contain moisture and are neutral or slightly acidic. Generally, microorganisms do not grow in foods that are highly acidic or highly alkaline. The pH value of a food, referring to its acidity or alkalinity, is compared with that of pure

■ **TABLE 15–1**
Acidity/Alkalinity of Foods

pH		
0	10,000,000	*High acid*, pH 2.0 and below: Limes, lemons,
1	1,000,000	vinegar, plums, gooseberries, pickles,
2	100,000	rhubarb, grapefruit juice, sauerkraut, most
3	10,000	fruits, ginger ale
4	1,000	*Acid*, pH of 3.7–4.5: Oranges, cherries, pears,
5	100	applejuice, tomato juice, buttermilk
6	10	
7	0	*Medium*, pH 4.5–5.3: Bananas, figs, asparagus,
8	10	pumpkin, spinach, beets, carrots, coffee
9	100	*Low acid*, pH 5.3–7.0: Butter, milk, sweet peas,
10	1,000	most vegetables, shrimp, salmon, meat
11	10,000	*Alkaline*, over pH 7: Ripe olives, soda
12	100,000	crackers, clam juice, egg white, red devil's
13	1,000,000	food cake, hard water, water softened by
14	10,000,000	sodium exchange

water, which has a pH value of 7, or neutral. The pH number indicates the hydrogen ion concentration and is stated as a logarithm. The lower the number below 7, the more acidic. The higher the number above 7, the more alkaline. As seen in Table 15–1, below a pH of 4 is 1,000 times more acidic than pure water. Most fresh fruits, berries, and wine contain enough acid (below pH levels of 4.6) to inhibit growth. Meats, fish, butter, milk, and vegetables are of a pH range conducive to bacterial growth.

Most hazardous foods, from the point of being able to support rapid bacterial growth are milk, eggs, meat, poultry, fish, and shellfish, or foods that contain one or more of these foods. Most fruits and vegetables, being slightly acidic, are not good hosts for bacteria.

Common culprits as hosts for food poisoning bacteria are cream and custard pies that are not held in refrigerated conditions. Gravies and ground meat dishes are also involved in many cases of food poisoning. Potato and egg salads carefully prepared and held refrigerated are nevertheless good hosts for food poisoning germs.

BACTERIA AND TEMPERATURE

Most bacteria, harmful or not, are destroyed by heat. For example, heat of 180°F is used in the final rinse of dishwashing machines. Chemical sanitation is most effective at temperatures between 75°F and 120°F. Three commonly used chemical sanitizers are chlorine, quaternary compounds, and iodine. If, for some reason, the usual dishwashing methods are not available, chlorine performs well if at least 50 parts per million of water are used for one minute. Dishes and utensils are immersed for one minute in solution at least 75°F in temperature.

Microwave heatings, as used in microwave ovens, acts by the agitation of water molecules in the food. Food is not heated properly because of unequal water distribution in the food and uneven microwave distribution in the oven. An important guideline to ensure that the safe internal temperature is achieved in microwave cooking is to add a minimum of 25°F to the recommended internal cooking temperature of food

■ **TABLE 15–2**

M i n i m u m   S a f e   I n t e r n a l   T e m p e r a t u r e s   f o r   V a r i o u s   H o t   F o o d s

Product	Temperature
Pork, ham, sausage, and bacon in a microwave	170°F (76.6°C)
All foods previously served and cooled that are reheated	165°F (73.9°C) within two hours
All poultry and game birds	165°F (73.9°C)
Stuffed meats	165°F (73.9°C)
Stuffing	165°F (73.9°C)
Pork, ham, and bacon in another heating element	150°F (65.6°C)
Potentially hazardous foods	140°F (60°C)
Beef roasts (rare)	130°F (54.4°C) for two hours
Beef steaks (rare)	130°F (54.4°C) (or as customer requests)

when prepared the conventional way. This means, for example, that chicken cooked in a microwave oven should have an internal temperature of 190°F instead of the usual 165°F recommended.

EVERY STAFF MEMBER A SANITARIAN

Because germs are ubiquitous in restaurants, management should set the tone that every staff member is also a sanitarian—a person constantly aware of the importance of personally controlling pathogens. There is a right and a wrong way of carrying utensils and serving food (Figure 15–1). Parts of food handling courses cover the subject.

VIRUSES

Viruses are another type of microorganism of concern to restaurant operators because they can cause food-borne illness such as hepatitis A and Norwalk virus. Viruses do not require a hazardous food in order to survive. They can survive on any food or surface, do not multiply, and are not as affected by heat or cold as are bacteria. They simply use the food or other surface as means of transport. Once the virus enters a body cell, it takes over, forcing the cell to assist in the production of more viruses.

Outbreaks of food-borne or water-borne diseases are usually caused by unfiltered drinking water, shellfish from polluted waters, and, especially, by poor personal hygiene. Foods not cooked after handling are those most likely to cause a viral disease. Examples include salads, baked products, milk, sandwich meats, fish, and shellfish.

CHEMICAL CONTAMINANTS

The increased use of pesticides has caused concern about the chemical contamination of foods. Besides pesticides, there are four types of chemical contamination that can occur at any point along the food supply chain.

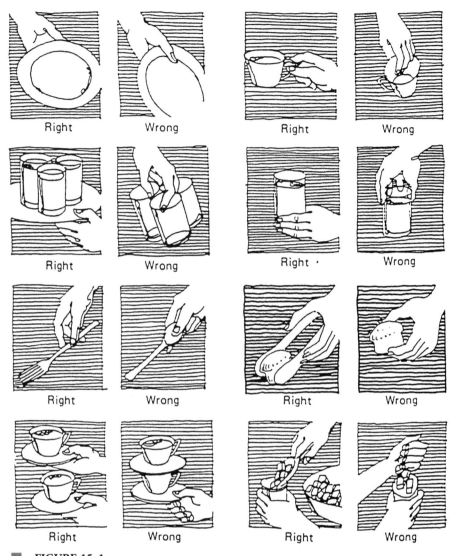

FIGURE 15–1

Sanitary ways to carry utensils and serve food. **Source: Applied Foodservice Sanitation, a certification coursebook,** *4th ed. (The Educational Foundation of the National Restaurant Association, 1995), p. 141.*

1. Restaurant chemicals like detergents and sanitizers, including polishes, caustics, and cleaning and drying agents, as well as similar products that are poisonous to humans

2. Preservatives and additives; overuse of preservatives like sulfating agents, which are used for maintaining the freshness and color of vegetables, fruits, frozen potatoes, and certain wines; nitrates, which are used as a curing agent to prevent growth of certain harmful bacteria and as a flavor enhancer

3. Acidic reaction of foods with metal-lined containers, particularly brass or copper, and zinc-coated containers

4. Contamination of food with toxic metals, copper being the main cause of toxic metal poisoning, particularly from carbonated beverages that traverse copper pipes[11]

PERSONAL SAFETY

Many outbreaks of food-borne illness are caused by humans who do not observe proper personal hygiene. By not washing hands frequently, especially after dealing with potentially hazardous foods, and by not wearing protective gloves when handling foods, employees may contaminate foods. Even a healthy person can carry microorganisms like staphylococci in their mouth, throat, and nose. Other microorganisms passed on by humans are shigella, *clostridium prefringens*, salmonella, and hepatitis A. The way to prevent outbreaks of food-borne illness caused by humans is to practice personal cleanliness.

HAZARD ANALYSIS OF CRITICAL CONTROL POINTS

Because of the necessity of avoiding any kind of illness among astronauts, the National Aeronautics and Space Administration (NASA) developed a program that attempts to ensure that space fliers do not become ill from food-borne diseases. The program, called Hazard Analysis of Critical Control Point (HACCP), presents methods for systematically ridding kitchens of pathogens. The system follows seven basic steps.

1. Identify hazards and assess their severity and risks.
2. Determine critical control points (CCPs) in food preparation.
3. Determine critical control limits (CCLs) for each CCP identified.
4. Monitor CCPs and record data.
5. Take corrective action whenever monitoring indicates a CCL is exceeded.
6. Establish an effective record-keeping system to document the HACCP system.
7. Establish procedures to verify that the HACCP system is working.[12]

The first step is to decide what hazards exist at each stage of a food's journey through the kitchen and to decide how serious each is in terms of overall safety priorities. On your own checklist, this may include the following items:

- Reviewing recipes; paying careful attention to times for thawing, cooking, cooling, reheating, and handling of leftovers
- Giving employees thermometers and teaching them how to use them; correctly calibrating the thermometers
- Inspecting all fresh and frozen products upon delivery
- Requiring handwashing at certain points in the food preparation process and showing employees the correct way to wash for maximum sanitation
- Adding quick-chill capability to cool foods more quickly in amounts over 1 gallon or 4 pounds

There are as many of these possibilities as there are restaurants!

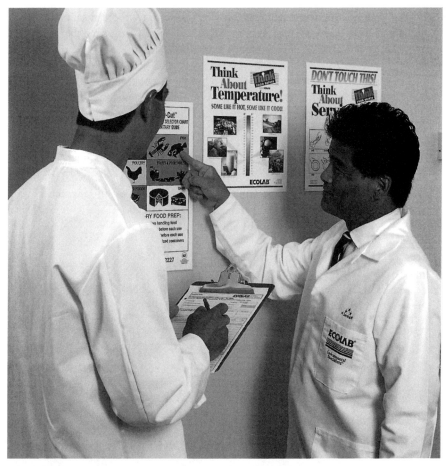

Setting up a cleanliness program is critical to food protection and the sanitation of restaurants. Reprinted with permission. © Ecolab, Inc.

The second step is to identify critical control points (CCPs). This means any point or procedure in your system where loss of control may result in a health risk. If workers use the same cutting boards to dice vegetables and debone chickens without washing them between uses, that is a CCP in need of improvement. Vendor delivery vehicles should be inspected for cleanliness; product temperatures must be kept within five degrees of optimum; expiration dates on food items must be clearly marked; utensils must be sanitized; and the list goes on and on.

The third step is to determine the standards and limits for what is acceptable and what is not in each of the CCP areas in your kitchen.

The fourth step in the HACCP system is to monitor all the steps you pointed out in step 2 for a specific period of time to be sure each area of concern is taken care of correctly. Some CCPs may remain on the list indefinitely for constant monitoring; others, once you correct the procedure, may be removed from the list after several months. Still others may be added to the monitoring list as needed.

Step 5 kicks in whenever you see that one of your CCLs (see step 3) has been exceeded and corrective action must be taken.

Step 6 requires that you document this whole process. Without documentation, it is difficult, at best, to chart whatever progress your facility might be making. If there is a problem that affects customer health or safety, having written records is also very important.

Finally, step 7 requires that you establish a procedure to verify whether the HACCP system is working for you. This may mean a committee that meets regularly to discuss health and safety issues and to go over the documentation required in step 6.

COMMON FOOD SAFETY MISTAKES

Some of the most common food safety risks in day-to-day food production fall into three key areas: time/temperature abuse, cross-contamination, and poor personal hygiene. Following are useful tips to avoid them.

Time/Temperature

Here's the drill: The danger zone in which bacteria thrives lies between 40°F to 140°F. Keep all cool foods below 40°F and all hot foods above 140°F.

- Invest in digital thermometers with long probes or thermocouples. (Some new thermometers even record temperatures for record keeping.) Make use of oven and refrigerator thermometers.

Sanitizing the dishwasher is an important step in maintaining a sanitary operation. Reprinted with permission. © Ecolab, Inc.

- Randomly take temperatures of sample food shipments to ensure that proper chilling temperature is maintained through transport. Food shipments that require cold storage must be chilled immediately.

- When cooling hot foods, place them into shallow pans and cool them with an ice bath or a cooling paddle, or use ice as an ingredient before placing them in the cooler. Placing hot foods in the cooler not only raises the cooler temperature, but many foods simply won't cool to 40°F within the four hours prescribed.

- Cook foods to the temperature recommended in the Food and Drug Administration (FDA) Food Code and reheat foods, one time only, to 165°F. Once foods are cooked or reheated, temperature must be held above 140°F.

- Prepare foods in batches; avoid leaving large quantities of food at room temperature during preparation.

■

Cross-Contamination

Most cross-contamination occurs in food preparation. It is not easy to engage in unsanitary food practices without realizing the dangers. Picking up a spoon by the bowl is like sticking your fingers in someone's mouth. Picking up ice has the same effect. Handling money definitely transfers germs to the hands. Sneezing in the hand has the same effect.

Have you ever seen a server grab a piece of pie and shovel it in his mouth while picking up an order for the dining room? He has almost certainly contaminated his hands. Dragging on a cigarette and failing to wash the hands afterward also means germs from the mouth go onto the hands.

- Buy a plentiful supply of color-coded cutting boards and dedicate the colors to specifics foods—chicken only, vegetables only, bread only, for example. Wash the board in hot water and sanitize after every use. When boards go black, that's bacteria growing in the scores. Throw them out!

- Buy nonabsorbent, washable mats to anchor cutting boards instead of using towels that can absorb contaminated juices. Replace mats between each cutting job.

- As with cutting boards, dedicate knives to specific foods and clean and sanitize them between all cutting jobs. Label the drawers where the knives are kept so that they stay dedicated.

- Wipe down the slicer blade with a clean, hot cloth between jobs and sanitize. Invest in an antiseptic block—a block of solidified sanitizer that you slice on the slicer.

- Clean and sanitize the counter between each cutting job.

- When storing foods in the cooler, follow this rule: Cooked foods and foods to be served raw go on top shelves, uncooked raw foods go on bottom shelves. This eliminates the chance of contaminated juices dripping onto ready-to-eat foods.

- Buffets are prime situations for cross-contamination. Tongs, ladles, and spoons get dropped, switched in the bins, touched by many hands, coughed on—you name it. They need to be cleaned and sanitized, or replaced, every half-hour.

Poor Personal Hygiene

Regular, thorough handwashing is one of the most effective safety precautions employees can take. The problems with this situation, however, are myriad. For one, many operations do not have handwashing situations in convenient spots in the kitchen. If employees have to walk a distance to get to a sink, chances are they will not.

And while they can use the washroom sink, they run the risk of recontaminating their hands on the doorknob. Using the scrub or pot sink is not always a solution, either; imagine employees washing chicken juices off their hands over a colander of lettuce or a newly washed pot.

So it is worth repeating: Make sure employees have convenient stations for handwashing. Technology can help even this kitchen basic: One company has developed a hands-free station that features infrared sensors.

Most employees do not wash their hands properly. It takes 30 seconds of thorough scrubbing with antibacterial soap and a nailbrush under hot-as-you-can-stand water to get hands clean.

To send the message home, try a demonstration with a special powder on the market. Have employees put this powder on their hands, wash, and then look at their hands in infrared light. The still-dirty areas will glow.[13]

APPROACHES TO FOOD SAFETY

Overall responsibility for foodservice has been given to the FDA. States and local health authorities draw up ordinances that specify standards and practice for the protection of employees and patrons and provide for regular inspection and enforcement of the ordinances. The FDA provides a model ordinance that is the basis for most local health ordinances.

A public health license to operate a restaurant is required; the license can be revoked if standards are not met or if a dangerous health hazard is found or suspected.

When operating a new restaurant facility or taking over an existing one, a sanitarian or other health officer makes an inspection and may call for changes such as the installation of sneeze guards over salad bars or changes in plumbing, floor coverings, and number or kind of toilet facilities. Most jurisdictions require a toilet for the people who are physically handicapped.

While the requirements and inspections may appear onerous to the operator, they should be welcomed as a means of safeguarding the public and avoiding problems that could destroy a restaurant. Some restaurant chain operators want more, not less food protection and monitoring and hire their own bacteriologists to perform regular bacteria counts on foodservice equipment and on such items as glass, china, and flatware.

Regular physical examination of personnel is an excellent practice, one that too few restaurateurs follow because of time and cost. At the very least, newly hired employees should be given physical examinations for no other reason than the protection of present employees and to learn of any physical limitations, and to counter claims that the disability was caused on the job. Some health departments provide free or low-cost exams.

That a person is examined and found healthy does not in any way reduce the necessity for following all the rules for food protection. Individuals can harbor an infectious agent in their bodies. These carriers can transmit the disease to others without themselves exhibiting symptoms. A number of outbreaks of disease have occurred through such carriers.

All states and many local communities monitor restaurants for cleanliness and adherence to food protection ordinances. Most, however, lack the staff to do more than a few inspections. Several states mandate that all foodservice employees complete a food protection course and become certified food handlers.

A number of municipalities have assigned their public health director the responsibility for seeing to it that every restaurant employee completes an elementary course in food protection. Certificates and pins are awarded to those who pass the course. With high employee turnover, however, it is virtually impossible to enforce health codes mandating such courses. Management interest in food protection and insistence on sanitation is the only practical way of protecting employees and the public from diseases that are most certainly present when hundreds of people sit down to eat in a public restaurant.

Many restaurants require kitchen staff to wear gloves when handling food. This lessens the risk of contamination. Uneven enforcement of regulations causes some confusion in the industry. For example, in some communities, public health officers do not permit tables to be set, prior to serving a meal, with glasses, cups, knives, forks, and spoons unless the glasses and cups are inverted and the knives, forks, and spoons are wrapped or otherwise covered.

FOOD PROTECTION AS A SYSTEM

Up to a point, the more sanitation practices that can be built into a system, the more likely they will be carried out. The system includes details that can be otherwise overlooked. Personnel trained in the system are carried along by it. One of the reasons for the success of chains like McDonald's is their emphasis on the sanitation system. "Why is that toothpick on the floor?" asks a McDonald inspector. "Why hasn't that table been cleaned?" "Why is the restroom not cleaned?"

To systematize sanitation practices, they should be built into the manager's daily schedule, as shown in Figure 15–2.

The Waffle House, Inc., an Alabama-based chain, provides a schedule that takes the manager through the day from 6:30 A.M., when he or she arrives and checks the building for appearance, until 9:00 P.M. when the cash register and supplies are checked when the manager leaves.

The first duty, on arrival, is to check around the building for paper, trash, and beer cans before opening. Five minutes later, the manager checks the front door glass, the floor, the booths, the rest rooms, and the floor behind the counter. At 10:30 A.M., the floor is swept and, at 2:00 P.M., mopped. At 4:30 P.M., the whole unit is gone over for cleanliness.

To take care of major cleaning, a weekly cleaning schedule is laid out. Each day something major is cleaned: the back bar on Sunday; grills and light globes on Monday; sidewalks and blinds on Tuesday; ceiling and booths on Wednesday; refrigerators and under the dishwashing machine on Thursday; display case, cigarette, and music machines on Friday; menus, office window, and parking lot on Saturday.

Each operator can design and copy a checklist that fits his or her restaurant. The checklist can be a reminder to check those things which, over time, may be overlooked. Without a checklist, the unacceptable becomes acceptable. The dirty carpet is overlooked; the soiled uniform becomes normal. If used on a regular basis, the checklist systemizes sanitation. Final responsibility for sanitation must remain a management priority.

Among the many corporations offering sanitation services is Ecolab, a global company of 76 years offering cleaning and sanitation products and programs, pest elimination and prevention, floor care, carpet care, and warewashing. It has been named one of the 100 best-managed companies by *Industry Week* magazine.

6:30 A.M.	Arrive at unit. Check around building for paper, trash, beer cans before entering.
6:35 A.M.	Use front entrance. Check front door glass for cleanliness. Check floor, sweep if necessary. Check booths and stools for dirt, crumbs, etc. Check restrooms for cleanliness, towels, and soap. Clean service if needed. Check floor behind counter. See if breakfast menus are out.
6:45 A.M.	Make out commissary order See that first-shift employees are in proper uniform before going on duty.
6:50 A.M.	Check cash register; take out night sales. Put in change as needed.
7:00 A.M.	Lower venetian blinds if needed. Take over grill or station to be worked.
10:30 A.M.	Have floor swept.
11:00 A.M.	Take cash register reading. Raise blinds if no longer needed. See that menus are changed. See that unit is set up for lunch; charbroiler, sandwich board, pies cut and displayed.
2:00 P.M.	Take cash register reading, replenish change in register; remove 1st shift sales from register; see that second-shift employees are in correct uniform. Raise or lower venetian blinds as needed. Sweep and mop floors, check restrooms. Leave instructions with employees for cleaning stainless steel, formica, booths, stools, etc. Take afternoon break, if possible.
4:50 P.M.	Check unit for cleanliness, floor, restrooms, grill area, etc.
5:00 P.M.	Take cash register reading. Take over grill or station to be worked.
8:30 P.M.	See that grill and waitress stations are clean and set up for 3rd shift.
8:50 P.M.	See if third shift is available for duty and in correct uniform.
9:00 P.M.	Check cash register, remove sales; replenish change. Check unit food and supplies. If short on food or supplies, restock if a commissary unit. If not a commissary unit, call your supervisor. Leave instruction with third shift for cleaning.

Weekly Schedule of Manager's Cleaning Duties

Daily Requirements
1. Sweep: 11:00 A.M.; 2:00 P.M.; 2:00 A.M.; or as needed.
2. Mop: 2:00 A.M.; 2:00 P.M.; or as needed.
3. Clean front door at least 4 times daily.
4. Pick up debris on parking lot.
5. Clean booths, chairs, and stools—frequently.
6. Clean bathrooms: 6:30; 11:30; 3:00; 1:00.
7. Sweep off outside walk.
8. Clean pie display case.

■ **FIGURE 15–2**

Sample manager schedule. **Source: The Chain-Restaurant Industry** *(New York: Wychoff and Sasser, Heath, 1978), 120–121.*

Sunday—Additional cleaning items:
1. Clean back bar.
2. Sweep off front walk.
3. Clean office window.
4. Pick up parking lot.

Monday—Additional cleaning items:
1. Clean return grills.
2. Clean and mop (well) under the back-bar.
3. Clean around the dumpster pad.
4. Wash light globes.

Tuesday—Additional cleaning items:
1. Hose down front and back walkways.
2. Clean blinds.
3. Clean front of counter and stools.
4. Clean waiting chairs.

Wednesday—Additional cleaning items:
1. Have windows washed, clean store front.
2. Wash booths and legs with Lux liquid.
3. Clean grills and burners

Thursday—Additional cleaning items:
1. Clean back-bar and shelves and drawers.
2. Clean refrigerators and drawers.
3. Clean ceiling.
4. Clean under dishwashing machine.

Friday—Additional cleaning items:
1. Clean return grills.
2. Pick up parking lot.
3. Clean pie display case well.
4. Clean cigarette and music machines.

Saturday—Additional cleaning items:
1. Parking lot.
2. Clean blinds.
3. Clean office window.
4. Check menus for cleanliness and condition.

FIGURE 15–2

Continued

One such form, developed for the Heritage Restaurants of Eugene, Oregon, is shown in Figure 15–3.

The experienced manager is constantly alert for sanitation deficiencies and reacts automatically to cues that say something is wrong:

- Soiled uniforms
- Body odors
- Dirty hands
- Hairnets or other hair restraints not being worn as required
- Someone fingering a pimple or scratching his head or face
- Someone sneezing in his or her hands

LOCATION: _____ DATE: _____ TIME: _____ DAY: _____

Does this Heritage Restaurant meet the following acceptable cleanliness standards?

	Yes	No		Yes	No		Yes	No
EXTERIOR			RESTROOMS (MENS)			DISH AREA (CONT.)		
Parking Lot			Floor			Garbage Cans		
Planters			Urinals			Floor		
Weeded			Stools			Walls		
Watered			Wash Basin			Ceiling		
Dumpster Area			Mirrors			Dish Racks		
Grease Area			Wastebasket			Mops and Buckets		
Front Door			Toilet Paper			Employee Table		
Walks			Seat Covers			WALK-IN		
Lights			Towels			Floors		
Signs			Soap Dispenser			Walls		
Back Door Locked			Other:			Ceilings		
Other:			RESTROOMS (WOMENS)			Racks Labeled		
INTERIOR			Floor			Containers		
Floors Swept			Stools			Labels and Dates		
Floors Clean			Wash Basin			FREEZER		
Door/Handles			Mirrors			Floors		
Greeting Sign			Wastebasket			Racks Labeled		
Floor Drains			Seat Covers			Containers		
Windows			Towels			STORE ROOM		
Window Sills			Kotex Dispenser			Floors		
Walls			Soap Dispenser			Racks		
Ceilings			Other:			Shelves		
Vents			KITCHEN			Walls		
Light Fixtures			Floor			Containers		
Light Bulbs			Walls			Labels		
Table Bases			Ceiling			OTHER:		
Chairs			Light Fixtures			OTHER:		
Counter Stools			Ovens			OTHER:		
High Chairs			Shelves			EMPLOYEES		
Counter Top and Front			Sinks			Waitress Appearance		
Other:			Work Tables			Uniforms		
EQUIPMENT			Mixer			Name Badge		
Cigarette Machine			Slicer			Hair		
Coffee Makers			Steam Tables			Cooks Appearance		
Cash Register			Filters			Hat and Scarf		
Cutting Bar			Grills			Clean Aprons		
Waitress Stations			Reach-ins			Utility Appearance		
Wait. Sta. Stock			Cold Table			SERVICE STANDARDS		
Wait. Sta. Cleaned			Grease Traps			Greeting		
Fountain Area			Other:			Service Times		
Pie Case Area			Other:			Cooperation		
Reach-ins			Other:			Customer Awareness		
Menus			UTILITY AREA			Cooking Times		
Salt and Peppers			Dish Machine			Service Priorities		
Sugar Dispensers			Sinks			Waitress Callbacks		
Creamers			Shelves			Managers Appearance		

COMMENTS: _____

Supervisor's Signature: _____   Manager's Signature: _____

■   FIGURE 15–3

Heritage Restaurants inspection report. Courtesy Heritage Restaurants

- Smoking in the dining room or kitchen
- Someone wearing an ornate ring or dangling bracelet that could get into the food or be a hazard around moving equipment
- Someone has a bad cold and needs to be sent home immediately
- Tabletop stains, cracked china, scratched glasses, cigarette burns on chairs and carpets

Uncorrected deficiencies soon vanish from the consciousness and are accepted by the management and employees—but not by sophisticated customers.

To emphasize the importance of cleanliness, Howard Johnson, the founder of the chain by that name, would appear unannounced at a parking lot or in a restaurant and pick up loose paper or cigarette butts, a practice certain to be instructive to the manager. Sanitation starts with the manager, who is the model for others to follow and emulate.

CONTRACT SANITATION SERVICE

Some hotels and restaurants turn over warewashing and general sanitation of food-service to outside companies on a contract. Environmental Sanitation Services (ESS), for example, a division of Economics Laboratory, has a number of contracts with hotels, country clubs, restaurants, and hospitals for doing all of the sanitation work. For a fixed amount of money per week, complete dishroom operation, bussing, laundry, and other sanitation requirements in the kitchen are taken over and managed by ESS. ESS becomes responsible for recruiting, hiring, training, and managing all of the personnel that have to do with warewashing and general utility work. If the operation has a laundry room, that too is usually a part of the package.

Ordinarily, current employees are retained and effort is made to reduce employee turnover and increase effectiveness. The company may have several contracts within an area of the city under one manager, and often will move employees from one location to another as needed. Recruitment is done with state and federal agencies and an effort made to employ people who are mentally and otherwise handicapped.

WAREWASHING AND FOOD PROTECTION

Warewashing is a critical step in the continuing battle to eliminate pathogens in the restaurant. Warehousing equipment operates in three phases: prewashing (also called scraping), washing, and sanitizing. Prewashing is usually done using high-pressure spray nozzles with a sink and leading through to a waste disposal system. Flatware is best soaked before washing. Overflow water from the wash tank is often used in the prewash.

Warewashing takes place at about 140°F, hot enough to dissolve detergents added to the wash water but not so hot as to bake food particles into the ware. The dirtier the ware, the more detergent needed, which adds urgency to removing most of the soil for storage as well.

The large warewashing machines are usually operated by two persons, one to feed the machine and one to remove the clean ware. Some machines come with a circular table that permits a merry-go-round of ware to move in and out of the machine. One person can load soiled ware onto racks, wait for them to return, and unload them.

The critical phase in warewashing is sanitation, either using water heated to 180°F or bacterial chemicals to destroy most of the germs present, as in low-temperature washing. A variety of equipment is available. Assuring the right temperature and power spray pressure are the problems for the high-temp machines. Booster heaters bring tap water to temperatures that, when sprayed onto the ware, are not less than 170°F. Hot water costs are high.

Low-temperature machines rely on iodine or quaternary ammonia to kill the germs. Machines using chlorine or quaternary ammonia compounds operate between 120°F and 140°F. Those using iodine as a bactericide heat water to 75°F. With cooler water, the air does not dry the dishes rapidly, so wetting agents are added in the final rinse. These sheet the water off, preventing droplets from forming. The droplets contain salts that, when dry, appear as spots on dishes, glasses, and flatware.

Low-temp machines cost less to buy and operate, sometimes less than half the cost of high-temp machines. They do not produce steam and operate without need for an exhaust system. Chlorine used in the chemical rinse can blacken metals such as pewter, aluminum, and silverware. High-temp machines do a better job of removing some stains, such as lipstick, and food soils, such as citrus pulp, cheese paste, and egg dishes.

In many communities, low-temp machines can be leased. Payment is based per rack through the machine. Computers are playing a role in warewashing. One machine speaks out in a firm voice instructing the operator on proper dishwashing procedures and how to shut down the machine. During operation, it comments on water temperature, level of soil in the water, the conditions of rinse jets, and the supply of the detergent and wetting agent.

In spite of computers and expensive equipment, warewashing remains a headache for the restaurant operator. After pot-and-pan washing, the job of warewashing is the least desirable in the restaurant. Persons with few other job options usually fill this low-paying job. Consequently, job turnover level is high, skill and motivation level low. The work is monotonous, the work area often noisy, hot, and humid.

Some options for making the job more interesting include:

- Upgrade the job by adding tasks such as keeping the parking area clean, cleaning the dining area, and training for other jobs, such as cooking or storeroom keeping. With added responsibilities, wages can be raised.

- Employ people for whom the work is challenging and so may be well satisfied with it.

- Employ part-timers who, because of shorter hours, will not find the work so repetitious.

- Rotate several utility persons through the job, making it less boring for each.

PEST CONTROL

From a sanitation viewpoint, pests are unwanted insects and rodents. Sometimes birds carry filth and disease into and around the restaurant.

Take a look at a fly under a microscope (Figure 15–4) and you will see that its legs are covered with sticky hairs that can carry bacteria and viruses that cause diseases such as typhoid, dysentery, tuberculosis, infantile diarrhea, and streptococcal and staphylococcal illnesses. A single fly can contaminate food with enough bacteria to cause illness. Lacking teeth, a fly spits on food particles to soften them, then sucks them up through a trunk like an elephant. Flyspecks are fly vomitus and swarm with bacteria and contaminates. One fly can produce thousands of offspring.

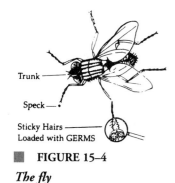

Trunk

Speck

Sticky Hairs
Loaded with GERMS

FIGURE 15–4

The fly

Cockroaches are just as unsightly and seem to appear from nowhere. A female cockroach can produce millions of offspring in her lifetime. Cockroaches are known carriers of salmonella bacteria and viruses that cause poliomyelitis.

Rats and mice transmit such diseases as salmonella and marine typhus. One fecal dropping can contain several million bacteria that can get into foods or appear as dust after drying out.

For most restaurant operators, the best way to control pests is to work with a licensed pest control operator who appears on a regular basis, is knowledgeable, and is equipped with approved pesticides. Trying to control pests in the restaurant is risky as the pesticides themselves can be dangerous and the control measures haphazard. In the excellent text *Applied Foodservices Sanitation*, published by the Educational Foundation of the National Restaurant Association and used for certification courses, the authors recommend developing an integrated pest management program (IPM).[14] The IPM program is a system combining preventive tactics and control methods to eliminate pests. The IPM system combines with good sanitation and food safety to make a comprehensive program of food safety.

The elements of pest control system include:

- Denying entry, food, water, and shelter to pests
- Checking all supplies entering the building for signs of pests
- Making a daily inspection of the kitchen and storeroom
- Keeping the kitchen and storeroom clean and free of places where pests can hide
- Storing all items off the floor and away from walls
- Building the pests out of the building by securing holes, cracks, or other possible entrances they might use
- Installing an air door over the back entrance to prevent flies and other insects from entering the kitchen
- Keeping the garbage area clean and sanitized

SUMMARY

Restaurants, like hospitals and schools, are public places where people from many walks of life and backgrounds come together. Every person carries harmful microorganisms or viruses that can be transmitted by food or drink. The restaurant operator is necessarily engaged in preventing that transfer of pathogens, a relentless war in which hot water, heat, refrigeration, and chemicals are used. Vermin and insects are excluded from the restaurant and cleanliness is part of the restaurant's credo.

The National Restaurant Association publishes a number of bulletins of value in food protection. Among them are:

- A Self-Inspection Program for Foodservice Operations on Sanitation and Safe Food Handling (40 pages)
- Food-Borne Illnesses Reference Chart
- Temperatures for Food Safeness (color chart)
- Don't Serve Illness to Our Customers (laminated chart)

- Know Your Health Officer (4 pages)
- A Food Protection Message for Foodservice Operators, Food Poisoning Case Histories (14 pages)

You can reach the NRA at 1 IBM Tower, Suite 2600, Chicago, Illinois 60611.

KEY TERMS AND CONCEPTS

Food protection system
Food poisoning
pH value (acidity/alkalinity)
Pathogen
E. coli
Salmonella
Clostridium perfringens
Staphylococcus
Shigella

Infectious hepatitis
Food infection
Outbreak
Quaternary compounds
Food disease carrier
Water hardness
Sanitizing temperature
Low-temperature warewashing

REVIEW QUESTIONS

1. Why is cleanliness a major concern for restaurant owners?
2. What can you, as a restaurant owner, do to avoid food poisoning in your operation?
3. Germs and viruses are prolifically active under what conditions?
4. Describe the three most common germs associated with food poisoning in the United States.
5. What is the significance of the temperatures 45°F and 140°F?
6. How can you tell if a person has a food-borne illness?
7. Compare the acidity/alkalinity level of different foods and their susceptibility to bacterial growth.
8. Describe the three phases of warewashing.
9. What can be done to control pests?
10. What is the purpose of systematizing warewashing?
11. If you are manager of a restaurant, what are your daily food protection and sanitation responsibilities?
12. As manager, how do you prepare for an inspection by the health department? In the unfortunate event of a food-borne outbreak at your restaurant, what steps would you take?
13. Draw up a plan to ensure a safe and sanitary restaurant.

ENDNOTES

[1] *The Safe Food Book: Your Kitchen Guide* (Washington, DC: USDA Food and Inspection Service, 1984).

[2] Sahra R. Labensky and Alan M. Hause, *On Cooking* (Upper Saddle River, N.J.: Prentice Hall, 1999), 20.

[3] Ibid., 21.

[4] Ibid., 22.

[5] Amy Spector, "Safety sessions: Avoid e-coli with better food-handling practices," *Nations Restaurant News* 30, no. 11 (1 October, 1999): 20.

[6] Richard Martin, "Foodmaker Rebounds Shows 2nd Profit in Row Sales Gain," *Nations Restaurant News* 29, no. 7 (November 20, 1995): 11.

[7] O.P. Snyder, *Encyclopedia of Hospitality and Tourism* (New York: Van Nostrand Reinhold, 1993), 205.

[8] Lucy Saunders, "Preventing Foodborne Illness," *Restaurants & Institutions* 104, no. 11 (1 May 1994): 186.

[9] *The Sanitation Operations Manual*, National Restaurant Association, 1200 Seventeenth Street, N.W. Washington, DC 20036-3097.

[10] *Applied Foodservice Sanitation*, 7.

[11] Ibid., 53–55.

[12] Costa Katsigris and Chris Thomas, *Design and Equipment for Restaurant and Foodservice* (New York: John Wiley and Sons, 1999), 209–210.

[13] Beth Lorenzini, "Avoid Common Food Safety Mistakes," *Restaurants and Institutions* 105, no. 21 (1 September 1995): 122.

[14] *Applied Foodservice Sanitation, A Certification Coursebook*. The Educational Foundation of the National Restaurant Association, 4th ed. 1995. p 46.

GLOSSARY

Action plan: Dictates how the marketing plan will be carried out. It assigns specific responsibilities to individuals and dates for accomplishment. An action plan is a detailed list of the steps necessary for carrying out the strategies and tactics designed for reaching each objective.

Amortize: To gradually repay a debt through scheduled periodic payments.

Appreciation: The increase in property value over time.

Back bar: The shelf or counter space along the back of a bar or counter area.

Bain marie: Double boiler or steam table.

Balloon payment: The bulk payment that retires a loan when minimal previous payments have not fully amortized.

Bay: Specific area assigned for workers to cover.

Booster heater: Supplies 180°F water for dishwashing machines.

Brazier: Heavy-duty stewing pan with tightly fitting cover.

Botulism: Toxin produced by some bacteria. It cannot be smelled, seen, or tasted, and cannot be destroyed by high temperatures.

Breakeven point: The point at which neither a profit nor a loss is made in operating a restaurant.

Bread strap: Four, six, or eight bread pans strapped or held together to make them easier to put in or take out of oven.

Breading machine: Manual or machine-driven device for rapid application of coating to raw foods such as chicken and fish.

Broiler: Equipment with heating elements above a rack on which food cooks.

Burnisher: A silver-polishing machine.

Buyout: The outright purchase, usually with borrowed funds, of a business, as by its employees or management; the acquisition of a controlling interest of a company's stock.

California menu: The name given to menus at many restaurants in which the guest can order any item from the menu at any time of the day.

Capital: Net worth of the individual or business; combination of fixed and liquid assets after the deduction of liabilities; the funds used to start up or capitalize a business.

Cash flow position: The presence or absence of surplus cash for recycling into business operations (sometimes known as positive or negative cash flow).

Chafing dish: A pan for preparing foods at tableside using portable or canned heating device.

Cheese melter: Similar to a salamander and used for melting cheese, browning, toasting, glazing, plate warming, and finish-heating items such as onion soup and Mexican specialties.

China cap: A cone-shaped strainer or sieve.

Civil Rights Law: Law stating that employers may not discriminate in employment on the basis of an individual's race, religion, color, sex, national origin, marital status, age, family relationship, mental or physical handicaps, or juvenile records that have been expunged.

Collateral (security): Personal or business possessions that the borrower assigns to the lender as a pledge of debt repayment. If the borrower does not repay the loan, the lender assumes ownership of the collateral.

Commercial kitchen equipment: Any piece of heavy-duty equipment sized and built to cook for as few as 50 or as many as 5,000 people.

Commissary: A large kitchen where foods are prepared to be served in quantity at another location or group of locations.

Communication mix: The variety of methods used to tell consumers about a product, including advertising, merchandising, promotions, public relations, and direct selling.

Compactor: Machine for crushing and compacting refuse; some crush bottles and cans as well.

Compartment steamer: A piece of kitchen equipment with cavities in which pans can be placed; food is cooked by steam.

Competition analysis: The analysis of a company's strengths and weaknesses within the market by comparing with competitors and environment.

Construction loan: Loan made in segments during a term loan.

Contribution margin (CM): The difference between the sales and the cost of the item.

Controllable expenses: Expenses that can be changed in the short term.

Convection oven: An oven that has fans inside to move hot air all around containers of food being baked, decreasing the baking time.

Conveyor: Moving belt that takes dishes or other items from one area to another; it can slant, turn corners, and go from room to room.

Co-op: A nonprofit institution that provides restaurants with food and supplies at lower cost than do the profit-oriented purveyors.

Convenience food: Food that comes in a form that makes possible storage in a minimal amount of space.

Creel: Rack with handle for carrying dishes.

Current assets: Cash or such assets as accounts receivable and inventory that are converted to cash in normal business operations.

Demographics: The characteristics of the market population in terms of age, income, education, sex, and occupation.

Depreciation: The process of writing off against expenses the cost of an asset over its useful life.

Desgustation menu: Features the chef's best dishes.

Detergent dispenser: A device for adding detergents to wash water in a dishwashing machine so that the desired strength of the wash solution is maintained throughout its operating periods.

Difference between marketing and sales: Marketing focuses on the needs and satisfaction of customers; sales focus on the distribution of products to customers.

Dishwasher: A machine for washing dishes.

Disposal: A machine to grind and flush food waste into drain lines.

Dolly: A small cart or wheeled platform used to move or transport heavy objects.

Dough divider: A machine used to cut rolls into uniform sizes from a piece of raw dough.

Dumbwaiter: A small elevator for transporting food between floors.

Equal employment opportunity (EEO): The legal right of all individuals to be considered for employment and promotion on the basis of their ability and merit.

Equal Employment Opportunity Commission (EEOC): The organization to which employees or job applicants may appeal if they feel they have been discriminated against.

Environmental analysis: The analysis of environmental factors that influence the organization and market. The factors are grouped under headings: political, economic, social, and technological.

Equity: (1) The value of a business or piece of property that is owned free and clear; (2) The money—equity dollars or investment—that purchases ownership.

Fabricate: To build in equipment in kitchens as opposed to installing separate pieces of stock equipment.

Filter: A strainer made of paper, cloth, or metal.

Fixed assets: Permanent business properties such as land, buildings, machinery, and equipment that are not resold or converted to cash in normal business operations.

Fixed costs: Expenses normally unaffected by changes in sales volume.

Floor machines: Powered kitchen equipment, as compared to separately installed pieces of stock equipment.

Food-borne illness: An illness caused to humans by consuming foods that carry bacteria.

Food checker stand: Place where food checker is located.

Franchise: (1) The authorization given by one company to another to sell its unique products and services; (2) The name of the business format or product being franchised.

Franchisee: Person who purchases the right to use or sell the products and services of the franchiser.

Franchiser: An individual or company that licenses others to sell its products or services.

Freezing unit: Place where frozen foods are stored, often a part of a walk-in refrigerator.

Front bar: Both the place where guests belly up to the bar and where the bartender prepares the drinks.

Glass washer: Machine with rotating brushes for washing glasses; most often used under bars.

Griddle: Large square or rectangle of heavy metal that can be heated to cook foods poured or placed directly on it, as pancakes or hamburgers.

Gross profit: Sales minus cost of sales in a standard accounting entry.

Hearth: Heated baking surface or floor.

Host or Hostess: A person who greets and seats the guest at a restaurant.

Hot plate: Counter-model electric heating unit, usually with two heating coils, used for heating, pan-frying, and sautéing.

Infrared warmer: Overhead warmer with quartz tubes that produce infrared waves; keeps food warm at or near point of service.

Ice machine: Equipment that makes ice in cubes, chips, or flakes; may also store ice after it is made.

Intermediate loan: Loan made for up to five years.

Job description: A description of the duties and responsibilities involved with a particular job.

Job instruction: Step-by-step details needed for training.

Job specification: Qualifications and skills needed to perform a job; also, the education and technical/conceptual skills a person needs to satisfactorily perform the requirements of the job.

Kitchen floor coverings: Surfaces usually made of quarry tile, marble, terrazzo, asphalt tile, or sealed concrete materials that are nonabsorbent, easy to clean, and resistant to cleaning chemicals.

Learner-controlled instruction (LCI): A program in which employees are given job standards to achieve and asked to reach the standards at their own pace.

Leverage: (1) The extent to which a business is financed by debt; (2) To boost a business's available fund by the injection of loan dollars.

Leveraged buyout (LBO): The use of a target company's asset value to finance the debt incurred in acquiring the company; a buyout using mostly borrowed money and in which the principals put up little or no money of their own.

Liquidate: To convert assets into cash.

Liquidity: The degree to which individual or business assets are in cash form or can quickly be converted to cash.

Loading dock: A platform outside an establishment, usually at the rear, where deliveries of food and supplies are unloaded.

Loan principal: The original amount borrowed or the unpaid loan balance, not including interest charges.

Magic phrases: Phrases used by the host or hostess to welcome or part with the guest.

Market assessment: An assessment that provides initial information helpful in planning the success and reducing the loss of the organization.

Market positioning: The placement in the general market that distinguishes a restaurant from others in terms of price and service.

Market segment: Population group with similar characteristics (needs, wants, income, background, buying, habits, etc.). A restaurant aims to address the wants and needs of specific market segments. When the product matches the desired segment's wants and needs, a successful marketing relationship is formed. Groups that respond in a similar way must be identifiable, measurable, and of appropriate size. In addition, they must be reachable by advertising media.

Marketing: The activities involved in developing product, price, distribution, and promotional mixes that meet and satisfy the needs of customers.

Marketing mix: The combination of the four *P*s of marketing: product, price, place, and promotion.

Marketing planning: The establishment of marketing goals and the design of marketing programs expected to be implemented in the future.

Microwave: An electronic high-speed oven.

Mixer: Mechanical equipment that revolves to mix ingredients; comes in variety of sizes with several speeds of operation; can be either on counter or installed.

Mobile: Describes portable equipment on wheels.

Module: A unit of measurement selected for equipment or furniture, such as modular pans to fit racks or refrigerator spaces, or chairs matching in size and shape.

Nappy: A shallow, open serving dish, sometimes having one handle.

Net worth: The book or on-paper dollar value of an individual or business when liabilities have been subtracted from assets.

Off-sale general: Authorizes the sale of all types of alcoholic beverages for consumption off the premises in original, sealed containers.

On-sale beer: Authorizes the sale on the licensed premises of beer and other malt beverages with an alcoholic content of 4% or less by weight.

Off-sale beer and wine: Authorizes the sale of all types of beer, wines, and malt beverages for consumption of the premises in original containers.

On-sale beer and wine: Authorizes the sale on the premises of all types of beer, wine, and malt liquor.

On-sale general: Authorizes the sale of all types of alcoholic beverages—namely, beer, wine, and distilled spirits—for consumption on the premises.

Oven: A piece of equipment designed to bake; a chamber for baking, heating, or drying, especially in a stove; may be in a range or separate, as in deck or stack ovens, or constructed with moving belts, as in revolving ovens; also see *convection oven.*

Paddle: A long metal implement used for stirring or mixing ingredients in a steam kettle.

Pan tree: Tree-like device for holding pans, usually overhead.

Pantry: A room for storage of food or china; also an area for finishing off foods, assembling foods on trays, garnishing.

Par stock: Level of an inventory item that must be maintained at all times. If the stock on hand falls below this point, a computerized reorder system automatically reorders a predetermined quantity of the item.

Partnership: Legally defined under the Uniform Partnership Act as any venture where two or more persons endeavor to make a profit.

Pass-through: A hot or cold compartment with doors on both sides where prepared food is placed to be picked up for service.

Pastry bag: Cone bag with a metal tip at the small end; used to decorate cakes, prepare fancy toppings, or insert fillings.

Pastry cart: Cart holding selection of dessert pastries to be served at tables from cart.

Pathogens: Bacteria that feed on nutrients in hazardous foods; if given favorable conditions, they multiply rapidly.

Pellet: A small heated metal disc placed under a dish to keep it warm; sometimes the disc is frozen and placed under dishes to keep them cold.

pH value: A measurement acidity/alkalinity relative to that of pure water; indicates hydrogen ion concentration and is stated as a logarithm.

Pickup counter: Place where kitchen workers place prepared food for pickup and serving.

Piece of the action: A term used by some restaurants in encouraging unit managers to acquire, through purchase, 20% of the store they manage.

Plus-minus-plus model: Disciplinary technique that starts with praise followed by criticism, then ends with praise.

Point-of-sale (POS) minicomputer: Machine that records the data of each guest order and can be programmed to provide a variety of data on demand.

Prime rate: The interest rate set by individual banks for their lowest-risk loans; usually short-term credit unsecured to their biggest, most creditworthy customers within a particular geographic area.

Product development: The marketing functions associated with the generation of new products and their introduction to the marketplace.

Product differentiation: The marketing strategy of calling the attention of buyers to those aspects of a product that set it apart from its competitors.

Product life cycle: A marketing management concept providing a graphic description of a product's sales history. It is depicted as having four stages: introduction, growth, maturity, and decline.

Product/service mix: Combination of product and services, whether free or for sale, aimed at satisfying the needs of the target market.

Proof cabinet: Container for proofing dough in preparation for baking or for holding prepared food. Some models have a built-in water reservoir.

Promotion: The activities by which restaurateurs seek to persuade not only first-time buyers but also repeat customers.

Rack: Open shelving designed to hold pots and pans, baked goods, and so on.

Ramekin: Shallow baking china or dish.

Range: A cookstove, usually a heated top; may also contain an oven.

Receiving room: Point at which incoming supplies are checked in, weighed, and routed to destinations within the operation.

Refrigerator: Reach-in and walk-in cooling units for cold storage of foods.

Retarder: Equipment used to slow down rising of bakery products.

Rotisserie: A cooking appliance fitted with a spit on which food is rotated before or over a source of heat.

Rule of 72: A simple method of calculating the number of years required to double money at a particular rate of interest. Divide the rate of return into 72 to obtain the result.

Salamander: A broilerlike stove with heat from above and a shelf below; has an open front so that dishes can be put on the lower shelf for glazing.

Salmonella: An infection caused by bacteria that live in the intestine of chickens, ducks, mice, and rats. May cause illness to humans. Can be destroyed at a temperature of 165°F or higher.

S corporation: Form of business that permits the business entity to operate as a corporation but allows it to avoid paying corporation taxes.

Scullery: A place where culinary utensils and tableware are cleaned and kept.

Self-leveling dispenser: Equipment that dispenses dishes, automatically keeping them at counter level.

Single-use real estate loan: Loan that, typically, runs for less than 20 years.

Slicing machine: Motor-driven machine for slicing meats and other foods.

Slip and fall: The action when a guest or employee slips on a wet floor or something on the floor, causing a fall and injury.

Soufflé cup: Cup used to cook souffléd ingredients; soufflés are made with enough egg whites to make them puff during cooking.

Speed gun: A dispenser for serving popular sodas and mixes for making up drink orders.

Speed rack: The rack where a bar's well brands are stored for speedy service.

Steam cooker (steamer): Equipment with steam-heated compartments in which pans of food are cooked. Some include a forced convection feature, with steam constantly moved by fan.

Steam-jacketed kettle: Kettle with double jacket that steam enters; the steam is used to heat the contents of the kettle.

Steam table: A table having openings to hold containers of cooked food over steam or hot water circulating beneath them.

Stockpot: A large pot in which stock, as for soup, or gravy, is prepared.

Stored labor: The technique of preparing food during slow periods for use during rush periods.

Streptococcus: A food infection found in contaminated nasal or oral discharges. It is spread by sneezing and poor food handling; it can cause scarlet fever and strep throat.

Target market: Market segment that a restaurant identifies as having the greatest potential for customers.

Term loan: A loan that requires only interest payment until the last day of its term, at which time the full payment is due; an intermediate or long-term secured loan granted to a business by a commercial bank insurance company or commercial finance company, usually to finance capital equipment or provide working capital.

Thermostat: An automatic device for regulating the temperature of cooking, heating, or cooling equipment.

Tilting braise/fry pan: A large, heated, multiple-use pan that can be tilted for emptying and cleaning. Can be used for braising, sautéing, frying, stewing, simmering, and boiling.

Tourist menu: Menu designed to attract tourists' attention to a particular restaurant or for acceptability to guests from foreign countries.

Toxin-mediated infection: Bacterial illness that has characteristics of both intoxication and infection.

Trunnion: A device that makes it possible to tilt cooking equipment, such as the trunnion kettle.

Tureen: A deep footed vessel with a cover from which cooked foods (as soup, sauce, or eggs) are served at table.

Under bar: The part of the bar under the front counter where the bartender prepares drinks.

Underliner: A doily or blotting circle placed under a dish or cup to absorb drops of moisture from condensation or spills.

Urn: A closed vessel, usually with a spout, for serving beverages, as tea and coffee.

Utensil: Tableware or kitchenware used in the storage, preparation, conveying, or serving of food (such items as scoops, scrapers, measures, knives, hand peelers, cooks' spoons, whisks, pots, and pans).

Variable costs: Expenses that change proportionately to fluctuation in sales.

Vegetable cutter: Device that cuts, slices, grates, and shreds vegetables; may include plates for cutting potatoes into french-fry and julienne sizes.

Vendor: Seller; supplier.

Virus: Type of microorganism that causes food-borne illness such as hepatitis A and Norwalk virus.

Walk-in refrigerator: A refrigerated area with doors through which people and carts carrying merchandise may enter.

Waterless cooker: Cooking utensil of heavy metal in which foods are cooked in their own juices.

Working capital: The excess of current assets over current liabilities, or the pool of resources readily available to maintain normal business operations.

2½ times rule: Measure the contact with each patron and party in the restaurant during the course of a meal. A hello when they come in equals ½ contact. A contact during the meal to obtain feedback equals 1 contact. A contact when the meal is over equals 1 contact. Adding them gives you a total of 2½ contacts.

INDEX

A&W Restaurants, Inc., 14
A la carte menu, 200
AAA Tour Book, 123
Acapulco Restaurants, 33
Accelerated depreciation, 163
Accessibility for disabled, 317
Accessibility of restaurant, location, 85, 88, 94
Accounting methods, 164
Acidity of food, and bacterial growth, 382–383
Advertising, 106, 121–124
    appeals in, 123
    budget for, 121
    cost and type of restaurant, 77
    in-house advertising, 122
    loss-leader advertising, 122–123
    mailing lists, 123–124
    travel guides, 123
    two-for-one-promotions, 122
    word-of-mouth, 121–122
    Yellow Pages, 123
Age discrimination, legal protection, 171, 316
Age Discrimination in Employment Act, 171, 316
Aging of meat, 34
AIDS, and restaurant workers, 318
Alcoholic Beverage Commission (ABC), 174
Alcoholic beverages, *see* Liquor
Alkalinity of food, and bacterial growth, 382–383
Aloha Table Service, 299
Alps Chalet, 68
American Culinary Federation, 15
Americans with Disabilities Act: Answers for Foodservice Operators, 317
Americans with Disabilities Act (ADA), 168, 316–317, 332
    Accessibility Guidelines, 317
Amoebic dysentery, 381
Anderson, Walter, 181
Anthony's Fish Grotto, 67
Antidiscrimination laws, listing of, 161
Appetizers, 196–197
    examples of, 196–197

Applebee's Neighborhood Grill and Bar, 23, 48
Aquaculture, 39
Asset corporation, 159
Atmospherics:
    marketing plan, 113–114
    theme restaurants, 114
Au Bon Pain, 49
Audits, for liquor control problems, 224–225
Auntie Anne's Anne Beiler, 48
Auto Sham, 266
Automat, 65–66
Aux Trois Freres Provençaux, 7

Bacillary dysentery, 381
Bacillus cereus, 381
Bacteria:
    bacterial illnesses, types of, 378–381
    control measures, 379, 381, 382
    from insects/pests, 397
    and pH of food, 382–383
    and temperature, 383–384
    See also Food-bourne illness; Food safety
Bakery-Café, 49–50
    characteristics of, 49–50
Bank loans, 132–133
    and Small Business Administration (SBA) loan, 133–134, 135, 137
Bar, 214–219
    areas of, 215
    bartenders, role of, 218
    basic inventory for, 218
    glass washing, 218
    handling inebriated patron, 370–371
    ice machine/ice bin, 216
    location and design factors, 214–215, 216–217
    speed gun, 217–218
Barteldt, Bruce, 132
Baum, Joseph, 42
Bayou, Mohamed E., 202
Becoming a Chef (Dornenberg and Page), 46
Behavior modeling, 347–348
Behavior modification, managerial use of, 353–355

Benihana, 44
Bennett, Lee B., 202
Bennigan's, 23
Bergeron, Victor, 59
Bern's Steak House, 188
Bidder, Alex von, 361
Big Boy, 23, 116
Black Angus, 35
Black Eyed Pea, 23
Blue Mesa, 192
Blue Point Coastal Cuisine, 93
Bob Evans Farm, 23, 318
Bolo, 181
Bookkeeper, role of, 294, 300
Border Grill, 46–48
Boston Market, 13, 23
Bottom-up method, task and job analysis, 306
Botulism, 378
Boulanger, M., 7
Brinker International, 25
Brinker, Norman, 25
Broilers, 263
Brown, John Y., Jr., 25
Buck, Dr. Peter, 31
Budgeting:
    cash flow budgeting, 288–289
    controllable expenses, 283–284
    fixed and variable costs, 283
    forecasting sales, 280–282
    gross profit, 283
    income statement, 282–283
    labor costs, 284–286
    operating ratios, 290
    pre-opening expenses, 287
    productivity analysis, 288
    rent, 287
    Uniform System of Accounts for Restaurants (USAR), 287
Building site, checklist for, 91–92
Burger King, 70
Burger restaurants, 29, 180–181
    cuts of meat/preparation, 181
    fat content of burger, 181
    food safety, 379

Business entity, 152–160
  comparison chart of, 159
  corporation, 156–157
  partnership, 154–156
  sole proprietorship, 152–154
Business expenses, tax deductible, 165–166
Business plan:
  and loans, 137–139
  outline for, 138
  and SBA loan, 139
Buy-sell agreement, in partnership, 158, 160
Buying restaurant, 5, 9

C&J Holdings, 48
Café Ba-Ba-Reeba, 63, 64
Caine, Michael, 42
California Café Bar and Grill, 256
California cuisine, 48
California menu, 200
Campanile, 63
Canned foods:
  can-cutting tests, 247
  fruits and vegetables, 247
Captain D's, 39
Carberry's, 49
Carl's Jr., 14, 26–27, 102
Cash flow budgeting, 288–289
  six month example, 289
Cash management, 288, 301–302
  and credit line, 301–302
Celebrities, restaurant owners, 42, 63
Census Tracts for Standard Metropolitan
  Statistical Areas, 84
Chain restaurants:
  location specifications, 89, 91
  See also Franchise; Restaurant categories
Chapeau, Dominique, 12
Charlie Trotter's, 37, 368
  degustation menu, 197–198
Chart House, 23, 69
  success factors, 121–122
Chattel mortgages, as loan collateral, 140
Cheese melter, 272
Chef-owner restaurants, 44–46
  ethnic restaurants, 45
  example of, 46
  most famous chefs, 196
  promotion of, 45
  women chefs, 46–49
Chemical contaminants, 384–386
  types of, 385–386
Chez Panisse, 47–48
  menu of, 205–206
Chicken:
  bacterial infections from, 378
  versus turkey in purchasing, 243
Child care leave, 170
Children:
  best kid's menu survey results, 194

  as employees, tax aspects, 166–167
  menu planning for, 193–194
  See also Minors
Child's Restaurant, 65
Chili's Grill and Bar, 23, 71
Chin Chin, 202
China Bistro, 41–42
Chinese restaurants, 41–42
  characteristics of, 41–42
  culinary styles, 41
Chinois, 63, 193, 202
Chipotle Mexican Grill, 34
Cholera, 381
Chuck E. Cheese's Pizza Parlors, 61
Cini, John C., 252
Cini Little, 252
Civil Rights Act of 1964, 172–173
  enforcement of, 315
  Title VII, 172
Clostridium perfringes, 378, 380, 386
Cluster concept, 86
Co-maker, of loan, 141
Co-op buying, 242
Coaching approach, training, 350–351
Coco's, 23, 71
Code of ethics, purpose of, 80
Coffee:
  brewing machines, 247–248
  types of, 247
Coffee shop:
  layouts of, 90
  markets for, 102
  space/seat requirements, 89
Coffeehouses, characteristics of, 23
Cohn, David, 155
Cohn, Leslie, 155
Collateral, forms of, 140–141
Color, in restaurant design, 95–96
Community, and building restrictions, 83–84
Competition analysis:
  elements of, 103–104, 107
  menu analysis, 181
  and pricing, 117, 188
Complaints, handling of, 370–372
Computer systems, 294–300
  decision-making questions, 295
  labor distribution summary, 295–298
  for multiunit restaurants, 295–296
  point-of-sale (POS) systems, 294, 298–300
Concept restaurants, *see* Restaurant concept;
  Theme restaurants
Consultants, role of, 73
Contamination:
  chemical contaminants, 384–386
  food-borne illness, 378–382
  viruses, 384
Contract services, legal aspects, 173
Contribution margin, and menu planning, 192
Contribution pricing, 117–118

Controllable expenses, 283–284
Convection steamer, 269
Convention ovens, forced-air, 266
Convertible bonds, financing method, 140
Cook-chill process, 262
Corner Bakery, 49
Corporation, 156–157
  asset corporation, 159
  business search expense, 160
  joint ventures, 158
  operating company, 159–160
  pros/cons of, 156–157
  S corporation, 157–158
  taxation, 156–157
Correll, John, 186
Cost-based pricing, 117
Country Market and Buffet, 51
Country Pride, 51
Coupons, promotional, 120
Coyote Café, 202
Cracker Barrel Old Country Stores, 23, 51
Creative Gourmets, 79
Credit:
  credit line, 301–302
  credit status information, 137
Crisis events, types of, 342
Criticism, manager to employee, 354–355
Croce, 153
Croce, Ingrid, 153
Crossroad Delis, 51
Cucina Paradiso, 44
Culinary Institute of America, 15
Current ratio, 301
Customer loyalty, rewards for, 118
Customer service:
  basic rules of, 366
  complexity of, 360–361
  customer survey on, 372
  and difficult customer, 370–374
  greeters, 362–363, 373–374
  importance of, 360
  servers, 361–366
  table setting, 367
  team system, 363–365
Customer space, and type of restaurant, 75–76

Daily specials, 200
Daniel, 36
Daniels-Carter, Valerie, 48
Deck ovens, 267
Decline of restaurant:
  buying losing restaurant, tax aspects, 164
  and concept of restaurant, 67–68
  demographic factors, 66, 84
  life-cycle approach, 65–66, 116
Decor:
  of concept restaurants, 59
  restaurant concept, 59–60
  and target market, 112

Deep-frying equipment, 264–265
Degustation menu, 197–198
Del Taco, 61
Delmonico steak, 34
Delmonico's, 8, 65, 202
DeLuca, Fred, 31
Demographic factors:
　decline of restaurant, 66, 84
　market assessment, 109–110
　market segmentation, 110
Demographic information, sources of, 84
Denny's, yearly sales, 23
Department of Labor (DOL), 315
Depreciation, 163–164
　accelerated depreciation, 163
　depreciation allowance, 163
　straight-line depreciation, 163–164
Design of restaurant, 94–96
　color, 95–96
　layout of dining area, 96
　lighting, 95
　and theme of restaurant, 94
Desserts, 194, 200–201
Difficult customer, 370–374
　handling of, 370–372
　teens as, 373
Diners, characteristics of, 23
Dinner house restaurants:
　largest chain types, 23
　service encounter, 361–362
　space/seat requirements, 88–89
Disabled persons, discrimination protection,
　316–318, 332
Discounts, promotional, 120–123
Discrimination, legal protection, 171–173,
　314–318
Dishwashing equipment, 274–275
　low-temperature dishwashing machines,
　275
　operational problems, 274–275
　warewashing guidelines, 395–396
Dive, 43, 63
Dobson, Paul, 121
Domino Pizza, 14–16, 39
Dorf, Martin, 44
Dornenberg, Andrew, 46
Downtown location, 87–88
Dram shop laws, 224, 349
Drucker, Peter, 105
Drug testing, potential employees, 333
Du jour menu, 200
Due diligence, and leasing, 133

Early-bird discounting, 121
Economic Development Administration
　(EDA), loans from, 140
Educational Foundation of the National
　Restaurant Association (NRA),
　350

Eggs:
　bacterial infections from, 380
　purchasing of, 244
　sizes of, 244
El Torito, 57, 102
Ells, Stephen, 34
Employee development:
　benefits of, 341–342
　combined with training, 343
　for decision-making, 342
　slogans, 343–344
Employees:
　child care leave, 170
　discharge, legal aspects, 173
　legal rights of, *see* Employment regulations
　managers, 169–170, 352–355
　orientation of, 338–339
　record-keeping on, 170–171
　taxes related to, 166
　tips, reporting to IRS, 173
　training, 339–351
　See also Staffing
Employer registrations, 161
Employment regulations:
　Age Discrimination in Employment Act,
　171
　Americans with Disabilities Act (ADA),
　316–318
　Civil Rights Act of 1964, 172–173,
　315–316
　Employment Retirement Income Security
　Act (ERISA), 172
　Equal Employment Opportunity Act, 173,
　315–316
　Equal Pay Act, 171
　Federal Wage and Hour Law, 169–171
　Immigration Reform and Control Act,
　316
　minors as workers, 171, 325–326
　National Labor Relations Act (NLRA), 173
　Wage Garnishment Act, 171
　wage and hour audits, 174
Employment Retirement Income Security Act
　(ERISA), 172
Employment testing, 332
Endorser, of loan, 141
Entrées, 200
Environmental Sanitation Services (ESS),
　395
Equal Employment Opportunity Act, 173,
　315–316
　scope of law, 315–316
Equal Employment Opportunity Commis-
　sion (EEOC), 171–172, 315–316
Equal Pay Act, 171
Equipment:
　depreciation, 163–164
　See also Kitchen equipment
Escherichia coli, 378–379

Ethnic restaurants:
　chef-owner restaurants, 45
　market for, 102
　theme-type, 43–44
Evaporative coolers, 273
Evvia Estiatorio, 44
Exxon Travel Guide, 123

Fado, 43–44
Failure rate, of restaurants, 8–9
Falls, liability for, 175, 258
Family restaurants:
　characteristics of, 23
　largest chains, 23
Farmer's Home Administration, loan from,
　140
Fashion Café, 63
Fast food restaurants, *see* Quick-service restau-
　rants
Federal employer identification number, 161
Federal regulations, *see* Employment regula-
　tions
Federal Unemployment Tax Act (FUTA), 166
Federal Wage and Hour Law, 169–171
Feninger, Susan, 46–48
FICA (Federal Insurance Contribution Act),
　166
Financial data, of marketing plan, 104
Financial management, 300–302
　cash management, 301–302
　ratio analysis, 301–302
　See also Budgeting
Financing:
　and fire insurance, 146–147
　leasing, 141–146
　loans, 131–141
　and return on investment, 165
　valuation of restaurant, 147
Fine-dining restaurants, 36–38
　characteristics of, 36–38
　economics of, 36
Fire insurance, 146–147
Fish, parasites, 381
Fixed costs, 283
　labor costs, 286
　pre-opening budget, 287
Flat Pennies, 43
Flay, Bobby, 181–182
Fleming's, 35
Flip, drink, 8
Floor coverings, kitchen, 258
Flying J's, 51
Food:
　flavor, importance of, 192–193
　product development aspects, 114–115
　as product in marketing, 102–103,
　112–113
　theft of, 292–293
　See also entries under *Menu*

Food-borne illness, 378–382
  bacterial, 378–382
  causes/types of, 378–382
  food handling errors, 381–382
  and high-protein foods, 379, 383
  most hazardous foods, 383
  parasitic, 381
  prevention of, see Food safety
  viral, 384
Food product specification, example of,
  235–236
Food purchasing:
  buying by specification, 238–239
  co-op buying, 242
  coffee, 247
  eggs, 244
  and food storage, 241–242
  fruits and vegetables, 244–247
  full-line distributors, 242
  meat, 243
  par stock, 240
  purchasing cycle, 237
  purveyor, role of, 237
  reorder point, 240
  specialty items, cautions about, 242–243
  standing orders, 240
  steps in system, 234, 236
Food safety:
  carrying utensils guide, 385
  cross-contamination prevention, 389
  gloves and food handling, 391
  handwashing, 379, 381, 386, 390
  Hazard Analysis of Critical Control Points
    (HACCP), 386–388
  health of personnel, 390
  inspections, 390
  preventing food-borne illness, 379,
    382–383, 386, 388–390
  public health license, 390
  serving food guide, 385
  system approach to, 391–395
  temperature and bacterial control, 378,
    382–384, 388–389
Foodservice Management Professional
  Credential (FMP), 350
Forecasting sales:
  method of, 280–282
  next day sales, 11
Forum of the Twelve Caesars, 42
Four Seasons Restaurant, 38, 361
Franchise, 10, 13–15
  international business, 14
  investment cost of common franchise sys-
    tems, 13
  largest chains, 22–23
  pros/cons of, 13–15
  by territory, 112
French, and history of restaurants, 7–8

French Culinary Institute, 15
Friendly's Restaurants, 23
Fruits and vegetables, 244–247
  canned, 247
  grades/standards for, 245
  selection guidelines, 244–245
Fuddrucker's, 87
Full-line distributors, 242

Gallagher's, 202
Gardenburgers, 192
Garnishment laws, 171
Gino's East, 63
Glass washing, bar, 218
Gloves, for food handling, 391
Goals and objectives, mission statement, 80,
  105
Godzilla, 59
Goin, Suzanne, 16
Goldstein, Evan, 119
Goldstein, Joyce, 119
Good Times Drive-Thru Burgers, 29
Grand Tavern de Londres, 7
Granita, 193
Great American Disaster, 63
Greeters, 362–363, 373–374
  attitude of, 373–374
  tact, importance of, 374
  wages of, 374
  waiting guests, handling of, 363
Griddles, 263–264
Gross profit, 283
Guarantor, of loan, 141
Guest checks, theft control, 293–294
Guest Service Solutions, 298–299

Hamburger, see Burger restaurants
Hamilton, George, 42
Handicapped persons, discrimination protec-
  tion, 316–318, 332
Handwashing:
  bacteria control, 379, 381, 386, 390
  method, 379
Hard Rock Café, 63–64, 66, 115
Hardee's, 14
Hazard Analysis of Critical Control Points
  (HACCP), 386–388
Health department permit, 167
Health inspection, 275–276
Hepatitis, food-bourne causes, 381, 384
Hiring employees, see Staffing
Home delivery restaurants, 50–51
  centralization of, 50
  operation of, 50
Hooters, 23
Horn and Hardart, 65–66
Host, see Greeters
Hot-food holding tables, 270

Hotel restaurants, fine-dining, 38
Hotel room service, from selected restaurants,
  50
Houlihan's, 23
Hours worked, federal regulation, 169–170
House of Blues, 43, 63
Houston's, 23
Howard Johnson's, 51
Hueblein Company, 26
Hughes, Lowry, 370
Hurst, Mike, 121

Ice:
  ice bin at bar, 216
  size guide, 272
Ice cream restaurants, 103
Ice machines, 216, 271–272
IHOP (International House of Pancakes), 23
Il Fornaio, 202
Image of restaurant:
  and marketing, 102
  and name, 57–58, 59
Immigrants:
  documents required for employment, 326
  legal, discrimination protection, 316
  undocumented, 326
Immigration Reform and Control Act, 316,
  326
In-house advertising, 122
In-n-Out Burger, 29
Income statement, 282–283
  with controllable expenses, 284
  example of, 282
  purpose of, 282
  Uniform System of Accounts for Restaurants
    (USAR), 287
Independent contractors, hiring of, 173
Infrared cooking equipment, 269
Ingraham, Billy, 181
Insects:
  bacterial disease from, 396–397
  pest control system, 397
Inspections, food safety, 390
Insurance:
  business insurance, types of, 160–161
  fire insurance, 146–147
  lease requirements, 146
  life, borrowing against policy, 146
Integrated pest management program (IPM),
  397
Interest rates:
  interest tax deduction, 131–132
  on loans, 131–132
  Small Business Administration (SBA) loan,
    134
Intermediate loan, time period of, 131
International business, franchise, 14
IRA plan, 164–165

Italian restaurants, 39–40
  characteristics of, 39–40
  northern Italian food, 40

Jack Dempsey's, 42
Jackson, Michael, 42
Job analysis, *see* Task and job analysis
Job description, 307, 308, 311–312
  importance of, 308
  job instruction sheet, 311–312
  job specification, 311–312
  writing guidelines, 308, 311
Job interview, 320–321, 327–330
  acceptable questions, 328–329
  interview and rating form, 321
  interviewing tips, 331
  multiple interview approach, 330
  purposes of, 320
  questions to avoid, 323–324, 327–328
Job specification, 311
  example of, 312
Johnson and Wales University, 15
Joint ventures, corporate, 158
Jordan, Michael, 63
Julien's Restaurator, 7

Karcher, Carl, 26–27
Kasavana, Michael, 202
Katsigris, Costas, 257
Kentucky Fried Chicken, 25–26, 188
  history of, 25–26
Keogh plan, 154, 164–165
Kitchen:
  dimensions for, 257
  efficiency, improvement tips, 255
  floor coverings, 258
  health inspection, 275–276
  open kitchens, 256–257
  planning layout, 252
  work centers, arrangement of, 255
  work flow diagram, 254
Kitchen equipment:
  categories of, 259
  and cooking skills, 261–262
  cost of energy related to, 261
  deep-frying equipment, 264–265
  dishwashing equipment, 274–275
  evaporative coolers, 273
  hot-food holding tables, 270
  ice machines, 271–272
  maintenance of, 274
  and menu planning, 186, 260–261
  pasta-making machines, 272
  refrigerators/freezers, 271
  selection issues, 259–260
  specialty equipment, 272–273
  steam cooking equipment, 269–270
  stove/oven, 262–270

trends related to, 253
used equipment, 273–274
Kobe beef, 35, 181
Kroc, Ray, 16, 58–59

La Fonda del Sol, 42
La Madeleine, 49
La Petit Boulangerie, 296
Labor costs, 284–286
  fixed costs, 286
  and productivity per employee, 77–78
  projected costs, 285–286
  variable costs, 285–286
Labor distribution summary, 295, 296–298
Lagasse, Emeril, 196, 202
Las Vegas, quality of restaurants in, 201–202
Lawry's, 70
Lazaroff, Barbara, 45–46
Le Bec Fin, 364
Le Champ d'Oiseua, 7
Le Cirque, 95
Learner-controlled instruction (LCI), 348–349
Lease assignment, as collateral, 141
Leasing, 141–146
  annual rate calculation, 145
  cost of leasing, 142
  and due diligence, 133
  financial responsibility for payoff, 145–146
  insurance requirements, 146
  language of lease, 144
  length of lease, 144–145
  maintenance agreement, 146
  municipal approval of lease, 146
  pre-signing questions, 142–144
  space, negotiation guidelines, 132
  tax avoidance plan, 164
Leftovers, 292
Legal aspects:
  business entity, 152–160
  employee related, *see* Employment regulations
  legal requirements, listing of, 161–162
  liquor laws, 174
  time-off for voting, 174
  wage and hour audits, 174
Les Dames d'Escoffier, 49
Lettuce Entertain You Enterprises, 63, 192
Liability:
  dram shop laws, 224, 349
  falls, 175, 258
  of partnership, 156
  personal, protective measures, 141
  of sole proprietor, 154
Life insurance policy, as loan collateral, 140
Lighting, importance of, 95
Limited partnerships, as financing method, 133
Liquor:
  control of losses/theft related to, 224–225

food to beverage sales percentage, 212
loss/theft methods, 225–231
profit-factor, 213
responsible alcoholic beverage service,
  223–224, 349
service, *see* Bar
state laws, 174
third-party liability, 224
wine, 220–223
Liquor license:
  applying for license, 213–214
  cost of, 213
  and purchase of liquor, 214
  types of, 213
Little Squirts program, 194
Loans, 131–141
  and business plan, 137–139
  and collateral, 140–141
  and credit status information, 137
  interest rates, 131–132
  non-bank sources, 139–140
  Small Business Administration (SBA) loan,
    133–137
  sources for, 132–133
  state programs, 162
  time periods of, 131
Local government, loans from, 139
Location of restaurant, 80–94
  adjacent complementary restaurants, 112
  building site checklist, 91–92
  for chain restaurant, 89, 91
  cost of location, 94
  downtown versus suburban, 87–88
  location criteria, listing of, 82, 85–86
  location information resources, 83–84
  location/concept match, 88
  and marketing plan, 111–112
  minimum population needed, 87
  new area/shopping center, 82–83
  and number of seats, 88–89
  restaurant row, 86, 112
  shopping mall location, 86–87
  takeover location, 92
  topographical surveys, 93
  traffic generators in area, 84
  travel time for patrons, 88
Lone Star steakhouse, 35
Loss-leader advertising, 122–123
Low-temperature dishwashing machines, 275,
  396
Low-temperature ovens, 266
Lucques, 16
Ludwing, Cleo R., 27–29

Macaroni Grill, 39–40
McDonald's, 14, 16, 181, 192
  concept/image of, 59, 70, 102
  yearly sales, 22

Magic Pan, 87
Mailing lists, for advertising, 123–124
Maintenance agreement, of lease, 146
Managers, 352–355
  as coaches, 350–351
  criticism of employees, approach to, 354–355
  effective, characteristics of, 352–353
  leadership aspects, 352
  minimum wage exemption, 169
  as partial owners, 355
  praising employees, benefits of, 353–354
  role of, 10
  tips for superior results, 352
  women, 49
Mangiano's Little Italy, 111
Marketing:
  competition analysis, 103–104, 107
  market assessment, 108–109
  market demand, 109–110
  market positioning, 110
  market potential, 110
  market segmentation, 110
  marketing philosophy, elements of, 106
  marketing plan, 102–105
  marketing strategy, 103–104, 107–108
  meaning of, 56
  Olive Garden example, 124–125
  and planning sequence, 108
  as problem solving, 107
  compared to sales, 106
  target market, 110
Marketing plan, 102–105
  atmospherics, 113–114
  differentiation of restaurant, 115–116
  food as product of restaurants, 102–103, 112–113
  location of restaurant, 111–112
  parts of, 103–104
  price, 116–117
  product analysis, 113
  product development, 114–115
  product positioning, 102, 115
  promotion, 118–124
Marshall, Gertrude, 33
Marshall, Ray, 33
Masa, menu of, 195
Meals on Wheels, 50
Meat:
  bacterial infections from, 378–383
  chicken versus turkey, 243
  purchasing of, 243
Melaniphy, John C., 83
Mentally challenged, hiring of, 317–318
Menu analysis:
  competitive analysis, 181
  item-by-item analysis, 202
  menu engineering approach, 202
  psychological factors, 202–203

Menu design, 203–204
  single page, 203
  two-or-more pages, 204
  type of paper, 204
Menu items:
  appetizers, 196–197
  daily specials, 200
  degustation menu, 197–198
  desserts, 194, 200–201
  entrées, 200
  matching/pairing of food/wine, 201
  new items, 194, 196
  salads, 194, 200
  sequence of items, 199–200
  soups, 194, 197
Menu planning:
  accuracy of items, 193
  aspects of, 180
  and availability of ingredients, 186
  and capability of chef, 186
  for children, 193–194
  and contribution margin, 192
  and flavor of food, 192–193
  and kitchen equipment, 186, 260–261
  nutritional aspects, 188, 192
  and price, 186–188
  pricing, 206–207
  role/responsibility for, 181
  and type of restaurant, 181, 194
  vegetarian selections, 192
Menus:
  examples of, 182–185, 189–191, 195, 198, 205–206
  types of, 199–200
Mesa Grill, menu of, 182–185
Mexican restaurants, 34
  characteristics of, 32–33
Meyer, Danny, 196, 361
Michalski, Edmund, 68
Mick, Rudy, 67
Micros 3700, 299
Microwave oven, 266, 268–269
  and internal cooking temperature, 383–384
  pros/cons of, 268–269
Miller, Eberhard, 202
Miller, Jack, 202
Miller, Mark, 202
Milliken, Mary Sue, 46–48
Minimum wage, exemption for managers, 169–170
Minorities Enterprises loans, 135
Minors:
  child labor laws, 171
  hiring restrictions, 325–326
  liquor served to, 174
  teen confrontations in restaurant, 373
Mission statement, 79–80, 105
  components of, 80
  goals and objectives, 80, 105

Mobile Travel Guide, 123
Monaghan, Thomas, 14–16, 39
Morton, Peter, 63
Morton's of Chicago, 202
Motown Café, 43
Mount, Charles Morris, 44
Mrs. Fields, computer system of, 295–296

Name of restaurant, *see* Restaurant name
National Labor Relations Act (NLRA), 173
National Restaurant Association (NRA), 167
National Sanitation Foundation, standards of, 253
New Orleans, 7
New Restaurant: Dining Design 2 (Mount), 44
New restaurant, building from scratch, 9–10
Nieporent, Drew, 196
Nobu, 24
Norwalk virus, 384
Nutritional aspects, menu planning, 188, 192

Occupational and health requirements, 161
Occupational Safety and Health Administration (OSHA), 173
Off-sale general liquor license, 213
Office of Federal Contract Compliance, 315
Olive Garden, 10, 40, 84
  marketing, 124–125
On-sale beer license, 213
On-sale beer and wine license, 213
On-sale general liquor license, 213
Open kitchens, 256–257
Operating company, functions of, 159–160
Operating ratios, example of, 290
Order taking, 367–368
Ordinaries, 8
Organization, 312–314
  organization chart, 314
  restaurant functions related to, 312
  unit restaurant personnel, 313
Orientation, goals of, 338–339
Outback Steakhouse Restaurants, 35
Overtime pay, federal regulation, 170

Page, Karen, 46
Palladin, Jean-Louis, 202
Palm, 202
Palmer, Charles, 202
Panda Express, 41, 42
Panera Bread Company, 49
Papagus, 63
Par stock, food purchasing, 240
Parasites, in food, 381
Part-time employees, and training, 341
Partnership, 154–156
  buy-sell agreement with, 158, 160
  corporate joint venture, 158

general partnership, 154
limited partnership, 154
pros/cons of, 156
taxation, 155–156
Pasta House Co., 40
Pasta-making machines, 272
Pathogens, *see* Bacteria
Paul and Bill's, 40
Payment of employees:
federal regulation of, 171
minimum wage exemption, 169–170
overtime pay, 170
Paypalt, Jean-Baptiste Gilbert, 7
Pegler, Martin M., 43
Penedo, Victor, 67
Pension plans:
legal protection, 172
See also Retirement plans
Perfringens, 380–381
Perfrongens, 381
Perkins Family Restaurants, 23
Permits and licenses:
importance of, 162–163
types of, 161, 167
Pest control, 396–397
integrated pest management program
(IPM), 397
Peter Luger Steakhouse, 34
Petrowski, Elaine Martin, 256
pH of food, and bacterial growth, 382–383
Physical exam, preemployment, 333
Physically challenged, hiring of, 317–318
Pizza, and Italian restaurants, 39–40
Pizza Hut, 14
Planet Earth, 63
Planet Hollywood, 42
Planning restaurant:
advertising/promotion costs, 77
common denominators and planning,
73
customer space, 75–76
labor costs, 77
levels of service, 74–75
market assessment, 108–109
planner/consultant, role of, 73
and purpose of restaurant, 73–74
relationship to restaurant concept, 78–79
sequence of activities in, 108
time of eating/seat turnover, 57
Plate House, 24
Plue Point Coastal Cusine, wine list of,
220–221
Point-of-sale (POS) systems, 294, 298–300
pros/cons of, 299–300
software for, 298–299
Police, calling in emergency, 370
Pork, parasites, 381
Positioning, marketing plan, 102, 115

Postrio, 193, 202
Praise, manager to employee, 353–354
Pre-preparation, par stock calculations, 240
Price, 116–117, 186–188
competitive pricing, 117, 188
contribution margin, 192
contribution pricing, 117–118
cost-based pricing, 117
and cost per seat, 76
customer income level and appeal of
restaurant, 102–103
factors affecting price, 116–118
food-cost percentage, 206–207
individual item method, 188
and level of service, 74–75
and menu planning, 186–188
price-value relationship, 117, 187
prime costs, 117, 207
psychological factors in, 202–203
and quality, 118
and supply/demand, 117–118
value-creating strategy, 186–187
weighted-average approach, 188
Prime costs, 117, 207
Problem solving:
and difficult customer, 370–372
marketing as, 107
Product analysis:
marketing plan, 113
products, levels of, 113–114
Productivity analysis, 288, 290
Profit:
gross profit, 283
liquor sales, 213
Promotion, 118–124
discounts, 120–121
examples of, 119–120
goals of, 118–119
and increased sales, 119
information source for, 119
for slow periods, 119, 120, 122–123
See also Advertising
Psychological factors, price perception,
202–203
Public health license, 390
Public relations, meaning of, 106
Puck, Wolfgang, 45–46, 193, 196, 201

Quality:
importance to customers, 180
and price, 118
Quality control, cooling controls, 11
Quick-service restaurants, 24–31
burger chains, 29
Carl's Jr., 26–27
history of, 24
Kentucky Fried Chicken, 25–26
L-K Restaurants, 27–29

Subway, 29–31
Wendy's International Restaurant, 26

Rainforest Café's, 42
Rally's Double Drive-Through, 110
Ratio analysis, 301–302
current ratio, 301
Real estate, as loan collateral, 140
Real estate agents, restaurant brokerage, 83
Real estate taxes, 146
Recruitment process:
Red Lobster example, 315
sources for employees, 327
Red Lobster, 10–11, 39
management selection flow, 319
recruitment process, 315
Red Robin, 23
Refrigerators/freezers, 271
Remi, 96
Rent, 287
annual rate calculation, 145
triple net lease, 287
Reorder point, food purchasing, 240
Research, demographic, 84
Restaurant, origin of word, 7
Restaurant Adventures, 294
Restaurant Business, 81
Restaurant business:
benefits of, 5–6
failure rate, 8–9
financial benefits, 16
historical view, 7–8
investment options, 9–10
liabilities of, 6–7
new business questions, 78–79
top sales by category, 22–23
Restaurant categories:
bakery-Café, 49–50
chef-owner restaurants, 44–46
Chinese restaurants, 41–42
fine-dining restaurants, 36–38
home delivery restaurants, 50–51
Italian restaurants, 39–40
Mexican restaurants, 32–33
quick-service restaurants, 24–31
seafood restaurants, 38–39
steakhouses, 33–35
theme restaurants, 42–44
travel centers, 51–52
truck stops, 51
with women chefs, 46–49
Restaurant concept:
adaptation of concept, 67
clear-cut versus ambiguous, 57
copying/improving approach, 68–69
decor, 59–60
defining concept, 60–62
design of restaurant, 94–96

Restaurant concept (*Continued*):
  development, sequence of events time line, 72
  elements of, 56
  examples of, 62–67
  and location, 80–94
  McDonald's example, 59
  market factors, 61–62
  meaning of, 56
  mission statement, 79–80
  modification of concept, 67–68
  multiple-concept chain, 70–71
  and name of restaurant, 57–58
  relationship to planning, 78–79
  symbology, 69–70
Restaurant designs, books about, 44
Restaurant and Fast Food Site Selection (Melaniphy), 83
Restaurant Growth Index, 81
Restaurant Interiors, 44
Restaurant name, 57–58
  filings for, 162
  and image of establishment, 57–58, 59
  name of owner, 58
  protecting name, 58–59
Restaurant row, 86, 112
Restaurants That Work (Dorf), 44
Restaurants Unlimited, 80
Restaurateur, qualities of, 12–13
Retirement plans, 164–165
  IRA plan, 164–165
  Keogh plan, 164–165
  tax deduction, 165
  tax-free compounding, 165
Return on investment (ROI), 165
Rib Rooms, 59
Ritz, Cesar, 69
Rivera, Dick, 32
R.J. Grunts, 63
Rodents, pest control system, 397
Roth, Doug, 362
Round Table for Women, The, 49
Roy's New York, 212
Ruben's, 71
Ruby Tuesday, 23
Ruth's Chris Steak House, 48, 118

S corporation, 157–158
  pros/cons of, 157, 158
  taxation, 157–158
Salads, 194, 200
Sales:
  forecasting, 280–282
  compared to marketing, 106
  sales volume, components of, 280
Sales-and-leaseback plan, financing method, 139

Sales mix, and price, 118
Sales tax permit, 161
Salmonella, 378, 380–381, 386
Sanders, Harland, 16, 25
Sanitation:
  bar glasses, 218
  cold-water sanitation, 275
  handwashing, 379, 381, 386
  pest control, 396–397
  sanitation service, use of, 395
  standards, 253
  warewashing, 395–396
  See also Food safety
Sanitation Operations Manual, 380
Schlotzsky's, 110
Schussler, Steven, 42
Scoozi, 63
Seafood restaurants, 38–39
  and farm-bred fish, 39
Seat turnover, 290–291
  and types of restaurant, 75, 76, 291
Securities, as loan collateral, 140
Seller's permit, 167
Servers, 361–366
  comments/responses of, 368–369
  competition among, 362–363, 365
  complaints about customers, 369–370
  effective, characteristics of, 362
  formality, level of, 366–367
  order taking, 367–368
  selling skills of, 365
  service encounter, 361–362
Service Corps of Retired Executives (SCORE), functions of, 135
Sex discrimination, equal pay, 171
Sexual harassment:
  forms of, 172
  legal protection, 172–173
Shigella, 386
Shoney's, 23
Shopping mall location, 86–87
  location in mall, 87
Single-use real estate loan, time period of, 131
Sirloin steaks, 34
Skillets, tilting skillets, 265–266
Slogans, employee development, 343–344
Slow periods, promotions during, 119–120, 122–123
Slow roasting ovens, 267
Small Business Administration (SBA), 135
Small Business Administration (SBA) loan, 133–137
  business plan for, 139
  guarantee on loans, 133–134
  information requirements, 136–137

interest rate, 134
  Loan Guarantee Plan, 137
  Low Doc Program, 134
  parties in, 133–134, 137
  qualifications of applicant for, 135–136
  Small Business Investment Companies (SBICs), 135
Small Business Investment Companies (SBICs):
  loans from, 135
  Minorities Enterprises loans, 135
Smith, Barbara, 16
Smith, Donald, 202
Smith and Wollensky, 202
Social Security taxes, 166
Sole proprietorship, 152–154
  pros/cons of, 154
  taxation, 152–154
Soups, 194, 197
Sous vide, 262
Spaghetti Factory, 57
Spaghetti Warehouses, 40
Spago, 45–46, 60, 63, 193, 201–202
Speed gun, 217–218
Splichal, Joachim, 202
Square One, 119
Squirrel Restaurant Management System, 299
Staffing:
  drug testing, 333
  employment legislation, 314–318
  employment testing, 332
  hiring objectives, 331
  job interview, 320–321, 327–330
  legal guidelines, 314–318
  minors, hiring of, 322, 325–326
  physical exam, preemployment, 333
  recruitment, 315, 319, 327
  selection process, 319
  steps in staffing, 314
  student workers, 322, 325
  substance abuse screening, 332
  and task and job analysis, 307
  telephone references, 330
  and type of restaurant, 322
Standard recipes, 204
Standing orders:
  food purchasing, 240
  purchase order, 240
Staphylococcus aureus, 380–381
Starbucks, 23
States:
  alcoholic beverage control, 213
  employee-related laws, 170
  loan programs, 162
  permits and license requirements, 161
  state and local taxes, 168

Steak, cuts of, 34–35
Steak and Ale, 35
Steak-Out Franchising, 50
Steakhouses, 33–35
    aging of meat, 34
    characteristics of, 34–35
    Las Vegas, 202
    sales figures, 35
Steam cooking equipment, 269–270
    convection steamer, 269
    steam-jacketed kettles, 269–270
Steam-jacketed kettles, 269–270
Steward, Julia, 48
Storage of food, 241–242
Stove/oven, 262–270
    broilers, 263
    conventional oven, 267
    deck ovens, 267
    forced-air convention ovens, 266
    griddles, 263–264
    infrared cooking equipment, 269
    low-temperature ovens, 266
    microwave oven, 266, 268–269
    slow roasting ovens, 267
    tilting skillets, 265–266
Straight-line depreciation, 163–164
Streptococcus infection, 381
Stuckey, Ethel, 51
Stuckey's, 51
Students, hiring of, 322, 325
Substance abuse, indicators of, 332
Subway, 29–31, 122
    capital requirements, 30–31
    franchisee responsibilities, 29–30
    history of, 31
    menu features, 30–31
Supply/demand, and price, 117–118
Symbology, restaurant concept, 69–70

Table d'hôte menu, 200
Table setting, 367
Taco Bell, 61
    discount value strategy, 120
Takeover of restaurant, 92–93
    conversion of restaurant, 84–85, 92
    lease clauses, 142
Tapas Barcelona, 44
Tapeworms, 381
Target market, 110
    meaning of, 56
    for restaurant concept, 61–62
Task and job analysis, 306–308
    bottom-up method, 306
    and hiring decisions, 307
    and job instruction sheet, 311–312
    task breakdown, 307–311
    top-down-method, 306

Tax forms and schedules:
    Form 1040, 152, 156
    Form 1065, 155
    Schedule C, 152
    Schedule K-1, 156
Tax-free compounding, retirement plans, 165
Taxation:
    accounting methods, 164
    business expenses, 165–166
    children as employees, 166–167
    corporation, 156–157, 159–160
    depreciation, 163–164
    interest rate deduction on loan, 131–132
    IRS publications, 167
    leasing-related tax avoidance plan, 164
    partnership, 155–156
    real estate taxes, 146
    retirement plans, 164–165
    S corporation, 157–158
    sales and uses taxes, 162
    sole proprietorship, 152–154
    state and local taxes, 168
    tax credit for van/bus, 166
    tax losses, 164
    tips, reporting to IRS, 173
Team system, for serving, 363–365
Telephone references, potential employees, 330
Temperature:
    bacterial control, 378, 382–384
    warewashing, 395–396
Term loan, time period of, 131
TGI Friday's, 23, 57, 63, 102
    training, 339–340, 344
Theft:
    general control measures, 291–293
    guest check control, 293–294
    ways to steal in bar/restaurant, 225–231
Theme restaurants, 42–44
    atmospherics, 114
    categories of, 43
    characteristics of, 42
    as concept restaurants, 59
    ethnic, 43–44
    examples of, 42, 43
Thomas, Chris, 257
Thomas, Clarence, 172
Thomas, David R., 16, 57
Tie-ins, 122
Tilting skillets, 265–266
Tinseltown Studios, 43
Tips, 355–356
    pooled tips, 356
    reporting to IRS, 173
    theories of, 355
TIPS (Training for Intervention Procedures by Servers), 224

Too Hot Tamales, 47
Top-down-method, task and job analysis, 306
Topographical surveys:
    for location of restaurant, 93
    visibility/accessibility, 94
Tourist menu, 200
Trader Vic's, 42, 59
Training, 339–351
    behavior modeling, 347–348
    coaching approach, 350–351
    employee development, 341–344
    importance of, 340
    learner-controlled instruction (LCI), 348–349
    and part-time employees, 341
    professional programs, 15, 350
    step-by-step approach, 344–345
    TGI Friday example, 339–340, 344
    theory, 345–347
    trainer skills/tasks, 346
Transportation of employees, tax credit for, 166
Trattoria del Lupo, 193
Travel centers, 51–52
Travel Centers of America, 51
Travel guides, advertising in, 123
Trichinella spiralis, 381
Tricon Global Restaurants, Inc., 71
Trotter, Charlie, 196
Truck stops, 51
Tupelo American, 155
Two-for-one-promotions, 122

Un Grand Café, 63
Unemployment taxes, 166
Uniform Partnership Act, 154
Uniform System of Accounts for Restaurants (USAR), 163, 287
Union Square Café, 361
United States, history of restaurants, 7–8
Urban Development Action Grant (UDAG) program, loans from, 140
U.S. Department of Agriculture:
    grades of fruits and vegetables, 245
    grades of meat, 243
Used equipment, 273–274

Vacuum-packing, sous vide, 262
Valuation of restaurant, components of, 147
Variable costs, 283
    labor costs, 285–286
Vegetables, *see* Fruits and vegetables
Vegetarian selections, menu planning, 192
Vibrio comma, 381
Victoria Station, 62
Viruses, food contamination, 384
Visibility of restaurant, 94

Voho, Jean, 202
Vongerichten, Jean-George, 196, 202

Wage Garnishment Act, 171
Wage and hour audits, 174
Wages, federal regulation, 169–170
Warewashing, 395–396
Warming tables, 270
Waters, Alice, 47, 48, 196
Wattel, Bob, 192
Weighted-average approach, price, 188

Wendy's International Restaurant, 102, 181
    history of, 26
White Castle, 181
Wian, Bob, 115–116
Wienerschnitzel, 370
Wine, 220–223
    matching/pairing of food/wine, 201, 223
    suggestions with various foods, 222–223
    wine list, example of, 220–221
Wolfgang Puck Café, 202
Women:
    chefs, 46–49

managers, 49
organizations for, 49
restaurateurs, 48–49
Word-of-mouth advertising, 121–122
Wynn, Steve, 202

Yellow Pages advertising, 123

Zip plus Four, 84
Zoning, 85, 161, 167
    importance of, 83